WHITE GOLD

ENGLAND'S JOURNEY TO RUGBY WORLD CUP GLORY

PETER BURNS

First published in Great Britain in 2013 by
ARENA SPORT
An imprint of Birlinn Limited
West Newington House
10 Newington Road
Edinburgh
EH9 1QS

www.arenasportbooks.co.uk

ISBN: 978-1-909715-08-0
eBook ISBN: 978-0-85790-694-6

Grateful acknowledgements are made to HarperCollins for extracts from
Full Time: The Autobiography by Jason Leonard and *Nine Lives: The Autobiography* by
Matt Dawson; Orion for *Richard Hill: The Autobiography* and *Clive Woodward: The
Biography* by Alison Kervin; Hodder Headline for *It's in the Blood: The Autobiography*
by Lawrence Dallaglio, *Winning! The Autobiography* by Clive Woodward, *Martin
Johnson: The Autobiography* and *Jonny: My Autobiography* by Jonny Wilkinson.

Every effort has been made to trace copyright holders and obtain their permission for
the use of copyright material. The publisher apologises for any errors or omissions
and would be grateful if notified of any corrections that should be incorporated in
future reprints or editions of this book.

British Library Cataloguing-in-Publication Data
A catalogue record for this book is available on request from the
British Library.

Designed and typeset by Polaris Publishing, Edinburgh

01010100 01101000 01100001 01101110 01101011 00100000 01111001 01101111 01110101
00100000 01100110 01101111 01110010 00100000 01100001 00100000 01110111 01101111
01101110 01100100 01100101 01110010 01100110 01110101 01101100 00100000 01100101
01100100 01101001 01110100 00101100 00100000 01001010 01110101 01101100 01101001 01100101

Printed in Sweden by Scandbook

ACKNOWLEDGEMENTS

Thanks, first of all, must go to my grandmother, Pamela Walker – for although she has lived in Scotland for over 60 years, she has always remained a true English rose; and as her heritage qualifies me under IRB rules to play for England, I therefore feel, by extension, qualified to write about England rugby's most glorious years.

Thank you to Tom English and Stephen Jones for supporting the idea of this book from the outset and for their kind endorsements of the finished product. Tom's marvelous account of the 1990 Grand Slam show-down between Scotland and England, *The Grudge*, had a significant influence on the style of this book, as did Michael Lewis's *Moneyball*, Alan English's *Stand Up and Fight* and John Carlin's *Playing the Enemy* (which became the film, *Invictus*). Matthew Syed's *Bounce*, Malcolm Gladwell's *Outliers* and Daniel Coyle's *The Talent Code* also inspired my approach – an eclectic mix, there's no doubt, but all had a part in the formation of ideas that went into creating *White Gold*. *Moneyball* was the first flash of inspiration – Clive Woodward is my rugby equivalent of Billy Beane – but these books all helped to fuel the fire.

A special thank you must go to Sir Clive Woodward for setting aside time to meet with me and for speaking so openly.

I am indebted to a long list of biographies, autobiographies, scientific studies, documentaries and dozens and dozens of newspaper and magazine columns which formed the basis for much of my research. A list of these sources can be found in the end-matter of this book – it is a long list and while I would recommend just about every one of the autobiographies and histories, for those who would like to learn more about the broader issues discussed herein – particularly those that draw on accounts and studies that go beyond the rugby matches themselves – I would nudge you towards *Bounce*, *Outliers*, *Winning!* and *The Talent Code*.

Thanks to all at Arena Sport and Birlinn Ltd who backed me on this project and have bought their renowned enthusiasm and high standards to bear on the end product. I hope that I have repaid their faith.

Finally, thank you to Annabelle, Isla and Hector who put up with me while I wrote this book. I'm sure that, by comparison, they think that England's journey was a walk in the park...

CONTENTS

PROLOGUE   1

PART ONE: GENESIS

    ONE: THE ANATOMY OF A PHILOSOPHY   11

    TWO: THE ANATOMY OF A BUSINESSMAN   45

    THREE: THE ANATOMY OF A COACH   65

PART TWO: REVOLUTION

    FOUR: THE ANATOMY OF AN UPHEAVAL   81

    FIVE: THE ANATOMY OF A WINNING CULTURE   117

    SIX: THE ANATOMY OF BUILDING A WORLD-CLASS TEAM   155

    SEVEN: THE ANATOMY OF EXCELLENCE   185

    EIGHT: THE ANATOMY OF PREPARATION   221

PART THREE: ASCENSION

    NINE: THE ANATOMY OF THE CLIMB   237

    TEN: THE ANATOMY OF THE SUMMIT   265

PART FOUR: HUBRIS

    ELEVEN: THE ANATOMY OF THE THEREAFTER   299

BIBLIOGRAPHY AND FURTHER READING   312

'Far better it is to dare mighty things, to win glorious triumphs even though chequered by failure, than to rank with those poor spirits who neither enjoy nor suffer much because they live in the gray twilight that knows neither victory nor defeat.'
Theodore Roosevelt

PROLOGUE

Happy the man, and happy he alone,
He who can call today his own:
He who, secure within, can say,
Tomorrow do thy worst, for I have lived today.
Be fair or foul or rain or shine
The joys I have possessed in spite of fate, are mine.
Not Heaven itself upon the past has power,
But what has been, has been, and I have had my hour.

Horace, Odes, Book III, xxix

Manly. Friday, 21 November 2003.

Within throwing distance of the golden sands that hem the eastern side of the Manly peninsula – a ribbon of land that juts out into the Tasman Sea on the north-east edge of Sydney Harbour – sits Manly Rugby Football Club.

A blustery wind was blowing in from the ocean on this late spring afternoon, rolling great white-crested waves on to Manly Beach and swelling the waters around a ferry that was carrying commuters from Manly Wharf to Circular Quay in downtown Sydney some seven miles away. The wind whipped up the sand on the beach and then swept inland, swirling across the pitch at the Manly Oval and then onwards towards the inland suburbs.

The view from club's stand, which faced east towards the Tasman, was one of the finest to be found in any sporting venue in the world – even on an unseasonably cold day like this when heavy slate-grey clouds cast a gloomy pall over the land below. The Oval had an unusual appearance, with temporary barriers erected all around its outer perimeter and patrolling security guards keeping a close eye as flocks of white-shirted fans gathered along the pavement, trying to get close enough to the barriers to peer through to the pitch at the centre of the Oval.

Huddled together in the stand, arms crossed against the wind, sat half a dozen figures. Frowns of concentration were etched across their faces as they peered down at the group of thirty men jogging around the field. There were two distinct teams of fifteen at work, running through a series of practice attack and defence moves.

After a babble of instructions, eight forwards on one side jogged lightly to the touchline for a line-out and seven backs assembled themselves into an attacking formation outside them. In opposition stood fifteen understudies, each with a yellow bib over his training gear, and in equally swift fashion they arranged themselves into a defensive configuration.

The murmur of Manly's traffic could be heard undulating in the background, mixing with the sound of the wind, the ocean, the occasional blast of horns from the commuting ferries and sporadic cries from the fans on the other side of the barriers. Down on the pitch the players barked instructions to one another – the attacking line-out code was called along with a corresponding backline move; each man in the defensive side called out who they were marking, while the inside-centre, Stuart Abbott – the general of the defensive line – reiterated the need for line-speed to close down the attack, and then readied himself to lead the charge as soon as the ball was released into play.

This was the England rugby squad. They were some twenty-eight hours away from the biggest match of their lives, the 2003 World Cup final, which was to be played against Australia, the host nation of the tournament, holders of the Webb Ellis Cup and the current world champions. Of all the outcomes of tournament rugby, to face the title holders – one of the undisputed superpowers of the world game – on their home ground in front of a partisan local crowd and under a welter of global media coverage, pressure and expectation, was as big as it could get.

Louise Ramsay, the England team manager, appeared from the tunnel beneath the stand and made her way up the steps to the group of seated observers. The first to greet her was Dave Alred, the kicking guru. 'Any news on the weather?' he asked, his eyes rising balefully to the dark clouds above them.

'More rain,' said Ramsay flatly, handing him a printout of the forecast.

Next to Alred, Andy Robinson, the forwards coach, nodded in brief acknowledgement but said nothing. For a moment a thin smile had registered on his lips as he cast his mind back just two months to Pennyhill Park in Surrey, where the squad had been training throughout one of the hottest English summers on record. Although training in such conditions had been hellish for the players, the management group had been delighted that the sweltering temperatures would match the conditions expected in Australia, glad that the team would be acclimatised before boarding the plane at Heathrow. So much for that theory. Since the team had flown into Perth some six weeks earlier, they had played almost exclusively in conditions that would have had Noah making final preparations to the ark. At this stage of the tournament the prospect of more rain was no surprise. The semi-final five days earlier had been played in a torrential downpour. Indeed, it had felt just like being back at Twickenham for an early February Calcutta Cup clash. As the forwards coach of the most effective and most experienced pack at the World Cup, Robinson was not remotely concerned at having to play in the kind of conditions typical at home during the autumn internationals or the Six Nations. Every player in the squad was comfortable with the ball in hand and over the previous few seasons England had developed a style of play never before practised by their predecessors: a heady combination of speed and width, flat passing, aerial bombardments, devastating running angles and brutal defence. But they had not forgotten the traditional cornerstone of the English game: brute power up front. If the conditions dictated a forwards-orientated slugfest, Robinson knew that he had some of the planet's finest exponents of granite-hard forward domination in his ranks.

His eyes didn't move from the players below as Ramsay and Alred discussed the possible wind conditions at the Telstra Stadium in central Sydney the following evening. He was watching his charges as they took their places at the line-out. In the middle of the line, Phil Vickery, the tight-head prop, feinted forward for a moment and then spun on his heels and took two quick steps towards the towering figure of lock Ben Kay. Steve Thompson, the hooker, drew back his arms and fired the ball in a smooth, spiralling torpedo that sailed in a high arc between the two contesting packs in front of him. Kay leapt, his jump propelled by Vickery, who gripped his legs just below his kneecaps and thrust him as high as his arms would stretch, while blindside flanker Richard Hill offered support from behind, his hands on Kay's hamstrings, pushing him as high as he could manage. In opposition, substitute prop Jason Leonard and flanker Lewis Moody boosted Kay's understudy, Simon Shaw, up to contend for the ball.

At the apex of the jump, Kay stretched out a hand and plucked the ball from the air before dropping it deftly down to the waiting scrum-half Matt Dawson, who immediately whipped the ball out to his backline. The whole process had taken little more than two seconds and had been executed to absolute perfection. *Like a well-oiled machine*, thought Robinson. Shaw's jump had been good, the supporting lift strong, but the slickness with which Vickery, Kay, Hill and Thompson had executed their routine had left the giant figure of Shaw grasping nothing but thin air.

'It's going to be pretty rough going,' continued Ramsay over Robinson's shoulder. 'Similar conditions to the semi.'

'Fine,' said Alred, and stood up. Wind and rain. Hardly a kicker's conditions of choice, but for the man that Alred worked with, who had first come under his guidance as a callow teenager, it would matter little. Come rain, wind or hail, England's stand-off, Jonny Wilkinson, could – and would – strike the ball with the same deadly accuracy and efficiency as he would on a calm, bright summer's day. No matter what.

Alred shoved a little sheaf of notes into the zip pocket of his windcheater and began to make his way down towards the pitch.

The 'captain's run' was drawing to a close. The coaches had long ago ceased to intervene at this stage of the team's pre-match preparation; it was a time for the players to run their final moves, to ensure that everything was working like clockwork. At this stage, the coaches didn't need to tell the likes of Martin Johnson, Lawrence Dallaglio, Neil Back, Hill, Dawson or Will Greenwood what to do. Indeed, none of the players out there – including the fifteen who were running in opposition – needed any further guidance from those in the stands. Every pattern of play was second nature; every call and move and reaction a natural progression from one to the other. They were a well-oiled machine indeed.

A ruck formed on the far 22-metre line and as Dawson bent to retrieve the ball from where centre Mike Tindall had placed it he heard the trigger-call for immediate distribution from Wilkinson and the ball was spun away from the breakdown almost as soon as Dawson had touched it.

Wilkinson shifted the ball to his inside-centre, Greenwood, who straightened the line, jinked and then dropped a soft little pass to full-back Josh Lewsey, who hit the line at an angle off Greenwood's shoulder and sliced straight through the onrushing defence. As his opposite number, Iain Balshaw – the last man in the defensive line – swept across to close down his space, Lewsey found that he had support runners on either flank – Jason Robinson on his left, Ben Cohen on his right. The two wingers were completely different in stature and brought contrasting styles of play to the strike-runner positions of left and right-wing, but both were equally lethal with ball in hand. After a small feint to Robinson, Lewsey fixed Balshaw with a half-step and then shifted the ball to Cohen and the six-foot-two, sixteen-stone speedster cruised in unopposed under the posts.

Johnson, the captain, was emerging from the ruck back on the 22. He nodded, a glint of satisfaction flickering for a moment in his dark eyes before his brow contracted into its habitual furrows, and with a wave of his hands he called the rest of his players to him. The run was over.

Alred began to make his way over from the touchline. After a few short words from Johnson, the huddle broke apart. Twenty-nine players headed for the showers. One remained.

Wilkinson.

At twenty-four, he was widely regarded as the best stand-off that England had ever produced. Indeed, many regarded him as the best player the world had ever seen. He was meticulous in everything that he did – from his training, diet, game preparation and analysis to the way he masterminded England's structure and play on the field. Never before had rugby union seen such a dedicated professional. He was the poster boy of English rugby and was adored across the country for his good looks, polite, unassuming manner and his virtually unerring excellence on the field – even though the latter was developed and maintained at a great personal price.

He began to walk slowly around the pitch, gathering up all the balls that had been used during the run-through before picking up a bag of extra balls that had been left on the pitchside. Alred met him there with a small blue kicking tee and they set off together towards the posts at the far end of the pitch.

As Wilkinson placed the ball on the tee – the seam of the ball aimed directly between the uprights, the ball tilted fifteen degrees to the left to open up the sweet spot for the first metatarsal bone in his left foot – he took a deep breath and slipped comfortably into a well-worn routine. In the secular world of sport, the two tall uprights and intersecting crossbar that made up a set of rugby posts were Wilkinson's altar; the metronomic routine that he went through as he placed first one ball on the tee and then another and another and another, with each flying straight and true between the uprights, was his carefully fashioned and delicately refined ritual.

The job of the rugby goal-kicker can be one of the loneliest in world sport. Dave Alred, who had helped Wilkinson to create and then hone his systematic technique, was there to ensure that his protégé was *never* alone; no matter the circumstances, no matter the conditions, no matter the pressure, he would never be alone when kicking for goal. The routine would always be there to keep him company, to focus his mind – not on the boiling mass of humanity in the stands around him, not on the roaring of tens of thousands of voices or the rolling clacks of hundreds of cameras aimed solely at him, or on the scowls and sledging and the sly digs from the opposition, but on the quiet practice fields, where his thoughts were calm and focused, where the only sound to be heard was of wind in the trees, occasional birdsong and the thump of a ball being perfectly struck on the sweet spot.

Wilkinson straightened, checked his alignment of the ball, took two steps backwards and then one to his right and leant forwards, his knees bent, his hands gently cupped together in front of him.

'Steady breathing,' said Alred softly. 'And remember the follow-through.'

Wilkinson tapped the end of his left foot on the turf, forcing his big toe tight into the corner of his boot, the pliable leather of his adidas Predator stretching tight against it. He tensed his foot, his toes stiffening as he curled and pressed down against the sole of his boot, the line from the tip of his big toe through the arch of his foot and up to his ankle locked solid.

Two steps. Contact. The foot continued up after the ball, the leg extending straight, the toes of the right foot, which had just a moment before been set solidly into the ground, now dragging on their tips through the grass as Wilkinson's centre of gravity followed the ball up and forward. He landed softly, his eyes still fixed on the target.

The ball flew end over end, straight through the middle of the posts. It was so perfect that it might have been struck from just a few metres in front of the uprights. But in reality Wilkinson was on the left touchline, more than forty metres away, on a tight angle.

'Well done,' said Alred. 'Next.'

Up in the stands, the small group of coaches had remained motionless.

Andy Robinson picked up the weather report that Alred had left on his seat. He studied it for a moment before passing it to his right, where the man responsible for masterminding England's passage to this moment sat, steadily watching Wilkinson working through his repertoire. Clive Woodward had been England's head coach since the late summer of 1997. Upon accepting the role he had become the figurehead of the largest and wealthiest rugby union on the planet. He had ascended to the position at a time when English rugby appeared in relatively rude health. From the late 1980s and through the early and mid-'90s, England had been the dominant team in the northern hemisphere. They had won three Grand Slams, contested the 1991 World Cup final and had reached the semi-final of the 1995 World Cup. Many of their players were considered the finest ever to have played for their country and a core of the team had just passed into legend after playing a central part in the British & Irish Lions' successful tour to South Africa that summer. But for all this success, for all their supremacy in Europe and for all the riches and resources at their disposal, England had never dominated on the world stage. At no point had they been considered the most outstanding team on the planet. At no point had the traditional superpowers in the world game – New Zealand, South Africa and Australia – cowered at the prospect of playing the men in white.

But over the six years of Woodward's reign all that had changed. A left-field appointment in the summer of 1997, Woodward had come to the job with an ambition to turn the entire structure of English rugby on its head, to carve a new path for the national team and all its contributory tiers, and to unshackle the traditionally staid play of the English so that they could, at last, emerge from the shadows cast by their illustrious opponents in the southern hemisphere and make their own, indelible mark on history.

But how had he managed to do it? How did he, his lieutenants and his players make such a fundamental shift in everything they did? How did they shake off ingrained styles, structures, expectations and deep-seated national and personal insecurities to discover a belief that they could be the best of the best – and establish the methods, support and environment to deliver on that belief?

Let's take the plunge.

PART ONE

GENESIS

ONE

THE ANATOMY OF
A PHILOSOPHY

'A journey of a thousand miles begins with a single step.'
Lao Tzu

CLIVE WOODWARD, aged thirteen, lay stretched out on his bed. He was fully dressed and on the floor beside him were two packed bags of clothes. Next to these, placed there as a last vestige of hope, was a mud-stained football. Woodward stared up at a poster above his bed. Alan Ball, Gordon Banks, Bobby and Jackie Charlton, George Cohen, Roger Hunt, Geoff Hurst, Bobby Moore, Martin Peters, Nobby Stiles and Ray Wilson: England's 1966 World Cup-winning heroes. He looked first at the face of Alan Ball and then at Geoff Hurst and recalled, as clearly as if he was again watching that history-making final on television with his father, Ball breaking away from the watchful eye of Karl-Heinz Schnellinger and crossing the ball towards Hurst, who thundered it against the underside of the crossbar for England's match-turning third goal.

Woodward had been only ten years old at the time but the World Cup final had seared itself on his memory and that goal, which restored England's lead, held a cherished place in his heart. He could recall with perfect clarity every movement of the players on the pitch as they overcame West Germany 4–2. It had been a seminal moment in his young life, a moment when football had embedded itself in his soul.

There was a creak on the stairs and Woodward blinked, his reverie broken. Another seminal moment was upon him.

There was a tap at the door and his mother poked her head into the bedroom.

'Your father says it's time,' she said softly. 'Are you ready?'

Woodward sighed and pulled himself to his feet. He picked up his bags and moved towards the door.

Unable to bear the look on her son's face, Joyce Woodward put her arm around him and squeezed.

'I'm coming back,' he said.

'I know that. Of course you are.'

But Woodward knew that she didn't appreciate *quite* how soon he intended to be back.

Outside, his father had started the car. Clive slung his bags into the boot, embraced his mother once more and then climbed into the passenger seat beside his father. They didn't speak as the car pulled away but he forced a smile and raised a hand to the dwindling figure of his mother as she waved from the roadside.

As the car turned the corner and the house disappeared from sight, Woodward tapped his feet in a light beat, as if he had a football at his toes, flicking it from side to side, curling an imaginary pass off the outside of his foot, bouncing a hundred keepy-uppies in a steady rhythm. He poured his thoughts into the game, shutting off the reality of what was happening. After thirteen happy years at home, he was leaving, off to fulfill an ambition that his father had long dreamed of for him: a private boarding school education.

Squadron Leader Ronald Woodward was a pilot trainer in the RAF, a respected and dedicated military man who loved his family and wanted the best for his children. He knew that his son was a talented footballer and he had heard the rumours that he was being scouted by a number of professional clubs, including Everton; but he also knew how few young prodigies actually make a successful career for themselves in football. What he wanted instead was a university education for Clive and a job as a lawyer or a teacher or a banker. Something with substance and longevity. He knew that his son was bright – but he also knew that he was being distracted by football.

When Ronald voiced his concerns about his son's errant behaviour at school to his commanding officer he had been advised that a position at the Welsh boarding school HMS Conway, on Anglesey, might be good for Clive's education and advancement in life. It was a naval institution, but Ronald Woodward had been training naval pilots for several years and his CO knew that strings could be pulled. As an added caveat, there would be no fees to pay – a perk of being an officer. Ronald barely thought twice about it. He had ascended to the rank of officer without a public school or university education – an achievement of real rarity at the time. He had always dreamed of a better start in life for his children and now here was an opportunity for Clive, set out on a silver dish. He returned home with a masterplan and presented it to his wife. There was no chance for her to argue – everything had already been set in motion. And if she wasn't to have a say about it, his son certainly wouldn't.

Clive Woodward was an intelligent young man but, as his father and teachers had noted, he struggled with a lack of focus. Flighty and impatient, his concentration often drifted off in class; all his attention was focused on his one great love: football. When thinking about, watching or playing the game, he would become utterly engrossed. He was already playing for the school under-15 side, a year ahead of his peers, and he was well aware of the rumours about the scouts. A life as a professional footballer was all he wanted in the world. But he also knew his father's feelings about the whole thing. A football career was not the path envisioned for him. No, that was a scenario for other people's sons.

And so it had come to this day: Clive Woodward's introduction to life at HMS Conway and a farewell to football – for at this all-boys institution there was no talk or thought of football. No, the game that ruled the hearts and heads on Anglesey was something else. It was rugby union.

'The only experience I had of rugby was watching a bit of it on TV. But it had always seemed slow and overcomplicated and had never really interested me that much,' said Woodward years later. 'So there's me, obsessed with football, and people saying I'm going to play for Man United and Everton and whoever, and that was all I wanted to do. I would sit in class and literally count down the minutes until I could be outside kicking a ball around. And the big thing that happened was that the headmaster at my school went out of his way to come to my house to see my parents and he told them that I was bright, but I was destroying my life because all I could think about was football. I was good but there was no family background to really understand professional sport, so what they heard was that I was ruining my life and they felt that they had to do whatever they could to change that. It was a tough decision to send me away, but they did it for my own good. My father was given a list of service schools that he could send me to and I think the reason he chose Conway was quite deliberate – they didn't play football there.'

The drive to Anglesey from their home at RAF Linton-on-Ouse, which was just outside Easingwold in North Yorkshire, took the best part of four hours and it was dark by the time the great concrete edifice loomed into sight.

In 1859, after a petition by the Mercantile Marine Service Association requesting that a school be set up to train young boys for life at sea, the Admiralty had commissioned the ship, HMS *Conway*, for this very purpose. It was originally moored in the Sloyne, off Rock Ferry, on the River Mersey in Liverpool. In 1941 Merseyside was targeted by Luftwaffe air strikes and the decision was made to sail the school ship to the Menai Strait in Anglesey. Twelve years later HMS *Conway* was being towed to Birkenhead for refurbishment when she was caught up in a storm, ran aground and was wrecked. Temporary tented accommodation for the pupils was set up at Plas Newydd on Anglesey, the country seat of the Marquess of Anglesey, before wooden huts were constructed as a makeshift schoolhouse and living quarters. These were in place for a decade until the new building, which became known as the 'stone frigate', was constructed.

While the original school ship had been a thing of beauty, the architects of the terra firma version had clearly decided that to emulate the ship in any way was undesirable. Instead they seem to have been inspired by the design aesthetics of the prison service. The main school was a large concrete oblong speckled with small windows. If Woodward had been dreading his induction to the school before, his anxiety went through the roof when he finally saw it. No home comforts, no football and now this: a prison block in the middle of nowhere waiting to embrace him in its cold, harsh grip.

Woodward said goodbye to his father in the entrance hall to the boarding house – a firm handshake and a brief locked gaze between them. Then Ronald Woodward turned and disappeared out into the night.

Clive was taken to his room on the third floor. As he threw down his bags he glanced out of his bedroom window and saw the twin red glow of his father's taillights as they bounced down the road on their way home. He swallowed. What the hell was he doing here?

It took only twenty-four hours for him to decide that enough was enough. If his initial thought had been 'What the hell am I doing here?' it had soon turned to, 'What the hell is Hell doing here in the middle of Anglesey?' He hated it that much.

'It was like bloody Alcatraz,' he recalled. 'The whole place looked like a prison, was run like a prison and it was out there on an island in the middle of nowhere. They were schooling boys who, by and large, were going to go on and serve out at sea, so the discipline was tough and everything was incredibly regimented. They wanted hard, tough cadets, so corporal punishment was high on the agenda – the teachers used to dish it out occasionally, but on the whole it was done by the senior cadets. If anyone stepped out of line in any way, they'd get beaten. And that whole culture of rough physical intimidation spread throughout the school. It was a tough place to be. They were the darkest days of my life.'

He escaped from the school grounds and caught a train at Bangor. When he eventually made it home, his parents were there waiting for him, having been alerted to his absence by the school. His father shoved him in the car and drove him straight back.

A few days later he tried again. This time Ronald drove him to York station and put him on a train to Bangor. A week later this round trip was repeated. Woodward was determined that he would break his father's will with this continual show of defiance. But in the end it was *his* will that was broken. The headmaster, Mr Basil Lord, was so infuriated at Woodward's insubordination that he ordered a senior cadet to unleash what was euphemistically called 'the Teaser' – a length of marine rope made of tarred hemp tied into a hard knot at one end; it was kept in a bottle of salted water and it was as hard as a metal bar. The thrashing was brutal and it was enough for Woodward to hold up his hands in defeat. He had to accept his lot. He had to try to assimilate.

'I was only thirteen when I went there and it was a long way from home,' said Woodward, 'and I ran away not because I hated it as such but because I wanted to play football. My parents couldn't understand it. They said, "You're mad, we're giving you the opportunity of a lifetime at a good school, don't throw it away." And was it a good school? It was an OK school – but it was tough because it had a military background.

'My parents are both dead now, but if my Dad was here I'm sure he would say, "I can't believe you are still going on about this. You've had an incredible academic, sporting, business and coaching career. Would you have done all of that if we hadn't sent you away to boarding school?" And I don't know. But I also don't know what would have happened with my football career – and like any big question, it tends to linger with you. But because I was good at sports and because rugby was the main game at Conway I got into it. It makes your life easier if you're good at the main game at a school – that's how you get respect from your peers and your teachers. I think that because I wasn't allowed to play football I wanted to show everyone that I could be the best player in the school at rugby. And that little niggle drove me – and it probably drove me through my entire career. In terms of motivation, I think every successful sportsperson has a drive in them that has been instilled by someone telling them that they can't do something, that they are too small or too skinny or too fat or too slow – it can be the slightest of comments – and proving that person wrong drives them for the rest of their lives. Look at guys like Brian Moore, Andy Robinson and Neil Back – they were told they were too small to play international rugby and every time they pulled on a jersey they wanted to prove that that wasn't the case and they did so with a furious, uncompromising will to win.

'Being good at rugby made being at Conway liveable. I don't think the school was much fun for kids that weren't good at sport. It was a tough place to be.'

It is little wonder that in an environment as oppressive as this Clive Woodward developed an instinct to rebel against convention and repression whenever he encountered it. It would be an instinct that would come to define him. As with many young children sent off to boarding school, he quickly learnt independence – and how to survive on his own wits. The psychological impact of his lost dreams to be a footballer cannot be underestimated. It was a crushing blow even more painful than a lash from the Teaser; and just as the corporal punishment was designed to harden and teach the young cadets, so too would this psychological wound form a bedrock in his psyche, ultimately coming to define significant aspects of his personality.

*

The day that Clive Woodward was born – 6 January 1956 – a schoolteacher in Perthshire, Scotland, stood up from the desk in his study in Patchell's, one of Glenalmond College's boarding houses, went to the window and looked out over Hockey Ground, the playing field at the front of the college.

It was a grey morning and a heavy mist clung to the glen as it so often did at that time of year.

Jim Greenwood raised a hand and wiped some condensation from the pane, the better to see the group of boys who were just appearing out of the haze in the distance. At this time of year many boys would go out running in preparation for the steeplechase, the school's cross-country run, but these boys were not in training for that. Being out this early meant only one thing: they were miscreants from one of the other boarding houses and were being duly punished for whatever mischief they had caused their housemaster; upon completion they would be forced to wash in a cold bath before being allowed to take breakfast and continue their day as normal. Such punishment had been an institution at the school long before Greenwood had taken up the position as English and French master in 1954, but it was a convention that he had no issue with for not only did it give a base layer of fitness to every boy in the school, but it was an additional piece of training for his rugby players – and he could now identify in the ranks of running figures four of his first XV. Adding this to the rigorous circuit training that he had introduced as part of each rugby training session, he knew that his players would be among the fittest in the country. And in rugby, that could go a long way in deciding the outcome of a match.

Greenwood had big shoes to fill when he rolled up at Glenalmond and took charge of rugby as part of his pastoral duties. One of his predecessors in the role had been John Gwilliam, who had taught history and French at the school from 1949 to 1952 and supervised the rugby programme – while also captaining Wales to Grand Slam victories in the 1950 and 1952 Five Nations.

For many, trying to replace a man like Gwilliam would have been a daunting task. Gwilliam's successor, E.B.A. Edwards, certainly found it so and after two years of poor results Ralph Barlow, the school warden, handed the reins to Greenwood. Fortunately for the new man, he wasn't short of rugby pedigree himself.

Born and bred in Dunfermline, Greenwood had read English at the University of Edinburgh before joining the RAF for his national service, during which time he played for Harlequins, the RAF and Eastern Counties. Although he played for the university as a student, he was dedicated to Dunfermline rugby club and then, once he started working at Glenalmond, to Perthshire Academicals. He was selected to play for Scotland against France at Murrayfield in January 1952, which resulted in a 13–11 defeat. He was dropped for the rest of the tournament and didn't gain his second cap until 1955.

The early 1950s was a dark period for Scottish rugby. In 1951 the side recorded a spectacular 19–0 victory at home against, coincidentally, John Gwilliam's Grand Slam holders. But between that glorious afternoon and the corresponding fixture in 1955 Scotland suffered an ignominious run of seventeen consecutive defeats, scoring just eleven tries, six conversions, and four penalties in five years for a paltry total of fifty-four points, and endured humiliation at the hands of the Springboks in 1951 – going down 44–0 in what became known as the 'Murrayfield Massacre'.

Greenwood, a fast and athletic 6ft 2in back-row forward, was recalled once again to face the French for the opening game of the 1955 Five Nations. This time the game was played at French rugby's fortress at Colombes – and he was named as captain. Although Scotland lost 15–0, Greenwood had been a revelation. In the next match, against Wales at Murrayfield, he was equally impressive as he led his team out of the darkness of that losing run to record a 14–8 victory, which was backed up by a 12–3 victory over Ireland at Murrayfield and then a narrow 9–6 loss to England at Twickenham.

His form in the 1955 championship earned him a place on Robin Thompson's 1955 Lions tour to South Africa, where he established his playing legacy for all time. Although selected as a No.8, he was converted to flanker and played in sixteen of the twenty-five matches on the tour. Crucially he scored tries in the First and Fourth Tests against the Springboks and was instrumental in securing the 2–2 series draw and the reputation of that touring squad as one of the finest ever to leave the shores of Britain and Ireland.

Warden Barlow had been more than a little reluctant to allow Greenwood the time off from Glenalmond to tour, but when the Lion returned his influence and charisma shone like a beacon for all the pupils at the school.

As one of his former colleagues recalled, 'He was a bachelor, as many of us were at the time, and was absolutely inspirational as a teacher. He had great personal charm and was never a rugby bore – in fact, I don't ever remember him talking about rugby in the common room unless we really pressed him. He had some wonderful stories from his time with Scotland and in particular his time with the Lions in South Africa, but you had to coax them out of him. At a time of conventionality, he was fairly unorthodox in his teaching methods. If it was a fine day he would take his class for a walk and would often take boys out of school for jaunts without telling housemasters. There was nothing sinister about it, he was just a free spirit who felt strongly that there was more to life and to teaching than could be learnt cramped up in a school room. Another colleague of ours, Peter Adam, always enjoyed telling the story about the time he had to make a dash down to Edinburgh just hours before an international match because Jim had left his rugby boots behind in his room in Patchell's. That was Jim – an inspirational man and thinker, with the odd flash that would remind us that he was still human.'

Greenwood smiled softly as the group of boys thundered across Hockey Ground, their hair plastered to their foreheads, arms a ruddy pink, legs splattered with mud. They were all working hard – the older boys vying for supremacy, the younger ones fighting to keep up and prove themselves to their elders. In a few hours they would be out there again, only this time under his tutelage. He loved those hours out on the rugby field with a group of players with minds completely open to his ideas, who would run around with unbridled abandon, lost in their love of the game. It was rugby at its purest.

He turned back to his desk. Piles of jotters were stacked all around his ink blotter, where a fat notebook heavy with scribbles and annotated drawings lay open beside a cup of steaming Ovaltine. He sat down and picked up a pen.

The simplest way to characterise team strategy is to specify the channel and manner in which players have been prepared for their first-phase strike. Once this model has been established, you have criteria for every practical aspect of team preparation. It brings coherence and purpose to all that you do.

He wrote for another ten minutes then put aside his pen and left his office. He didn't have a class for over an hour, so he changed into his running gear and set off through the mist into the glen.

Years later his Lions teammate, Phil Davies, would recall sitting in their room in South Africa in 1955 and hearing from Greenwood about his training regime. 'He was years ahead of his time, Jim. He would sprint alternate telegraph poles down the glen and back. No one trained like that – certainly not in the UK. Probably not anywhere in the northern hemisphere. You would hear stories about some of the South African farmers on the high veld working the land and then going on these great long training runs, or of New Zealanders who would run around the hills and lift tree trunks and so on. Jim was like that – but also different. Even before sports science had ever entered rugby he was training like a sports scientist would approach the game. He would run until his lungs were on fire, but it wouldn't be a mindless dash across the wilds, he would do things that were relevant to rugby – changes of direction, hitting the ground and getting back to his feet at once, back-pedalling, sprint acceleration, the works. Everyone trains like that now, but not then. Jim was doing these things before anyone else. And he *thought* about the game.'

Three years later, in 1959, Greenwood left Glenalmond to take up a position at Cheltenham College before moving on to Tiffin School in Kingston upon Thames where, in 1967, he decided that the time had come for him to do something with all his scribbled notes on rugby. The journal that he had been writing in his second-floor room in Patchell's had become two, then three, then four volumes. His thoughts on the game were prolific and it was sometimes a battle to transfer them all from his excited mind to paper. But it was a battle well fought and his first publication, *Improve Your Rugby,* was the result.

It was a period of contrasts in British sport. The year before, a ten-year-old Clive Woodward had watched in rapture, along with half of the world, as the England football team had lifted the World Cup at Wembley. While that tournament was taking place, however, the Lions were enduring a torrid time in New Zealand.

The tour was a hotchpotch of disasters from the outset. Scotland's Mike Campbell-Lamerton had been chosen as captain and, even though he was well regarded by those that knew him, he was far from the outstanding choice at lock – and the basic requirement for any Lions captain is that their Test place should never be in doubt. The coach was John Robins, a Lion on the 1950 tour to New Zealand and a lecturer in physical education at Loughborough College. Although experienced and clever, he was sidelined by Campbell-Lamerton, who felt that running training, leading the team and performing all manner of off-field duties should remain the captain's responsibility.

The tour began well with a run of six unbeaten matches against Australian provincial sides and two resounding Test victories over Australia in Sydney and Brisbane, but the fate of the 1966 Lions spiralled dismally once they crossed the Tasman and arrived in New Zealand. They were soundly beaten in all four Test matches, becoming the first Lions side to be whitewashed in a series.

The tour wouldn't have registered as even a blip on young Woodward's radar, but it hurt Greenwood deeply to see the Lions so humiliated. They had played poorly and with little intelligence save for the odd creative spark from players like Mike Gibson and David Watkins. The style they adopted was the complete antithesis of his own rugby philosophy. But why sit there and complain about it if he wasn't going to do anything to try to advance matters? *Improve Your Rugby* was the first step – if he could get even a handful of players to change their attitudes on how to play the game, to look for space and to try to exploit it, then at least he had made something of a difference. Even if it was just at the grass roots level. Because the way the game was being played at that time was killing rugby union.

The following year he left Tiffin and life as a schoolteacher and moved into higher education. He took up a position as an English lecturer at Loughborough – where he would become a colleague of John Robins – and with it he took charge of rugby at the colleges. Although no one would have foreseen it at the time, it was a move that would change rugby union throughout the world.

*

HMS Conway's 1st XV were playing Birkenhead Grammar at home. After a messy line-out on Birkenhead's 25-yard line there was a ruck in midfield and the ball was then shipped to the Birkenhead full-back, who cleared it downfield with a thumping kick. But his aim was poor and instead of the ball drifting out of play over the touchline, it held its line infield and was caught cleanly by one of the Conway centres who had read the situation as the ruck was forming and had dropped back deep to cover the kick.

Those watching on the sidelines held their breath. Whenever this particular player touched the ball in open play like this, spectators would look on admiringly and think, 'This boy's different'; this long-limbed youth who glided around the pitch, who had no appreciation for the traditional structures of a game. He didn't understand the patterns of play – or at least the patterns of play that had been ingrained into his teammates' minds by years of coaching. He would gather the ball from a clearance kick like this deep in his own half and traditional tactical thinking dictated that in such a situation he should hoof the ball back upfield into opposition territory. But this boy took the catch, looked up, scanned the field and saw space – as a footballer would. While his teammates were equipped with blinkers, his vision stretched to the peripheries. He saw the whole pitch, could sense the congested channels, the pockets of space and could anticipate the movement of both the opposition and his teammates – all in just a few infinitesimal moments. It was an instinct born out of his obsession with football and the perpetual motion of the protagonists in that game. When he transferred that instinct to rugby, opportunities unfolded before him like no other player in his side – and he had the pace to exploit those opportunities. Off he would dart, his long legs carrying him easily across the turf. At times his speed could take him all the way, at other times he would jink and swerve, change pace and direction or, if the need arose, extend a long, sinewy arm and keep a would-be tackler far enough away from making solid contact to either ease through a gap or buy enough time and space to offload the ball to a support runner. He was poetry in motion.

But that wasn't to say that Clive Woodward couldn't kick either. Again, the fundamental principle of his first sporting love meant that he had a kick like a siege gun – and a pinpoint accurate one at that.

He was slightly built but could also hit hard in defence. If he had his way he would always have the ball in his hands or at his feet, but if the need arose to make a tackle, he wouldn't be found wanting. All the frustration at his lost dreams, all the railing that he would do in the privacy of his dorm room at the unfairness of his situation, all would explode out of him as he dipped his shoulder and clattered into an opposition runner.

He could also make mistakes, of course. That was only to be expected of a player so new to the game, whose natural thinking was aligned with an entirely different sporting discipline, and for someone who liked to play as daringly as he did. *Overenthusiasm, thinking ahead of those around him, challenging the perceived wisdom and the supposed basic tactics of the way rugby should be played.* These were traits that would both inspire and dog his playing career, and they were traits that would define his professional life thereafter.

And so it was that the boy who would never have chosen to play rugby found that rugby was a perfect fit for him, even if it took him years to admit it. The game wasn't his dream but it would become absolutely central to his life.

He was small but fast and had at first been placed in the scrum-half position, but his ability to break tackles and avoid contact thanks to his blistering speed meant that, after a brief spell playing fly-half, he was moved out into the centres.

When he was in his second-last year at school he was made first-team captain and held the role for two seasons. It was a testament to his abilities that this new boy to rugby was so readily accepted by his teammates and coaches.

It was a talent that was not only recognised at Conway. In February 1974 he was selected for a trial in Cardiff for the Welsh Schoolboys side. He was the only player from North Wales to get the call that year; it was a moment of genuine pride for both Woodward and Conway, but it would soon become a memory that would live long in his psyche for all the wrong reasons.

'One of my North Wales coaches drove me down to Cardiff for the trial. I played for the Possibles. The Probables, who we were up against, had some players who would go on to have stellar careers – the half-back combination of Terry Holmes and Gareth Davies alone went on to be greats of Welsh and Lions rugby. But even though I was only in the Possibles, I had a good game and the selectors took me aside for a chat afterwards. It was clear that I had impressed them, but things went cold as soon as they asked where I was from and I told them that I was from North Yorkshire. As soon as I said that, the conversation was over. I was English and they weren't going to play an English boy in their team.'

Years later, a Welsh journalist brought up the trial and asked why it was that Woodward had not played for the Welsh Schoolboy side.

'I said that I had to withdraw because of injury. I didn't want to make a fuss about it in the press. But the real reason gave me a special, private motivation which I used whenever I faced Wales – both as a player and a coach. It may sound bitter but that whole experience had a profound effect on me at the time. I was young and I was angry. And I carried that anger with me for a long time.'

The whole situation was unusual and would never happen now. In the modern game, particularly in the northern hemisphere, club and regional selectors care not a jot for a player's country of birth; if they are good enough and are committed to the cause, they are in. The same is often true of international selection – if a player makes the grade, all that matters is their desire to play for the national side and that they are qualified to do so (by birth or through the birth-place of one of their parents or grandparents, or through a three-year uninterrupted residency in the country they wish to represent). But it was a different time and the episode left its mark on Woodward.

Another unusual element was that he had been allowed to go to the trial at all. Conway had often prevented its pupils from attending local representative trials or from appearing for representative teams, as it would mean too much time away from the school. But Conway's days were drawing to a close. In the summer of 1972 it was announced that the school was to close in July 1974, at the end of Woodward's final year. As the processes for decommissioning began and the staff members started to contemplate life after Conway, many of the old strictures were relaxed – and so it was that Woodward was allowed his shot at playing for North Wales and his trip south for the Cardiff trial was given the go-ahead.

At the end of the year Woodward took his leave from the school and as the old doors closed behind him, they did so for the last time.

It had been a torrid few years but Ronald Woodward had got his wish. His son had buckled down and got on with his schoolwork. Even if he might not have admitted it at the time, playing rugby had taught Clive valuable lessons about leadership, group responsibility and about the value and importance of teamwork. Rugby had come easily to him and even the pain and anger caused by the Welsh Schoolboys fiasco had taught him to always keep his feet on the ground and his head up. Above all, Conway had taught him how to roll with the punches.

He left school with three A-levels and applied to Durham University to read law. He felt that he had done well in his exams but his results weren't enough to gain him a place on the course. He was at a crossroads. Did he wait for clearing and try to get in in the second tranche of applications? Did he defer for a year? Did he resit his exams? Or did he try something else altogether? He spotted an advert in a newspaper one morning and, on a whim, applied for a management traineeship at NatWest Bank in London. He was accepted.

He moved down to work in the Richmond branch of NatWest in September and, a short time later, turned up at Harlequins. They were one of the founding clubs of the Rugby Football Union back in 1871 and their ground, the Stoop, stood in the shadow of Twickenham, the home of English rugby. Woodward was an unknown quantity when he arrived for his first training session one bright September evening, but his style of play was a natural fit for the club. Harlequins had a tradition, known globally, for champagne rugby both on and off the field. They played an expansive, fast game and the social scene was legendary. They had strong ties to the financial centre in the City and they attracted both a wealthy and gregarious type of player. Rugby was all about fun at Harlequins; in the face of the attritional style of rugby so prevalent throughout English rugby at the time, the free-flowing play encouraged at Quins was a breath of fresh air – particularly to players like Woodward.

There were a number of England internationals in the Quins ranks at the time. The captain, Nick Martin, had been capped by England in 1972 and although he would play only once for his country, he was a hugely influential figure at the club. His full-back, Bob Hiller, was the incumbent England No.15. Hiller went on to win a total of nineteen caps and had toured with the British & Irish Lions in South Africa in 1968 and in New Zealand with the legendary side of 1971, who became the first (and so far only) Lions tour party to win a series against the All Blacks. Also playing was centre David Cooke, who was selected for England's tour to Argentina in 1973 (only for the tour to be cancelled after concerns about the players' safety) and was eventually capped in 1976. Adding to this wealth of experience was the coach, former All Blacks fly-half Earle Kirton.

Kirton was a favourite son of Otago rugby in New Zealand and it was much to the chagrin and bemusement of the Otago faithful that his talents had been only marginally recognised by the national sectors. A fast and creative fly-half who was elusive on the break, he had also been an excellent tactical kicker with an inventive mind for the game, particularly in attack.

After several bright seasons with the University of Otago and Otago province, Kirton had been selected for the South Island team in 1963 and performed so well against the North Island that the opposition captain Wilson Whineray (who was All Blacks captain at the time) announced during his post-match speech that he hoped that the national selectors had taken note of Kirton's performance. It would prove prophetic and Kirton was selected for the All Blacks' end of year tour to Britain and Ireland.

He made his New Zealand debut in a midweek fixture against Newport, but he gave an underwhelming performance and it has since been suggested that this coloured how he was viewed by the selectors thereafter. He played another twelve times on tour – but as the schedule included thirty-six matches in total, this was a relatively small number of run-outs.

He continued his good domestic form when he returned to New Zealand, playing for Otago, South Island, South Island Universities and New Zealand

Universities, but was not selected for an All Blacks squad again until 1967 and for a return tour of the northern hemisphere. This was a much happier experience and he went on to become the leading stand-off on the tour, winning the playmaker role for all four Tests against England, Wales, France and Scotland and scoring two tries against England at Twickenham. He picked up further Test caps against Australia, France and Wales before finishing his career after the 1970 tour to South Africa, where he played twelve matches, including two Tests against the Springboks.

After the tour was concluded Kirton moved to England to take up a postgraduate course in dentistry and began playing for Harlequins. His playing career in the UK included appearances for Middlesex and the Barbarians and when he finally decided to hang up his boots, he was persuaded by the Harlequins hierarchy to take on a coaching position at the club. By the time the eighteen-year-old Clive Woodward turned up in 1974, Kirton was well established as the first-team coach.

Rugby in Britain and Ireland was in buoyant mood at the start of that season. The Lions had just returned from a twenty-one-match tour of South Africa in which they had gone unbeaten – the only blight on their 100 per cent record coming in the fourth and final Test against the Springboks when they were denied victory at the death thanks to a dubious refereeing decision and had to settle, instead, for a draw. The team, captained by Ulsterman Willie John McBride, would become known as the Invincibles and are roundly regarded as the greatest tour party ever to have represented Britain and Ireland. Both the 1971 and 1974 Lions squads had combined power and dynamism in the forwards with mesmeric back play out wide; it was a golden period, with the Welsh sides throughout the decade fielding some of the finest players ever to grace the world stage. While English rugby was some way behind their rivals across the Severn, the knock-on effect of the exuberance of both Welsh and Lions rugby was palpable. It was, in many ways, alien to the style so prevalent throughout England at the time, but it was inspirational to the new generation of players coming into the senior game – Clive Woodward among them.

After the oppression of his life at Conway, the feeling of freedom that Woodward enjoyed in London was seismic. He was young, independent, relishing the challenges and opportunities of his new job and expressing himself in the most wonderful ways every Saturday in a Harlequins shirt. The influence of Kirton, in particular, cannot be underestimated. He encouraged expression and creativity on the field and moved Woodward back into the fly-half position. If Woodward thought an attack was on, even if it was deep in his own territory, his coach backed him. And if it didn't always work, it didn't matter to Kirton – he would rather Woodward tried these things a dozen times each half to no effect, if it paid off once or twice a game – for those one or two moments could mean the difference between winning and losing. But he also instilled tactical awareness, game management and a kicking strategy in Woodward – classic New Zealand fly half traits – and his experience of playing in the wild conditions so often found in Otago transferred easily to the harsh conditions of an English winter, and they were lessons that he passed on to his young protégé.

Rugby union was in something of a state of flux through the late 1950s, the 1960s and into the 1970s with the International Rugby Football Board constantly tinkering with the rules. Rugby visionaries like Jim Greenwood were not alone in lamenting the style of play that was dominating rugby throughout the world. In 1966 the RFU president, Gus Walker, voiced the feelings of many when he said, 'The standard of play in top games in the last two or three seasons has been in general, but certainly not exclusively, disappointing.' This was epitomised by the 1963 Five Nations encounter between Scotland and Wales in Edinburgh, which the Welsh won 6–0, but which will be remembered for the extraordinary statistic that there were 111 line-outs; at the time, the ball could be kicked directly into touch from anywhere on the pitch and a line-out would be held at the point where the ball crossed the touchline.

'I played in that famous match,' recalls George Stevenson, the Scotland winger. 'Or rather that *in*famous match. The Welsh scrum-half, Clive Rowlands, just kicked to touch every time he got the ball. I think that was one of the first times I played on the wing for Scotland and in those days the winger put the ball in at the line-out. I touched the ball more that day than I had ever touched it in any match before, but it was only to throw the ball in after Rowlands had kicked to touch again. What a dreadful game. They changed the rules after that, making it illegal to kick directly to touch unless you were in your own 25.'

England won the 1963 Five Nations but in doing so scored only four tries throughout the entire championship. Rather than accept any criticism of this statistic, the RFU revelled in their team's victorious tactical acumen and celebrated their success. In 1971 the value of a try rose to four points, making scoring a try worth more than a successful kick at goal for the first time in the history of the game. But this did little to change the general style of play in England at the time. England tended to produce one of the biggest packs of forwards in the world game, only ever matched for size by teams from France, New Zealand and South Africa. Winning was of such importance to the RFU that national selectors and coaches would encourage a limited England game plan, playing to the traditional forward strength of the team. Even with the increased value of the try, an expansive style was rarely, if ever, implemented.

But this style held little truck with Earle Kirton and the players that he coached at Harlequins. The club's traditional player base tended to be men with high-flying but stressful careers and rugby provided a break from the rigours of working life – but only if it was played in a spirit of adventure and with freedom. This was a philosophy actively encouraged by Kirton and embraced by Clive Woodward, who started his career at Harlequins playing for the club's fourth team, but quickly had a meteoric rise through the ranks and within a month of joining the club, and still aged only eighteen, was selected to start at stand-off for the first team.

Although there were no leagues in England until 1985, when the John Smith's Merit Table was introduced, a national knockout tournament had been introduced to club rugby in the 1971–72 season. This increased level of competition complemented the existing 'friendly' matches that were traditionally arranged between clubs across the country and with the major clubs in Wales. While the new knockout tournament added a much welcomed structure to the season, it remained of secondary importance to the long-standing rivalry matches – particularly those played against the Welsh sides. The status of these matches was reflected in the club's stadium choice; Woodward's first start came against Cardiff and was played not at the Stoop but at the towering edifice that loomed over Harlequins' home ground and which would bear witness to some of the most significant matches in Woodward's life: Twickenham Stadium.

Among the opposition that day was Gareth Edwards, the Cardiff, Wales and Lions scrum-half who has been regularly named as the greatest ever to play the game. Edwards was a central cog in the success of the all-conquering Wales teams of the 1970s and had been crucial to the Lions' unprecedented success in New Zealand in 1971 and South Africa in 1974 (while he had also toured South Africa with the Lions in 1968). To be playing at Twickenham against such an illustrious opponent was a daunting debut for the young Woodward, but he took to the experience like a duck to water.

'Playing for Quins was a real eye-opener,' he recalled. 'I was nervous at first, of course, but to play alongside a guy like Bob Hiller was such a help. He had confidence in me – or appeared to – and that gave me the reassurance of my abilities that I needed. I was playing against internationalists every week – mainly English ones, but there were Scots, Irish and Welsh players appearing for English clubs then as well, and of course when we played the Welsh club sides they were full of internationalists. To come up against someone like Gareth Edwards in your first senior game was quite an experience! But when I came through that – and the other games in my first season – and felt that I had played well, then I began to think seriously that I might have a shot at playing on the international stage alongside or against players of his calibre. It helped that I scored a try in that first game and it settled the nerves a little.

'I loved the style of play that we were developing as a team under Earle Kirton. It was free-flowing and so enjoyable to be part of. But at the same time, I felt unsettled in my life; I was getting itchy feet with my job at the bank after just a couple of months. I had my A-levels and I still wanted to go to university – and even if law at Durham was beyond me, I wanted to study *something*.'

It was a Thursday night in early November. Training had not long finished and, as was customary, several Harlequins players had headed to a local pub for a bite to eat and a few fortifying pints after a hard session. As the veterans in the team insisted, it was always good to have a couple of drinks to ease stiff limbs in preparation for the weekend's match.

Woodward returned from the bar carrying a tray of ales, handed them out to each of his teammates and then settled back into his seat beside his flatmate Paddy McLoughlin, a lawyer who played for the Quins fifth team, and David Cooke, who were in mid-flow as Woodward sat down.

'He was a Lion, wasn't he?' said McLoughlin, gratefully scooping up his pint glass.

'Yeah, and a bloody good one,' replied Cooke.

'Back-row?'

'That's right. One of those hard bastards they always seem to produce. Massive engine – he could run all day.'

'Who's this?' asked Woodward.

Cooke glanced at Woodward. 'There's this Scottish guy, an ex-internationalist, up at Loughborough.'

'What, the PE college?'

'Yeah. He's a lecturer. Coached me when I was there. He's a genius.'

'A genius?' asked Woodward sceptically.

Cooke smiled. 'Well, if you have an appreciation for thinking man's rugby – yes. Earle's mad for him.'

'How the hell does Earle Kirton know some old Scottish bloke up at Loughborough?'

'Like I say, he's a genius. It's bloody ridiculous, but hardly anyone's heard of him here. They love him in New Zealand. And South Africa. All over the bloody world. He's a pioneer.'

Cooke took a sip of his pint. 'You know this Total Football that they're always going on about. From that Dutch guy at Ajax...,'

'Rinus Michels?' said Woodward quickly. He couldn't help himself. Cooke had his undivided attention now.

'Rinus Michels, right. Well this guy's the rugby equivalent. He's all about fifteen-man rugby – and I mean fifteen-man. He wants every player to be able to handle and kick, to see space, to run. The works.'

'Sounds a bit much to me,' laughed McLoughlin.

'Sounds bloody fantastic,' said Woodward. 'And it makes total sense. Have you ever seen Ajax play? It's incredible. The Netherlands were playing the same style during the World Cup in the summer.'

'Yeah, I remember,' said Cooke with a smile.

'The fluidity is amazing. There are no fixed positions, everyone moves to use the space in the best, most creative way they can, interchanging where they are on the pitch, what they do. You can have strikers in defence, defenders breaking out into attack, the midfielders all over the place. As long as everyone buys into it, it can be unstoppable. Someone like Johan Cruyff is able to orchestrate those incredible attacks because he can pop up wherever he wants on the field, wherever he thinks there will be space – and everyone reacts to him. And why couldn't it work in rugby? If all fifteen guys are able to play like stand-offs, then you could attack from anywhere. From set-piece, from broken-field play, from counter-attacks, it wouldn't matter. As long as everyone was working hard to get themselves into the right positions you could spin the ball to wherever the space might be and then attack.'

'I knew you'd like the idea,' said Cooke, now breaking into a grin. He paused and raised an eyebrow. 'So what are you going to do about it?'

'What do you mean?'

'Listen, I've not brought this up for the sake of a cheery little chat, Clive. A few of the other young guys at the club have applied to Loughborough. The colleges are being merged into Loughborough University next year and they're starting a new three-year degree in sport science. And guess who's running it?'

'This Total Rugby guy?'

'This Total Rugby guy. I know you want to get a degree – but you don't know where or what in. You could do a lot worse than to have a look at this BSc at Loughborough. I had a great time there – and we had a hell of a team: me, Fran Cotton, Steve Smith, Louis Dick, Clive Rees and Dick Cowman all played. Loughborough is the best university for sports in the country. And if you want any more proof that it's a good idea, I'd talk to Earle.'

At training the following Tuesday, Earle Kirton was standing by the touchline as the players filed out of the changing room to begin their warm-up. Woodward emerged from the warmth, his breath clouding around him in the chill evening air as he made his way across to his coach.

After a few minutes of conversation, Woodward hit him with the question.

'Of course I bloody know him, mate,' said Kirton. 'The man's a rugby god. Jeez, I can't believe you *haven't* heard of him.' He fixed Woodward with a steady gaze. 'So you're thinking about Loughborough are you?'

'Just thinking.'

Kirton nodded slowly. 'A degree's a good thing to have, Clive. Loughborough's a good place to get one. And that man up there will teach you more than you could ever imagine about rugby and fitness, the science of your body and how it applies to the game. There's none finer.' He sniffed and looked out across the pitch. The grass was crystallising in the early-evening frost. 'If I was you I wouldn't even think twice about it. Yeah, if I had my time again, I'd give anything to be coached by Jim Greenwood.'

*

After an hour and a half's journey from London, the train pulled in at Loughborough station. It was just over two weeks until Christmas and a group of carol singers greeted Woodward as he left the station and made his way towards a bus stop for the brief ride that would take him to the university campus. It was a beautiful winter's day in north Leicestershire, the sky a brilliant blue, the air crisp and clear.

As he took his seat on the bus, Woodward glanced again at the sheet of paper that contained the information about his interview. He double-checked the time and then studied again the campus map that had been sent to him in the post a week earlier. He was buzzing with nervous energy.

When he finally arrived at the campus it took him a few minutes to get his bearings, but he soon found himself in the sports hall. He introduced himself to the receptionist and was pointed to a line of chairs. He took a seat.

Ten minutes later the door to the hall opened and in walked a man in his fifties, dressed in a tracksuit. He had cropped white hair and a chiselled face which, despite his age, showed that he was still physically very fit.

'Jim Greenwood,' he said, with a soft rolling cadence. 'Come with me.'

He led Woodward to his office and directed him to a chair before taking a seat on the other side of his desk.

'How are you enjoying Harlequins?' asked Greenwood, steepling his fingers.

'Very much, sir, thank you.'

'I've heard a lot about you. Not seen you play yet, but the reports are good.'

'That's nice to hear.'

All the nervous tension that had been building in Woodward's body was melting away. In just a few words the Scot had put him totally at ease.

'So tell me about some of the games you've played in. Give me some highlights.'

And so Woodward told him. They chatted for half an hour, with Woodward recounting his career highlights from Conway and then at Harlequins. He told Greenwood how much he enjoyed working under Earle Kirton and Greenwood nodded in appreciation.

'So,' said Greenwood at last, 'what element of your game do you think you need to work on the most? What *can't* you do?'

Woodward thought for a moment. 'Well,' he said, 'I can't kick very well off my left foot.'

Greenwood smiled. 'And here I was thinking you were a footballer! Come with me.' He stood, grabbed two rugby balls from a bag by his desk and walked out of the room, Woodward trailing behind him.

Greenwood turned down a corridor and made his way to a side door. When he pushed it open Woodward saw that they had come out by one of the university football pitches.

'Your body is like a machine,' said Greenwood, 'and the best machines are well-balanced and finely tuned. It's not rocket science – it's simple biomechanics. That's what you're going to learn here – both in the classroom and out on the training field.' He flicked a ball to Woodward. 'Kick this with your good foot. Nice and relaxed.'

Woodward took the ball and, careful to keep his balance in his leather-soled shoes, swung his foot at it. Although his non-kicking foot slid slightly on the grass, he made a sweet contact with the ball and it spiralled through the air, landing some thirty yards down the pitch.

'Very nice,' said Greenwood. He tossed a second ball to Woodward. 'Now, go through each step that you did there again – but slowly and don't actually kick this time.'

Woodward made a small adjustment with his hands, angling the ball at a slight right-to-left diagonal, set his shoulders square, took a step, planted his non-kicking foot as firmly as he could on the ground and then swung his right foot. As instructed, he didn't release the ball from his grasp.

'So, thinking about your body as a machine, have a close look at every aspect of your kicking process. You angled the ball right to left to open up the sweet spot for the arch of your foot. You set yourself square to where you wanted to direct the ball. You made sure you had a solid base with your left foot and then you swung through the point of contact with your right foot. A textbook spiral punt. Pass me the ball.'

Woodward passed him the ball and it was immediately spun back to him. 'Don't even think about it,' called Greenwood as the ball fell into Woodward's hands. 'Kick it with your left foot.'

Woodward adjusted the ball, planted his right foot, pivoted his body and kicked. He skidded on the grass and sliced the ball horribly off to his left.

Greenwood wandered over to collect it. 'Your balance was all wrong. You angled the ball OK in your hands, but you swung your upper body at it and brought your foot round at the same time. Your right foot was set badly and the momentum was turning in an uncontrolled pivot. Biomechanics. Your body is a machine, remember. You kicked with precision with your right foot, every aspect of the kicking process under control. You just need to learn to mirror those movements, to have as much control and poise when working the other side of your body as you do when working with your more natural side. Everything in your body needs to be balanced, to feel connected and under control. That's what you'll learn here. It will require a commitment to hard work and a constant dedication to improve. But if you give me that, I'll give you the results you're looking for. Let's try the kick again.'

They worked on the kicking for another ten minutes. Every time Woodward went through the motions, Greenwood made small adjustments. It took perhaps fifteen or twenty strikes but then he nailed it – a perfectly executed spiral punt off his left foot. And it was no fluke – Woodward felt the movement and balance as comfortably in the left side of his body as he felt in his right when kicking with his stronger foot. Again and again Greenwood passed him the ball and, alternating his kicking foot as instructed, Woodward fired off spiral punt after spiral punt. It was one of the most satisfying feelings he had ever experienced.

Some thirty years later, Greenwood would fondly recall that first meeting. 'I was impressed by Clive straight away. I'd heard good things about him before he came for his interview and I wasn't disappointed. He was very absorbent of ideas. He recognised very early how important small details were to the bigger picture of achieving success. At Loughborough we were focused on honing excellence in the basic skills – whatever the sporting discipline you were involved in. Without that attention to detail and to the fundamentals of your sport, you can't achieve anything great. The key to the question that I asked him – about what he wasn't good at – is to admit to a weakness in your game. That is often a very hard thing for athletes to do. But it is invaluable. If you can admit to your weaknesses, identify them, analyse them and then do everything you can to go out and improve yourself, then you are preparing yourself in the best possible way for a competitive environment. When a rugby player is out on the pitch in the heat of the battle, there is nothing a coach can do to help them. If they understand every aspect of their play and have principles and methods to fall back on, then they can control the outcome of their performance.

'I was a teacher rather than a coach. I tried to get people thinking. I wanted each player to be his own coach, and I encouraged each player to expand their awareness, to find truth wherever it lay. All coaching is one-to-one: there's a place for the motivational speech, but it's far more effective to talk to people individually. I liked to break down teams, plays and players and examine each as individual components, looking for areas of strength and weakness and working out how to improve each part. It's like a jigsaw. Then, when you have your targets figured out you go out and you work as hard as you can to improve. And you just keep doing it again and again and again.

'It was my mantra that my players would always work harder than anyone else. We would make sure we covered every base we could in our preparation, which meant that we always had that strong foundation to fall back on whenever we came into difficulties during a match. Looking at how Clive developed as a player, a businessman and then a coach, I'm pleased to see that it was a philosophy that clearly rubbed off on him.

'Sebastian Coe was at Loughborough at the same time as Clive. He had a wonderful athletics coach in George Gandy and Clive used to go and watch Gandy put Coe through his paces. Again it came down to attention to detail and hard work. They spent a lot of time concentrating on preparation, nutrition, recovery, building strength and stamina. These were things that were alien in rugby union but which we were starting to introduce at Loughborough.

'The rugby that I most enjoyed playing was fast and open and that is the style that I always wanted to encourage as a coach. I wanted every player in my teams to be able to handle the ball comfortably, to be able to offer something in attack, in defence and as a support player. This meant, of course, that they had to have huge fitness levels and had to work hard all the time on their skills. But if they did that then I would build a game plan and a structure where they could all play and enjoy a truly fifteen-man game of rugby. That's what the game should be about – that's the game that, ultimately, every player wants to play and every spectator wants to watch. It doesn't mean spreading the ball wide at every moment; it's about decision-making and player judgement. It's about creativity in the tight channels and exchanges as much as it is about opening up space and gaps for breaks in the wide expanses or on a counter-attack in broken play. Again, I think that's where my instinct to teach rather than coach kicked in – I always wanted my players to *think*. I wanted them to be able to change tactics at will, to adapt to any game situation and to react to opportunities when they arose – not just adhere to the strictures of a clearly-defined game plan.

'What I like about the approach that we had at Loughborough was that there could be no cutting corners – everyone worked as hard as anyone else. No one got by on a bit of flash talent. That meant that our players tended to be level-headed. That's something that I certainly noticed in Clive. He was a player capable of real individual brilliance but he was also very level as a character. You always get highs and lows in sport – it's an emotional business to be involved with. But that ability to be level-headed is so important to long-term success. If you don't buy into the hype, then you can weather the storms when they break. And if you have a long career there will always be storms.'

Woodward left the interview absolutely buzzing. He had dreams of playing for England and now he could see a pathway to achieving that dream – and the next step lay in Loughborough. Just before the end of December he received a letter from the college. His application had been accepted and he would be starting his first year the following autumn.

'I was ecstatic,' recalled Woodward. 'Jim was such an exciting guy to be coached by. His whole ethos was different to anyone else coaching in the UK at the time – with the exception of maybe Earle Kirton at Quins and Chalkie White at Leicester. He always loved to say that 'there are no rules in rugby', meaning that we should never just accept the ingrained style of play that was fashionable at the time – which was a relief because it was a torturous period in English rugby. The national team was dreadful and they played such a depressing style of ten-man rugby. During my four years at university I think England only managed six wins in twenty-two games. Jim said that any side in the world could be beaten as long as you had several ways to play the game. If you only had one way, as England did at the time, opposition teams could work you out very quickly and easily nullify any threat that you might pose. It was a lesson that I would always remember. The way he saw it, every player on the pitch had a role to play in attack and defence, even if they were nowhere near the ball. I loved it. It was everything I had been looking for since I first began playing rugby.

'A few weeks after my interview with Jim Greenwood, I had my first taste of playing for England when I was selected for the England Colts, the under-19 side, against Wales at Twickenham. I was up against several players that I knew from the Welsh Schoolboys trial – and I played directly against Gareth Davies. It was a pretty dire game; we won 9–6 and even though I scored the only try of the game, we were playing a dreadful style that was endemic in the England set-up at the time. I had been warned about it by David Cooke, who was playing in the centre for England in that year's Five Nations. "The game plan is to kick the ball if we're anywhere other than inside the opposition's 25-yard line," he said. "Then, when we're there, the forwards keep the ball until they can't bludgeon their way forward any more, and that's the moment that the backs get the ball to play with – which is pretty much the worst ball to have, especially when you've hardly touched it before then. It usually all goes wrong and we butcher any chances to score. The old joke is that if you're picked as an outside back for England you should bring a hat and some gloves to keep you warm until you touch the ball. We're told that we can only run the ball from other areas of the pitch if we're twenty points up – but with that style of play we're never twenty points up." And that was pretty much exactly the style of play I was ordered to orchestrate when I was playing for the Colts. The whole system got to me; I was young and it was an incredible experience to be pulling on an England shirt and to be playing for my country, but the set-up and the style of play nagged me. It was the antithesis of what I had heard Jim Greenwood talk about during my interview. I couldn't wait to get to Loughborough in the autumn.

'I played for Jim for three years, captaining the squad in my last two seasons. No man has done more in our time to single-handedly transform the modern game of rugby than Jim Greenwood. He published *Total Rugby* in 1979 when I was there and it has become a classic all over the world. It remains the only coaching manual I have ever read and I have referred to it constantly over the years. He was a visionary and was the premier strategist on the game during his lifetime.

'He would get so angry if we walked off the field and he felt that we hadn't risked everything out there, if we hadn't tried things. He would say, "We're not getting paid for this, why would you want to do anything other than enjoy yourself out there? You're not under any pressure. The only pressure is from me and I'll only be annoyed if I feel you haven't tried things." He was obsessed with trying to play rugby differently. He was an amazing, amazing man. We were small because we were a bunch of students, but he felt that if we were fit enough, fast enough and skilful enough we could play anyone and beat them. It was fantastic. It was probably the only time in my career that I was as close to being a professional as it was possible to be. We trained properly, we ate properly and as a coach he was a genius. A pure genius. And you just learned so much from him – not just in terms of technique but in the philosophy of how to play and how to enjoy the game to its fullest.'

It wasn't only the rugby coaching that would shape and influence Woodward's thinking. The degree in sports science included coaching, medical studies, psychology, nutrition, analysis and fitness – all things that were way ahead of their time as far as British sport, and particularly rugby union, was concerned.

'My time at Loughborough was everything I had hoped for and more,' said Woodward, 'although there were some tough times there, too. I broke my leg twice in five months during the 1976 season and was out for a year, which was very difficult to deal with at the time.'

Stuart Biddle, who was head of Woodward's degree course and president of Loughborough's Athletic Union, recalled how impressed he had been with how Woodward coped with his injury setbacks. 'He was an outstanding player and he made huge strides in his game under Jim Greenwood's tutelage. What most impressed me, though, was how he dealt with the injuries that cost him a whole season. He never lost his hunger for the game and he came back stronger, captaining the side for two years and leading them to the UAU Championship titles [the Universities Athletic Union managed inter-university competition across the UK] in 1977, 1978 and 1979 and to victory at the Middlesex Sevens. That 1978–79 season was particularly memorable as the side only lost two matches in the entire season.'

As much as Jim Greenwood was a huge influence, he was not the only one that Woodward came across while at university. 'Loughborough was such a fascinating place to be because of all the other talented sportsmen and women who were studying and training there,' he said. 'I used to love going to watch Seb Coe train, which I did quite a bit when I was injured during the '76 season. Just as Jim Greenwood had been the attraction for me to go to Loughborough, so George Gandy would have been the attraction for Seb.

I can still remember some of the brutal training that Gandy made him do – a dozen or so consecutive 300-metre sprints, with only a 100-metre jog around the bend to recover between them, with Gandy barking at him all the time. The whole approach both men took was incredibly professional – strength and conditioning, diet and analysis, the focus on the biomechanics of Seb's body and how it could all be adjusted to help him run faster. They did everything they could to give him a physical and psychological edge. And it paid off – it was all part of the road to him breaking twelve world records and winning both gold and silver medals at the 1980 and 1984 Olympics.

'I absolutely loved my four years at Loughborough and I really enjoyed that I only played for the university team. There was quite a bit of pressure to play for one of the established clubs and the England selectors told me that they couldn't pick me if I was only playing for Loughborough – but it was a decision that felt right for me. It was only when I graduated that I thought about where to play next and what I might do career-wise. I went back to London and rejoined Harlequins, but I remember chatting to Jim about what I might do and he suggested looking into a management training scheme with Rank Xerox.'

'They were an American company and I heard how good their graduate training schemes were,' said Greenwood. 'As much as I knew he had enjoyed his PE degree, a management training scheme with a company like that would open up a lot more options for him. As he has gone on to speak and write about, his experience with Rank Xerox had as big an impact on his life and coaching career as anything I taught him rugby-wise.'

'Despite how much I had enjoyed my degree, I wasn't interested in a teaching career,' said Woodward. 'NatWest had promised that I could return to work for them after graduation, but the banks sector had lost its lustre for me. Earle Kirton had gone back to New Zealand by then as well and it felt like the end of an era for me.'

Fortunately the decision of where to play next was an easy one to make. One of the biggest clubs in the country was Leicester, which was only a few miles from Loughborough, and they were being coached by another visionary who was determined to buck the national trends. Herbert 'Chalkie' White was a hard taskmaster in training but he was always willing to encourage his players to attack and play the game as they saw fit. Like Greenwood, he didn't prescribe to restrictive game plans. While he never felt that he was a great coaching innovator, he was open-minded in his approach and trusted his players' judgement. If they felt that it was on to attack, he backed them – no matter the field position or what stage the game was at. It was a liberating approach for his players and they often more than repaid the faith that he put in them.

White took a pastoral approach to his player management. He was not a bawler or screamer. He understood that his players were all in full-time jobs and that they should be looked after as best they could when they stepped inside the Leicester gates. In midwinter he introduced the initiative of the groundsman welcoming the players to training with piping hot mugs of tea.

'It was these little things that can make a huge difference to the players and to the general environment of a team and a club,' said Woodward. 'Chalkie was also a great guy to talk to. He was always ready to listen to ideas that you might have. He might disagree with them, he might argue with you over opinions or points, but he would always listen. From a player's point of view, that kind of open rapport with a coach is hugely important.

'He had a talented team there, but he would say, 'Look, we're not getting paid to play here, we should enjoy ourselves and we should look to entertain, because that's why people are coming to watch.' And I think you have more chance of winning if your team is genuinely excited about going out to play. As a player it was great, you really looked forward to each game and the chance of going out and expressing yourself rather than going out to bludgeon your way through a game.

'Earle, Jim and Chalkie had massive influences on how I played and then how I coached. They were so positive – especially when compared to the way the England team was coached, which was so bad. The tragedy for me was that neither Jim nor Chalkie coached England and they absolutely should have, especially Jim. Looking back now, Jim should have been made England coach and then when he stood down, Chalkie should have replaced him. It was such a waste that they never got the chance – and they both wanted to do it. They were both hugely ambitious but they didn't fit the mould at Twickenham; the RFU were never going to have guys that thought so differently coaching England. It really was a tragic waste.

'So I was really pleased with where I was going to be playing rugby post-Loughborough, but I still needed to find a career. Jim's recommendation of

Rank Xerox had piqued my interest and this was further enhanced when Leicester arranged for me to meet Alan King, the regional branch manager for Xerox in Leicester. Although King was a big Leicester fan, he didn't make the interview any easier for me – but I was delighted when I was finally offered a job. Xerox was a hugely competitive, driven company that demanded furious competition among its employees for results. It was a high-pressure environment, but I loved it and soon began to thrive. I probably played my best rugby while at Loughborough, largely because it was as close to being a professional player as you could get at the time, but it was when I joined Leicester that my rugby career really took off.'

Leicester were one of the traditional powerhouses of English rugby and were just launching a dominating run in the national knockout competition. They won the John Player Cup in 1979, 1980 and 1981 and had a team laced with internationals, with hooker Peter Wheeler, prop Steve Redfern, scrum-half Nick Youngs, fly-half Les Cusworth, centre Paul Dodge and full-back Dusty Hare forming a talented spine to the team – with Wheeler, Dodge and Hare all British & Irish Lions.

'We didn't have the biggest pack of forwards at the time,' said Peter Wheeler in an interview with *The Guardian*'s Richard Williams in 2003. 'But we were playing an open, expansive style of rugby that inspired everyone. We scored a lot of tries from all over the place. The best coaches try to be pragmatic, and we happened to develop that style because we had a lot of good backs and not much in the way of forwards. I'd be pretty sure that while Clive was at Loughborough he'd have spotted the sort of squad we had, and realised that it would benefit him.'

'Clive had bags of flair,' remembers Les Cusworth, 'but it was Paul Dodge that kept a talented backline together and made Clive look a better player. Chalkie White was a pioneering coach, in the mould of Jim Greenwood, and he helped Clive a lot. Chalkie and Paul were significant factors in Clive's development and really helped him push on to gain his international recognition.'

'They were a great combination in the centre, Paul Dodge and Clive,' recalled White before his death in 2005. 'In many ways Paul helped Clive to become the player he did: if Paul hadn't been there, Clive might have looked quite ordinary. Clive had bags of pace, which is invaluable, he was brave in the tackle and wasn't afraid of anyone, but he could be flighty and Paul kept him in line. They formed what many pundits considered one of the most effective centre partnerships in world rugby at the time and they carried that on to the Test stage.'

Woodward joined the club in 1979 and went straight into the Leicester first team. He scored fourteen tries on his way to selection for the England squad in that year's autumn internationals, before winning a place on the bench against Ireland in the 1980 Five Nations opener at Twickenham, by which time he was the club's leading try-scorer. He made his debut in that match when he replaced Tony Bond and England went on to record a 24–9 win. It would be a memorable Five Nations for many reasons. Woodward established his place in the team thanks to Bond's injury and England went on to dominate the competition, winning their first Grand Slam for twenty-three years and playing an almost unrecognisable brand of expansive rugby in the final game against Scotland. It seemed as if England had uncovered a new attacking élan that had eluded them for decades. They followed up their victory over the Irish by defeating France 17–13 in their first ever win at the Parc des Princes in Paris, Wales 9–8 at Twickenham, before clinching the Grand Slam in epic style at Murrayfield 30–18.

Unfortunately, the success of that season would prove to be a flash in the pan with the expansive style the consequence of overwhelming forward domination over the Scots rather than a specifically pursued tactical approach. As Woodward explained, 'That season is largely remembered for the attacking play in the Grand Slam clinching game, but it wasn't all like that. We won the first game against Ireland playing in our usual ten-man fashion. I think that for the twenty or so minutes I was on, I touched the ball once – and was penalised for holding on in the tackle.

'We played well out in Paris, scoring tries through winger John Carleton and my centre partner for that game, Nick Preston. Dusty Hare kicked a penalty and John Horton at stand-off kicked two drop-goals. It was all the backs scoring the points, but the forwards did a magnificent job against a big French pack, which was led by the great Jean-Pierre Rives.

'The win against Wales was huge because they had been the outstanding team throughout the seventies – but it was a tight game. Dusty Hare kicked like a machine to give us the win, but it was a battle of attrition and we were given a real help early on because Paul Ringer, their flanker, lost his rag and was sent off after fourteen minutes. Paul Dodge came back into the team for that game and it was great to be able to continue our club partnership together for the last two games.

'So we went up to Edinburgh for the final game and it is the one that is always shown on the highlights reel – and for good reason as we played superbly. But because it is the game that lives long in the memory it creates a false impression of how we actually played throughout the tournament. We were largely playing ten-man rugby still with a dominant pack, but because the pack demolished the Scottish forwards so effectively, we had more ball then usual to throw about.'

England did more than throw it about. They cut devastating running lines, with Mike Slemen and John Carleton lancing in off their wings or putting on the after-burners out wide, John Horton and Paul Dodge pulling the strings in midfield and Dusty Hare kicking two conversions and two penalties. Slemen and scrum-half Steve Smith both scored a try, while Carleton was in brutal form, scorching over for a hat-trick. Up front, the power of veterans like Fran Cotton, Peter Wheeler, Bill Beaumont, Maurice Colclough, Roger Uttley and Tony Neary was destructive. But at the epicentre was Woodward. With the platform created by the forwards, England were constantly on the front foot and the Scottish defence was run ragged. In the openings that were created on the wide Murrayfield pitch, Woodward was at his creative, elusive, mazy best.

'I remember coming into the changing room at half-time and the game had been so fast in the first half,' said Woodward, 'and Fran Cotton got all the players around and he said, "Before anyone says anything, what the fuck happened to keeping it tight?" And everyone just burst out laughing and he had this big grin on his face. It really was fantastic the way we were playing, everyone was enjoying themselves so much. And Scotland were a great side – they had guys like Jim Renwick, Andy Irvine, John Rutherford, Roy Laidlaw, David Leslie and John Beattie playing – but we just blew them away. They came back at us in the second half but we kept playing and it was just a fantastic spectacle, the way rugby is supposed to be played. But it just happened – it wasn't planned, there was no magic formula.

'It was a strange experience to be part of a Grand Slam in your first season as a Test player. I remember sitting in the changing room after Bill Beaumont had been carried from the field and there were guys there in tears over what we had achieved. I was delighted with how I had played and felt that we were at the beginning of a new era. But unfortunately that didn't happen.

Winning the Grand Slam was like winning a one-off cup final for the veteran players. Guys like Fran Cotton and Roger Uttley were legends of the game, particularly after their efforts in South Africa with the Lions in 1974, and Bill Beaumont was one of England's and the Lions' greats. But it was almost as if they had achieved all they wanted to achieve with that Grand Slam. Bill was selected as captain for the Lions tour to South Africa in the summer of 1980, but he had to retire two years after that. Roger retired after the Grand Slam and Fran retired after 1981 Five Nations. As opposed to the beginning of a new era, it was actually the end of one. And from a personal point of view, I don't think I ever played as well again as I did that day in Edinburgh; instead of pushing on to develop that fast, expansive game that won us the Slam, we reverted to type again.

'It was a huge disappointment.'

TWO

THE ANATOMY OF
A BUSINESSMAN

'Success is about having money and fame,
but excellence is being the best you can be.'
Mike Ditka

I N THE SUMMER of 1980, Clive Woodward was one of nine Englishmen
selected for the Lions tour of South Africa – their first excursion to the
Republic since the historic tour of 1974. But just as Willie John McBride's
Invincibles had left London under a cloud of political controversy, so too did
Bill Beaumont's class of 1980.

By 1980 contact between South Africa and the rest of the sporting world
had almost entirely ceased. In 1976 the All Blacks had toured in the face
of such international opposition that Abraham Ordia, the president of the
Supreme Council for Sport in Africa, had stated that the forty-six member
countries that made up the council would boycott the 1976 Montreal
Olympics if the tour went ahead. When the Games began in July, athletes
from several of the member nations did indeed walk out in protest, while
threatening that the Commonwealth Games in Edmonton in Canada in
1978 would descend into further chaos if sporting contact with South Africa
was maintained.

Things escalated in 1977 with the Gleneagles Agreement, which saw the
Commonwealth of Nations unanimously agree to discourage sporting contacts
with South Africa.

Despite rugby union being one of the key sports that the Commonwealth
leaders were most keen to deprive South Africa of (along with cricket), the
Lions committee and the four home unions held firm in the face of the swell

of political pressure and confirmed in January 1980 that they would proceed with their tour as planned.

The power of the Springbok badge, which had loomed over world rugby for more than a century, was emblematic of the apartheid regime for both sides of the divide in South Africa. Rugby in the Republic was white-dominated and it represented the values of traditional rugged strength and masculinity that the white population (particularly the Afrikaners) vehemently felt defined them. But to the non-white population – all 40 million of them – that same badge and the green and gold of the Springbok strip were symbols of their oppression. Whenever the Lions toured, they were supported vociferously by small pockets of non-white supporters in the crowds. It was a case of *the enemy of my enemy is my friend* and every time the Lions were victorious it was celebrated wildly as a wound to that symbol of apartheid.

Before the 1974 tourists had left their base in London, their hotel had been besieged by pickets led by the anti-apartheid demonstrator Peter Hain and hounded by the national and world press. The resounding triumph of the tour drowned some of this out but the Lions were under even greater media scrutiny by the time they came to tour South Africa again in 1980.

More than a hundred years of reciprocal touring between the home unions, France and New Zealand meant that the rugby union bond with South Africa was deeply embedded. To cast them out into the wilderness would be to cast out a member of the family – or so the thinking went. Furthermore, while other sporting bodies had withdrawn contact with South Africa, the International Rugby Football Board continued to encourage tours for fear that not doing so would result in rugby in South Africa abandoning the strictures of amateurism and turning fully professional while in isolation. With the advent of professionalism just fifteen years later in 1995 and the seemingly inexorable global growth of the game ever since, it seems utterly incongruous that official bodies would rather sanction – indeed actively encourage – tours to a country run by such an oppressive regime than risk one of its member unions falling under the 'shadow' of paying players to take part in the higher echelons of its domestic game. To reflect on those days now is to see a moral compass spinning wildly in the wrong direction.

'In those days apartheid was a raging subject and we got a lot of abuse, but I had a very simple philosophy,' said Syd Millar, the manager of the tour.

'Rightly or wrongly I felt that politicians should not interfere with sport. We asked the South Africans to play mixed teams, which they did. We asked for mixed crowds, which we got. So we thought that was a step forward and more than the politicians were achieving. I remember one press report at the time, which said the UK had improved their trading position with South Africa by tens of millions and thinking, *why isn't that causing as much fuss?*

'You could argue for hours about the rights and wrongs of going on that trip, but my point of view is that we did achieve various things and I along with others spent a lot of time speaking to blacks and coloureds and finding out how we might help them in rugby terms, so it was a positive experience and I have no regrets.'

'In my innocence, and it's no defence at this stage of my life,' recalls the Lions' Irish fly-half, Ollie Campbell, 'I was cocooned in this sort of rugby world that I was living in and all I wanted to do was play rugby. I was that innocent. I was almost oblivious to the political controversy that was raging at that time. It's a very weak defence, it's almost uncomfortable, it's almost embarrassing saying it now, to be so unaware of the repercussions but I was so immersed in the game I was virtually oblivious to the whole issue, strange and unbelievable though that may sound.'

So it was that the 1980 tour was conducted under a vitriolic shadow of political opposition, even if there was, eventually, some relief from the media spotlight when the tour was overshadowed by the bigger international news story that the USA were to boycott the 1980 Moscow Olympics.

It was the shortest tour in Lions history, with eighteen games packed into a ten-week schedule – and while the shortened period away would become the model for future tours, it would soon be realised that the number of games scheduled was far too many for such a small window. Injuries soon began to mount up, particularly among the backs, and a record number of replacements were called up to join the tour.

Clive Woodward had joined the tour on a high, the Grand Slam in one pocket, the John Player Cup in the other. And he had started his new job at Rank Xerox, which was opening his mind to a whole new way of thinking.

'I shared with Clive on that 1980 Lions tour and he was a Rank Xerox trainee at that time,' recalls John Beattie, the former Scotland No.8. 'I remember he accepted a call, and then immediately said "Hang on" and laid the phone down for thirty seconds, then went back on the line and finished the conversation. I asked him afterwards what that was all about and he said, "We've been told to always be in control of every situation – so that's me getting my time to think, and he's on the defensive." So he was a guy who had been taught how to be a leader. He was a really nice man – but I remember thinking, "Wow, you're different."'

'Throughout that tour he was always energetic, positive, imaginative, full of ideas about the endless possibilities of the game of rugby,' recalls Ollie Campbell. 'He trained and played with a smile, always gave the impression that he was enjoying himself thoroughly and he was great fun too. Beyond playing with him on that tour, I will always remember him for that mesmeric, outrageous, breath-taking and impossibly brilliant try he scored against Scotland at Twickenham in 1981. It is surely one of the greatest individual tries ever scored at that famous and historic ground. He was such a talented player.'

While many of the tour party felt a distinct level of discomfort with both the apartheid system and the abject poverty that they encountered as they toured South Africa, and despite the injury problems, they enjoyed considerable success on the field. The Test series was lost 3–1 but this was a poor return for the Lions; they were dominant up front but, as was the case with England, the backs were given very little licence to thrill – which was criminal considering the running ability of players like Woodward, Jim Renwick, Andy Irvine, Mike Slemen and John Carleton.

'We had a plan to play ten-man rugby,' recalls Scotland centre Renwick. 'And that is what we were going to do. But if you arrive with two or three different ways you can play then it makes life easier for you when plan A doesn't work. On a tour like that, plan A is not going to work all the time.'

'Syd Millar, the manager, Noel Murphy, the coach, and myself as captain were all forwards,' remembers Bill Beaumont. 'And we decided that we would take on the Springboks up front. During that period our rugby had probably become too preoccupied with forward domination at the expense of back play, and as captain in 1980 I hold my hands up. When you are on top in the forwards it is easy to say, "Let's keep it here," and one or two of our backs got frustrated because there is no defence against quick front-foot ball, as the Springboks showed us. In South Africa we were a bit one-dimensional – the forwards kept the good ball to themselves, and then gave the backs the bad ball and said, "Do something with it." I have to accept responsibility for that.'

The Lions deserved to get more out of the Test series, but with injuries taking their toll, so too did luck desert them – and Clive Woodward in particular.

'Clive played in the centre in the Second Test and got in on the wing for the Third Test,' said Renwick. 'He was probably a bit like me from the point of view that he wasn't happy with the way the back play was going, and I think he felt there should have been a backs coach. At Leicester, where he was playing, Chalkie White was the backs coach and he was actually in South Africa at the time and there was some chat amongst the players about trying to get him involved, but it never came to anything.'

'A Lions tour is like a three-year university degree crammed into three months,' said Peter Wheeler, Woodward's Leicester, England and Lions teammate. 'When you are living so closely together, sharing such an intense experience, you cannot hide anything. Whether it's strengths, weaknesses or foibles they will be found out and examined.' Unfortunately, the truth of this statement would be hung around Woodward's neck like a millstone.

'We were 2–0 down in the series and had to win the Third Test at Port Elizabeth to stay in it,' recalls Beaumont. 'The weather was terrible, with lashing rain and a howling gale. With about ten minutes left to play, we were 10–6 up after Bruce Hay had scored a try and Ollie Campbell had kicked two penalties. Then disaster struck... Clive Woodward normally played centre but had been selected on the wing and made the kind of mistake that is typical when someone plays out of position. He chased after a loose ball and tapped it into touch and then turned his back and ran off to get back into position. I was about thirty yards away and hammering across the pitch and it was one of the worst moments of my career because I could see exactly what was about to happen. Clive was jogging away and his opposite number, Gerrie Germishuys, picked up the ball and took a quick throw-in to their flanker, Theuns Stofberg, who passed it back to him, and Germishuys belted up the wing to score in the corner. Naas Botha kicked the conversion and for the third time in three Tests we had been the cause of our own downfall.'

It was a slip in Woodward's concentration – a trait that had dogged his youth but which he had learnt to largely overcome. It was deeply unfortunate for both Woodward and the Lions that it should rear its head at such a crucial moment in the Test series. Regrettably, it wouldn't be the last such lapse that would haunt his playing career. The Lions completed the series with a morale-boosting win, 17–

13, with tries from Clive Williams, John O'Driscoll and Andy Irvine combining with the kicking of Ollie Campbell to save them the humiliation of being the first Lions side to be whitewashed in a series in South Africa, but Woodward was not involved with the match-day squad and would never again play a Test match for the Lions.

Returning from the tour, with his playing reputation still very much intact despite his error in the Third Test, Woodward plunged himself into his new career. But it wouldn't be long before another lapse in concentration would cost him dear in the sporting arena.

17 January 1981: England opened the defence of the Grand Slam title against Wales at the Arms Park in Cardiff.

The final seconds of the game were ticking down and England had worked themselves into position to record an historic victory – their first in Cardiff for eighteen years – with a slender lead of 19–18.

After a midfield move off a Welsh line-out broke down, Robert Ackerman, the Wales right-wing, collected the loose ball in his own half and popped it to J.P.R. Williams, the Wales full-back, who looked to salvage the attack. He swerved back towards the blind side and, as the England defence pushed up to meet him, he passed the ball outside to his scrum-half, Brynmor Williams, who hoisted an up-and-under to relieve the pressure. It was fielded by Dusty Hare, the England full-back, who attempted a clearance kick of his own, but he was clattered by tight-head prop Graham Price as his leg swung for the ball and all he managed was to slice it into the charging body of Wales's open-side flanker Jeff Squire. The ball ricocheted around and eventually fell back into the arms of J.P.R. Williams, who carried it a few vital yards further downfield. He was finally hauled to the ground and a melee of bodies collapsed around him as Brynmor Williams desperately scrabbled for quick ball and the England defence did all they could to stifle its release. Brian Anderson, the referee, blew his whistle as the ball failed to emerge and he awarded Wales a scrum some twenty metres from the English try-line.

The stands all around the old ground were shaking with the noise from the crowd, the lamps that lined the South Stand trembling from the vibrations of song and cheer and stamped feet as the partisan home crowd roared encouragement to their team.

Down on the pitch, England hooker Peter Wheeler barked at the rest of his forwards for one last superhuman effort in what had been a brutal forwards-orientated arm-wrestle for nearly the full eighty minutes of play. As they assembled themselves in formation for the scrum, England captain Bill Beaumont roared for them all to keep their heads. 'No penalties!'

Behind the scrum the message was repeated. From scrum-half Steve Smith all the way out to winger John Carleton, the call was repeated again and again: 'No penalties! Knock them down, drive them back, they're not getting through! No penalties!'

In the centre, Clive Woodward set himself in a half-crouch beside Paul Dodge. It was imperative that the Welsh midfield was shut down quickly. *Get up in their faces, be aggressive, give them no time to think. If we give them space they might conjure a gap, find half a space and get an offload in; then they would be in behind our defence and that would spell real trouble. Shut them down fast. Give them no room to breathe.*

There was a thump as the front-rows collided. Brynmor Williams fed the ball and hooker Allan Phillips heeled it back cleanly to his back-row. Gareth Williams, the No.8, controlled the ball at his feet and then bent his back into the drive to help the rest of his pack as the English forwards put on the squeeze, looking to disrupt the ball at his feet.

Woodward's eyes were fixed on the central midfield axis of stand-off Gareth Davies and centres Steve Fenwick and David Richards. *Up in their faces. No time to breathe. No time to think. Shut down their attack before it even gets started.* Brynmor Williams bent down to retrieve the ball, paused for a moment, and then snapped upwards, his arms sweeping out towards Gareth Davies.

Woodward was out of the traps like a greyhound. But before he had taken even three strides he could instinctively tell that something was wrong. There had been no movement on either side of him: both Dodge and Carleton had remained where they were in the line. He looked at Brynmor Williams, whose hands were empty and was now appealing desperately to the referee for offside as the crowd broke into raptures and cheers.

The referee blew his whistle at the same moment that Woodward recognised the cool chess move that Brynmor Williams had played against him: the scrum-half had dummied the pass; the ball was still at Gareth Williams' feet, and Woodward had sprinted into the offside trap. Penalty Wales.

As Woodward stood beneath the posts, his stomach in his boots, he watched

Steve Fenwick, the Welsh captain, line up the ball. The stadium went eerily quiet. Fenwick kicked and the crowd erupted. 21–19 to Wales.

England had one last throw of the dice in the very final moments of the match when they were awarded a penalty. But Dusty Hare, who had rescued the game for England at Twickenham the previous year with a similar match-winning kick, could not repeat his heroics and England's bid to repeat their Grand Slam achievement was over after just one encounter.

Just as Woodward had allowed his concentration to slip in the Third Test in South Africa with the Lions, so too had he allowed it to slip in the Cardiff cauldron.

Woodward continued to feature in the England midfield for several more seasons, with mixed results. The rest of the 1981 Five Nations saw England record wins over Scotland and Ireland before losing to France 16–12 at Twickenham. They had a successful tour to Argentina that summer, winning the first Test and drawing the second, before defeating Australia 15–11 at Twickenham in January 1982.

Woodward appeared in the 9–9 draw against Scotland in the 1982 Five Nations, which was Bill Beaumont's last game for his country. Steve Smith took over the captaincy and they lost 16–15 to Ireland, but they bounced back after that setback and Woodward scored a magnificent individual try in a thumping 27–15 win over France in Paris, before beating Wales at Twickenham 17–7 in the final match of the championship.

In 1983 England had a horror show in the Five Nations and finished with the wooden spoon. Their best result had been a 13–13 draw with Wales in Cardiff. Woodward played only one match because of injury (a loss to Ireland at Lansdowne Road), so it was something of a surprise when he was selected for the Lions tour to New Zealand ahead of his centre partner Dodge, who had played in every game in the championship – which was to be later lamented by the former Lion and rugby historian Clem Thomas: 'Imagine leaving out Paul Dodge, amongst many other terrible errors of judgement!'

The 1983 Lions tour was typically tough and brutal, as has always been synonymous with touring New Zealand, and was not a particularly happy one either. There were divisions in the party from the outset over the choice of captain – Ireland's Ciaran Fitzgerald – and over the omission of several leading lights among the home nations, Dodge among them.

Looking back on that tour, Jim Telfer, the coach, regrets the structure of the management and coaching set-up. 'I thought at the time I was good enough to be the coach,' he said. 'I thought I had enough experience to take on the All Blacks. But I learnt that I just wasn't good enough at that stage to get the best out of the players.

'I don't know who would have been good enough because New Zealand were streets ahead of us in terms of how they developed players and played the game. We deserved to be beaten. And it was a pretty sad tour by the time we finished.

'I was the only coach, which meant I had to take charge of the backs. I had never coached backs in my life so I had to delegate a lot to guys like John Rutherford, Roy Laidlaw, Clive Woodward and Ollie Campbell.'

As has been pointed out by both Les Cusworth and Chalkie White, many felt that Woodward was at his best when he played alongside Dodge and his partner's absence may well have affected his performances on the tour. He played largely for the midweek team and wasn't selected for any of the Test sides. Even by his own admission, Woodward wasn't playing as well as he could have – but there were a number of players, pundits and supporters who felt that he could have made a difference to the Lions' chances in the Test series.

'Part of the selection problems lay in the fact that Jim Telfer was an out-and-out forwards coach and Willie John McBride, the manager, was also a forward,' recalled Roger Baird, the Scotland winger, who appeared in all four Tests. 'By 1983 every team had two coaches, so it was terribly short-sighted. We ended up sorting the back division out amongst ourselves, and consequently I felt we had the balance wrong in the side. John Rutherford should have played stand-off instead of Ollie Campbell, and Clive Woodward should have had a chance to play in the Tests – but you needed a backs coach there to push both those selections. John played brilliantly in the centre, but we could have done so much more with him at 10 and someone like Woodward outside him.'

The 1983 Lions shared the ignominy of their 1966 forebears by being whitewashed in the Test series. The first three Tests were relatively close-run affairs, but the All Blacks ripped loose in the fourth to hammer the Lions 38–6, the heaviest Test defeat in the Lions' history.

'Saturday, 16 July 1983 – the date of the Fourth Test – remains one of the saddest days in my life,' said Telfer. 'A 38–6 defeat, a 4–0 series loss, there was no coming back from that. The dreams I had held three or four months earlier were in tatters. I was very disillusioned with coaching and with rugby and I was also totally against the whole Lions concept by this stage: it was so difficult to get the team together and prepare properly before going into the biggest Test matches these players would ever experience.

'I couldn't fault the players, because they'd given everything, but they'd come through a system that wasn't good enough to prepare them for the levels of excellence of that All Blacks team, who were just better – both technically and tactically. But for all that I still felt that the fault lay with me because I'd failed to work around those deficiencies and differences. I'd failed to find a way for us to win – and there is always a way to win.'

Appropriate preparation. It was a bugbear so often felt by not only the Lions but also within the England set-up. In the years that have passed since he played, Clive Woodward has often highlighted the lack of time that the players had together as one of the key reasons why England struggled to dominate the world game in the way their resources should have allowed them to. The 1983 Lions tour added yet more grist to his mill over this issue – and it would be one that would remain central to his entire career. There were a number of other issues that affected morale – accommodation and food were consistently poor, there was little or no back-room staff, they trained brutally hard and they had to slog it around New Zealand in the dead of winter, playing some of the hardest teams on the planet in the most dreadful conditions. To say that it was a tough tour is an understatement and the lack of simple home comforts took its toll on the players and management. The Lions is the pinnacle for British and Irish rugby players – they are the best of the best, the elite; but the support environment for them was anything but elite and many felt, Woodward included, that their efforts were hamstrung by the crude organisation of the tour.

*

It is a curious fact that as free-spirited an individual as Woodward had been in his youth and when playing competitive sport, he had, by 1983, become relentlessly, even obsessively, driven by his business career. After the disappointments of the Lions tour and the gradual decline in his England career, he took great solace in pouring himself into his work life.

The environment at Xerox was hugely competitive – even more so than a rugby Test match or even a Lions tour. Daily results on the sales performance of every rep Xerox had in the country were posted on a large league table that could be seen by every employee as soon as they entered the office.

'Unlike in rugby, the pressure to perform here was relentless,' wrote Woodward in his autobiography, *Winning!* 'The daily 8 a.m. meetings stick in my memory. If we weren't meeting our targets, you'd think the world had come to an end. It was brutal. But that's why Xerox was successful... it was a no-excuses environment. If you didn't make the sales calls, if you didn't get the business, there was absolutely no sympathy. It was sink or swim.'

This was a very different way of thinking to anything that Woodward had encountered before. Football had given him sporting freedom and imagination, rugby had provided a conduit to international stardom, his three most influential coaches in Earle Kirton, Jim Greenwood and Chalkie White had given him masterful instructions in how to play rugby at its most beautiful. Now Xerox was giving him a ruthless, hard edge, where nothing but the results mattered and only excellence was acceptable.

There is no doubt that his status as a rugby player helped to further his career – first with winning the job at Xerox, but then with making client appointments. 'He was quite shy to begin with,' recalled Alan King when interviewed by Alison Kervin for her biography of Woodward. 'But he worked hard and soon learnt the ropes – and by God he could open doors with his rugby status. He was such an asset for us in that way.'

It was classic eighties yuppism at work in the Xerox office: big money, hugely male orientated, results at all costs. With the exception of the financial incentives, it was a rugby environment in all but name. And if you couldn't handle the pressure, if you didn't deliver the results, you were out the door. It was cut-throat – like life at Conway, like life as a Test match rugby player – and it appealed to Woodward's intensely competitive nature. For a man desperate to prove himself, it was just what he needed. And it was a simple work-and-reward philosophy – work your bollocks off, get the job done and you will reap the rewards. His experience in a team environment was also crucial – he was no lone gunman, he needed his colleagues to step up to the mark and work as hard as he did, so he had to foster relationships and encourage those around him. Collective responsibility and collective excellence would lead to collective reward. Patterns in the sand.

*

After a summer of misery with the Lions, Woodward was back in England colours in November to once again face the All Blacks. Against all expectation, they pulled off a remarkable 15–9 victory at Twickenham, their first for ten years over New Zealand and only their third ever, to mark some revenge for the desolation of the Lions tour.

Despite the glory of that victory, Woodward played in yet another disappointing Five Nations campaign in 1984, which saw England record just a single win – against Ireland at Twickenham – before appearing in his last Test, a dispiriting 25–15 loss to Wales at Twickenham. He was only twenty-eight, an age that many would regard as the beginning of the peak three or four years of an international's career. But it was not to be.

Woodward never formally retired from the England side, instead his Test career fizzled sadly out with non-selection. For all that he was something of an enigma as a player, he was also a game-breaker and it was a sad end to a career that never really delivered on its undoubted promise – hampered, unquestionably, by the conservatism of the England Test scene. The frustration of the whole environment has haunted him since; Test rugby is the ultimate honour for any player – but save for the odd glimpse when he was able to display his genius, it was an arena of broken dreams.

What is most impressive, however, is that he did not mope around, nor did he seem to pine for the limelight as it faded from his life. Instead he turned his focus ever more ferociously on his business career and flourished as part of one of the best performing Xerox teams in the UK.

In the summer of 1984, after six years at the Leicester office, he received a job offer from the Xerox operation in Sydney (where his former mentor, Alan King, had not long since relocated). He flew out for a recce and fell in love with the prospect of life in Australia, and shortly afterwards he and his new partner, Jayne, moved out there, taking up residence in Manly. Not only was Manly a stunning setting with an easy commute to central Sydney, but it was also home to one of the finest rugby clubs in the world. Alan Jones had just left the position of head coach at the club to take charge of the national team (and guide the magnificent '84 Wallabies on their Grand Slam tour of Britain and Ireland), and had left behind an excellent coaching and playing structure that appealed immediately to Woodward.

He arrived at the Xerox office in Sydney with grand plans to transform it into a replica of his old Leicester office – target-driven, hungry for success, relentlessly ambitious. But it came as a major shock to him to discover that his new colleagues had no desire to adopt such an approach. He turned up in a suit and tie and found his sales force in shorts and sandals. They had no interest in topping sales charts, in his proposed 8 a.m. daily meetings, or to be as unerringly driven as his colleagues and staff had been in Leicester. At first he was bullish, determined to force them to fit the mould that he knew could deliver results, but he hit resistance at almost every step.

As he was soon to learn, the priorities of his staff were simply different to his own. They didn't care about league tables and proving themselves to be the best. They just wanted to do their job and enjoy their lives away from the office. It was like Conway, but in reverse – here he was the disciplinarian with draconian views of how things should be done, facing an almost carefree institution that would not bend to his desires or wishes. And just as he had done at school, so he had to do in Sydney – he learnt to adapt.

Changing his hardline focus, he strove instead to make the office a fun place to be – veiling his targets behind humour and light-hearted approaches (such as changing his office into a Hawaiian-themed hut for a day). It took time but he gradually won his staff over and began to make great strides in the efficiency of the office and his team's ability to hit – and even surpass – their targets. It was a hard lesson for him to learn because he constantly had to mask his frustrations at the lack of importance placed on success in the workplace. But with perseverance he managed to make a difference.

Away from the office, however, he discovered that the Australian psyche was not endemically bereft of a furious drive for success. That, he discovered, was reserved for the sporting environment.

While generalisations can often be hollow and misleading, in this instance it is probably fair to pull out a broad brush and state that there is a winning mentality in Australia that is prevalent across all major sports in the country

– particularly at international level. There is an entrenched belief that they should win every encounter they enter into. That's not to say that they are deluded in this belief – their fierce competitiveness, along with skills honed in largely ideal weather conditions, allows them, more often than not, to back up that confidence with results. It is a cultural difference, particularly in rugby, between the hemispheres. The All Blacks, Wallabies and Springboks expect to win every game they play, no matter who it is against. The northern hemisphere teams hope to just keep in touch when they face their southern rivals and, maybe, sneak the odd win. While Woodward had to adapt to the laissez-faire attitudes at work he subsumed himself in the sporting culture of Australia and relished the style of attacking rugby – on hard, fast grounds, invariably played with a bone dry ball – which encouraged speed and skill from every player for the full eighty minutes.

He soon saw how much importance the whole country placed on success in sport. It was a medium that allowed them to show themselves off to the rest of the world, which in turn fostered positive feelings at home. It was a culture that extended from games played by children in the street to political policy.

At Manly, full of the joie de vivre of the style of rugby played at the club, he moved back to his old position of fly-half and was eventually to captain the side. There were a number of internationals in the team at the time: Phil Cox at scrum-half, his brother, Michael, on the wing, Steve Williams and Peter FitzSimons at lock, Ross Reynolds at No.8 and Bill Calcraft at flanker.

It wasn't long before Phil Cox and Woodward struck up a tremendous playing partnership. 'We'd had the odd player from Wales, Ireland and England, but never an international from Britain,' recalled Cox, in an interview with Richard Williams. 'He was great to have around the club because of his experience and, being an international, the boys looked up to him. Our coach insisted we ran with the ball, the tracks were hard, and I think that's why Clive enjoyed himself so much, having come from the soft pitches and the ten-man game in England.'

It was, as Cox intimated, like manna from heaven for Woodward, even if the first few games were much tougher than he might have expected. His first game was against Randwick, one of the powerhouses of Sydney rugby. Randwick were coached by Bob Dwyer, who had been head coach of the Wallabies from 1982–83, and they had in their armoury three weapons that had been revolutionary in transforming Australian rugby into a world force: the Ella brothers, Mark, Gary and Glen.

Growing up in La Perouse, an Aboriginal community in Sydney, in the 1960s and '70s, the Ella brothers had spent every moment they could playing sport. While they were incredibly talented at a whole range of sports, particularly cricket, it was rugby that had truly captured their hearts. Playing for hour upon hour on Tasman Street amid a bubbling mass of other children, the Ella brothers developed an attacking style of perpetual motion, flat attack play, lancing late running angles, short pop passes and looping support runs, all held together with pinpoint passing accuracy.

From the chaos of street rugby, this style was adapted to the more organised structure of a fifteen-a-side game at Matraville High School in Chifley by the rugby master, Geoff Mould, and the school first XV went on to win the prestigious Waratah Shield in 1976 with Mark, Gary and Glen pivotal to the team's success. In 1977 all three boys were selected for the Australian schoolboys side that toured Britain – and went undefeated in sixteen matches. It is ironic that the style of play utilised by the Australian schoolboys had its roots in Jim Greenwood's Total Rugby. While Greenwood was largely ignored by the rugby establishment in the UK, his ideas were gospel in Australia and combining the fifteen-man rugby philosophy with the talent of players like the Ellas, Andrew Slack, Michael Lynagh and the burgeoning genius of David Campese, Australian rugby was on a steep upwards curve.

Upon leaving high school, Bob Dwyer, who was close to Mould, persuaded the Ellas to join Randwick, where their revolutionary game tore apart the Sydney league. In 1980 Mark won his first cap for the Wallabies and was joined on the international scene by his brothers in 1982.

In simple terms, the Ellas' attacking strategy was organised with all the backline players standing flat to the gain-line, with numerous changes of angle and direction all coming at the last moment, right in the face of defence. For players accustomed all their lives to facing a deep lying attack and consequently having a lot of time to line up a tackle – which was invariably made at a side angle, around the knees – this new attacking formation was completely bamboozling. The defender had no time to react to the change of pace or direction of the ball carrier or to track the lines of the support runners. With Mark Ella pulling the strings at stand-off, the Wallabies destroyed every defence they faced on the 1984 tour to Great Britain and Ireland and will be remembered as one of the greatest attacking sides the world has ever seen.

Playing in the Sydney league, where the flat-line attacking style was being adopted by various teams and expertly executed at Randwick, Woodward came across a style of rugby that at first shocked and then utterly enthralled him – even if it took him a little while to get his head around it, particularly in defence. Not only were the attacks he was trying to defend against devilishly difficult to track, the flat-line approach also meant that attackers and defenders were often smashing directly into one another.

'I had never made a front-on tackle in my life,' recalled Woodward, 'and suddenly every time they had the ball from a set-piece I was having to make one – or try to make one. I was run over a lot in that first game. It was a physicality that I hadn't encountered before – and the speed was just mind-blowing.' It was as if every philosophy that he had aspired to under Kirton, Greenwood and White was, at last, being brought to fruition. It was intelligent, fast, expansive and highly skilled. It was Jim Greenwood's vision of Total Rugby.

But it wasn't just Dwyer, the Ellas and Randwick that were rewriting rugby in Australia. Alan Jones had been head coach at Manly before taking up the role of head coach for the Wallabies in 1983, and the structures, mantras and philosophies that he had put in place were still very much in evidence at the club when Woodward joined.

Jones did not have much of a playing CV himself, but he transferred his considerable business skills to the sporting environment to startling effect. Peter FitzSimons was enticed from Sydney University to Manly by Jones in the early 1980s. FitzSimons went on to win seven Wallaby caps before beginning an illustrious career as a rugby journalist, broadcaster and author. In his book, *FitzSimons on Rugby: Loose in the Tight Five*, a collection of some of his finest articles, he recalls his first experiences of Alan Jones. 'Right away he was different. His was not an ad hoc rugby training that you made up as you went along, but rather it was precisely prepared and slickly executed. Each drill flowed smoothly into the next, each training session having its own cohesive theme. We danced to his whistle, but even that early in the Year of Jones, there was a sense that he seemed to know what he was doing. This wasn't a bloke who thought we might have half a chance to win the competition if we got it right. This was a bloke who said – and *meant* it when he said it – "We are going to win this competition, and this is how we are going to do it."

'The first rule we had to understand, and it wasn't one of those rules of the unspoken variety, was that it had to be "his way or the highway". We could discuss things all right, but we were to be under no illusions as to which one of us had the final say. Alan did.'

For anyone with even an inkling of how Clive Woodward developed as a coach, this portrait of Jones could be instantly transferred to Woodward's approach in later years.

'Alan Jones's most fundamental principle of rugby,' wrote FitzSimons, 'was eliminating errors. "The difference between professionals and amateurs is that the professional is dedicated to the total eradication of error," Jones was extremely fond of saying. "It has nothing to do with how much money you're earning, and everything to do with not repeating the same mistakes."'

Jones would analyse the game more than any coach in the league, constantly taking notes during games and then applying his analysis in training the following week. This analytical approach was deeply embedded into the culture of the club when Woodward joined Manly. At the start of training each Tuesday night each player would be handed a typewritten analysis of the previous Saturday's game, with tailored notes on their own performance – what they did right and what they needed to work on. As Woodward would subsequently do, Jones transferred his business knowledge and skill base into a rugby environment.

'Did he know a lot about rugby?' FitzSimons questioned of his coach. 'What I have no doubt about is that he knew a lot about motivation, about the principles of getting fifteen people together and functioning smoothly. And whatever he might not have known about the game was compensated for by the experts he called in to take us for particular training sessions.'

This philosophy of bringing in experts in certain aspects of the game was unheard of at the time in rugby union. Indeed, when Woodward adopted the Alan Jones blueprint in his coaching career some ten years later, he was ridiculed. Yet again, the southern hemisphere giants were showing the way years ahead of their northern counterparts. But this was the reason that Woodward had moved to Australia, even if he hadn't realised that it would have such a bearing on his later life. He had gone to experience a new life and culture and to learn. He had found that he had to adapt to the circumstances that he found himself in and, while he had gone with a mind focused on furthering his business career, it was the global influences on his rugby that really made the long-term difference.

'I broke my jaw against Warringah, which was the big local derby,' recalled Woodward, 'and I was lying there in the hospital bed and the first person who came to see me was Alan Jones. He came in with a guy called James Black, who was the Wallaby full-back, to see how I was doing. And I was like, "Wow, thanks so much for coming to see me." And we chatted away for a while and he eventually worked into the conversation that he thought I would soon be playing for Australia. At the time I was just like, "What? What are you talking about?" But he was just applying business principles to his new role as Wallaby coach. He saw me as a potential asset who could make his team better and there was nothing in the rules at the time to stop me from changing my international allegiances to Australia. I ended up going to a Wallaby training session, but it just didn't feel right and I didn't pursue it after that – and Alan understood that. But it was intriguing to see him thinking outside the box like that.'

While he was in Australia, Woodward took the time to visit the world-famous Australian Institute of Sport in Canberra. Just like his experiences at Manly, his tour around the AIS's sixty-six-hectare campus in the northern suburb of Bruce had a profound effect on him. As Woodward wandered around the huge multi-sport campus, he could see that the AIS was Loughborough writ large on a massive, national scale.

In 1973 Professor John Bloomfield was commissioned by the Australian government to construct a plan to increase the professionalism of elite sport in the country. Bloomfield and his team conducted a number of studies of successful sports institutes in Europe and concluded, in *The Role, Scope and Development of Recreation in Australia*, that a national institute of sport should be established to monitor and develop elite athletes. This report was not acted on initially, but following Australia's disastrous participation in the 1976 Montreal Olympics, where they managed to win only one silver medal and four bronze medals before finishing thirty-second overall in the table, moves were made to put Bloomfield's plan into action. On 26 January 1981, Australia Day, the Australian Institute of Sport was officially opened by Prime Minister Malcolm Fraser.

By the 1984 Los Angeles Olympics, the work of the AIS was already in evidence as Australia dramatically improved on their performances in Montreal and also at the 1980 Moscow Olympics, and in 1985 the federal budget increased the Institute's funding by 60 per cent. By the 1986 Commonwealth Games in Edinburgh, seventy-five current and former AIS athletes competed in the Games and won nineteen gold, sixteen silver and seventeen bronze medals.

In 1987 the AIS brought rugby union under its umbrella and established centres in Brisbane, Sydney and Canberra. Through scouts, recommendations and personal applications, the AIS identified talented young athletes across a range of sports and monitored their progress at school, club and at national level, bringing them in for elite training sessions and providing them with programmes to develop their fitness, strength, speed, conditioning, diet and so on. What impressed Woodward the most was to see another Loughborough trait transferred on to a much larger canvas – the sharing of knowledge across sporting disciplines. Just as he had been fascinated watching Seb Coe's training under George Gandy, the AIS had adopted a system where every sporting programme would pool its collective expertise and new findings so that every athlete under its aegis could become the very best that they could be.

Within just a few years of its inception, the AIS's rugby centres were producing Wallabies in the shape of Tim Horan, Phil Kearns and John Eales, who would go on to lift the 1991 World Cup before being joined by AIS graduates Jason Little, George Gregan, Matt Burke, Ben Tune and Joe Roff to form the core of the 1999 World Cup-winning side. There is no arguing with the phenomenal success of Professor Bloomfield's brainchild – and it was a structure that Woodward envied greatly.

*

In 1987 Woodward's playing career began to wind down towards retirement. Feeling that he had achieved all that he could with the Xerox office in Sydney, Woodward left the company and started working for Portfolio Leasing, a company whose modus operandi was based on the most profitable side of Xerox's business – the leasing of office equipment to businesses around the country. He hand-picked a very effective sales and administration team, adopting a crossover philosophy between his management style in the UK and Australia, and was soon making a huge success of the new venture. His networking and people skills were exceptional and he ensured that his staff all felt part of one big team striving for collective excellence – which would be rewarded on a regular basis if they achieved their targets. The drawback was that the business was hugely time consuming and there was little or no time for rugby any more and so, without much fanfare, he finally hung up his boots.

The Woodwards (for he and Jayne were now married and had had their first child) continued to live in Australia for a further two years until the siren call of home proved too much and they returned to the UK in late 1989. Portfolio Leasing were desperate to keep him, so they arranged for a transfer to their London branch. This proved to be only a temporary arrangement, however, as Woodward was as disenchanted with the London branch of Portfolio Leasing as he had been with the Sydney branch of Xerox – and he soon sought to spread his wings independently. In February 1990 he left Portfolio Leasing and set up his own company, Sales Finance and Leasing, based in the converted garage of his new family home in Pinkneys Green, just outside Maidenhead. As he had done in Australia, he chose a small team of employees and led them on an aggressive drive to build the business. Within a very short space of time they had developed the leasing business into a multimillion-pound concern and moved out of the garage and into a proper office space. It was an incredibly impressive start for such a new venture – its success due to the culmination of years of accumulated knowledge and acumen, Woodward's leadership of a carefully selected team that he trusted completely, his own grand ambition and vision, and hour upon hour of hard work by all concerned. It would prove to be a powerful blueprint.

THREE

THE ANATOMY OF
A COACH

'Two roads diverged in a wood, and I –
I took the one less traveled by,
And that has made all the difference.'
Robert Frost, 'The Road Not Taken'

HENLEY RUGBY CLUB'S Dry Leas ground in the world-famous
rowing regatta town of Henley-on-Thames, Oxfordshire, is a postcard
setting, as quintessentially romantic a home of English sport as can
be imagined. On a mild August night in 1990 a gentle breeze shifted through
the trees that lined the river a few hundred yards from the ground, carrying all
the rich smells of summer across the beautifully manicured pitches towards the
old clubhouse. But something unusual was taking place to disturb the usual
calm of this rural idyll.

The speakers built into the stand as part of the club's PA system crackled.
A whine of feedback howled through the quiet evening and startled a flock of
birds into flight from the riverside foliage. The door to the clubhouse swung
open and out trooped every playing member of the club, ready for pre-season
training, the studs of their boots clacking on the dry ground as they made
their way down to the area of the pitch just in front of the stand and formed
themselves into a series of makeshift rows.

A young woman, dressed predominantly in Lycra, followed them out
and then took up a position in the space between the rows of players and
the stand. She was beaming at their bemused and, in some cases, palpably
terrified faces.

'OK!' she called out with a clap of her hands. 'Just follow my lead – this is
going to be so much fun! Just try to keep up… and enjoy yourselves!'

She waved an arm to a figure in the clubhouse who turned to a CD player hooked up to the PA system and pressed play.

'The Power' by Snap! screeched out of the speakers, filling the evening air, and the Lycra-clad aerobics instructor began her routine – and forty men in a ragbag assortment of different rugby shirts, T-shirts and shorts tried to keep up as best they could.

Leaning against one of the posts watching proceedings, a clipboard in one hand, a whistle draped around his neck, and with a satisfied smile on his face, stood Clive Woodward.

Just six months earlier, Woodward had known little or nothing about Henley RFC, the club just a few miles from his new home in Pinkneys Green. Then, one evening, completely out of the blue, he received a call from an old Loughborough teammate, Mike Poulson, who was a player-coach at the club, which played in South-West Division Two. Poulson had heard about Woodward's return from Australia and wondered if he would be interested in coming down to the club to give a talk to the players about his time Down Under. At first Woodward was reluctant but he could think of no real reason to decline the request.

He turned up one evening and observed training, gave a small talk to the players about his experiences in Australia and made a few suggestions on how to improve one or two aspects of their training. He enjoyed the interaction and the response he had from the players. After attending a few more training sessions on this casual basis, he started to watch their games on a Saturday and he and his family soon got heavily involved in the social scene at the club. It was a relaxing change of focus from work and the Woodwards enjoyed the welcoming embrace of the club community. As the summer approached, Poulson cornered him at a club barbecue and asked him if he would be interested in taking on the head coach position for the following season. Much to Woodward's own surprise, he agreed.

While he had been in Australia, the RFU had moved to establish an organised structure to the whole club game in England by setting up a pyramid league system. There is little doubt that the concept of taking part in a competition that would matter week in week out, with relegation and promotion at the end of the season, would have appealed to Woodward's competitive instincts. There would be a tangible sense of achievement, of driving for a goal, which stimulated a very basic instinct in his psyche – and he was soon completely hooked by coaching. As he had done with his business career, he threw himself into the challenge; he was as focused on making a success of his time at Henley as he was of making a success of Sales Finance and Leasing – and, consequently, there would be no half-measures in his attitude or his dedication.

He approached coaching as Alan Jones had – in a businesslike manner, drawing on all his experience, all his accumulated knowledge and all his resources and folding them into a philosophy inspired by his love of football and the attitudes of Earle Kirton, Jim Greenwood and Chalkie White – and in direct contrast to that of his England playing days. Above all else he wanted his players to enjoy their rugby, to have fun with the ball and to play with smiles on their faces. A tight, forwards-orientated game plan wouldn't achieve this. An aspiration to play Total Rugby would. It was a lofty ambition to have for a team in such a lowly league as South-West Division Two, but he saw no reason to limit his ambitions for the team just because of the league they were playing in.

Having tried and failed to come in and foster his own way of doing things in the Xerox office in Sydney, he knew that he had to take time to understand the playing culture at Henley and what the players wanted. He would then build that into his plan for developing their game and aiming for promotion from the league. He also realised that the key to success didn't just lie with the first XV squad. Henley was a club and he needed to involve (or at least make feel involved) every player in every team, all the committee members and volunteers, the supporters, sponsors and the players' families. They were all part of the club and if they worked together then there would be a solid bedrock from which to build consistent and continued success.

One of his first tasks was to set about analysing the team's previous tactical structures and the players at his disposal. In so doing he recognised that they had talent but that their basic skills were flawed and they could be forced into making serious errors if pressed by an aggressive defence, if they were tiring towards the end of a game or if play broke down and became disorganised chaos. So from the first pre-season training session he went back to basics, focusing on simple handling drills and getting the fundamental tactical elements of the game right. If the game broke down it wasn't the time to panic – when the defence is caught wrong-footed, when predictability goes out of the window, it is the perfect opportunity to attack.

He wanted to make sure there was fun in everything that they did. Thus the aerobics instructor. It was additional fitness and co-ordination work for his players, hidden in the guise of fun. It also allowed his players an opportunity to shed inhibitions in front of one another, have a laugh and, as a result, bond as a team. It was his first outside-the-box piece of coaching; it would not be his last.

One of the main objectives, however, for focusing so specifically on developing their handling skills was his ambition to introduce the flat-line back play that he had learnt in Australia. It would be difficult for his players to learn and then implement the style and it was high-risk because if it went wrong they would be horribly exposed in defence. But he also knew that there were high rewards for the team if they got it right – no defence they would come up against would be able to handle it if they executed accurately, and the players would derive so much enjoyment from it.

He knew that it was important not to override the senses with a flood of new ideas, so he gradually introduced things at training over a period of time. This allowed the players to adapt to each new phase of their development and also kept them fresh and interested throughout the entirety of the season.

There is a story that Woodward tells in his autobiography that demonstrates perfectly his efforts to get the players thinking differently – while also forcing them into executing his tactical shift to the flat-line all-out attack.

'A month or two into the season I banned any form of kicking during play. Without kicking, you have to play the ball in your hands. When the pressure was really on, that was actually the time to keep hold of the ball, not kick it away. But a lot of the players were terrified of playing under pressure… That's the time when people with less skill tend to collapse under the pressure of it all. Pressure is wonderfully revealing in that way. When the pressure is on, there is just no place to hide on the pitch. I loved it. The players hated it – at first – but very quickly we became good at playing this way. If we did not become skilled at this very quickly we would be at the bottom of the table, but if we could get it right we'd be at the top. It was compelling.'

An analysis of this story is revealing for it not only gives a fascinating insight into Woodward's psychology but also the management style that would come to define his coaching career. It shows his inherent belief in what has been termed a 'growth mindset', a psychological approach that is often inherently present in the most successful individuals in life, from business to music to education to sport.

Carol Dweck is a professor of psychology at Stanford University who has dedicated much of her career to researching and understanding the growth mindset. Her illuminating book, *Mindset*, pitches the notion that there are two types of mindset when it comes to an individual's intelligence, talents and personality – a fixed mindset and a growth mindset.

In a fixed mindset, an individual believes that their basic qualities, such as sporting talent, intelligence or ability to play music, are inherent traits – natural abilities that they are born with. If they believe that they are naturally in possession of these traits, they do not work with the relentless dedication required to achieve consistent levels of excellence in their given field; when they come up against obstacles or experience failure, they blame the limitations of their apparently inherent nature. Those with a growth mindset, however, believe that through sustained and dedicated effort these qualities can be developed; when they come up against obstacles or experience failure, they teach themselves new ways to improve and push themselves onwards to greater success. The growth mindset is perhaps best summarised by Thomas Edison when he said, 'If I find 10,000 ways something won't work, I haven't failed. I am not discouraged, because every wrong attempt discarded is another step forward.'

So it was the case with Woodward and his coaching philosophy. By placing an almost complete ban on kicking at Henley he encouraged his charges to find other ways to negotiate their way out of a problem, to think differently – to think *positively* about the game at all times. They had to find space, they had to identify weaknesses in the opposition, they had to think their way out of trouble and they had to develop their handling and running skills to allow them to execute their escape strategies. Although Carol Dweck spent two decades studying fixed and growth mindsets, she did not publish *Mindset* until 2006, so Woodward had no knowledge of her studies. It is fascinating to see that he is typical of someone with a growth mindset – a subject that we will return to later.

Henley narrowly missed out on promotion in Woodward's first full season in charge, but their game dramatically improved and they won the last eight matches of the season, as well as the Oxfordshire Cup. They were still in a transitional phase under his guidance and there were some inevitable teething problems as they adapted to the new style of play he was trying to implement, but they were developing all the time – Edison would have been proud. And the way they were training and playing was attracting a lot of attention in rugby circles; by the end of that first season there was a groundswell of new players eager to join the club.

Turning his focus to his second season at the helm, Woodward continued his player development, knowing that the most successful teams are ones that are led by the players themselves with only guidance from the coach. Player empowerment was crucial for this to happen. He assigned responsibilities to senior players for various key aspects of the game – line-outs, scrums, penalties and defence – and gave them copies of Jim Greenwood's *Total Rugby* for encouragement. Thereafter they would make reports at pre-training meetings, analysing their areas with regard to the previous week's game and offering solutions on how to improve aspects of their play. He was determined to replicate Greenwood's vision – just as he had experienced it in Australia.

It wasn't only on the training ground and in matches that he implemented new standards at the club. He insisted that the team wore matching off-field team-wear so that all the players felt as one – and showed a united front and professional appearance to the opposition teams and their own supporters. He also asked that the players try to remain as responsible as possible when it came to drinking after away games. He didn't want anything to bring embarrassment to the team or to distract from their focus on winning. He aimed for high standards across every facet of their association with the club.

While the Henley players were making great strides towards playing the flat-line attack, the technique was still in need of some refinement. In another show of lateral thinking and of bringing in outside expertise, Woodward recruited two former teammates from Manly, Rob Gallacher and James Perrignon, to join the club for the 1992–93 season. The primary reason was to help continue the development of the flat-line back play, but their quality and experience also helped to significantly raise the standards of those around them in both training and in games. As a reflection of just how good the imports were, both continued to play for Manly's first team for a number of seasons after their return to Australia and, in a further testament to his quality, Gallacher was eventually selected for the Wallaby squad.

Henley went unbeaten throughout that second season and comfortably won promotion to South-West Division One. This launched a run of unprecedented success as they continued to push on through the leagues year by year, winning the Oxfordshire Cup every season before eventually breaking through to the national leagues in 1994. Their success was turning heads all over the country and *Rugby Special* showcased a feature on them – with an interview with Woodward at its core. The club's playing numbers had grown out of all proportion to the base that had been there when Woodward arrived. It was, without doubt, a remarkable success story.

*

After a long and difficult season in 1994–95, London Irish were relegated from England's First Division. Amid the gloomy pall that hung over the club, their coach, the former New Zealand hooker Hika Reid, quit his position and several top players, including a number of Ireland internationals, began to jump ship to other clubs that were still in the top flight. All of a sudden the club were rudderless and staring into oblivion. With no coach, a sudden vacuum in the senior player department, and a culture of disappointment and defeatism now deeply rooted throughout the club, London Irish were facing the prospect of a drastic and continued downward spiral. For one of the world's grand old clubs, everything looked to be falling to pieces; they were in a deep crisis.

Ann Heaver, who worked for Woodward at Sales Finance and Leasing – and, in truth, by 1995, was essentially running the whole operation with Jayne Woodward while Clive spent the majority of his time and energy concentrating on rugby – was a passionate London Irish fan. Acutely aware of the club's plight, she had an epiphany: Woodward should apply for the available head coach role. She contacted Mike Gibson, the Ireland and Lions legend who was in charge of the playing side at the club, spoke glowingly of Woodward as a boss, a man and of his success with Henley, and suggested that Gibson get in touch with him – which he duly did.

When being shown around the club's impressive stadium at The Avenue in Sunbury-on-Thames, Woodward explained to Gibson that he would be interested in taking on the job, but only if he was allowed to do things his way. He had to have complete control of how the team was organised and run, complete control of selection and even control of player recruitment – including the ability to bring in players who had no connection to Ireland. They were reasonable demands, totally in keeping with anything that any modern coach would expect to be granted. These conditions, and the last in particular, would prove thorny, but the club acquiesced to his demands and he was named head coach in the summer of 1995.

One of his first acts at London Irish was to examine the playing roster and clear out the dead wood, including encouraging the last remaining international on their books to move on – his public indecision about whether to stay or go was proving a huge distraction during pre-season preparations. Woodward had already proved himself an astute team builder in both business and rugby and he readily understood the negative influence that someone who is not 100 per cent dedicated to the cause can create.

He brought music and enjoyment to training and playing, just as he had done at Henley. The team trained to music, ran out on to the pitch before matches to music and music blared when they scored. Not only did it create an alien and intimidating environment for visiting teams, but it raised the spirits of the home players and encouraged a party atmosphere among the large, passionate and vocal support. Home games at London Irish were played in a carnival atmosphere – and the positive feelings that this engendered spread from the vociferous crowd to the players on the pitch.

The first season was almost a carbon copy of his first season at Henley. The team gradually bought into Woodward's new way of thinking – which again he introduced incrementally – and they consolidated their position. And just as Henley had done, London Irish finished the season strongly, with their tails in the air. Woodward had managed to prevent a spiral into disaster, which can so often happen when a team is relegated and knows nothing but the feeling of defeat and desolation. The following season would be all about focusing on winning the Second Division and returning to the top flight.

He pulled off an incredible coup by persuading two of the brightest talents in Ireland to join the club – full-back Conor O'Shea and second-row Gabriel Fulcher – much to the irritation of the Irish Rugby Union, who were trying to attract and keep all their top players in Ireland. And just as Gallacher and

Perrignon had made a significant difference to Henley, so too did O'Shea and Fulcher make a huge difference to how London Irish performed. But the move to bring these two players to the club had motivations other than just improving the player pool. Woodward was acutely aware of the club's heritage and its identity with its fan base. While insisting on having the power to bring in whoever he wanted, no matter their nationality, he also recognised that there was a lack of quality Irish players at the club; in order to elevate the team out of mediocrity, to give the fans something to really bond with and feel pride in (which would, in turn, lift the spirits of the players on the pitch) he needed to build on the Irish identity within the squad. So once O'Shea and Fulcher were on board, he set about recruiting several more players from Ireland. Among those that he brought over were future Lions Jeremy Davidson, Malcolm O'Kelly and Rob Henderson and players who would enjoy stellar careers with Ireland, including David Humphreys and Victor Costello. At one stage, there were thirteen players in the Ireland squad who were playing at London Irish.

'There's no doubt that Clive helped transform the club,' said Kieran McCarthy, the club's manager, in an interview with *The Guardian*'s Richard Williams. 'He had some really radical ideas, many of which we couldn't put into practice because we didn't have the money at the time. But by 1996 he had helped bring over Irish internationals such as Conor O'Shea, Gabriel Fulcher, David Humphreys and Niall Woods which was a pretty amazing coup at the time.'

Woodward continued his philosophy for playing the flat-line attack at London Irish and he made training fun – but there was always a clear separation between him and the team. He was the boss and his call was the only one that mattered. He picked the team and it didn't matter how senior the player was, if they were having a dip in form, weren't training hard enough, if they were making costly mistakes during games or were not sticking to his game plans, then they would be dropped – and considered for selection again only when the issues had been addressed.

Again he returned to Greenwood's vision of Total Rugby. It took time for the players to adjust and there was a seminal moment before one league game when, just as the team was about to leave the changing room, Woodward lined them up in alphabetical order and told them to swap their shirts so that they were lined up 1 to 15 down this new order. It was a small psychological trick but it had a wondrous effect. Just this small change from the entrenched structures that they were all so used to set the players' minds free and they went out and played as fully rounded rugby players, unrestrained by the restrictions of their traditional playing positions. They all looked to attack, to pass, to identify and target space. It had worked even better than Woodward had expected and he was delighted.

'Clive was always trying to get players to think on their feet,' said McCarthy. 'In one game we sent out a team with different numbers on their backs. O'Shea, a full-back, wore No.2, Clive arguing that he wanted the players to be able to play anywhere. He was quite a character.'

They won promotion back to the First Division at the end of the 1995–96 season, just in time to begin the first full season of professionalism in England. But Woodward didn't get the chance to guide the team through this major transition.

At the AGM in July a motion was put forward to have a new clause written into the club's constitution that stated that only someone of Irish descent could be involved with the management of the team (with any exceptions to this to be made at the discretion of the committee). Woodward felt that it was a deliberate ploy to remove him from his position, despite his achievements with the first team. In many ways it was Woodward's history with the Welsh Schoolboys repeating itself.

While the chairman tried to defend the motion and offered the caveat that the ruling, should it be passed, wouldn't apply to Woodward, he felt that the xenophobia at the heart of the issue was too much for him. It felt like too much of a betrayal for what he had done, it touched a still-raw nerve and it showed him in a single moment that the club was not yet ready for the direction or the professionalism that Woodward wanted to drive through. His interest was in the players and focused on rugby – he had never had any interest in the politics of the club. But now politics was being forced on the rugby side of things and it was too much.

Alison Kervin interviewed Kieran McCarthy, rugby manager at London Irish at the time, for her biography of Woodward. McCarthy recalls the incident quite differently, stating that the motion had been put forward as a way of ensuring the Irish heritage was maintained at the club in the new professional era. Because the club had had to become an incorporated business, and as a result had had to remove certain clauses in their constitution that called for officers of the club to be of Irish birth or descent, they still wanted to make sure that the overall ethos at the club remained true to its Irish origins. 'All it meant was things such as the green shirts, the Irish music, the association with Guinness and the celebration of St Patrick's Day were kept. Nothing heavy,' said McCarthy. But Woodward obviously didn't see it that way. 'He was too rash,' continued McCarthy. 'He lashed out without listening properly.'

After several weeks of apologising and reassurances, Woodward was persuaded to continue. The motion at the AGM hadn't been passed but the whole experience had disillusioned him. He would not be at the club for much longer. Sales Finance and Leasing was continuing to expand rapidly and he was still only part-time as a coach. Woodward realised that he was over-stretching himself so he brought in an assistant coach. He chose Willie Anderson, the former Ireland second-row, and had the club employ him full-time. It was a sensible idea but it was also the death knell for Woodward's time at the club. In October he turned up for training but was prevented from entering the changing room by a committee member who informed him that he had been replaced as head coach by Anderson. It was an ignominious end to his time at the club.

Looking back, Woodward is philosophical about his time with London Irish. He had relished the challenge of taking on a top team that was in trouble and turning their fortunes around. He had saved them, but not only that, he had developed as a coach and he had continued to prove to himself that his idealism to play Total Rugby could be achieved if a group of players bought into the idea. And perhaps most importantly, he learnt never to let politics interfere in his involvement with rugby again – although he had no idea at the time how that lesson would ultimately come back to haunt him.

*

For the previous two seasons, as well as coaching at London Irish and running his company, Woodward had been one of the England Under-21 coaches. Don Rutherford, the technical director of the RFU, had been impressed by the Henley story and by the way London Irish were rallying themselves in the Second Division and when Woodward had been invited to Twickenham to make a presentation of his methods to a group of coaches in 1994 Rutherford had been bowled over by his ideas and his enthusiasm. The RFU had been looking for a new coach for the Under-21 side and it occurred to Rutherford that Woodward might be the perfect choice.

He had phoned Woodward with the offer of the position and Woodward was hugely enthused by the proposal – but on one condition: he had to choose his own coaching team and his would be the final say on training, tactics and selection. It took some negotiation but Rutherford was so intrigued by what Woodward had to offer as a coach that he agreed.

Woodward invited Andy Robinson of Bath, who was still playing for the club but was looking to cut his teeth in coaching, and Mike Poulson from Henley to come on board as assistant coach and manager respectively. A compromise had been made with Rutherford over former England prop Jeff Probyn's involvement in the set-up – Rutherford had wanted him as manager, Woodward had wanted Poulson, so in the end Probyn was made forwards coach.

As the appointment of Mike Poulson as England Under-21 manager also demonstrates, one of Woodward's strongest traits was a loyalty to those that he liked, respected and whose skills he appreciated. Over the years he would show this trait over and over again, while never forgetting the ruthless edge that is often a given in a competitive business environment. If he was required to make a difficult decision regarding an individual, he would rarely shy away from it, no matter how conflicted he might be personally over the issue. He understood that to succeed in both business and sport there was a time and a place for loyalty and a strong bond with individuals, but there was also a necessity for ruthlessness if the grand design required it.

It is important to bear this attitude in mind for all that is to follow.

Thinking back to Peter FitzSimons' recollections of Alan Jones, it is remarkable how similar he and Woodward were as coaches – despite the two having never worked together. Where with Jones it had been 'his way or the highway', at Henley, London Irish and with the England Under-21s, it was very much a case of 'Clive's way or the highway'. But this is not to say that both men were unreasonably draconian – rather it is illustrative of a business leader in action in a sporting environment. Just as the boss of a company might be willing to listen to input from his staff, it is the boss who is ultimately responsible for the key decisions in the business, who needs to drive the company forward and who is in control of the larger success or failure of the company – and they are the ones who are ultimately accountable. Woodward believed in his vision, he articulated it brilliantly to the players, coaches and committee members and his passion and belief swept them all aboard alongside him. But he never forgot that it would be his head on the line if results went against him, just as it would be if, as a businessman, his company ran into difficulties and began to fail.

The Under-21 team worked very well together and his partnership with Robinson was particularly fruitful. Their similar philosophies to the way the team should play, along with their unbridled competitiveness, meant that they struck up a tremendous working dynamic.

After leaving London Irish, Woodward had resigned himself to the fact that he would have to continue to limit his involvement in rugby to a part-time basis only – his own business was doing too well for him to consider a full-time move into coaching. So it was with this understanding that Robinson phoned him one day just a few weeks after Woodward had left London Irish. Robinson was a fellow graduate from Loughborough and had been as influenced and inspired by Jim Greenwood as Woodward had been. Robinson was a fiery former England open-side who had played for Bath for his entire career before stepping up to become head coach in 1997 – the first full-time professional coach the club had ever had – with the departure of Brian Ashton after a disappointing season. Robinson's Test career had been limited to just eight England caps, but that was primarily because he had had the misfortune of competing for the number seven shirt with Peter Winterbottom, considered by many to be one of the finest open-side flankers ever to play for England. Robinson, however, was very highly regarded as a player, undoubtedly talented (he was a Lions tourist in 1989) and hugely influential in the great Bath sides of the eighties and early nineties.

Outwardly Robinson and Woodward were quite different, but they were kindred rugby spirits. When Robinson learnt that Woodward had become a free agent he realised that a marvellous possibility had emerged and asked Woodward if he would be interested in becoming a part-time coach at Bath. For Woodward, it was exactly what he had been looking for. Bath were one of the leading sides in the country, they liked to play an expansive game and played at perhaps the most stunning ground in England, the Rec. They had significant financial backing and superstars on their roster in the shape of Jeremy Guscott, Phil de Glanville, Jon Callard, Mike Catt, Adedayo Adebayo, Victor Ubogu and had just signed the Welsh legend Ieuan Evans. There were also young internationals of the future in Mark Regan, Mike Tindall and Matt Perry. It was an ideal situation.

'When Clive came to the club for a short time, Bath were in turmoil,' recalled Matt Perry. 'Our coach, Brian Ashton, had been sacked and there were cameras everywhere: a BBC documentary was being made about us. Clive looked upon the club as a business and brought a sense of professionalism to the place. He was also a hands-on backs coach and every coaching session was different, with little ideas such as turning up in smart rather than casual clothes to make us feel professional – ideas that didn't go down too well with some of the older hands. Clive had this thing about creating the right image, and about players taking responsibility once they had crossed the whitewash and were on the pitch.'

Woodward employed a driver to ferry him from the office to Bath twice a week, allowing him to work during the journey, and he and Robinson forged an impressive working relationship, relishing the talent at their disposal. 'It was a magic time,' recalled Woodward. Once again he had helped to turn around an ailing team, had brought freshness to an organisation and instilled professional standards. He loved the work-rugby balance that he had established. Little did he know quite how dramatically that balance was about to change.

PART TWO
REVOLUTION

FOUR

THE ANATOMY OF
AN UPHEAVAL

'The difference between the impossible and the possible
lies in a man's determination.'
Tommy Lasorda

JACK ROWELL HAD been the England head coach since 1995 and
presided over the bitterly difficult transitional period as rugby union
changed from an amateur to a professional sport. He had enjoyed
tremendous success as a coach, first during a glorious sixteen-year period at
Bath when the club had won eight John Player/Pilkington Cups and five
league titles, then with England when he succeeded Geoff Cooke in 1995.
During his tenure England won twenty-one of their twenty-nine matches,
including two Five Nations Championship titles, a Grand Slam and a famous
defeat of Australia in the 1995 World Cup quarter-finals.

Rowell himself was, like Woodward, a very successful businessman and
throughout his reign he coached England on a part-time basis. During the
amateur years this was fine, but once the game crossed the Rubicon it became
increasingly unsatisfactory that a team of full-time professional players were
being coached by a part-timer.

It might not have been an issue had England's results continued to excel
– but they had not. At best England were treading water and the RFU
were aware that, with professionalism in other countries bound to drive up
playing standards and off-field organisation, England had to have an equally
impressive (if not more so) professional structure in place. Cliff Brittle, the
chairman of the RFU management board, met Rowell to discuss whether he
would be interested in taking on the role full-time. Rowell was not. He agreed

to continue in his part-time capacity until the RFU selected a replacement – but his tenure had become a stopgap.

The whole process for selecting the new head coach of England was done behind closed doors. The position was not advertised. The Rugby Football Union was made up of a council of fifty-seven unpaid volunteers who ran the game through a management board. Don Rutherford was the director of rugby and he worked closely with the chairman of the management board. When it was announced, in confidence, to the council that there would be a hunt for a new coach it took less than twenty-four hours for the story to leak to the press. It was obvious that there were just too many people involved in the council for the process of selecting a shortlist and appointing a final candidate to remain a secret.

Brittle gathered a small group of trusted advisers – Rutherford, Bill Beaumont and Fran Cotton – and the four of them set about identifying a list of possible successors to Rowell. They would keep their progress strictly confidential.

After the resounding success of the 1997 Lions tour to South Africa (where Fran Cotton had been manager), several of the senior England players voiced their backing for Ian McGeechan to be Rowell's replacement after the Scotsman had so impressed them as Lions head coach. But this option was soon shot down in flames; McGeechan was head coach at Northampton at the time and when the RFU approached them with their proposal to buy him out of his contract, Northampton owner Keith Barwell demanded nearly half a million pounds in compensation. Adding this buy-out fee to the £100,000 or so per annum in McGeechan's salary was all too rich for the RFU.

They considered Richard Hill at Gloucester, but he was too inexperienced. They looked to New Zealand, where Graham Henry was enjoying huge success with the Auckland Blues, winning the first two titles in the newly formed Super 12 competition. Rutherford had previously flown to Auckland to offer Henry a position with the Under-21 and England A squads and with an advisory role to the national team. The idea was that Henry would eventually succeed Rowell as coach. But Henry was, for the time being, happy in his position and wanted to stay in New Zealand.

Thoughts turned inwards to Peter Rossborough, the England A coach who had also been considered as a replacement for Geoff Cooke before Rowell was appointed... and to Woodward. To say that the cupboard was bare is probably unfair but there is no doubt that his name was not top of many pundits' list. But the more Brittle, Rutherford, Beaumont and Cotton thought about it, the more the idea of Woodward appealed. They needed someone to come in and manage the professional set-up of the England team. In everything he had done he had proved himself to be a blue-sky thinker who was not afraid to fly in the face of tradition or parochial opposition to achieve his goals. Cotton had a vision for Club England, where the national team would operate in as professional an environment as any club in the land, with constant monitoring of its players. Having seen the extraordinary impact that former rugby league players had had on the Lions tour, Cotton was also keen to fast track more into the England set-up. What the job needed was something that Woodward had been bringing to every side he had been involved with since picking up a whistle – a rugby man with a business brain, a professional manager as much as a coach.

Cotton, who had fought in the trenches for England and the Lions alongside Woodward, was sent to discuss the job with him. They met halfway between their homes, at the N.E.C. in Birmingham.

'As soon as we met I knew that he wanted the job,' said Cotton. 'I could see his excitement and his focus. It was a gamble we were taking with him – but I had a strong feeling that we were making an intelligent choice.'

'I was probably more surprised than anyone when they chose me,' said Woodward. 'But there must have been reasons that even I wasn't aware of. Whatever they saw must have been potential because I certainly wasn't prepared for the job at the time. I knew that if I could survive the first two or three years, I'd work out how to do it.'

*

Marlow, west London. Tuesday, 16 September 1997.
Set among sprawling grounds on the bank of the River Thames and once home to members of the English nobility and aristocracy, the 800-year-old Bisham Abbey and manor house had, by the end of the twentieth century, become one of the finest sports centres in the UK.

Used as a training base by more than twenty English elite sports organisations, it boasted indoor and outdoor tennis courts, international standard hockey, rugby and football pitches, a nine-hole golf course, an array of conference and meeting rooms and excellent medical facilities. Bisham Abbey had been a training venue for the England rugby team for decades and the condition of the pitches was among the best in country; interestingly, however, despite its position at the heart of English sport, there was no gym on site nor any weight-training facilities, and the accommodation block was run-down and tired looking. For all that, it was easy to see why the RFU had selected it as a training venue – it suited many of their needs, was easily accessible from the motorway and it had a comfortable boarding school atmosphere, which harked back to the established roots of the game in England.

In a small room behind the indoor tennis centre an assembly of journalists and camera crews were shuffling into position as they prepared themselves for a press conference that had been called by the RFU to announce the new head coach of the England national team.

When all were settled and the cameras and lights were fixed on an empty table at the head of the room, Richard Prescott, the RFU's media director, pushed through a side door and addressed the floor.

'Ladies and gentlemen,' he said smoothly. 'I hope you are all comfortable. We will begin proceedings in just a moment, but I would like first to thank you all for attending this exciting new beginning for English rugby.'

He grasped the handle of the door and pulled it open, continuing, 'I am delighted to introduce Don Rutherford, Cliff Brittle, Bill Beaumont, Fran Cotton, Roger Uttley and the new head coach of the England rugby team, Clive Woodward.'

The six men strode in and took up their places at the table. Woodward sat in one of the centre chairs with Uttley, Brittle and Rutherford to his left, Cotton and Beaumont to his right.

As Woodward stared into the bright camera lights, trying his best not to squint, he looked to pick out some familiar faces in the audience – but at first all he could see were shadowy silhouettes. It felt like he was in some kind of Soviet show trial. As his eyes grew accustomed to the glare he was able to determine the features of the faces in front of him, some of whom he knew, but many he did not. They were all sitting with pens poised above notepads. *There's not a doubt in the mind of anyone in this room*, he thought, *that I am anything other than a desperate left-field appointment.* Not even in his own mind, he realised.

In an instant his thoughts turned to what the gathered throng must be thinking as they stared at him. He had never been a head coach in the top division of the English league; his coaching CV, although littered with success, had never been tested outright at the top of the England club game. But he checked himself; this was no time for self-doubt. He took a deep breath and thought of the incredible success enjoyed by Alan Jones, who had little or no rugby background before he took over at Manly. Unlike Woodward, Jones hadn't even played at the elite level but he had brought other assets to the job and within a year had led Manly to victory in the league Grand Final before taking over the Wallaby job and guiding them on their 1984 Grand Slam tour and to further greatness beyond. Experience as a rugby coach was not necessarily a prerequisite for success in the top job – as long as you approached things in the right frame of mind, uninhibited by that lack of experience and with enough belief in your convictions to see through your new ideas with complete confidence. *Complete confidence…* that was what he had to exude.

After today he had just eight weeks to prepare for a brutal four-match autumn Test series against New Zealand (twice), Australia and South Africa. It was a tall order for any coach, let alone one fresh into the job; but those were the cards he had been dealt and when he accepted the job he had picked them up, prepared to play with every ounce of wit and ingenuity he possessed.

A hand went up in the darkness and Prescott nodded.

'Clive,' came a gravelly voice, which he recognised as belonging to Stephen Jones of *The Sunday Times*. 'In just a few weeks you are facing the three best sides in the world over four consecutive weekends. How are you going to mould a team in that time to take them on? What are you going to do differently to Jack Rowell?'

Woodward smiled thinly. 'There's no time to implement anything drastically different between now and the first game. I need to get to know the players and they need to get to know me, so we'll start simply. We'll start with the basics. And then we can look to build from there.'

It was an honest answer, if a little underwhelming, but the floor seemed to appreciate it. Woodward could feel a trickle of sweat running down his back. He was glad that he hadn't tried to grandstand and make a sweeping statement about how he was going to revolutionise the team in preparation for the autumn Tests; it would have been a lie and everyone gathered there would have known it – there was, as he had said, simply no time to do anything like that. The task ahead of him over the next few weeks was gargantuan and it wasn't going to get any easier after that. From November to November in that first year alone, England would play sixteen Tests, including ten against the three southern hemisphere giants. As challenges go, it was like standing at base camp, staring up at the west wall of Everest. He took a deep breath. He had to make sure that he sounded confident that he was the right man for the job – as the next question so pointedly emphasised.

'How do you feel that you were the RFU's second choice for the job?'

Woodward raised an eyebrow and this time broke into a grin. 'I don't think I was anywhere near second choice. Fifth choice might be more accurate!'

To his great relief a rumble of laughter filled the room and it had genuine warmth to it. 'Listen,' he continued, 'I am under no illusion as to how hard this job is going to be, how much pressure of expectation there is. And rightly so. This is England and our fans are right to expect that we should be going into every match expecting to win. It's a big responsibility but I'm hugely excited about the opportunity that I've been given and I wholeheartedly believe that I am the right man to deliver the results that will place England at the top of the world rankings.'

'And what style of play will achieve that?'

Total Rugby. That was the answer he wanted to give. *The most exhilarating rugby you've ever seen. I don't just want us to win games, I want us to smash every opponent we face off the park. I want each of you to fill your column inches with reports that say how grotesquely one-sided each game we play is, that no team out there can live with us...* 'Results are the only barometer that I'll be judged by,' he said levelly. 'At international level, that's all that matters. We will analyse each team that we come up against and will form a plan for how to beat them. It's that straightforward. We will aim to win every match we play. And once we have a winning formula, then I'll entertain thoughts on building some style into the performances. But Test match rugby is about winning first and foremost.'

'But with so little experience, why do you think you're the man to do that?'

Woodward's nostrils flared but he did not allow himself to get riled. 'I'm England's first-ever fully professional coach. I'm not afraid about doing whatever is necessary, going to whatever lengths are required to make my time in charge a success. I won't leave any stone unturned. As you all know, I spent some time playing out in Australia at Manly and I spent a lot of my time studying the set-up that Alan Jones had established at the club and how he transferred his skills – not his rugby skills, but his business and political skills – to his job with the Wallabies. He had hardly any track record in rugby before Manly, but there's no doubting how well that transference of skills and other life experiences worked out for him and for Australia. I have a different background to Alan, but I see no reason why I can't bring similar success to England.'

'And who will your captain be?'

'I have yet to decide. We have a number of outstanding candidates. Martin Johnson has obviously just had a fantastic summer leading the Lions, but I don't want to rush into any decisions on that front. I need to sit down with all the senior players, discuss how we are going to go forward and assess who I think will work best as the captain throughout that process.'

*

Woodward had invited seventy of the top players in the country to Bisham Abbey for a meeting following his unveiling as the new head coach. They were gathered in the cafeteria beneath the old chapel, sitting at long tables amid the musty smell of old food. Woodward didn't want it to be a long session but he felt that it was important for them to meet as soon as possible so that he could lay out his vision for the team going forward.

Woodward entered the cafeteria and nodded a greeting to one or two players as he, Roger Uttley and John Mitchell, his new assistant coach, passed them and climbed a set of creaking stairs to the Elizabethan Room – a meeting chamber adjoining the chapel. The Elizabethan Room was long and narrow with sun-bleached wood panelling and chipped, peeling paint. A stale and slightly dank smell permeated the air.

The players began to file in after them and took up seats where they could, but there weren't enough seats for all the players and management staff, so some had to sit on tables or on the floor. As Woodward looked around, he was aware how tired and old the Bisham Abbey experience felt – it was anything but the elite surroundings that reaching the pinnacle of your rugby career merited.

He glanced at the faces of those near the front of the room. The senior players had taken up their seats there – Martin Johnson, Lawrence Dallaglio, Matt Dawson, Jeremy Guscott, Neil Back, Richard Hill, Mike Catt and Jason Leonard. There was an expectant look on their faces – but also something else. Fatigue. He looked further back through the room and saw the same on the faces of other players. And he knew exactly why.

While the Lions had been in South Africa, Jack Rowell had led England on a two-Test tour of Argentina, where they won one match and lost the other – which, considering the size of the English contingent on the Lions tour, was a very respectable outcome. But in an extraordinary decision, the RFU had also organised a one-off Test against Australia in Sydney – and had insisted that the English Lions fly out to join the squad as soon as the Test series against South Africa was concluded. It was one fixture and tens of thousands of air miles too many for an already stretched and fatigued squad and the repercussions of that match stretched well beyond the 25–6 loss to the Wallabies. Although the true cost of such a gruelling season wouldn't become apparent until the summer of 1998, Woodward was facing a room of men who were, although no doubt thrilled to be involved again in the England set-up, mentally, emotionally and physically exhausted.

'The strange thing about that time,' recalled Matt Dawson, the scrum-half who had just made his name in South Africa with the Lions and would become an integral part of Woodward's team, 'was that Jack Rowell knew that he was going to be leaving. It wasn't one of those shock coaching changes. Clive came with good credentials, he'd played for England and the Lions, he'd played down in Australia and of course he'd played for Leicester. He knew all about the England set-up and the RFU and all the committee men that ran things there. He came with all these ingredients and a completely different style of management, which some might have thought of as controversial, but I just found it so refreshing. It may have taken a few years for the players to really get used to it all, but it was such a breath of fresh air.'

When the room settled, Woodward stepped forward.

'Good afternoon, gentlemen. My name is Clive Woodward and I am the head coach of the England rugby team.' He held out a hand to the men beside him. 'This is Roger Uttley, the team manager, and John Mitchell, the assistant coach.'

Roger Uttley smiled under his thick moustache and inclined his head, while John Mitchell, shaven-headed, ice-eyed and chiseled-chinned, nodded once.

Uttley was a rugby legend in England and across the British Isles. He had won twenty-three caps for England between 1973 and 1980, playing in both the second-row and back-row, and played in all four Tests with the Lions on their undefeated tour of South Africa in 1974. Born in Blackpool, Uttley had played for Fylde, Gosforth and Wasps. After acting as an assistant coach to Ian McGeechan on the Lions' triumphant tour of Australia in 1989 he joined Geoff Cooke's England coaching staff and helped to guide Will Carling's team to the final of the 1991 World Cup. He was appointed manager of England in 1997, just a matter of months before Woodward's appointment – but the appointment, like that of Mitchell, was only part-time, with Uttley combining his managing duties with his career as a teacher at Harrow.

John Mitchell was a more unconventional choice as assistant coach. Born in Hawera in Taranaki, New Zealand, the thirty-three-year-old former captain of Waikato had played several seasons in both France and Ireland before moving to England to become a player-coach for Sale in 1996. Just a year later he was appointed as England's assistant coach by the RFU – although strangely this was done before Woodward's appointment. Despite being relatively new to the English game and certainly green as a coach, Mitchell was widely recognised as a player and coach with a razor-sharp intellect, a granite-hard character and in possession of magnetic leadership skills. Woodward had driven up to see him shortly after he was given the head coach role. 'We talked about our philosophies and ideals,' recalls Mitchell, 'and the marriage was created. Clive created a special environment and we got on very well from the start.'

'I want to thank you all for being here today,' continued Woodward to the assembled players. 'I am hugely proud and excited by what lies ahead for this squad – you are the elite from which we'll draw the best of the best over the coming years. The aim is for us to be the best team on the planet and I have every confidence that the players in this room can deliver on that ambition.' He paused. 'But to do that, we have to be prepared to do things completely differently to the way that they have been done before. Nothing you have done in your careers will prepare you for what lies ahead. To get to the summit we are going to have to prepare properly at the base camp; we have to pare everything we have thought about rugby right down to the basics, to strip away bad habits and to think and act differently, to set new standards of excellence and be willing to embrace new ideas. We will not be looking to emulate our rivals in the southern hemisphere; we will be looking to surpass them. Our ambition is to be the dominant rugby-playing nation on the world stage, to set the bar for others to follow. As a nation we have underachieved in the past. Forget Grand Slams and World Cup finals. Forget heroic one-off victories against the All Blacks or the Springboks or the Wallabies. We want to be the best in the world – consistently and undisputedly. Our ambition from this moment on is to win the 1999 World Cup. That is our sole focus. And I know that we can do it.'

*

The following Monday, Woodward climbed into his car and set off for Twickenham. He was dressed in a suit and tie and carried a briefcase with him as he entered the reception area at the stadium. He was greeted by the receptionist – who didn't recognise his name when he gave it and seemed to have no expectation of his arrival.

Woodward smiled tightly and hid his embarrassment.

'If you could tell Don Rutherford that I'm here to see him, it would be great,' he said.

A few minutes later Rutherford appeared in the reception area.

'Good morning, Clive, good to see you,' he said, shaking Woodward by the hand. The welcome was warm but Woodward could detect that Rutherford was flustered and seemed slightly bemused. 'What are you doing here?'

'I'm here for work,' replied Woodward, equally perplexed. 'If you could show me to my office, I'll get started – there's no need to trouble you further. I'm sorry, I didn't mean for you to even come all the way down here.'

'Your… office?' Rutherford looked blank. 'But I thought we'd agreed that your remit was to visit the players at their clubs. The head coach usually works from home, you see…' He trailed off. Woodward was still staring blankly at him.

'But Don, this is a professional position now. I'm in charge of the whole England set-up and you're *paying* me. This is a full-time position. I need an office. With a phone and a computer. And a secretary.'

Rutherford's eyes widened. 'Well… I don't think…' he stuttered. But he broke off again in the face of Woodward's piercing, unblinking stare.

This was not the start that Woodward had envisioned. But by the end of the day he had persuaded Rutherford to comply and he had been provided with an office, a telephone, a computer and a secretary, just as he had requested – albeit a secretary he had to share with two others. But it was a start. And like the first falling pebbles on a mountaintop, the landslide of change would soon gather momentum.

*

Woodward sat in his office and surveyed a folder on his desk that listed profiles of each of the players that he wanted to include in his first proper squad session. Of the seventy that he had addressed at Bisham Abbey after his appointment, he had whittled them down to thirty-five. Of those, twenty-two would make his first Test match squad.

Examining the current access he had to players, he roughly calculated that he would have only fifty sessions in any one season. The Test players could play anything up to fifty matches a year for club and country. Adding vital rest and recovery periods to this equation meant that there were very few opportunities for him to try to gain more time with the players. That is where one of the fundamental weaknesses of the set-up in England reared its head. With the advent of professionalism in 1995 the clubs in England retained their autonomy. In the two decades that have passed since then, only two or three have ever ended a season operating in profit. In the absence of self-sufficiency, the majority rely on wealthy benefactors and philanthropic owners to survive. Some have failed to stay afloat, most noticeably London Scottish, who went into administration during the 1998–99 season and were subsequently demoted nine leagues by the RFU. It is one of rugby's great stories that the club has progressed back through the leagues year by year and, at the time of writing, lie in the Championship, one tier below the Aviva Premiership. But while the autonomy of the clubs lifts a huge financial burden from the RFU – which has largely been shouldered by every other major union in the world, with the exception of France and Argentina – the priorities of the club owners and sponsors is not to ensure the success of the national team by prioritising player rest periods and tailoring their training and fitness programmes to the international windows, but the success and survival in the league and cup competitions that they are involved with. Just as Woodward had recognised that a lack of appropriate player preparation time with England and the Lions had hamstrung their chances to achieve anything approaching consistent success (never mind establishing greatness), so he could see – even more sharply – the debilitating flaws in the structure of the England game that confronted him as a coach.

The first full training day with the squad was two weeks after that initial meeting at Bisham Abbey. In that time he had set about drawing up a long-term plan for the team's ambitions. He had already presented a similar document to the RFU when applying for the job – now he began to add meat to the bones. This document was never really completed – because it was constantly worked on, tweaked, revised and expanded. The plan, like Woodward, never stood still – and just as Jim Greenwood's jotters of notes had grown and evolved over time, so too did Woodward's working plan for the England team.

'I was the first professional national coach so in that sense I had a blank sheet of paper,' said Woodward, 'which was good because I was starting from scratch. But the flip side was that experience tells me that the first two or three years of any new venture are the toughest, and if you're smart you come in after three years when some other idiot has taken all the initial crap. However, it was a fantastic opportunity for me and I jumped in with both feet. I had various ideas but the bottom line was that I had to win Test matches otherwise I wouldn't survive.'

What he had seen at the Australian Institute of Sport had lodged itself firmly in his mind. He had marvelled at the pooling of specialist knowledge that he had first witnessed at Loughborough and seen taken to a new level at the AIS. So he set about identifying specialists in scrummaging, line-outs, defence and fitness.

'One of the major things that he did was to put a fantastic coaching group together,' said Richard Hill. 'He tried to look for the very best experts in their fields – the guys who were the best at coaching scrummaging, line-outs, defence and so on – guys who could lead the best players and make them better. That, of course, had its own challenges because each coach wanted to have some quality time with the players to work on their core skills; if you want to be the best coach, if you want to be a world leader in your specific coaching area, you want to have a good amount of time with the players – you don't want to get to a World Cup and say, "My area was a let-down." So we had all these coaches who would want maybe thirty minutes a day with us, but you can't train that much as a rugby player. Three-hour sessions just do not happen; even two-hour sessions were a stretch. Clive was very adept at managing that workload so that we got the benefit of the specialist coaching but without overworking our bodies.'

'We hadn't had backs, forwards, defence, attack, scrummage and kicking coaches before,' said Jason Leonard, the prop forward, 'let alone throwing in coaches, tactical analysts and all the other people who suddenly became associated with the team. I realise now that it was the right thing to do but, at the time, we were a bit alarmed at how quickly everything was changing and what all these new and varied coaches were going to do. Some of the players had visions of the coaches all wanting to have their input, and us having to train ten hours a day to allow them all to contribute. Luckily the whole thing was managed by Clive, and he made sure that the coaches all had their input and that we got the most out of them.'

'He was obsessed with detail and changing things that you would never have even thought of before,' said Hill. 'I remember one of the first things he did was to bring in a TV make-over company to revamp the changing rooms at Twickenham. We were all asked what sort of things we would like, from the paint colour to whether we wanted cubicles. We were locked out of the place in the build-up to a Test match and then shown in before the game and we were all bowled over with how much it had changed. We went in and it was all bright and spacious, with huge pictures on the walls and plaques with our names on them above individual cubicles. It was completely different to the old barren concrete blocks that had been in there before and it certainly made you feel like you were a part of an elite environment.'

'And he made the away changing rooms worse!' recalled Dawson. 'He made them as dull and cold as possible. Then you'd walk into the tunnel and line up next to the opposition before running out and there would be all these plaques to great England victories that went right back to the first internationals dotted all along the walls, and on the doors to the pitch in giant writing were the words: THIS IS FORTRESS TWICKENHAM. At the time as a player I didn't really appreciate all the little things that Clive did but you look back now and think, *he was a clever so-and-so...*'

Woodward had always been irritated by the fawning attitudes that northern hemisphere players, teams and unions had towards their counterparts in the southern hemisphere. He had witnessed at first hand the skills and attacking élan of the Australian players when he had played at Manly, but he had also realised that they were human and not necessarily any better than the players he had played with at home. It was just their environment – from the weather conditions that allowed for a more free-flowing game, to a well-honed competitive atmosphere – that allowed the Australians, New Zealanders and South Africans to develop a winning attitude and a positivity to their rugby that could cow a less ambitious side and make the crucial difference between winning and losing. Over more than a century, the three southern hemisphere giants had enjoyed a dominance not just over the individual home nations but also over the Lions and the Barbarians. Their superiority extended from training and playing styles, to structural organisation of competitions, to importing players. As a result the northern hemisphere sides had come to almost automatically bow their heads to their southern rivals. Woodward had had enough.

As Leonard recalled, 'I remember that when the New Zealand team put together a booklet of their training drills, coaches in England got hold of it and we all copied it slavishly for years. Clive's theory was that we should find a way that worked best for England and not copy what other rugby nations were doing. We should establish the England way of doing things, and let other countries copy that.'

Woodward wanted to develop the England Way. He wanted *his* team to become the trend-setters, he wanted *his* team to become the team with the revolutionary practices that other teams would want to emulate. Because he knew that if they didn't do that they would never become the best team in the world.

'Clive came in and wanted to change how we were playing, to move away from the stereotypical English game dominated by the forwards,' said Martin Johnson. 'In fairness, we had already started that under Jack and he just moved us further down the track. He insisted, in those first games, that we play without a game plan as such – in fact, the term "game plan" was banned from being mentioned – and that we were to play off the cuff whenever we could. At first it was all a bit chaotic but in retrospect I can appreciate what he was trying to do – he was wanting us to free our minds and to think differently. It was a bit much for me at times – rugby is a simple game when you really break it down and if you want to be successful the key is to execute your basic skills as well as possible, but I can't deny that his approach was also really refreshing.'

Woodward had so many things that he wanted to implement, so many ideas that he wanted to convey, so many changes he wanted to make. But the lessons from the Sydney Xerox office had, fortuitously, left an indelible mark. He knew that many of the players he had met in the Elizabethan Room doubted his credentials, that they were exhausted by Test rugby and that they were well aware of the challenges awaiting them that autumn. If he was going to achieve anything, he needed to win their trust. It was Henley, London Irish and Bath all over again. Do not flood the senses, do not slip straight into overdrive – win their trust, give them time to understand your vision, let them believe in you and they will follow you anywhere.

*

Dave Reddin was working on a part-time basis as a fitness adviser to the England team. Woodward knew that to play Total Rugby at the elite level of the game would require the team to have incredible fitness levels. But if they could push beyond that to become the fittest and most powerful team in the world then they would be taking a major stride towards his goal to make them a dominant global force. If they could play at a speed that no other team could live with, if they could physically intimidate their opposition and if they could maintain that dominance for the full eighty minutes and beyond, then he knew that, save for human error, they would be in a position to win just about any encounter they entered into – and win well. So one of Woodward's first moves was to install Reddin full-time. He stressed to the players that their time with England was not to build their strength and fitness – they didn't have enough training time available to permit that. Instead Reddin would work with every player to construct a training programme – which would fit with their club commitments – that would allow them to get in the peak physical condition required of them. If they failed to adhere to the plan, they would not be considered for selection.

Over the course of the next few months he added Phil Larder as defence coach, began to utilise Dave Alred as kicking coach in a more regular fashion than had been the case under the previous regime, brought in Phil Keith-Roach as scrummaging adviser and Tony Biscombe as video analyst.

As he had first done at Henley, he set about empowering the players as much as possible by assigning them individual responsibilities for key areas of the game, from line-outs to defence. A number of them were already established stars of the world game for both England and the Lions – indeed the success of the 1997 Lions had propelled a large core of the team into the stratosphere.

As well as putting together his first squad of players and beginning to build up his back-room staff, Woodward also had a major call to make over who he was going to name as captain. Martin Johnson seemed the obvious choice after successfully captaining the Lions in South Africa and the media speculation was heavily in his favour. The other option that Woodward was considering was Lawrence Dallaglio, the young captain of Wasps, who had led his team to the league title during his first season at the helm before becoming an iconic figure on the Lions tour.

'I was a lot more talkative than Martin,' said Dallaglio in *It's in the Blood*. 'That was more Clive's style. In the early years, he was full of ideas and I think he liked to feel he could discuss them with his captain… What I particularly liked was Clive's vision. He didn't want England to be the best team in just Europe, he wanted them to be the best in the world. That meant beating the southern hemisphere countries and doing so regularly. It meant winning the World Cup, and even though I was young and didn't know much, I could see we were never going to do that without a radical change of attitude. And Clive definitely wanted to be the man to bring about this change.'

Dallaglio was twenty-five years old and, despite his profile soaring after the Lions tour, he was beginning only his third season as an England player. But he was passionate and forthright and seemed open to new ideas, while Johnson was more rugged and sceptical in his approach to the game. Both men had clear leadership assets and, while public opinion was that the job was surely Johnson's, it may well have been a case of Woodward making a statement of intent by deciding to go against the grain and select Dallaglio.

The Lions tour hung over the England squad in more ways than simply the issue of who should be the captain. Many of the Lions in the England squad were struggling for form and fitness at the start of the 1997–98 season, largely owing to exhaustion and the inevitable comedown from playing a part in such a momentous tour. Woodward knew that one of the very first things he had to do was to reinvigorate their enthusiasm for the England environment. He had stated in that first meeting at Bisham Abbey that he wanted the players to realise that this was a new chapter for English rugby – and so he continued with that theme.

When the players were settled into their seats in the Elizabethan Room for their second meeting, Woodward welcomed them and put up a slide on an overhead projector. Then he turned to a large, ruddy-faced man and introduced him as Humphrey Walters. He was a management consultant recommended to Woodward by Uttley and considered one of the best in the business at advising on leadership, team-building and performing under pressure. He had recently returned from the 1997 BT Global Challenge – a ten-month yacht race going the 'wrong way' around the world: sailing against the trade winds and tides, covering 33,000 miles and setting new standards in endurance. After an experience like that, he certainly understood the challenges that groups could experience under intense physical and mental duress. 'Clive wanted someone who the players and management could relate to, who had done something, knew how things worked in action and was not a bullshit merchant,' said Walters. 'The round-the-world race was for ordinary people, but they became extraordinary people. It was this process that interested me and Clive and I wanted to bring its lessons to the England management, making them a unit who live and breathe excellence. And right from the start he wanted the team and the management to kick aside their usual mentality of what a rugby environment was and think differently.'

The slide that was displayed read:

> Finished files are the result
> of many years of scientific
> study combined with the
> experience of many years

'Can I ask you all to please stand up for a moment,' said Walters, addressing the room.

There was a scraping of chairs and every man rose to his feet.

'Now,' continued Walters. 'Please sit down if you only saw one f in this sentence.'

No one moved.

'OK. Please sit if you only saw two fs.'

Again, not a muscle twitched.

'Please sit down if you only saw three fs.'

There was a scuffle and general exhalation as each man returned to his seat.

Walters smiled. 'How interesting. You all fall in with what 98 per cent of the population see when presented with this sentence. Three fs.'

There were some quizzical glances shared among the players. What was all this kids' stuff?

'And that shows that 98 per cent of the population and 100 per cent of you do not pay enough attention to detail. There are, in fact, six fs in that sentence. But when your eyes scanned over the words, your brain did not register the fs in the three *ofs*. I have been brought in to help focus our attention on details. They may seem of little importance, but small details can make a huge difference to your performance as a player both on and off the field.'

'What is also of huge importance,' said Woodward, 'is that we change our way of thinking. We cannot say that something is right just because it is being done the way it has always been done. We have to look at every aspect of our environment, our training and our preparation and consider if we are doing it in the best way, if we are missing any fine details. Because if we find them, then we are going to have an edge on our competitors; they are still going to see three fs, but we might just see six, and that could make all the difference between winning and losing, from being the fifth best team in the world to being the undisputed No.1.'

Richard Hill, who Woodward would later say was the first name on any team-sheet he picked, said, 'As sportspeople we think we can offer a lot to a business in terms of profile and leadership and so on, but Clive came in with a business approach to sport and it made a huge, huge impact. He brought in management consultants and over the years we did all sorts of different tests with these guys, from mental examinations to spatial awareness to practical exercises. It was all team-building and expanding our horizons beyond the basic blinkered view of your normal rugby environment.'

Although many of the ideas that Woodward would come up with over the years wouldn't necessarily work out as planned, his enthusiasm and his relentless drive to pursue any lead that might give them the edge made the players open to trying out each new idea as it came along. He was single-handedly instilling a growth mindset into the playing group and in so doing allowed their rugby horizons to expand further than they had ever done before. He called it 'six f thinking'. Woodward worked closely with Walters on developing the elite atmosphere and environment for the England team for two key reasons. First, it provided an environment of no excuses: if the players travelled first-class, stayed in five-star hotels and had the best training equipment and specialist coaches, physios and doctors around, they could never come off the pitch and blame anything other than their own efforts for a substandard performance. Second, it created a 'pull strategy' that motivated the players to do all they could to gain access to and then remain within the England environment. It was an exclusive club and if they wanted to be part of it, they would have to work harder than they had ever worked before to stay there. And they had to know that if their standards slipped, no matter who they were, they would be out. It was a powerful combination and again encouraged a growth mindset among the players: they wanted to improve themselves and there is no more effective learning stimulus.

'The great thing with Clive's England set-up,' said Austin Healey, 'was that you could phone the guys up in the week and they'd be there at your house in six hours. They'd do video analysis with you, or take you out on the pitch and train you, or advise you on any and every little detail of your game.'

When the meeting was adjourned, the players were told to pick up a copy of a book on their way out of the Elizabethan Room. It was called *Building the Happiness-Centred Business* by Dr Paddi Lund. Lund was an Australian dentist who had revolutionised his business practices and had devoted much of his energies towards identifying and improving what he called 'critical non-essentials'. The theory has subsequently been adopted by sports teams and businesses all around the world, but it was relatively unheard of in 1997 and captured Woodward's imagination as powerfully as the teachings of Humphrey Walters.

While attending a three-day conference featuring the American marketing guru Jay Abraham in London in 1996, Ann Heaver had discovered *Building the Happiness-Centred Business*. She read it from cover to cover throughout the conference – much to Woodward's annoyance at the time. But when she handed him the book and insisted that he read it, he experienced an epiphany almost as powerful and influential to his career as Jim Greenwood's *Total Rugby*. Lund had been depressed at work and on the verge of suicide; pulling himself back from the brink he analysed his life and decided to make some drastic changes at work so that he, his staff and his clients would actually be happy in that environment. It had stunning effects. His practice became something of a private members' club; sophisticated, relaxed and welcoming. His satisfaction at work soared – as did his profitability. Woodward was captivated by the concept. He knew the power of positive thinking and of a happy environment in sport – but it had never been articulated quite as clearly as Lund had done in his book.

'I remember hearing the odd comment from the players that I was mad giving them the book,' said Woodward. 'But I don't think I was mad. The message was very simple – if a dentist could turn his entire business upside down, doing the same with rugby is not going to be very difficult. I said to them, "We are so conservative, so stuck in our ways, we've got to open our minds up." And I just used Paddi as an example that this can be done – you can change the way you look at things and how you run your organisation. And it can't all come from your leader or your coach, the players have to buy into the idea in order for it to happen and for it to work. And the more you can get your team totally thinking about it, the more good ideas will come through from everybody. But you've got to get your whole team in on it and not just sitting there with their arms folded. You can't just have the coach coming out with idea after idea after idea, you need to get some interactive engagement. Yes, the coach leads it, but we called it "Paddi thinking" and we got the players to question everything. The big question was always why – why are we doing this, why do we do it this way? Why do we stay here, why do we train this way? Because now we are professional there is no excuse – we have to question everything we're doing and to get better than everyone else. People talk about changing for the sake of changing and that's important not to do, but you've got to question everything and work out what needs changing and what doesn't. And that's why I used Paddi as an example: if a flipping dentist can do it – and there can't be that many ways to run a dental practice – then why can't we as a rugby team do the same thing?

'You don't just bring it all in at once – it's a gradual thing. I took one or two of the senior guys aside for a private chat and I explained what I planning. I wasn't looking for approval, but I wanted to help them to understand what the rationale behind my thinking was.

'It was a hugely exciting time because you have one chance and you've just got to go for it. And I wasn't scared of it; I think that's where running my own small business really helped. I started that from a garage and then I employed a couple of people and we took risks and we lost money and we made money, we mortgaged the house, and we did all sorts of stuff – and by that stage you're used to just getting on and doing things. I wasn't a big corporate animal, I was small businessman – which is what a rugby team is, you're running a small business, you have 30-odd people in a room, it's not a huge operation. That's how I used to think about it with the players: "It doesn't really matter what's happening out there," I'd say, "it's just here in this room that matters – it's down to us whether you like it or not." As an England coach you're at the sharp end, you can't affect player development; we're here now, we're the end result – and we have a job to do. And that's the message you've really got to get across: it's now or never. You either look back in twenty years' time and say, "That was great," or you have what I have with my playing career and you look back and say, 'I wish we had done it better.' That's one thing that I can get across to people, whether they are Olympic athletes, rugby players, footballers, golfers or whatever – you only have one shot and you have to give it everything you can. And you are a long time retired. But it isn't easy. You can sit in that room and think you're quite good, but there are rooms of players in New Zealand, Australia, South Africa and France and they all think they're pretty good too, and those are the guys that you have to beat. But I think I did get that message across to them and they trusted me. And I wasn't afraid to try things. I got this tag of the "mad professor" which I don't like because there was nothing mad about the things we tried, they were all carefully thought out and had a specific purpose; I prefer the term "maverick", which has also been used, because what we were doing was different and no one else was trying it – but it wasn't madness. All I wanted to do was to ensure that we weren't going to die wondering. And some of the more conservative players maybe thought some stuff was a bit daft, but I still don't think any of it was. It was maybe something that no one else had done before but it wasn't daft, and I think that that's what a lot of the players actually liked – they liked being challenged.'

While touring Australia in the summer of 1996 with the Under-21s, Woodward went to meet Lund at his practice in Brisbane. It was a meeting that inspired him as much as reading the book and Lund's philosophy would form as important a cornerstone to his coaching mantra as those of Kirton, Greenwood and White.

In what has become a widely recognised practice in the sporting world in recent years, Lund opened Woodward's eyes to the importance of critical non-essentials (CNEs). In the context of the England team this will be discussed in more detail later, but for Lund it meant offering his clients a range of luxury teas and coffees upon arrival, insisting on having his staff and customers talk politely to one another at all times and ensuring that his staff knew his clients' names and faces so well that a client would never have to give their name upon arrival at the practice. By adding CNEs into sport, a coach, manager or player is creating an environment in which tiny marginal gains can be achieved that ultimately improve overall performance, giving them a crucial edge on their competitors.

'You don't win a Test match because you've got better clothing than the All Blacks,' said Woodward on critical non-essentials some years later. 'You don't win a Test match because you turn up on a bus with a big red rose on the side of it. But when you add up all the hundreds and hundreds of tiny details that we added, it gives you an edge and it does make a difference. And in Test match rugby, it's those edges that can be the difference between winning and losing.'

Woodward knew that if the England players spent more time fine-tuning their game and considering hundreds of tiny assets that could improve their fitness, diet, physique and preparation – improving things that no other team had even considered improving – then they would give themselves a potentially defining advantage over their competitors. As he would often say to the players, 'It is impossible to improve one thing by 100 per cent. But you can improve 100 things by 1 per cent and give yourself a crucial edge.'

Again, Woodward's focus on incremental improvements in myriad tiny details aptly demonstrates the power of Carol Dweck's growth mindset theory in practice. By encouraging his players to take control of their performances and creating a structure that would not only support them but which would allow them to flourish, he provided a framework with achievable targets that could significantly improve their fitness, conditioning, diet, mental well-being, and their physical and mental preparation for Test match rugby – which would ultimately set them in better stead for winning on the Test stage than ever before. But it would be a long road.

*

England's first game of the autumn was against Australia at Twickenham on 15 November – a fitting opposition for Woodward to face in his first Test match as an international coach.

Woodward had sent a message of intent to the Wallabies, and to the rugby world at large, by making a trip to Buenos Aires to see Australia play Argentina. The game was not televised, so he went in person to analyse the Australians. It was an impressive demonstration of the lengths to which he was willing to go to ensure that he and his team were properly prepared.

He was up against a coach who was almost as green as he was on the Test stage. Rod Macqueen had only recently been appointed as head coach of Australia and the match at Twickenham would be just his third in charge. Although Macqueen would go on to have a decorated tenure, he had a mixed start – winning the first Test in Argentina but losing the second in Buenos Aires as Woodward watched from the stands.

While Woodward had been intent on making the England set-up as professional as possible, he was also keen to experiment, with an eye firmly locked on the 1999 World Cup. As well as naming Lawrence Dallaglio as his new captain ahead of Martin Johnson and the previous incumbent Phil de Glanville, he named five new caps: Matt Perry, David Rees, Will Greenwood, Andy Long and Will Green. It is easy to understand the rationale behind this when examined in hindsight – Woodward was experimenting with new players to see if they could cut it at international level – but it also contradicted what he had said about focusing on results and building his team from a winning foundation. Woodward would often contradict himself while in charge of England; sometimes his sudden changes of heart would pay off for his team, at other times they would backfire.

Martin Johnson was unconvinced by Woodward's 'new broom' approach for that first Test. 'For a game like that,' he wrote in his autobiography, 'you want to pick your most experienced players, but Woody wanted to bring in some new players to freshen things up and he selected Will Green at tight-head over Darren Garforth and Andy Long over Mark Regan. I can understand that he wanted to show he had his own way with selection, but it is a huge, huge call to pick two guys to have their debuts against one of the best sides in the world. If you struggle to set your foundations up front, the rest of your game is going to struggle – and it was a huge ask for those two guys. It was too soon for Andy and he was replaced by Richard Cockerill at half-time. Will had a difficult game as well and, although he was a good player, he was never a front-runner again. I think Clive learnt a lot from that first selection – although he also made some good ones, capping Will Greenwood after he'd had a good

Lions tour and giving Neil Back a shot in the No.7 shirt. Australia were a little limited in that game but they scored two tries to nil; we held on to draw 15–15 with them thanks largely to Mike Catt's boot.'

'It was tough, going straight into a fierce environment I'd never been in before,' recalled Andy Long of his nightmare debut – after which he was dropped straight back into the Under-21 squad. 'Then to fall out of it like I did – not going down to England A or being supported. Things could have been different. Don't get me wrong, I loved the experience. That week leading up to the Australia game was just amazing. It was the dawn of a new era, Clive Woodward coming in, so it was a really big week. Running out at Twickenham was amazing for me and my family. It was awesome. But who knows what might have happened if I'd been drip-fed into it.'

The Andy Long story is revealing in two ways. First, it shows that Woodward could be rash in some of his decisions and that not all of his ideas paid off; that is only natural – when he made so many changes and introduced so many new ideas, not all of them would work. But it also showed how ruthless he could be if things weren't working. He wasn't afraid to admit his mistakes and do something immediately to try to rectify a situation. It was incredibly tough on Long and he made only one further appearance for the national side, after which he reflected, 'Clive said afterwards, "I wanted to get you off that one cap." I think it was on his mind.'

Despite the stalemate, many fans and pundits were pleased with a solid if unspectacular start, but for both sets of coaches and players it was a disappointing result.

And it wasn't about to get any easier. Next up they faced the All Blacks at Old Trafford. The RFU had decided to take the game to Manchester to help encourage the growth of the game in the north of England. The match at the Theatre of Dreams was a sell-out as New Zealand fielded a team of modern-day legends; that crop of All Blacks made up arguably the greatest team never to win the World Cup. Among those who faced England that day were Christian Cullen, Jeff Wilson, Frank Bunce, Andrew Mehrtens, Justin Marshall, Craig Dowd, Olo Brown, Ian Jones, Josh Kronfeld, Taine Randell, Robin and Zinzan Brooke and the global superstar, Jonah Lomu. The bookmakers and the newspaper pundits had predicted something of a massacre, but New Zealand, despite scoring three tries, were never able to completely break free from England.

'We surprised ourselves with how well we competed,' said Johnson. 'I think they had become an even bigger test in our minds than they actually were.'

As well as giving the England players the much-needed insight that they were not light years behind New Zealand in terms of quality, the match at Old Trafford was notable for two other things that would have a huge bearing on the future of the team's performance. The first was the introduction to the team of Phil Larder, the defence coach. He was initially invited to join the team for just a week to familiarise himself with the environment and to meet the players, but he was soon inducted into the ranks as a full-time member of the back-room staff.

The second was the introduction of a new back-row combination that would come to be known as the Holy Trinity – and which again demonstrated Woodward's ruthless side. 'We started with a back-row of Richard Hill at 7, Tony Diprose at 8 and me at 6,' said Dallaglio. 'Clearly, Clive felt the back-row hadn't performed in the first half and at the interval he came into the changing room, looked at Diprose and said, "Right, you're off." Turning to Neil Back he said, "You're on." It was brutal. Rugby substitutions didn't happen like that, at least not in an England dressing room. That was the start of the successful back-row of Hill, Dallaglio, Back.'

The third leg of the autumn challenge saw England return to Twickenham to face the world-champion Springboks, still smarting from their series defeat in the summer to the Lions. And the South Africans exacted their revenge on the English Lions with a 29–11 victory, the home team's heaviest defeat at Twickenham.

For the final match of the series, the All Blacks came to Twickenham for what many claimed was the best game the old ground had ever seen.

Before the match, Woodward was fired up. After a moderate start with the draw against Australia, he had seen his team picked apart by slicker, fitter and stronger opponents – but they had not been crushed. He knew that they weren't as far away from their illustrious opponents as some might have suggested before the autumn began. In another example of Dweck's growth mindset, of casting off indoctrinated ways of thinking and so find new paths to success, he instructed them to abandon all sense of a game plan and to 'just have a crack at them from anywhere'. It was Henley and his 'no kicking rule' all over again. In many respects it was what Martin Johnson would later call 'naive thinking from Woody', but it also had a tremendously liberating effect on his players.

'It was a brilliant approach,' said Dallaglio, 'almost as if Clive was saying, "Do whatever the hell you want." We went out and just blew them away in the first half an hour. Phil de Glanville knocked someone over, the ball fell loose and I hacked it on to score. Then our wing David Rees got a beautiful try when he chipped over Jonah Lomu's head, raced past him, regathered and had his teeth smashed in the act of scoring. De Glanville got a third and we were in the extraordinary position of being twenty-one points clear of the best team in the world. We had them completely shell-shocked, rattled like I've never seen the All Blacks rattled.'

'Paul Grayson was at stand-off,' said Woodward, 'and I remember during the week standing in a team meeting and saying to him, "We have nothing to lose now, we've not had a great autumn, we've drawn one and lost two, so we have to try and do things differently now. I want you to push up flat to the gain-line on attack, I want you right up in the All Blacks' faces. And I mean *right* up there." And the whole team was listening in to this. I said, "I don't care what you think about this or how you feel, you're going to do it. And if you don't, I'm going to pull you off. I don't care if we're only five minutes into the game, I'll sub you for someone who *will* do it." And that's what we practised all week. And Grayson was awesome. That whole performance stemmed from him standing flat and passing so well. It really was fantastic. He said it was the most terrifying thing he'd ever done – but the All Blacks didn't know how to handle it.'

'But even after that magnificent effort, you only had to look at the scene in our changing room at half-time to realise why we were miles away from the best countries in the world,' said Dallaglio. 'After playing at the higher tempo that Clive demanded, we were physically shattered after forty minutes. I felt sick and was retching, other guys were in an even worse mess and it was plain that forty minutes of rugby at that pace was more than we could cope with. We knew we couldn't sustain that level of performance through the second half and Clive must have looked at us and thought: "We're not fit enough, we're not strong enough, we're simply not good enough." He knew, as we knew, that to win a World Cup you've got to play back-to-back Tests at the level we couldn't even sustain for forty minutes. It was carnage in the changing room. No one could speak. Players were sprawled on the floor, others were vomiting into the bins and it was simply a question of allowing players to regain some semblance of physical normality. We should have gone out and closed the game down, but instead we started falling off tackles and allowed them to get into our territory. One try came, then another and, at the end, we were happy to hang on for a 26–26 draw.'

Will Greenwood had made a similar observation about England's physical inferiority to the South Africans the week before: 'I don't know whether the stats bear out my impression, but I remember thinking how much bigger and more powerful than us the South Africans seemed that day. Perhaps it's a trick your mind plays on you when you are beaten, but it certainly felt a little like boys against men… If we gained anything that afternoon, it was the realisation that we had a vast amount of work to do if we were going to turn the tables on the southern hemisphere and start bullying them.'

This lesson was the most important that England took away from that brutal autumn. In many respects they knew that they could play at the level required to compete with – and even surpass – their southern hemisphere rivals. But their physical conditioning was not up to par and without that base they were building on sand. It was with this in mind that Woodward began to hand greater resources and influence to Dave Reddin.

Reflecting on that autumn series with characteristic bluntness, Johnson said, 'Looking back, we weren't a good enough team to beat those sides at that stage. We might have defeated the Aussies if we had had a really good day, but the New Zealanders and the South Africans were a level above us. It had been a pretty tough baptism for Clive: four games, two heavy losses and a couple of draws. If that wasn't enough, our first game in the 1998 Five Nations was France. In Paris.'

*

It was a bitterly cold afternoon in Paris in early February. The training pitch that England had been assigned had frozen solid and the team had had to change plans and train in the garden of their hotel. As the team bus swept down the Périphérique towards the glittering new Stade de France in the suburb of St Denis, there were serious concerns that the game might be cancelled. Even though the French had spent more than £270 million on the new stadium that would be central to their hosting of the football World Cup that summer, it had been built on an old industrial site that contained potentially explosive pockets of methane and engineers had been unable to fit the ground with undersoil heating. As it transpired, the game went ahead as scheduled, but the pitch was rock solid and an icy wind whipped in from the north to chill the warm glow that still radiated from Woodward's squad following their last encounter with the All Blacks.

The French had swept all before them on their way to a Grand Slam in 1997, crucially winning at Twickenham and at Murrayfield. They had suffered a heavy defeat at the hands of the Springboks in the autumn and they were desperate to right the wrongs of that fixture. So here England were; after a bruising autumn playing the top three teams in the world, they were off to Paris to play the fourth best. The challenges just didn't let up.

Intriguingly, despite the fact that Woodward's team had yet to secure a victory, the bookmakers and pundits had pencilled in a Grand Slam next to England's name. This was owing to the euphoria of the last autumn Test against the All Blacks – but it seemed to have been put to one side that they had managed only a draw after the All Blacks had hit back from England's strong start. And that was at Twickenham. Travelling to Paris was quite a different undertaking.

Despite the wintry conditions, the battle that afternoon was heated, with an enormous French pack furiously fired up in their intent to make their new home as fortress-like as the old Parc des Princes had been for Les Bleus. Behind this collection of behemoths, which included the monstrous Christian Califano and Franck Tournaire propping on either side of the inspirational captain Raphaël Ibañez, the towering Olivier Brouzet and Fabien Pelous in the second-row, and the emerging genius Olivier Magne at open-side, there was the impish genius of Thomas Castaignède at stand-off. He controlled the pace of play like an old master, bringing the exceptional talents of Christophe Dominici, Christophe Lamaison, Stéphane Glas and Philippe Bernat-Salles into play as he saw fit to terrorise the English defence. The final scoreline of 24–17 more than flattered the visitors and it served as a marker as France marched on to claim a second consecutive Grand Slam.

The ledger against Woodward's England now read: played five, won none. The draws against Australia and New Zealand had been respectable and some of their play had been very encouraging in terms of vim and excitement, but the pressure on the new regime to convert that promise into results was already mounting. They needed to turn the tide and turn it quickly.

'There was some consolation in the fact that we had played the best four teams in the world,' said Johnson. 'But essentially it wasn't good enough. As we faced Wales at Twickenham there was a lot of pressure on the team to do well – and we certainly felt it.'

Wales fielded a powerful and dynamic team full of Lions and they roared into an early lead with two tries from former rugby league centre Allan Bateman in the first twenty minutes. But then, at last, things began to click for England. Despite their setbacks, Woodward had never abandoned his desire for Total Rugby and for his players to attack from anywhere on the field. He had stated to the team that he wanted them to 'inspire the nation' – and there is little doubt that the attacking élan that afternoon did just that as the home team ran in eight tries to romp home 60–26.

It was the spark that lit up the remainder of the tournament as England overpowered Scotland 34–20 at Murrayfield and then dispatched wooden spoonists Ireland 35–17 at Twickenham to win the Triple Crown.

The fixture schedule of the previous eighteen months had been remarkable in its intensity. For the leading England players, there had been games against Italy, Argentina and a New Zealand Barbarians side in the autumn of 1996, the 1997 Five Nations, the Lions tour, the one-off match against the Wallabies in Sydney, the four-Test series in the autumn of 1997 and the 1998 Five Nations, as well as all their club commitments. In the summer of 1998, for some inexplicable reason, and with the World Cup just one season away, the RFU had organised one of the most taxing tour schedules ever conceived: seven matches, including four Tests. These were against Australia, New Zealand (again twice) and South Africa on their own turf.

'Clive recognised that because of the previous year's Lions tour, England's top players hadn't had a proper break from the game for almost two years,' said Dallaglio. 'In the Lions season, I played fifty-two matches, the last three but one against the Springboks in the most punishing series I'd ever been involved in. I was desperately in need of a long break. Jason Leonard, Martin Johnson, Richard Hill and Neil Back couldn't have felt any better than I did.'

In the end, seventeen leading players were unavailable for the 1998 summer tour, either through injury or fatigue – the latter being listed as injured by their clubs, who saw that their most valuable commodities were about to break down under the workload. Twenty of the squad of thirty-seven would be making their England debuts and only six players had won more than ten caps

– tour captain Matt Dawson, Ben Clarke, Austin Healey, Graham Rowntree, Garath Archer and Steve Ojomoh.

Woodward and his coaching staff looked at the schedule ahead of them and the personnel at their disposal and knew that they were on a hiding to nothing. They were about to face the three strongest sides on the planet, again, at full strength and this time in their own back yards – with players that were at best second or third choice. The media and the rugby unions in Australia, New Zealand and South Africa were incensed that England were sending such a weakened squad, claiming that in doing so they were not only breaking an agreement made by the RFU to send their strongest squad, but that they were also devaluing Test match rugby. Dick McGruther, the chairman of the Australian Rugby Union, was so furious that he publicly announced that it was 'the biggest sell-out since Gallipoli'. While McGruther's statement was callous, there is little doubt that, privately, Woodward would have struggled to disagree with the sentiment.

One positive to emerge before the tour party departed, however, was the addition of Brian Ashton, whom Woodward brought in to his back-room staff as attack coach. Ashton was widely regarded as one of the brightest brains in the English game and, although he had just endured a short and painful stint as head coach of Ireland – where he had been let go after just a single season in charge – Woodward knew that he was just the man he was looking for to bring a new attacking edge to his team. Continuing with his Total Rugby philosophy, Woodward didn't want his players to think of themselves as forwards and backs when it came to open play – he wanted fifteen rugby players spread across the pitch. Phil Larder had been recruited as defence coach, now Brian Ashton was there to make every player an attacker in his own right.

Ashton had played scrum-half for Tyldesley, Fylde and Orrell, then also for Montferrand in France and Roma and Milan in Italy, but had never managed to win a cap for England. The closest he got was sitting on the bench for the 1975 Five Nations and on the tour to Australia that summer; they were the days when substitutes could only be made if there was an injury and he never made it on to the pitch.

His coaching career began while he was a history teacher at King's School, Bruton, in Somerset. He was an assistant coach with England from 1985–86, but felt so frustrated with the political influence of the RFU committees over the team that he resigned and returned to coaching King's. During his years at the school he developed a policy, almost identical to Woodward's in his early coaching days, which almost completely banned kicking in the school's first XV. News of this all-out attacking school side soon reached Bath and Jack Rowell recruited Ashton on a part-time basis as attack coach. After guiding the outrageously talented Bath backs for several of their most successful seasons he was recruited to the Ireland post, but his philosophies were not well received – by the committee men at the IRFU more than the players – and he was soon replaced by Warren Gatland, whereupon Woodward swooped for his services and brought him back into the England fold.

'Clive and Jack Rowell were similar,' recalled Ashton. 'They made me attack coach and told me to get on with it. If it became too mad, they would rein me in, but with Clive you had to go a long way off the beaten path before he'd say you'd gone too far.

'What I tried to do was to give a team a framework. We had to have solid set-pieces and solid restarts, we had to look to win the tackle area, our kicking strategy had to be spot on and our defence outstanding. But you must also give top players the chance to bring something in when appropriate. That is what liberating players means. You give them a framework but when they are out there and it is not working, they can say bugger it, we are going to change it.'

His brilliance as an attack coach was soon recognised among all the senior players – as was the new idea that every man on the field should be comfortable with the ball in hand.

'Brian Ashton was very good,' recalled Jason Leonard. 'He is credited with being just a backs coach, but he also did a great deal of work with the forwards as we all tried to become more complete, more "total" players. Under Clive, there was no room for "forwards" and "backs" – we were all players who had to get out there and do whatever it took to win. The forwards had to break down defences as well as the backs, but we always used to do it by barging through the middle. Brian would say things like, "Why do you have to run through someone, why can't you run round them? Why can't you find some space to run in? I can't understand why you would want to run at a bloke who's sixteen stone when you could just run round him."'

'Clive was a visionary and he let me get on with it,' said a self-effacing Ashton. 'We had a great platform, and a great balance. Those players enjoyed being challenged.'

'He's more than a backs coach,' Jonny Wilkinson said of Ashton. 'He's an attack guru, an inspiration in his understanding of running lines, space and width.'

'He was very meticulous but also had a way of keeping the game simple and enjoyable,' said Jeremy Guscott. 'For example, the skills involved in working an overlap, or beating a man, have not changed in one hundred years. What Ashton did with us was to give us drills with endless variations and problems to work out. If we were practising a three-on-two he would bring in defenders coming in at different angles so that it was more like a maze – and the maze was different every week. Some coaches can easily come across like bad salesmen and you can hear their hollow patter. But Brian earned our respect by always putting a lot of effort into his training routines.'

So while Ashton's arrival provided a silver lining to the pre-tour preparations, because the squad was so underpowered there nevertheless remained a dark cloud hanging over the party as they set off from Heathrow for Brisbane – for what would become known as the Tour of Hell.

*

Jonny Wilkinson was only eighteen years old when he was selected for his first England squad session in the autumn of 1997. To have watched the young fly-half-cum-centre play for Newcastle Falcons during the 1997–98 season and for England Under-21, an observer would have seen a focused, highly-skilled and audaciously talented young player undoubtedly destined for great things. When he eventually stepped out into the Test arena, for a brief five-minute debut during the 1998 Five Nations, he seemed to the manner born. But the ease with which he appeared to acclimatise himself to Test match rugby was surface-deep only. To read his autobiography, *Jonny*, is to gain an astonishing and brutally honest insight into a painfully shy and deeply self-conscious individual. Despite his undoubted natural abilities and the faith shown in him by the England selectors, Wilkinson confessed to feeling like a fraud among the famous faces with whom he mingled when he first joined up with the national team.

When the squad gathered at the Petersham Hotel in Richmond, he would hide in his room at every opportunity, would agonise over who to sit next to at meal times, would stutter and then fall silent when trying to speak with senior players, and would feel a deep stab to his confidence at even the most light-hearted of playful put-downs.

He took solace in the familiar face of kicking coach Dave Alred, whom he had been working with since his mid-teens. After training the two of them would stay on for several hours working on kicking drills and routines, alone under the floodlights in the middle of a silent and empty Twickenham Stadium, until eventually returning to the hotel for a late dinner, just the two of them, the other players and coaches having eaten several hours before.

Woodward could see that Wilkinson was shy and didn't like speaking in front of the other players in meetings, but he needed a confident player at stand-off to command the run of play and to boss those around him. He could see that Wilkinson had it in him to be a huge asset for the England team, but he needed him to come out of his shell. To help with this, Woodward would often make a point of asking Wilkinson questions or for his opinion of certain attacking strategies when in team meetings. From Woodward's perspective it made perfect sense to encourage the young man to speak openly in front of his teammates, but those meetings became a source of deep dread and anxiety for Wilkinson.

It is extraordinary to imagine how Wilkinson overcame this deep crisis of confidence to become the attacking general of the England backline. He was capped off the bench against Ireland at Twickenham in the last match of the 1998 Five Nations as an emergency winger after Mike Catt suffered a hamstring injury, and in so doing became the youngest player to play for England in seventy-one years. He played that first season as a centre at Newcastle, with Rob Andrew at fly-half, and that was where he was selected in the England squad, but the coaches for both club and country always envisioned the centre position as a stepping stone towards the No. 10 shirt. And that was exactly where he was selected for the first Test of the Tour of Hell – against Australia in Brisbane.

For thirty minutes the game was close – on the scoreboard at least. England scrambled like madmen and held the Wallabies to 6–0. But over the course of the next fifty minutes, the floodgates well and truly opened as the hosts ran up a further seventy unanswered points to record the heaviest defeat England had suffered in Test match history.

'We were doing quite well to begin with, albeit defending a lot,' recalled Graham Rowntree, the prop. 'But it ended up being a total disaster. It was hard to take but we were pretty honest with ourselves afterwards and spent a couple of days studying the video. John Mitchell was fantastic and sorted out a few things up front. A week later we played New Zealand in Dunedin and even with only seven forwards – Danny Grewcock was sent off – we did all right.'

'Looking back on that tour – and there's no escaping how horrendous it was in terms of results – there was still a great deal of value taken from it,' said Roger Uttley. 'Firstly we found out that several players weren't up to scratch and they never featured in an England squad again. But then, on the other side of that, we had guys like Jonny Wilkinson, Josh Lewsey and Phil Vickery playing their first full Tests against the southern hemisphere big boys and you had guys like Matt Dawson really having their leadership abilities and their resilience put to the test. You don't learn anything by winning all the time.'

The tour had a profound effect on Wilkinson in particular. He confesses to weeping and screaming in his hotel room after the 76–0 defeat in Brisbane, utterly ashamed by what had happened and pinning a large proportion of the blame on his own shoulders. But then he had an epiphany. 'Then I get it,' he writes in *Jonny*. 'That 76–0 is a bit like kicking with Dave Alred. Dave shows you what being the best is; he makes you realise how much work you have to do and how far you have got to go. The Australians have just done the same. They have shown me what being the best looks like. They've shown me what I want to look like too, and how much work I have to do in order to be that way. And now that I know, I make a promise to myself – I am never going to feel this way again. I'm never going to feel so helpless, never going to feel so second-rate, never going to allow myself to feel as unvalued as that. Never. The day we were defeated 76–0 is one of the worst and most important days of my life.'

It was a significant psychological shift for Wilkinson. He went from passively trying to just make his way in the England set-up without causing any unnecessary waves, without drawing any undue attention to himself, realising that he could have a controlling influence on proceedings, that his destiny – and that of his team – was ultimately in his own hands. And it wasn't just Wilkinson who experienced an epiphany from the tour.

'That was the lowest point in the history of English rugby and I was in charge of it,' said Woodward. 'It didn't matter that I'd only been doing the job seven months from a standing start. That was the time when I had to be absolutely convinced that I could pull this thing around. A lot of resolve came out of that experience. I'd been to the bottom of the pit and I was determined to be bloody-minded and fight hard to get a team of people around to make England competitive.'

The squad flew out of Brisbane and crossed the Tasman Sea for two Tests against the All Blacks and midweek matches against New Zealand A, the New Zealand Rugby Academy and the New Zealand Maori.

After disappointing losses to New Zealand A (18–10) and the New Zealand Rugby Academy (50–32) they travelled to Dunedin for the first Test against the All Blacks. England's hopes were seriously hampered after Grewcock was sent off and then Jonny Wilkinson was injured during the forty-third minute, which ended his tour. New Zealand ran in nine tries to record a 64–22 victory, their biggest winning margin against England.

While few obvious positives could be taken from an experience like that, Humphrey Walters, who was travelling with the team, picked up one that he would use as part of the refurbishment of the players' area at Twickenham.

'When you get off the bus in Dunedin and walk into the stadium, you are greeted by the words, YOU ARE NOW ENTERING THE HOUSE OF PAIN,' explained Walters. 'When I saw it I turned to Clive and said: "We need something as intimidating as that." So when we got back we hung a big sign that every opposition player would see when they arrived at the ground: YOU ARE NOW ENTERING FORTRESS TWICKENHAM.'

The tour was already a nightmare, but it was overshadowed by tragedy when Woodward received news shortly after the Dunedin Test that his father had died. Leaving the tour in the hands of his deputies he flew home for the funeral. He missed the 62–14 midweek loss to the New Zealand Maori, but returned in time for the second Test against the All Blacks, this time at Eden Park in Auckland.

'On the flight back to New Zealand, for the first time, I looked at my situation as my father would and knew what he would be asking me: was I really doing this job properly or just trying to keep everyone happy? Losing my father put many things into perspective. In many ways it was time to take the gloves off and stop pussyfooting around with the dozens of people who were playing with the politics of English rugby.'

England lost the second Test 40–10 but there was a new steel in Woodward's resolve to do anything within his power to help the team succeed as they flew to South Africa for the final leg of this impossibly tough tour.

On arrival in the Republic, the team headed to the Holiday Inn Garden Court Hotel near Newlands Stadium in Cape Town, where they would be playing the Springboks. It was the same hotel that the Lions had stayed in the year before and the South African Under-21 side were also in residence at the same time as England. Despite this, Woodward felt that the accommodation and facilities fell way below his expectations for an elite sports team. So he decided to do something about it. He made some calls and, putting the entire cost on his own credit cards, moved the team across town to the exclusive Mount Nelson Hotel at the foot of Table Mountain, nicknamed the Pink Palace. He felt that he could not ask his team to give their best if they were not given the best. It was Paddi Lund's theory of the importance of critical non-essentials put into practice on the largest scale the RFU had yet seen. England lost to the Springboks, but the 18–0 scoreline was the best of the tour and was impressive after all they had been through and given the players they had at their disposal. The RFU eventually picked up the bill for the Pink Palace and Woodward quietly celebrated the precedent of higher standards. Now that the bar had been raised to that level, they couldn't go back.

There was no doubt that, on paper, the tour was an unmitigated disaster. But from the ashes of the hammerings, some phoenixes were to rise. The tour had seen the emergence of a new resolve never to let a run of results like that happen to the team again; it had allowed the management a chance to separate the wheat from the chaff in terms of which players could or couldn't cut it at Test match level; and it had given valuable game-time to Jonny Wilkinson, Josh Lewsey, who could play full-back, centre or wing, and prop Phil Vickery – all of whom would play vital roles for England in the years to come.

'Defeat makes you a stronger person,' said Uttley. 'The only good thing about that trip is that the players remained competitive. It hardened the notion, too, that if we were going to be successful we had to learn to win down there. The lessons learnt by the likes of Wilkinson, Lewsey, Dawson and Vickery were invaluable for the seasons ahead.'

FIVE

THE ANATOMY OF
A WINNING CULTURE

'I've missed more than 9,000 shots in my career. I've lost almost 300 games.
26 times, I've been trusted to take the game-winning shot and missed.
I've failed over and over and over again in my life. And that is why I succeed.'
Michael Jordan

STEVE BATES WAS a chemistry teacher and rugby master at Lord
Wandsworth College in Hampshire. He had enjoyed a prosperous playing
career as a scrum-half for London Wasps, playing alongside England
and Lions fly-half Rob Andrew for many seasons and earning himself a cap for
England against Romania in 1989, while also touring with England to South
Africa in 1994 and making several appearances for England A over the years.

Bates had seen many talented players pass through his teams over the years,
but there was one young lad that he felt was quite different from all the others,
one young lad who had something about him, who he really felt could go all
the way. A lad by the name of Jonny Wilkinson.

Wilkinson had been playing mini-rugby almost since he was old enough to
hold a ball. Encouraged by his father and spurred on by his close relationship with
his older brother, Mark, he was soon playing for teams above his age grade. Indeed,
from the age of eight onwards, he almost exclusively played in sides that were for
boys a year or more older than he was. In a country like New Zealand this is not
unusual and often, thanks to the Polynesian influence, youth teams are delineated
by weight grade rather than age because of the physical maturity that Polynesian
children reach before their Caucasian counterparts. But in the northern hemisphere
such an occurrence is a lot less common – and particularly so for Wilkinson, who
was no overgrown physical specimen. As a stand-off or full-back he was regularly
the smallest player on the field. But despite this, he was able to cope with playing
in such an environment because of two things: audacious skill and tremendous

bravery. The former he worked on obsessively and will be discussed more closely shortly. The latter was fuelled by a deeply ingrained competitive streak and by an acute sense of self-doubt. While this may sound contradictory, it is not – the two traits go hand in hand. Wilkinson was an anxious, often overwrought child who obsessively overanalysed his life, judging every facet of his existence by a barometer of success and failure; but success to him meant absolute perfection, failure was anything that deviated from that. His life was haunted by seemingly never-ending incidents where he felt that he came up short, was exposed physically or mentally or let someone down. It plagued him incessantly and drove him to work longer and harder than ever before so that he could stamp out his perceived imperfections. The drive to overcome these shortcomings not only meant that by the age of nine he could comfortably spiral punt and kick goals with both feet, but that when it came to a competitive game he would throw himself at the challenge with total commitment in an effort not to expose any weakness or let his teammates, coaches and family down. And all of this was done while often being so cripplingly nervous about failing that he would be physically sick with nerves before a game – even when just playing in a Sunday morning mini-rugby tournament.

As he progressed through school and eventually moved to Lord Wandsworth College he continued to play for the first XVs in the year above him until he moved into his senior years and came under the wing of Steve Bates.

Wilkinson was without doubt the hardest trainer Bates had ever seen. He was just insatiable. He never got bored, always gave 100 per cent and seemed to just soak up anything Bates said to him like a sponge. He was ticking every box and Bates could already see him continuing his rise through the England age group teams and eventually reaching the highest position in the land. But Bates also knew that there were thousands of boys across the country with that same dream, all vying for the same shirt. He knew as well as anyone how hard one had to work to make it at a top club and to then attract the attention of the national selectors. He had experienced the euphoria of representing his country in a Test match – and the agony of his international career ending there. In a country with so many players, it was easy to slip between the cracks, become disillusioned with rugby and eventually just drift out of the game. Looking at Wilkinson, Bates knew that it would be a crying shame if that fate were to befall him. So what could he do to help?

Having trained and played alongside Andrew, who had won seventy caps for his country and played in five Test matches for the Lions during the 1989 tour of Australia and 1993 tour of New Zealand, and who was regarded as one of England's finest ever stand-offs, Bates knew exactly what it had taken for Andrew to scale the heights that he had done in his career: a work ethic second to none. But Bates knew a little secret of Andrew's; his teammate was recognised the world over as one of the best kickers in the game – but he had had help with his kicking, having employed a specialist kicking coach by the name of Dave Alred to assist with his training.

Alred had played full-back for Bath and Bristol in the 1970s and also enjoyed stints playing rugby league for Sheffield, before giving up rugby in 1978 to play American Football. He played for the Minnesota Vikings for three seasons and it was there that his fascination for coaching kicking blossomed. He returned to the UK to coach Great Britain's rugby league side in the mid-eighties and enjoyed periods working with the Wallabies and in Aussie Rules, before taking up a role as kicking coach with the '97 Lions. This was particularly successful as the Lions clinched the series thanks to the unerring boot of Neil Jenkins and a late drop-goal from Jerry Guscott to seal the Second Test. Much of Alred's expertise is transferable across a number of sports because his focus is not just on technique and biomechanics, but on the psychology of performing under pressure and the mantra that all practice must be of the highest quality. As well as working in the various oval ball codes, he has worked with Joe Cole at Chelsea and Luke Donald, Padraig Harrington and Paul McGinley in golf. He is, without doubt, regarded as one of the world's best, if not the best, in his field.

Bates knew that if Wilkinson was to really make it on the world stage as a fly-half then he would have to develop his kicking to a world-class level. And so he arranged for Wilkinson to have a private session with Alred.

When he broke the news to his young charge, Wilkinson was unconvinced. He was both confident that he was good enough already as a kicker and also shy about meeting a perfect stranger. But after some gentle persuasion from Bates he reluctantly agreed.

A week later, Wilkinson and his father drove to meet Alred at the training grounds at Bristol University. They found him out on a pitch with a pile of balls, a flip chart and several plastic cones dotted around the field.

Alred was in his forties, dressed in a tracksuit and boots and looked fit and strong. To the relief of the socially awkward Wilkinson, they almost immediately got down to business – although to Wilkinson's surprise they didn't start kicking balls around straight away. Instead, Alred directed him to the flip chart and began to talk through the essential mechanics of kicking, the movement and balance of the body, the flight path of the ball. Wilkinson had never dreamed that kicking could be broken down into so many components and that each component could be finely tweaked and refined. But if Wilkinson had been impressed by Alred's theory, it was nothing compared to seeing him in action.

They walked out on to the pitch and then came to a stop some 50 metres from two cones that had been set five metres apart from one another.

'If you bear everything I've just shown you in mind,' said Alred picking up a ball, 'you will soon see that you can be in complete control of the ball. Complete control. No hit and hopes, no general satisfaction that the ball is sort of where you wanted it to be. If you can learn to control every aspect of the kick, you can control precisely where the ball goes.' And with that he took one step and struck the ball. It made a sweet, clean thump as it hit the bridge of his foot and spiralled away through the air with a *fffffoooommmm*. It was a thing of beauty as it arched high and then dropped, smack in the middle of the cones. It was a perfect kick.

'Now your turn,' said Alred, a white-toothed grin breaking brightly across his tanned face.

Wilkinson picked up another ball, set himself and then kicked. The ball made more of a *duuumph* noise when he connected and the spiral was wobbly and unkempt as it swept away from them – to fall both short and wide of the cones.

Without another word Alred picked up a third ball, stepped and struck. It was identical to his first kick.

In that moment, Wilkinson was sold. 'As I watch him,' he recounts in *Jonny*, 'I feel this enormous respect and confidence in him. It's already clear to me that this is a truly special guy, and if I'm really serious about wanting to succeed, I need to learn from him everything I possibly can.'

Over the coming years Wilkinson worked tirelessly on his kicking, his strength, his fitness and his understanding of the game. Not for individual glory, rather because the team needed him to. He did it for his mates, for his brothers in arms alongside him in the trenches. He would practise his kicking for hours after every training session, setting himself a number of kicking challenges which, if he ever missed a kick, he would start again from the beginning until he had completed the task with 100 per cent success. There would never be a day off for him – he even famously practised for three hours in the snow on Christmas Day.

In the seminal book *Bounce: The Myth of Talent and the Power of Practice*, Matthew Syed, England's former table tennis No.1 and now a *Times* journalist, brilliantly brings together a number of scientific studies and social and psychological theories about the development of world-class talent to explode the widely held premise that champions are born naturally talented and predisposed to genius. He draws on a number of works, including Carol Dweck's growth mindset theory, and explores a wide range of disciplines, including music, sport and academia, to prove that champions are the product of their environment and thousands of hours of dedicated, quality practice rather than natural child prodigies. It is fascinating to hold up several of the theories in *Bounce* and apply them not just to the England rugby team under Clive Woodward but to Jonny Wilkinson in particular.

As Syed espouses when discussing the 'talent myth', Wilkinson was not the product of some fabled natural gift at birth that set him on the road to stardom. He did not just pick up a rugby ball and naturally spiral punt off both feet, spin pass the ball twenty feet with an easy flick of the wrists or know the best area of the field to kick a ball based on instinct. Instead, as his compulsive obsessions show, his talent was the product of many thousands of hours of dedicated and focused practice. Malcolm Gladwell's book *Outliers* postulates that the success of outstanding performers – be it Bill Gates or the Beatles – was down to the '10,000-hour rule'. Gladwell cites the work of K. Anders Ericsson, a psychologist whose studies of a group of violinists at the Berlin Music Academy revealed that the only factor separating the outstanding from the very good and the mediocre was how much they practised. Neither the age at which they began training nor their family background mattered much – it was simply a case of the number of hours devoted to serious practice. This 10,000-hour rule is the basis for much of both Gladwell and Syed's suppositions and is reinforced by Wilkinson as a test subject: for 10,000 hours of quality practice is considered the minimum time required for the acquisition of expertise in any complex task – from playing the violin, to becoming a chess grandmaster, to being a multiple Commonwealth Games table tennis champion in Syed's case, or to becoming the world's greatest kicker of a rugby ball in Wilkinson's. High-quality practice correlates directly to scientific studies on the development of world-class skillsets and can transform the body and brain to allow an individual to achieve world-class standards of excellence and, importantly, consistency.

Reverting to Dweck's theories, Wilkinson also showed an impressive growth mindset and appetite for new information – he wanted to know as much as he could to improve himself as a player. From a very early age he showed a deep desire to become the world's best rugby player, but he never once thought that he was naturally gifted enough for it to just happen for him. His deep self-doubts pushed him ever onwards and he absorbed information insatiably. He was not alone in the England environment in having this open-minded drive for self-improvement. As Woodward writes in *Winning!*, 'I've never met a quality player intent on winning who didn't want to hear about ways he could improve his game. The greatest compliment I can give to players like Martin Johnson and Jonny Wilkinson would be to tell you of their thirst for knowledge. They are sponges for new ideas and real quality coaching.'

And this was why Alred so enjoyed working with Wilkinson. The boy loved to learn and he worked tirelessly to improve himself. He had already put in thousands and thousands of hours of kicking practice at home on his own, with his brother and father, at school and with various representative teams. Now it was a case of refining his technique; and from there Wilkinson would happily continue to put in the hours of work, forever chasing perfection.

'At the highest level,' said Alred, 'kicking is 40 per cent technique, 60 per cent mental. Test match kickers will have honed their techniques, but the difference between the truly great kickers and the others is the ability to cope with the pressure of the situation. Jonny, for example, is mentally very strong – he can block out all the external factors, everything in that stadium, and kick the goal. It says a lot about him. We developed a number of different techniques to help him with that focus. The sweet spot that you want to hit is around three or four inches up from the tip of the ball. So that's the area you want to strike with the hardened ball of your big toe. But to get real accuracy with that, you want to focus on a specific target within that sweet spot, so I would ask Jonny to pick out an individual stitch and aim for that. It's partly about technique, partly a mental exercise. If you hit that stitch and hit it hard, then it should be the ideal strike. But it's also a way of dealing with the pressure. If you're concentrating hard on trying to find the stitch, then you naturally block out everything else that's going on around you. If you're solely focused on that stitch, then nothing else should distract you.

'Then we looked at the target. Again, we focused on narrowing the target down. You don't just want to focus on some vague space between the posts –

there is too much margin for error, too many things to distract you. In Jonny's case we made up an imaginary woman sitting in the stands right between the posts, holding a Coke can. She sits some thirty yards behind the posts and Jonny does two things – first, he imagines a blue line attaching the ball to the Coke can, and second, he visualises knocking the can out of her hand with the ball. That's his target. Another way to think of it is like aiming to kick a barn door – you need to aim for the keyhole to guarantee hitting the door. If you can hit the keyhole, you know that hitting the door is just a formality. With Jonny, I always expect him to kick his goals, but what we get fussy about is whether we've hit the keyhole – or, in his case, the Coke can.

'So he sets himself, looks along the blue line, sees the Coke can, then returns his focus to the stitch on the ball. When he begins his approach to the ball, all his focus is on the stitch, the hardness of his foot and the follow-through of his leg. All the power of the kick comes from his body weight, not from the swing of his leg. It's like a golf swing – the power of the swing comes from the rotation of the waist; in rugby, the power of the kick comes from the rotation of the hips. When Jonny is readying himself for the kick he hardens his toe and bangs it against the ground. This pushes his toe to the extreme edge of his boot and also replicates the feeling of striking the ball. Then he centres his weight. I got the idea from baseball – it's a technique used to centre the body's balance, to reach a comfortable equilibrium so that you are in complete control of your body. It is vital that players understand how their weight is distributed and have a point of reference for what it feels like to be totally balanced and centred – for Jonny, the crouch does that and his raised hands is all about him finding his central balance; it's a focal point for him, a reference that tells him he's ready.

'The next step is to imagine the power of his balanced weight sitting behind his navel. It's like a hot glow and he focuses that power into his leg and down into his foot. When he is ready he approaches the ball; you want to come round in a J shape so that you are square on to the ball when you strike it. You want to be looking to step through the kick so that the weight and momentum of your body is what drives the power through the ball – just like a golf swing. And like a golf swing it's important to keep your head down. If you do all that, you'll hit the Coke can.'

Wilkinson first played international rugby for England Under-16 before progressing to the Under-18 A side and from there to the full England

Under-18 team that went on to win a Grand Slam – with Wilkinson scoring a last-minute forty-yard drop-goal against Wales in the final game to secure the clean sweep. On the back of that championship, he was selected for the Under-18s' tour of Australia, which saw them clinch a resounding 38–20 win over their Australian counterparts at the North Sydney Oval. When he returned home, his rugby education continued to rocket ever upwards.

With the advent of professionalism in 1995, Sir John Hall had bought Gosforth RFC/Newcastle Gosforth, rebranded them as Newcastle Falcons and moved swiftly to make the Division Two side a force to be reckoned with. He recruited Rob Andrew as both a player and as director of rugby and, as well as signing a host of international players such as Pat Lam, Tony Underwood, Dean Ryan, Alan Tait, Nick Popplewell, Garath Archer, Gary Armstrong and Doddie Weir, and rugby union's first million-pound signing in All Black Va'aiga Tuigamala, assigned the role of head coach to Steve Bates. In their first season, Newcastle won promotion to the First Division and Bates moved to recruit his young protégé from Lord Wandsworth College to join their ranks. Wilkinson was incredibly nervous about making the move from his home in the south of England to the north-east, but he was thrilled by the opportunity and would soon flourish in the ultra-professional environment at Newcastle.

He was a student of the game and, with such illustrious and experienced teammates around him, immersed himself in their collective knowledge.

Unlike most fly-halves before him, Wilkinson dedicated himself to the hard yards, to the dark and dirty parts of the game. He realised that the weakest link in a side's defensive chain was usually down the fly-half's channel. No.10s are traditionally slight players, who pass on shoddy ball, kick the leather off it to relieve pressure and run only when gaps open up for them. No matter the time of year or whether they are playing on the boggiest, quagmire-like pitch, the fly-half in any game is invariably barely mud-splattered come the final whistle. Tackling was not what fly-halves were on the pitch to do – that was a job for the back-row to do for them. But Wilkinson realised that to play like that would make him a weakness in the team and would require another player to work even harder to cover for his deficiencies, potentially opening up spaces in the defence elsewhere. And he couldn't allow that. So he threw himself into weight training, honed his technique and abandoned any notion of self-preservation to become a defensive rock. He didn't just absorb the impact of the offensive runner, he would halt them in their tracks with a juddering hit and drive them backwards into the turf. Some of the hits that he put in were extraordinary – they lifted his teammates' spirits, brought the crowd to its feet and lowered the heads of the opposition – all in a moment of power, timing, perfect technique and, most crucially, unerring bravery. The cost to his own body would prove to be devastating, but it is unlikely that even the briefest consideration for his long-term health would have flitted through his thoughts.

But his dedication to the cause in preference to personal safety went beyond defensive tackle duties. He would throw his body anywhere he felt his team needed it to be: into rucks, onto loose balls, towards the swinging boots of opposition players as they tried to clear their lines.

And then there was the kicking. Rob Andrew, his predecessor in the England No.10 shirt and his mentor at Newcastle, along with Andrew's fly-half contemporaries Grant Fox, Michael Lynagh and Joel Stransky, had taken a dedication to kicking practice to a level never before seen in the game. But Wilkinson took it into the stratosphere.

Wilkinson's ability to deliver time and time again under the most severe pressure meant that, as time progressed, opposition teams very soon learnt to avoid giving away needless penalties anywhere in their own half. And in so doing, Newcastle (and, in due course, England) found that the ball would emerge more quickly from rucks, that mauls would seldom be pulled down and that space would open up for them across the field. Thanks to Wilkinson's endeavours, the opposition were forced to play more closely to the rules and England were given the time to control the pace of the game, to dictate which areas of the field they played in, and the space to dismantle any defence they came up against. And if they couldn't break down the defence, if that defence stayed honest and true and wouldn't give up a penalty, Wilkinson would retreat back into the pocket and drop a goal. The scoreboard would tick on with a sense of unrelenting inevitability. There was no one in the world who could keep the points mounting like Jonny Wilkinson in his pomp.

But Wilkinson's obsessive dedication would prove to be even more harmful than the reckless abandon with which he threw himself in the path of rampaging runners. He would suffer serious groin problems, shearing the muscle away from the bone thanks to his repetitive kicking motion, twice tear a medial knee ligament, break a shoulder and suffer a lacerated kidney. But the most damaging fallout was psychological. Read any interview with Wilkinson since he emerged on the scene or read any of his own biographical works and you will see before you a lost and troubled soul, an obsessive, wedded to his passion for his sport and his unerring quest for perfection – a quest that brought him global fame, success and adulation, a quest that made him an inspiration and a hero to millions, a quest that set him in the pantheon of sporting icons, but a quest that has haunted his life. 'I've had days where, having already been out for around two hours, I've wanted to finish with six kicks, fairly easy ones, and then I was going home,' said Wilkinson in the documentary *Perfect Ten*, 'and those six kicks have taken an hour and a half. I get very stubborn and I refuse to leave until those six kicks are perfect – because it felt like a challenge someone was putting to me.'

Protected to some degree by the low profile of rugby in the north-east of England while at Newcastle, Wilkinson shunned the spotlight as much as he could before eventually making the leap to join Toulon in the south of France in 2009. There, although the locals and the press were feverish about his presence at the club, he was eventually able to establish a sanctuary away from the clamour and start to find a path towards peace. He became a central cog in a Toulon team bursting with world-class talent, a local hero and a legend across France, a match-winner time and time again. In 2013 he helped Toulon claim the Heineken Cup; in the quarter-final, semi-final and the final of that tournament, he enjoyed 100 per cent accuracy with his goal-kicks. His dedication to training and his pursuit of perfection hardly dimmed at Toulon, but there was a sense that he had begun to find more balance in his life. Whether he has found enough will be put to the test when he finally hangs up his boots and walks from the pitch for that final time and into retirement. His has been a life lived for rugby. For those millions who have looked on with open-mouthed awe at his dedication and skill, there is nothing but hope that he can find a life of contentment and happiness beyond the rugby arena.

But for where we are in this story, many of these woes lie in the future. Here we are in the spring of 1999 and Jonny is nineteen years old. Boyishly handsome, with barely a blemish on his clean-shaven face, he is nervous in the international environment but anxious to show his esteemed colleagues exactly what he can do. He is a child among figures like Johnson, Back, Guscott and Leonard. But as a stand-off, he must be the one to boss them around on the field, to dictate play, make tactical decisions and establish the rhythm of the game.

He looked around the faces in the room at the Petersham Hotel. These were his childhood heroes, players he dreamed of emulating – not playing with. And certainly not telling them what to do.

Clive Woodward pushed open the door at the back of the room and marched in with Roger Uttley, Brian Ashton, Phil Larder, Phil Keith-Roach, Dave Reddin and Dave Alred hot on his heels. As the entourage took their seats at the head of the room, Woodward stood forward and welcomed the squad to the meeting.

'We'll head to the bus shortly,' said Woodward, referring to the coach that would ferry the team between the hotel and the nearby training grounds owned by the Bank of England. 'But first I want us to go over the attacking strategies that we'll be running through at training.'

He moved to a flip board and turned to a new sheet. He looked up.

'Jonny, could you come up here and talk us through some of the moves you think we should be employing in their red zone off set-piece play, please?'

Wilkinson's stomach dropped. *Not again…*

He swallowed hard, stood up and, averting his eyes from the faces of the other players, moved towards the flip board. He took a black marker pen from Woodward, who gave him a brief but reassuring pat on the shoulder before taking his seat next to Ashton.

Amid the fallout from the Tour of Hell and his recovery from injury, Wilkinson had been dropped from the squad for the 1998 Autumn Tests, but was brought back into the fold for the 1999 Five Nations. The coaching team recognised that he was still too insular for their liking and felt that if he wasn't comfortable telling the senior players exactly what he wanted from them, then he wasn't ready to run the game from stand-off. But he was too talented to leave out, and so they moved him back to centre and played Paul Grayson at 10, allowing Wilkinson to learn from his more experienced colleague. Wilkinson was a project, a work in progress. Woodward continued to bring the focus in meetings back to Wilkinson, moving him to the front of the room and asking him questions; during training runs he would stop play and ask Wilkinson his thoughts, would ask him to analyse what they were doing and whether they were executing the correct moves at the correct time in the correct part of the pitch. Wilkinson hated it all – but he was slowly getting used to it. His ambition to play for England, to be the best that he could be, was so powerful that he forced away his fears and his doubts as best he could, gradually becoming inured to the attention and slowly beginning to feel more comfortable in his surroundings.

But he still hated having to stand up in front of everyone. He looked at the blank sheet of paper and silently began to draw symbols and arrows of movement on the board. But he knew he had to speak up, so he cleared his throat and began – taking deep, slow breaths between sentences to try to steady his quavering voice. And as he began to drill down into the detail of the moves, he felt himself relaxing; his voice became more assured and his wrist began to flick quickly and easily across the sheets of paper as he illustrated sweeping attacking lines, changes of direction, pockets of space and areas of weakness in the opposition defence. For a while he slipped into a comfortable zone and was able to forget everything else in the world except the game.

Only when he had finished and turned to face the room again did the anxiety return. What if they disagreed? What if they thought he was childishly naive? What if they thought he was a fraud? He looked at Dallaglio and Johnson, then over to Dawson, Hill and Back, who were all sitting together. They were all nodding. They were happy – and a wave of relief flooded over him.

'Well done, Jonny,' said Woodward. 'Everyone happy? Good. Then let's go.' And with that the meeting was over. The players filed out of the room, ready to begin putting Jonny's moves into practice.

*

Six men were sitting together in a meeting room at the Petersham Hotel: Lawrence Dallaglio, Martin Johnson, Jason Leonard, Jeremy Guscott, Matt Dawson and Paul Grayson. All six were Lions – Johnson and Leonard the veterans of two tours, Guscott of three, and each had played on the 1997 tour of South Africa. They formed a senior group of players within the England team. Sometimes they would be joined by Phil de Glanville, Richard Hill and Neil Back; sometimes the group would be distilled down to just Dallaglio, Johnson and one or two of the others. But today there were six.

It was a week before the opening round of the 1999 Five Nations – the last time the championship would be known as that before it became the Six Nations in 2000 with the inclusion of Italy. England had had to sit out the first round of matches and all their focus was on playing Scotland at Twickenham in two weeks' time.

The meeting room had a special status within the England camp. It was known as the 'war room' and it was for serious discussions only. No phones, no jokes, no messing around. The team room was the place for socialising, relaxing, and spending an enjoyable time together. It represented an important psychological compartmentalisation – it separated downtime from the serious business of professional athletes. The war room was the equivalent of a company's boardroom and Woodward was explicit in his desire to make it as focused as possible. It had a cool and businesslike atmosphere – when the players were caught up in thundering chaos of a Test match, they could return to the strategies and tactics discussed, refined and honed in the war room; it was an oasis of calm that they could cling to in moments of bedlam.

The six men were leafing through the latest inserts into the England 'black book' to discuss its content before presenting it to the rest of the squad. The book had been commissioned by Woodward and Humphrey Walters shortly after their first meeting. It was, as Woodward describes, 'an everything-you-need-to-know manual about playing rugby for England'. The A4-sized black leather-bound book was embossed with the England rose and the words *This is England* on the front. It had ring-binding inside so that pages could be removed or added and the content had been written in full consultation with the players; and it evolved constantly over time. As well as explaining standards of behaviour, dress codes, information on meeting times, training schedules and other expectations that players coming into the England environment should adhere to, it also contained material expressing what it meant for the players to represent their country, and the team's philosophies and goals. Central to the whole document was a key phrase beside an image of the Webb Ellis Cup: *How do you want to be remembered?* It was a powerful document as well as a practical one.

The new pages that the six men were reviewing contained a list of 'Teamship Rules', which had been put together over the previous nine months. These were rules that had been set down by the players for the players. Near the top of list was a note about punctuality. *Lombardi Time*, it read.

Martin Johnson smiled at that. It had been his idea, inspired by his great love of American Football.

Growing up in Leicestershire, Johnson had been adept at a whole range of sports. He was blessed with incredible stamina, which he inherited from his mother, Hilary. She had been a Great Britain ultra-marathon runner (an ultra-marathon is run over a distance of 100km) and had often worked

Johnson and his brother, Will, to a standstill on family holidays and weekend breaks, making them run up and down sand dunes with her, doing hill sprints, interval training and circuits – and carrying on for hours after her boys had collapsed with exhaustion. Johnson's physique (he would grow to a height of 6ft 7in), fitness and hand-eye co-ordination could have made him a decent central defender in football, or seen him carve out a career in tennis, basketball or rowing; but his two great loves had been rugby and American Football.

He had progressed quickly through the schools rugby system, representing England at every age group and it was that success that ultimately made him opt for rugby over American Football. But his passion for the latter never waned and he would spend hours poring over annuals, histories and biographies of the great NFL dynasties and players, and staying up late into the night to watch Monday night football games beamed from across the Atlantic.

His rugby career really began to take off when he travelled to New Zealand to play for Tihoi in King Country when he was nineteen. He had been spotted by the Tihoi coach, John Albert, when England Schools had travelled to Australia for the three-way tournament with Australia and New Zealand. England had won both their games against their illustrious opponents and Albert had been impressed by the imposing figure of the young Leicester second-row. After just a few games for Tihoi, he was invited to a training session with the King Country provincial side and within ten days was playing his first game for them. He played throughout the season for King Country and was, much to his own surprise, then selected to train with the New Zealand Under-21 side. Although he didn't make it into the main Under-21 team on that occasion, he joined College Old Boys Marist in Taupo the following season and was again selected for the Under-21 squad for a trial match. He put in a much improved performance and at the end of the trial found that he had been selected for the side, which was coached by John Hart, who would later coach the All Blacks at the 1999 World Cup. The Junior All Blacks went on an undefeated three-match tour of Australia and in the game against their Australian counterparts Johnson lined up against John Eales, who would become a formidable opponent over the years ahead.

Johnson returned to England in October 1990 and worked his way into the Leicester first team. He won his first cap for England in the 1993 Five Nations against France at Twickenham and was a late replacement on the Lions tour to New Zealand later that summer. Despite not being an original selection, he impressively fought his way into the Test side for the series.

'As soon as Martin Johnson came out to New Zealand, it was clear that he would be in the Test side,' recalled Peter Winterbottom, the England flanker. 'And it was clear that he should have been on tour from the start – he was that good.'

Johnson's career continued to blossom on his return and he became a mainstay in the England team. He experienced a great deal of pain in an England shirt, not least the hammering that England suffered at the hands of the All Blacks in the semi-final of the 1995 World Cup, when Jonah Lomu, aged just eighteen, rampaged past – and over – the England defenders time and time again to score four hugely impressive tries. But there tended to be more highs than lows when he pulled on a white shirt. He was part of a Grand Slam-winning side in 1995 and picked up a Five Nations championship title in 1996. He was named as captain of the 1997 Lions and went on to become only the fourth man to lead a series-winning tour party since the Second World War.

He had been disappointed not to claim the England captaincy under Clive Woodward, but he was also philosophical about Dallaglio's appointment ahead of him.

'Clive and I weren't that similar,' said Johnson in an interview with Alison Kervin. 'We always got on because we both wanted to win and that's what made the relationship work when I did become captain, but it didn't surprise me when Lawrence was his first choice as captain. I suppose I've got my feet on the ground a bit more. Clive would have his barmy ideas and I'd just stand there and look at him.'

Johnson looked down at the words *Lombardi Time* printed on the paper in front of him. Vince Lombardi was the doyen of American Football coaches, having led the Green Bay Packers to five championships in seven years in the 1960s, including winning the first two Super Bowls in 1966 and 1967, and coached the New York Giants and the Washington Redskins. The National Football League's Super Bowl trophy is named in his honour. 'Lombardi Time' was a tribute to the NFL legend's penchant for punctuality; it meant being at a meeting ten minutes early, so that everyone was ready to go at precisely the scheduled time.

Beside Johnson, Jerry Guscott was scanning further down the document. He read the words *No Mobile Phones* with a wry smile. Guscott was the longest serving England player in the room – when he had come into the side in 1988, mobile phones had barely been heard of.

Described by the great BBC commentator Bill McLaren as 'the prince of centres', Guscott had burst on to the international scene as a one-cap bolter on the 1989 Lions tour to Australia after scoring a hat-trick of tries for England in a 58–3 win over Romania in May of that year. His delicate grubber kick behind the Australian defence, which he gathered himself to score, had won the Lions the crucial Second Test match to tie the series, and he had gone down in Lions legend again when, in 1997, he kicked the late drop-goal to win the series-clinching Second Test against the Springboks. Between those two momentous occasions he had won Grand Slams with England in 1991, 1992 and 1995, won the Five Nations in 1996 and toured with the Lions to New Zealand in 1993.

Beside Guscott sat the barrel-framed prop Jason Leonard, who had been an England regular since 1990. Known as the 'Fun Bus', he played a huge part in keeping morale high in the England camp, but played an even more important role on the field as the cornerstone of the scrum and with his vast experience. By the time he retired from international rugby in 2003, he was the world's most capped player – a remarkable feat considering the brutal attrition endured by players in the front-row of the scrum.

Paul Grayson and Matt Dawson, the half-backs, smiled easily as they flicked through the pages. The two were clubmates at Northampton and had played together for England since making their debuts in December 1995, in England's win over Samoa at Twickenham.

Dawson had, in many ways, mirrored Guscott's Lions story: he had been the third-choice scrum-half for England when Ian McGeechan, his club coach, selected him for the 1997 Lions tour. Many felt that his inclusion in the tour party had been nothing other than pure nepotism. But that was to underestimate McGeechan's genius for talent spotting. While appreciating that luck had played its part when the Lions' leading No.9, Rob Howley of Wales, was injured and ruled out of the tour during a midweek game, Dawson's play in South Africa more than merited his inclusion in the Test team – which he proved still further when he broke from a scrum in the First Test, set off down the blindside and seemingly into no man's land as five Springbok defenders closed in on him. In one of the most audacious pieces of play ever witnessed on the Test scene, Dawson feigned to pass the ball back infield with an overarm lob. All five defenders bought the dummy and halted in their tracks, giving Dawson a clear run to the line to score a decisive try that brought the Lions back into the game.

He played in all three Tests and scored another delightful try in the third Test, returning to England a hero.

Grayson had had a less fortunate tour. He had been selected as a probable Test starter in the No.10 shirt but a thigh injury picked up against Border in East London ruled him out of the tour. But his pedigree was such that as soon as he had returned to full fitness he was back in the England fold, running the show again from stand-off.

As the other five players in the room worked their way through the new inserts, Lawrence Dallaglio was still staring fixedly at the first page. His large square jaw was locked tight and he blinked one or two times, trying to quell a rising tide of emotion.

The opening line of the document had three simple words. *Inspire the Nation.* That was the mantra that Woodward wanted his team to always hold close, with an understanding that a nation's mood, its hopes and its dreams could be raised or dashed by the performances of those who represent them on the international sporting stage. It went hand in hand with the question, *How do you want to be remembered?* But a few lines down from *Inspire the Nation* was a sentence that read, *And never forget who you are doing this for. It is for all those people who have supported your efforts to get here. Your friends and family, your teachers and your coaches.* It was a simple sentiment, but emotive. And for Dallaglio, one word in particular shone from the page and played a painful melody on his heartstrings. *Family.*

Dallaglio thought about his elder sister, Francesca. He thought about her every day – and she was *always* there in his mind when he prepared himself to play rugby. Francesca had died when she was just nineteen, the youngest of the fifty-one souls who perished in the *Marchioness* riverboat disaster on the Thames in 1989. Her body had been found several miles away by Battersea Bridge four days after the pleasure boat, which had been playing host to a private birthday party, sank following a collision with the dredger *Bowbelle.*

'The night before, we all sat down as a family and had dinner together and talked about the party, which I was also invited to – but I had a headache and decided not to go,' recalled Dallaglio. 'The next morning my mum woke me in a terrible panic and said, "Have you heard the news? The *Marchioness* has sunk and they haven't found your sister yet."

'It was an incredibly traumatic few days. It blew me away. And it blew my family apart. It was horrific.

'Losing a member of one's family is a terrible thing, particularly for us, having been very close-knit. I became quite driven after that. I thought, *I now actually need to pull my finger out and do something that's going to bring everyone together.*

'I was a good sportsman at school, but rugby wasn't my life. I certainly wasn't destined to play for England. I didn't even play for the first XV at school. But I became a man on a mission after I lost my sister. Part of that might have just been me growing up. It's very hard for me to understand. Was I successful as a result of the fact I decided to grow up, or as a result of the fact my sister died?

'If you find the right emotional touch-points, the power of what you can achieve is phenomenal. In every game I've ever played, I always thought about my sister at some point.'

Dallaglio was an immensely patriotic player, who always played with his heart on his sleeve. He was passionately driven by the death of his sister, determined to try to honour her memory and her ambition to be a ballet dancer by achieving success on the rugby field. While his mother campaigned tirelessly to have the disaster investigated as an avoidable accident, Lawrence strove to make the name Dallaglio one that would be on the lips of every rugby fan in the world.

Now that he was England captain, he knew that if he could lead his team to the success that Woodward envisaged for it, then the name Dallaglio would be known all around the world. He could think of no greater tribute to Francesca than that.

But first they had to get the team – and the country – over the hangover from the Tour of Hell. They had managed to go some way towards that in the autumn when the senior players came back into the side. 'Five months after losing so heavily to the Aussies,' said Dallaglio, 'we fielded our best side against them at Twickenham and lost 12–11, which was a far more realistic measure of the difference between the teams. A week later we beat South Africa 13–7 and we went into the 1999 Five Nations believing we were good enough to win every game.'

Dallaglio, his fellow players and the management all knew that the Five Nations was going to be the measuring stick of where they were as a team. Was the Tour of Hell a real indication of where they were in the world standings, or could they build on the win against South Africa and show themselves to be a true global force going into the summer tour of Australia and into the World Cup thereafter? The win over South Africa had ended the Springboks' incredible record-equalling run of seventeen consecutive Test victories. It had been Woodward's first win as a coach over a southern hemisphere giant and England's first since beating Australia in the 1995 World Cup quarter-final. The players felt that this was the real England coming to the fore, but the Five Nations would prove the litmus test.

*

In October 1998, Francis Baron was appointed by the RFU management board as the first full-time professional CEO of the union. His appointment introduced a new corporate culture into the union and the way it ran its business. Baron had decided to take up the offer from the RFU after watching the Tour of Hell on TV; he never wanted to see English rugby laid so low again.

He was the former managing director of WHSmith's media division and had been headhunted from the travel group First Choice, where he had been chief executive, to address the RFU's multimillion-pound deficit. In the two years prior to his appointment the RFU had lost more than £10.3 million. It could not continue to lose money at that rate and his first task was to audit the staffing levels within the RFU.

'It was not a good start to the professional era, but it was a major business challenge,' he said. 'My wife said I was nuts.'

His business focus instantly commended him to Woodward and what Baron did brilliantly was to recognise the creative spark that was so fervent in the coach. He gave Woodward the room to express that creativity – while simultaneously keeping a tight rein on how much money he could spend.

A few months after his appointment, Baron called all the staff in the RFU for a series of review meetings. He had spent his initial time in office examining the structure of the organisation and, with the backing of the management board, set about making sweeping changes. There were thirty-four redundancies – most significantly Roger Uttley and Don Rutherford. Having analysed each position, Baron had concluded that for the RFU and the England team to fully flourish there was no room for part-timers. The organisation had to be for professionals dedicated full-time to instilling a corporate ethos of excellence across every facet of the organisation. There could be no exceptions, no room for anyone whose focus was not entirely fixed on pushing England to the forefront of the world game.

Rutherford had worked for the RFU since 1969; he was only three years away from retirement and qualification for a full pension. When Baron gave him the news of his redundancy he instructed him to clear his office with immediate effect. By the time Woodward arrived for his own meeting with Baron – when the latter explained the casualties of the cost-cutting exercise – Rutherford had already left the building. Woodward never contacted him afterwards, instead thanking him in a public statement for all his years of service. Not contacting Rutherford directly was something that Woodward later bitterly regretted.

Uttley, however, was a slightly different case. As he was a teacher at Harrow and not based at Twickenham, Baron suggested that Woodward break the news to Uttley in person. Baron had typed every redundancy letter himself to ensure that news of the cull did not leak before that fateful morning. He handed Woodward his letter to Uttley and Woodward got straight in his car and drove to Harrow.

In his autobiography, Woodward glosses over the antagonism that existed between him and Uttley throughout their time working together and takes a magnanimous line in praising his former teammate's work as England manager. Uttley, however, has always been a lot more candid about their relationship and, while it is always important to bear in mind that the slighted man is likely to lean towards bitterness, his opinions of Woodward are interesting to reflect on.

'He's a clever, shrewd bloke who'll try and manipulate all sorts of situations,' said Uttley in an interview with Alistair Grant in *The Sunday Telegraph* in 2006. 'He was extremely hard to work with,' he said to Alison Kervin for her biography of Woodward, 'extremely hard to please. I hate to criticise Clive because it seems like sour grapes. It was a very difficult two or three-year period for me – very up and down. He could be a charming man but there were times when he wasn't charming at all. In fact, there were times when he could be extremely hard work and unpleasant... When Clive had to head home from the Tour of Hell for his father's funeral, the hotel was a different place without him. There wasn't this feeling of panic. You weren't worried all the time that he would burst in with his next demand. The players all looked more relaxed. It reminded me how enjoyable international rugby can be.'

Uttley issued a statement shortly after Woodward delivered the news in which he said, 'I had no idea this would happen to me. It's deeply disappointing and I'm fed up at not being allowed to follow through a job I was told eighteen months ago would lead up to the World Cup.'

It was an unpleasant end for Rutherford, Uttley and their thirty-two colleagues. But it showed that Baron, Woodward and the new-look RFU meant serious business.

*

In the same month that Baron was appointed, Woodward set off to the US on an information-gathering trip. Inspired by his time at Loughborough and what he had witnessed at the Australian Institute of Sport, Woodward had developed a fascination with examining other sports in detail to see whether there were any aspects of their accumulated knowledge that could be applied to rugby. No doubt encouraged by both Martin Johnson's obvious obsession with the game and by Dave Alred's first-hand experience, Woodward arranged to spend time with two American Football organisations to study their practices.

'Playing American Football was an unbelievable experience for me,' said Alred. 'The focus and professionalism was light years ahead of English sport. It really switched me on to the importance of performing under pressure. I was fascinated by the way a player could slot eight out of eight kicks one day and not hit a barn door the next. Spending time in the US had a profound effect on Clive as well – although in a different sphere to me.'

'The game had gone professional and I knew virtually nothing about professional sport,' said Woodward, 'so I wanted to go and see people that did. We were sponsored by Nike and so were the University of Colorado and the Denver Broncos, so I arranged a visit through them so that I could spend a couple of weeks watching how they ran things – and it was fascinating. I went out to Boulder to start with to see the University of Colorado. The head coach was brilliant and let me sit at the back of the room through all the meetings and attend all the training sessions and so on. One of the big things I learned happened on the first day. We went into a building and on one floor was the offence and on another floor was the defence – in American Football you basically have two teams which come on and off the field depending on whether they are attacking or defending. And I can't tell you what it was like sitting in a team meeting with all of the players there the day after a game when the side has just lost 50-49; the offence guys are going crazy because they've scored forty-nine points, but the defence have thrown the game away by leaking fifty.

'The specialisation in coaching struck me profoundly and it was then that I realised what we had to do – we had to get specialists in to coach specific parts of the game to the very best standard available. And then we had to think like those two teams within the team in the NFL – when we had the ball we were all focused on offence, but when we lost it we had to switch our mindset completely and become the defensive team, we had to suddenly become a different animal. We used to call it "ice" when we lost the ball – your thoughts turn to ice and you immediately address where you've got to be and what you've got to do. And you switch back and forth throughout the game.'

The experience in the US was invaluable – not only for the new ideas that it engendered, but also for reaffirming his belief in building a team of specialist coaches in various fields to ensure that every aspect of England's game was the best it could be. There was also a reaffirmation of everything that both Humphrey Walters and Paddi Lund had taught Woodward – that attention to detail was crucial to sporting success. At the University of Colorado, an institution where crowds of more than 53,000 would gather in the Folsom Field stadium during the college football season to watch the Colorado Buffaloes, there was a huge message printed on the locker room wall: GREATNESS IS ACHIEVED THROUGH ATTENTION TO DETAIL. It was like manna from heaven for Woodward.

'I can't remember going to a club or being involved in a coaching situation where anyone taught me how to sidestep or swerve, where precisely you need to put your feet to make it happen, how balance affects the dynamic,' said Woodward in an interview with Paul Ackford in *The Sunday Telegraph* about his trip. 'We're still in the culture where that skill is perceived as natural. In the States we saw people coaching one-on-one on how to lose their marker in tight areas, which is essentially what rugby is all about. The coaches were able to simplify complex skills into the smallest biomechanical movements. It's one thing knowing your rugby, another thing entirely being able to teach it.'

Woodward returned home more focused than ever on building a back-room team of specialists in every position imaginable. Over the next two years he would add to his already impressive team with the inclusion of Simon

Hardy, who became throwing coach in 1999 and full-time line-out coach in 2000. He also employed the team's own chef (after heeding the warning of the 1995 All Blacks, some of whom suffered from food poisoning on the eve of the World Cup final, which they lost to South Africa) and utilised the services of Sherylle Calder to develop the players' peripheral vision.

In December 1998 Woodward equipped every player and coach with their own laptop. By connecting them all by email and having Tony Biscombe send the players clips of their play or analysis of their opposition, Woodward was able to bridge part of the gap between the players and the England set-up when they were out of the camp on club duty. And from a team-building perspective it allowed the players to stay in touch socially and to chat online, whereas before that they had returned to their clubs in isolation from one another.

'Woody used every conceivable trick in the book to fund performance,' said Baron. 'He was brilliant at it. He made lots of demands – he wanted more coaches and a better environment for everyone involved with the Test side. He was convinced that if he got what he wanted the team would win. The England Test side is our shop window, it generates the most income for the RFU and it puts us on the world map. If we were to succeed as a business, the Test side had to have success. Woody believed that this was what it took and we believed in him, so he got what he wanted.'

During the build-up to the 1999 Five Nations, the work done by the specialist coaches was starting to pay dividends – and none more so than that of Dave Reddin.

After completing undergraduate and master's degrees in sports science at Loughborough University, Reddin worked for the Sports Council at Loughborough for five years before joining Leicester Tigers in 1994. In 1996 he began working with the England team under Jack Rowell and with the various England age group teams. His involvement with the Under-21s saw him join forces with Woodward and Andy Robinson for the first time. As discussed previously, he was one of Woodward's first full-time appointments in 1997.

'The potential to be a champion is in the genes,' said Reddin in an interview with Vern Gambetta, 'but the environment determines whether someone makes it or not. The wrong training can make a huge difference. With the best athletes, I think we must constantly assess what we can really add, unless we understand their sport as they do. Many coaches suffer by forcing their doctrine on their athlete. I'm always surprised about how little of the right training it takes to make a significant difference, and how much of the wrong stuff it takes before things go really wrong. In other words, training is the icing on the cake for the best athletes, whose talent tends to win through almost in spite of the training sometimes.

'It was a great moment when Clive introduced the laptops to the team as it meant that I could easily communicate with all the players and send them training information – and they could send me back results for analysis. Athletes thrive on feedback in my experience. Without feedback it can be tough to engage the athlete. Using feedback systems, for example jump mats, micro-muscle lab, Rob Newton's Ballistic Measurement System and so on really helps as it gets the athlete engaged through competition with themselves and the rest of the squad.

'Throughout my time with the England squad I did a lot of analysis – I videoed training so that I could study the players' biomechanics, I talked to their club fitness coaches and to the players themselves about their training, I examined their previous programmes and looked at their movement patterns. I then tried to get to the fundamental movements and actions and energy systems which were important for each player, depending on their position, age, biomechanics and so on. For older guys like Jason Leonard, there was no point in trying to teach him too much new – it just wouldn't work and he would get frustrated; but his work ethic was incredible. The young guys were great at learning new lifts from me, but they learnt work ethic from the senior guys. Then you get guys like Jonny Wilkinson who were both those things combined – you don't have to beat Jonny with a big stick to train. You have to beat him with a stick to stop him training.'

In consultation with the leading clubs, Reddin's goal was to see England's elite players once a week. Because of some of the distances that were required to travel between clubs, it didn't always work out that way, but on the whole he pretty much managed it and the email communication was a huge help with developing his programmes. By the spring of 1999 they were still a long way from where he wanted them to be, but they were on the road.

*

England dominated the opening twenty minutes of the Calcutta Cup clash against Scotland at Twickenham, racing into an early 14–0 lead with tries from full-back Nick Beal and winger Dan Luger, both converted by Jonny Wilkinson. But Scotland roared back into contention with two tries from Alan Tait and a sixty-yard effort from stand-off Gregor Townsend, all converted by Kenny Logan. England responded with a further converted try by Tim Rodber, but the real difference was Logan's kicking from the tee, as he missed several opportunities for Scotland to record a famous win. In the end England held on to secure a 24–21 victory.

'What gave us the edge was a young man of nineteen playing in his first Five Nations start for England,' said Woodward. 'He was playing at centre, his name was Jonny Wilkinson, and it was his place-kicking that gave us the points we needed. In addition to an excellent kicking game with three conversions and a penalty, none easy, Wilkinson made two try-saving tackles in the second half when we were hanging on by our fingernails to a three-point lead.'

'Scotland were a good side that year and they had played a game already, beating Wales,' recalled Johnson. 'That was our first of the tournament and it was a shaky start, but it was still a win.'

The second match of their campaign was in Dublin where a strong Irish pack had many pundits fancying them for the title, but after a hard-fought battle, England emerged 27–15 winners.

What many saw as the key encounter of the tournament was next: Le Crunch against the French at Twickenham. It was not a spectacle but England did what they needed to do and, thanks to Wilkinson knocking over seven penalties, they emerged as 21–10 victors – their first win in four seasons over the French, who were chasing an historic third consecutive Grand Slam.

'It was a typical English performance of that period,' admitted Martin Johnson in his autobiography. 'We were a better defensive side than we were an attacking force, which perhaps frustrated Clive a little. He wanted us to thrill the crowd with all-out "total rugby", but we weren't really ready for that.'

'Despite Clive's desire to play "heads-up" rugby,' said Richard Hill, 'we were probably improving much faster as a defensive unit. A lot of that had to do with Phil Larder. He certainly changed my approach. I had thought I was a good defensive player before he came along but I got quite a wake-up call… Phil, with his rugby league background, very quickly made us question everything, by asking us to consider what we wanted to achieve from each and every tackle. Did we want to knock guys backwards to deny them yardage? Did we want to stay on our feet afterwards? What if your opponent was running straight at you rather than at an angle? Did you want to isolate the ball-carrier by turning him, thus stopping him presenting the ball back to his teammates? After that, we began examining our techniques in detail, from the positioning of our feet to our body angles. It all seems obvious now but his approach was much more scientific.'

Wales were the host nation for the World Cup that autumn and the Millennium Stadium in Cardiff was still under construction, so Wales opted to play their final 'home' matches of the Five Nations at Wembley Stadium – the home of English football. Going into that last round of the championship, England had a Grand Slam on the cards and the deciding fixture was to be played at the most iconic ground in English sport – the ground where Woodward had dreamed of playing as a child, where he had always imagined himself lifting a cup. It may not have been the Jules Rimet trophy that he would be hoisting aloft if they won, but the Five Nations' version was not a bad substitute; it all seemed to be written in the stars.

Wales, after promising so much at the outset of the season, had had something of a mixed tournament. They had lost to Scotland and Ireland, but had then defeated France 34–33 in a thriller at Stade de France and had backed up that victory by thumping Italy 60–21 in a friendly in Treviso.

As he had done against Scotland, Dan Luger burst away to score an early try at Wembley and he was followed over the whitewash by Richard Hill and Steve Hanley. 'We should have been cruising by half-time,' admits Johnson, 'but whenever they got within thirty or forty yards of our line we seemed to be penalised, usually for technical infringements or offsides that were marginal at best, like guys being pinged for offside when they had just come up very quickly in the defensive line.'

With the score standing at 25–18 to England at half-time, Woodward and his team still felt comfortable. It had been their own errors gifting the Welsh a foothold in the game. If they could cut those down during the second half, they knew that the Grand Slam was theirs.

But after the referee blew his whistle to begin the second forty minutes, things began to unravel as the Wales full-back Shane Howarth slid over the English line at the corner and Neil Jenkins continued his immaculate kicking by slotting the touchline conversion to tie the score at 25–25.

Wilkinson nudged England back in front with two penalties but then came the first of two decisive moments in the match.

The clock had ticked to seventy-five minutes. England were awarded a penalty halfway between the Welsh 22 and the 10-metre line. A penalty kick at goal would stretch their lead to 34–25, more than a converted try clear of their opponents. Lawrence Dallaglio glanced up at the posts and tossed the ball to Wilkinson. 'Go for the corner,' he said. 'We'll take the try.'

It was a bold move but it was what Woodward had wanted from his captain – a man who was willing to put himself out there to inspire the nation, to take the tough decisions.

'At the time we were six points clear,' recalled Dallaglio in *It's in the Blood*, 'but I was a disciple of Clive's have-a-go philosophy. Both of us were naturally opposed to the lack of adventure traditionally associated with England... The key mistake was my belief that, at that point in the game, Wales weren't going to go down to the other end of the field and score a try. I should have known better. In hindsight, it was a big mistake.'

Ninety seconds later, after a powerful rolling maul, Mike Catt hoisted a garryowen in front of the Welsh posts, which was only just gathered by Welsh centre Mark Taylor. Tackled in the process of taking the catch, Wales were awarded a scrum; Rob Howley swept the ball to Jenkins who put in a booming kick, and the Welsh lines were cleared.

Wales had survived. But time was running out for them and England were still six points ahead. Wales needed a converted score to steal the victory. Save for a few rampages from the giant brothers Scott and Craig Quinnell and Howarth's try, the English defensive line had held firm all afternoon. The talismanic figure of Scott Gibbs, a hero of the Lions tour two years previously, had been well-marshalled by the English midfield and back-row and his efforts to scythe through their ranks in the way that Alan Tait had done at Twickenham just a few weeks earlier had been met by staunch English tackles time after time. There seemed no way through.

But then Tim Rodber smashed Colin Charvis in a huge tackle forty metres from the Welsh line, which the referee deemed as high. Jenkins stabbed the resultant penalty down to the English 22.

There were two minutes remaining.

The Welsh second-row, Chris Wyatt, won a shortened line-out and Howley fed Scott Quinnell. The No.8 juggled the ball and managed to slip it to Gibbs, who hit a hard flat line and burst through Rodber's tackle, fended off Neil Back, arced his run around Matt Dawson, slid past Wilkinson and skipped past Matthew Perry, raising his arm in triumph as he dived over the line. The score stood at 31–30 to England.

Jenkins lined up the ball for the conversion. Stepping back, he picked a bit of mud from his studs, wiped his palms on his shorts and subconsciously waved a guiding hand towards the posts. Three steps. Contact. It was a perfect Dave Alred kick. The ball sailed straight and true. 32–31 to Wales.

There was less than a minute left on the clock as England kicked off. They were lucky. Wales spilled the ball and England were awarded a scrum. There was still time for them to snatch the win. Dallaglio controlled the ball at the base and Dawson fed Catt, who struck a drop at goal. It went wide. Howarth gathered, called the mark and then rifled the ball into the sea of red beyond the touchline. Andre Watson blew his whistle and the game was over.

To make matters worse, not only had the Grand Slam slipped through their fingers, but so had the championship; because of their superior points difference, the title went to Scotland.

'Inside my head,' said Dallaglio, 'a voice said, "Bottle this feeling, mate, and I guarantee it will help you in the future." The changing room was like a morgue – complete silence. Guys sat in stunned bewilderment. How did we lose that? We had blown it and we knew it. If you looked around, some guys were quietly shedding tears. What hurt most was that we had contrived to lose a match when we were the better team. I blamed myself for the decision not to kick for goal. Over the following years we would learn how to build a winning score, brick by brick.'

'I cannot imagine a worse memory of that,' wrote Matt Dawson in *Nine Lives*. 'The combination of it being my first Grand Slam game and its being played at Wembley Stadium, a mecca for every Englishman. It had been such an inspiring place to be… Later that evening the England squad went back to the Petersham Hotel in Richmond for dinner and a few drinks. Clive stood up and said, "I believe good things come out of bad days. In time, this will do us the world of good."'

*

As part of their World Cup preparations, England were travelling to Australia for a training camp and a one-off Test against the Wallabies. But before they left, a storm erupted that would shift the focus firmly away from the playing side of English rugby.

At the beginning of the year, 1999 seemed to promise everything to Lawrence Dallaglio. He was captain of England, the team had just recorded a famous win against South Africa, they were favourites for the Five Nations, his partner Alice was due to have their second child, England were to tour Australia with a full-strength team in the summer and then in the autumn there was the World Cup, where a large proportion of England's games would be played at home. To top matters off, he was now something of a celebrity – the name Dallaglio carried serious commercial weight and there appeared to be all manner of sponsors keen to sign him up for endorsement deals. But this, it would prove, was the pride before the fall.

It was late May when Dallaglio was told by his agent that Gillette wanted to pay him £500,000 to front a new campaign, but that they wanted three of their executives, Peter Simmons, James Tunstall and Louise Wood, to meet him in person to discuss the terms of the contract. He met them twice and over the course of the meetings they plied him with drinks and encouraged him to tell as many lurid stories as he knew about the off-field life and antics of elite rugby players. Thrilled by the lucrative offer that was on the table and keen to impress them in any way he could, Dallaglio talked and talked and talked. He spun long tales of his misspent youth and under the beam of their grinning faces and the glugging sound of endlessly flowing alcohol, his tales grew increasingly exaggerated and outrageous.

'During my childhood in Barnes, I'd hung out with guys who knew a lot about gangs and the recreational drug scene,' revealed Dallaglio in *It's in the Blood*, 'and as the chat shifted in that direction, James and Louise gave the impression they found this stuff fascinating. So I took what I knew, exaggerated it, put myself into various stories I'd heard and tried to be the guy they wanted me to be. When it comes to bravado, I can give it with the best of them.'

On Sunday, 23 May the *News of the World* published a Dallaglio exposé, revealing the three Gillette executives to have been nothing more than undercover journalists.

'When it was revealed that Peter Simmons, James Tunstall and Louise Wood were all working for the *News of the World* and that every conversation had been taped, I felt sick,' he said. 'And it all made a different kind of sense... They set the trap and I didn't so much get caught as throw myself headlong into it.'

Dallaglio called Woodward, desperate to explain that it was all a terrible mistake, that the stories that were now being read at breakfast tables all around the country were nothing but tall tales told under the influence of too much booze. He made the call in hope rather than expectation – why would Woodward believe him? This was surely the end of his international career; perhaps even the end of his time as a professional rugby player.

'You've been a bit of a prat, haven't you?' said Woodward, having been forewarned of the story when the *News of the World*'s editor, Piers Morgan, phoned him for a comment the night before the story broke. Woodward had refused to comment and then spent several hours desperately trying to get hold of his captain. When Dallaglio explained what had happened with the sting, Woodward didn't think twice. 'Pack up everything, bring Alice and the kids and come and stay with us.'

Woodward opened his home as a refuge to Dallaglio and offered him as much support as he could. He called other senior team members, explained the situation, and the team as a whole closed ranks around Dallaglio. It was an incredible moment of unity.

Two days after the publication of the story, the RFU held a press conference at Twickenham and Dallaglio admitted his stupidity before publicly resigning as England captain. There was little else that he could do – and the captaincy passed to Martin Johnson.

'In the weeks that followed the publication of the stories, my concern wasn't so much the newspapers but the Rugby Football Union, who felt they had to investigate the allegations,' said Dallaglio. 'After an initial gathering of evidence, they decided to charge me formally with bringing the game into disrepute.' If there was one element of the affair that he most resented, it was the RFU's decision to allow the media to attend the internal disciplinary hearing that followed publication of the story, which, to Dallaglio, gave it the feeling of a show trial. 'It gave it a legitimacy it didn't merit, but it was the RFU's desire to be seen to do the right thing,' he told David Hands of *The Times* in a 2012 interview on the affair.

But the RFU were also desperate to make sure that Dallaglio was available for the World Cup. They backdated his suspension so that its duration affected only the tour to Australia and he was available for selection for the first World Cup warm-up game in August.

'When the team departed for Australia with Martin as the new captain, the disappointment for me was simply not being able to travel with the team. When you are all in that group, each contributing in his own way, it doesn't matter that much who is or isn't captain. Martin knew that, when I was back in the team, I would give him the same 100 per cent support he had given me. It wasn't complicated – what mattered was being part of the team; the rest was peripheral. Martin was the new captain, he had my support.'

Dallaglio appreciated above all the way that Woodward had stuck by him and drawn the wagons around him within the team. It showed not only the regard he was held in by his coach and his peers, but also the loyalty of the group. While Woodward could be ruthless with team selection, cutting players that he felt were dead wood from the international scene altogether, he was also steadfast in his support for players within his inner circle. Such loyalty would form the bedrock for the team moving forward.

'I could complain about the methods of the newspaper,' said Dallaglio, 'be annoyed about the RFU turning the hearing into a media circus, but the reality is that the hearing brought me down a peg or two – well several, actually. I needed to focus on the things that mattered: those close to me and my rugby. But I was a pretty angry man; angry with the newspaper, angry with the RFU, angry with myself. But if you can channel anger correctly, it can be a help. I was determined to play the best rugby of my life.'

*

Before the summer tour to Australia, Woodward took Wilkinson to one side and told him that he was considering moving him back to stand-off. But having watched him playing for Newcastle over the preceding weeks, he was concerned that Wilkinson was running the ball too much.

'I need you to think more carefully about your kicking game,' he said. 'It's one of the most important weapons in a stand-off's armoury. We need to be able to control territory around the field – which means you need to control territory around the field. Can you do that?'

Wilkinson nodded. He would do anything for the team. And he felt comfortable that he had the skills that Woodward was looking for.

'Good,' said Woodward. 'And if you're going to be leading the side at stand-off, I need you to start leading things more in meetings. I want you to start making presentations about our tactics and game management. It won't be rocket science, just reaffirming the tactics that we will all be coming up with and making sure that everyone understands them.' This time Woodward didn't leave his statement hanging as a question. This is what he required from his stand-off and if Wilkinson wanted that No.10 shirt, this was what he had to do.

Wilkinson's stomach felt leaden. He swallowed. And nodded.

Almost exactly a year on from the Brisbane drubbing on the Tour of Hell, England took to the field in Sydney to play Australia. It was the one hundredth Test match between the two countries. The Wallabies were largely the same team, with a core of world-class excellence. England, on the other hand, were quite a different force to the one that had last played Down Under. Wilkinson was again at stand-off, but he had the cool presence of Jeremy Guscott and Mike Catt alongside him in the centre, Matt Perry at full-back and warriors in the forwards in the shape of Jason Leonard, Martin Johnson, Tim Rodber, Richard Hill and Martin Corry, while the bench was packed with experience in Matt Dawson, Ben Clarke, Victor Ubogu and Phil de Glanville. While England once again faltered, the performance was startlingly different to Brisbane in 1998 and they fought all the way before succumbing 22–15.

'It was a big game in the lead up to the World Cup and we'd proved we could compete,' reflected Woodward. 'But our fitness and performance under pressure let us down in the second half again. During our stay at Couran Cove before the match, Dave Reddin had been working incredibly hard with players on fitness and nutrition, but clearly this is not something that could be done on such a short time span.'

Reddin had launched his world-class performance concept while at Couran Cove, a training facility on the Queensland coast used previously by the Wallabies. It was a programme that would take several years to come to fruition, but its introduction was the cornerstone for what was to come and, for the majority of the players there, it opened their eyes to what was to be expected of them in terms of physical preparation, diet and the general organisation required to be a world-class athlete.

While the team were at Couran Cove, Reddin arranged for his colleague, Dr Adam Carey, to hold a seminar on nutrition at Twickenham for the wives and girlfriends of all the players so that they were fully aware of – and able to support – what the conditioning staff wanted the players to be eating.

It was disappointing to be heading home on the back of a defeat but Australia had been playing on thier own turf and, as they were to prove over the coming months, they were a world-class unit. For England the game proved a good run-out for the players as they began to ramp up their World Cup preparations – but it also kept their feet on the ground.

After witnessing the collapse against Wales and the close-run loss to the Wallabies, Woodward realised that the one area in which he had yet to prepare the team thoroughly was psychology.

As part of their preparation for the World Cup, Woodward and Humphrey Walters arranged two training camps with the Royal Marines for forty-eight players, from which he would select the World Cup squad – one ten weeks before the tournament, the other just four and a half weeks out. The sessions were designed to build teamwork, give the players a good physical workout (while not burning them out or risking injury) and to bond them in adversity. It would also teach them the value of learning to think correctly under pressure, and develop their leadership skills and decision-making when placed under physical and mental duress – all aspects that they would have to contend with during a Test match.

The Marines, like Robert Burns, know that even the very best-laid plans can go wrong and that crucial to success is the ability of their soldiers to adapt to any situation presented to them. They call it 'dislocated expectations'. The course designed for the England team set out to test their capacity to adapt, lead and perform under extreme pressure.

'For rugby teams, the training sessions that military personnel put themselves through are a good test of how strong the team is as a unit and how confident and communicative the individuals are,' wrote Jason Leonard in his autobiography. 'There may not be much similarity on the surface between the Marines and the England rugby team, but the reality is that within every good team there are core values which are the same whether you're fighting a war or playing a match – for example: trust, determination and communication… As we completed tasks we were observed by assessors who specialise in analysing how people cope under pressure. They were looking to see who the team players were, who were not great team players, who was willing to listen and who was willing to give advice. In life it's no different to rugby – there are some people who are open to new ideas and responsive to instruction, whilst there are others who will not listen to what they're being told, acknowledge blame or seek to improve. Under the pressure of an alien environment and in potentially life-threatening situations, these characteristics come to the fore very easily.'

Perhaps most importantly, however, the team learnt about the 'jumping out of a helicopter' test. Would the players look at each of their teammates and be prepared to jump out of a helicopter behind enemy lines with them – believing in one another enough, trusting in one another enough, not to let themselves down? If they didn't have that complete trust, if there was a weak link in the chain, should that individual be involved with the England team? These were the individuals that Woodward and Walters were looking to identify and weed out.

Woodward labelled these weak links another way – as 'energy sappers'. He analysed the entire squad and identified which players were 'energisers' and which ones were 'energy sappers' – and looked to cut the dead wood from the tree. He told the squad that he would not accept negativity within the group – that even the odd moan or grumble could instil a poison that could spread quickly through the squad and completely undermine everything they had been working towards.

'Looking back on the list of guys involved at that training camp,' said Woodward, 'the most remarkable thing was that over 50 per cent of the guys there were in the World Cup squad of 2003. That shows just how much time and commitment needs to be invested in learning to perform under pressure and developing leadership skills across an entire group. It was the same for the Wallaby sides of 1995 and 1999, the Springboks of 2003 and 2007 and the All Blacks of 2007 and 2011. By 1999 we were nowhere near where we needed to be – as it showed.'

*

'The build-up to the World Cup tournament was like nothing I have experienced before or since,' wrote Martin Johnson in his autobiography. 'Back in England, we continued our training camp, spending the whole of the summer and early autumn together, working hard on our fitness and skills. We were probably stronger and fitter than we had ever been, but we felt a massive weight of expectation on all of our shoulders. Clive had always insisted he be judged on the World Cup, which put a lot of pressure on him and us.'

England played two 'Premiership All Stars' sides, a kind of Barbarians of the league, at Twickenham and Anfield, which were won 92–17 and 67–14 respectively, before two Tests at Twickenham against the USA and Canada.

The USA match was won 106–8, another rout that hardly prepared the side for the rigours of a knockout tournament. The Canadians offered a sterner test but they too were swept aside 36–11.

The 1999 World Cup had a bizarre format, which was subsequently revised. There were five pools of four teams, from which eight quarter-finalists would emerge. The pool winners would automatically qualify for the quarters, but the runners-up from each pool would have to play an additional play-off match against another second-placed side. England knew that if they defeated the All Blacks they would get a full week's recovery and an easier path through to the final. If they lost, they would have to play a midweek qualifier and then face each of the southern hemisphere giants in consecutive matches to lift the trophy.

Though the tournament was being held in Wales, the Welsh Rugby Union had promised England, Scotland and France that they could host matches if they supported their bid. This meant that there were fixtures held in the Scottish Borders, Edinburgh, Manchester, London and Paris. It was a dislocated tournament as a result but it gave those nations a crucial home advantage during the pool stages – something that England hoped would give them a critical edge over their rivals.

England's opening game against Italy followed a similar pattern to the warm-up games as the Azzurri were defeated 67–7. The third match in the pool was against Tonga and, after the Pacific islanders were reduced to fourteen men, England powered to a crushing 101–10 victory. But the key fixture was England's second pool match – against tournament favourites New Zealand.

'I realise now that I made a fundamental mistake in selection,' said Woodward of that game against the All Blacks. 'I played Wilkinson at fly-half with De Glanville and Guscott in the centre. I should have played Grayson at fly-half with Wilkinson and Guscott in the centre. Selection is the most important part of this job. Selection wins or loses you more matches than anything else... Jonny had played most of the season at centre, with Paul Grayson at fly-half. Playing Grayson at fly-half would have given us real leadership and experience, which Wilko was still acquiring.' It was perhaps an unfair reflection to blame the loss on the selection of the fly-half. Wilkinson was far from the lone culprit as the All Blacks powered their way to victory. While the management had analysed New Zealand's strengths – particularly the threat of giant wing Jonah Lomu – and concluded that a tight kicking game was the best route to success, looking to turn Lomu by kicking over him and pressing him hard and fast in defence to prevent him building up speed and momentum, Lomu was not the only weapon in the All Blacks' armoury. The fact that some of Wilkinson's kicking was not as accurate as it needed to be is a fair point, but it did not result in the game-changing try – which did, indeed, come from Lomu, who was as devastating as ever.

'As in the 1995 semi-final,' wrote Matt Dawson in *Nine Lives*, 'it was Jonah Lomu who was the difference. With the scores tied at 16–16 the ball headed in his direction, and before it even reached him I had this feeling of impending doom. It was one of those moments when you look up and your heart sinks. I could tell he was going to skin Jerry Guscott on the outside, and then it would be me in his path. I tried to go high and generally get in the way. He swatted me off but I stayed on my feet. Then Matt Perry went in and got boomed, then I tried again by jumping on his back. He didn't even break stride. Even Lawrence Dallaglio could not stop Jonah, who went over the line with three of us clinging to him.'

'I remember, as a child, I was being chased and I ran into the road and into the side of a car,' said Guscott. 'A split-second earlier and I would have been squashed, but I hit the side of the car and I bounced off it. I was shocked and didn't really know what had happened. It was exactly the same when I tried to tackle Jonah at Twickenham. I didn't quite have the right angle on him and he just brushed me off as if to say "Go away".

'I don't think any international rugby player would openly admit to a fear of tackling him, you just hope you don't find yourself isolated in a one-on-one against him. To stand a chance of stopping him, you have to get the right angle, and your technique has to be so precise. Head-on, you have to hope he falls over you. From the side, you have to go low and try to tackle him round his ankles, because his thighs are so big. But he has such a huge reach and such a powerful hand-off that it's hard to get anywhere near him.'

New Zealand pushed on to win 30–16 and earned themselves a quarter-final spot against Scotland in Edinburgh. The defeat left England with the harder route to the final – one that they had hoped to avoid. They had to play Fiji in a quarter-final qualifier at Twickenham and then, if they came through that, they had to travel to Paris for a quarter-final with South Africa.

Although the scoreboard against Fiji suggested a comfortable win, it proved to be a bruising encounter and several players picked up knocks and injuries – including the iconic centre Guscott, who strained his groin. After the medical staff assessed his injury the prognosis was that his injury would prevent him from playing again until after the conclusion of the tournament; in light of this, Guscott officially announced his retirement from the international game the following day. It was the end of an era.

That same day, Thursday, England travelled to Paris for just two days of preparation before facing the Springboks at Stade de France. The South Africans, meanwhile, had topped their pool after defeating Scotland at Murrayfield in their first match and had been able to field a second-choice XV against Spain and Uruguay before travelling to Paris for a full week of quality preparation.

'I spoke to Nick Mallett, then their head coach, some time later,' said Johnson, 'and he said that once they had beaten the Scots they spent the next three weeks preparing for us. Their squad players had all had a good run-out and they were mentally and physically fresh, whereas guys like myself and Lawrence had started every game and we were all knackered.'

Woodward had looked at the tapes of England's pool game against the All Blacks and decided that Grayson should wear the No.10 shirt. It was a controversial call, but after Wilkinson's average performance against New Zealand, Woodward was probably damned if he did, damned if he didn't when it came to fly-half selection. But it wasn't the England No.10 who made the headlines in that game.

Nick Mallett, with his fresh, powerful squad, had got his tactics spot-on. The Springboks forwards nullified their opponents in the set-piece and at the breakdown, securing quick clean ball for their scrum-half, Joost van der Westhuizen. He in turn fed his fly-half, Jannie de Beer, who boomed long touch-finders into England's territory if play was anywhere near the South African try-line. And when the Springboks moved into England's half, de Beer retreated deep into the pocket behind the ruck and fired off drop-goal after drop-goal. The accuracy and distance of his kicking were remarkable. He said in the aftermath that he had felt touched by God that day – and his kicking really did have an otherworldly feel to it. He just didn't ever look like missing.

'His kicks were going over from miles out and we just couldn't get pressure on him to try and affect his accuracy,' said Johnson.

'You could tell they had worked it out,' said Dallaglio. 'England defend well, so let's set up drop-goal chances. What really annoyed me was the fact that none of us could get near de Beer, who sat so far back in the pocket that he was untouchable.'

'Once they nosed ahead we had nothing left,' said Johnson. 'And although we fought as hard as we could, we just weren't able to come back.'

While agreeing that de Beer's drop-goals were decisive in securing the result, Will Greenwood was more analytical in his appraisal of the difference between the teams. 'South Africa were just bigger and better than us,' said the centre. 'De Beer's goals were no more than a statistical blip diverting attention from the plain fact that we were well beaten on the day.'

'Clive must have thought he was out of a job,' said Richard Hill. 'He had asked to be judged on the World Cup and we had fallen short of England's performances in 1991, when they reached the final, and 1995, when they got to the last four. Clive, though, was adamant he could still do something with us. It would have been very easy for the Rugby Football Union to replace him, but they stuck with him and it proved the right move. It gave the team stability and gave us the chance to develop as a group.'

'You learn from experiences like that,' said Dallaglio, 'and over the following seasons, Clive never let us forget how we felt on the journey home from Paris. Any booklet he produced for us carried photos of us at the end of that game and there was one wonderful shot of Backy crouching down on all fours, utterly distraught... Another photo showed Johnno and I looking hopelessly over our shoulders at a de Beer drop-goal as it flew between the posts. Clive touched a raw nerve and when he saw us wince with pain, he touched it again and again.'

Clive Woodward in action for England during the tour of Argentina, June 1981. *Getty Images*

Above left: Earle Kirton, the former All Black fly-half who became Woodward's Harlequins coach. He encouraged Woodward to attack from anywhere on the field.

Above right: Jim Greenwood. 'He was an amazing, amazing man,' recalled Woodward. 'A pure genius. I learned so much from him – not just in terms of technique but in the philosophy of how to play and how to enjoy the game to its fullest.'

Left: Chalkie White holds the JPS Cup with his Leicester players in May 1981. 'Chalkie was a great guy to talk to,' said Woodward. 'He was always ready to listen to ideas that you might have. He might disagree with them, he might argue with you over opinions or points, but he would always listen. From a player's point of view, that kind of open rapport with a coach is hugely important.' *Getty Images*

Left: Alan Jones. The Wallaby coach loved to think outside the box and was arguably the first rugby coach to introduce business principles to the sporting environment – an approach that would prove inspirational to Clive Woodward. *Getty Images*

Above: England unveil their new coach. From left to right: Roger Uttley, Bill Beaumont, Clive Woodward, Frank Cotton and John Mitchell. "When I started in September 1997, I wouldn't say it was through default as such, but it kind of just happened out of leftfield. And you just start. It's like running a small business, you're just in it and you're flying by the seat of your pants. You think you're doing all the right things but you don't really know – you're just doing it." *Getty Images*

Left: A new captain and a new era. Lawrence Dallaglio leads his team out to face Australia at Twicken- ham in the autumn of 1997 in Clive Woodward's first match in charge. *FotoSport*

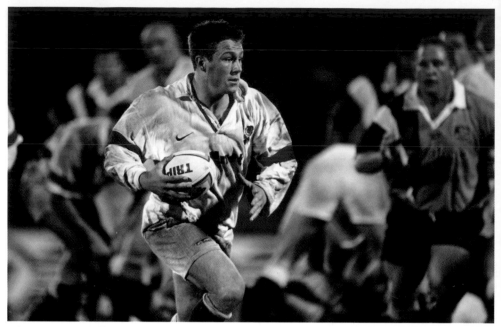

Above: Jonny Wilkinson in action against Australia on the 1998 Tour of Hell. Although he was devastated by the results, the tour would have a huge impact on him. 'I make a promise to myself – I am never going to feel this way again. I'm never going to feel so helpless, never going to feel so second-rate, never going to allow myself to feel as unvalued as that. Never. The day we were defeated 76–0 is one of the worst and most important days of my life.' *Getty Images*

Below: Returning to Twickenham after the Tour of Hell and with their front-line players returned to the starting line-up, England turn the tables on South Africa to win 13–7. *Getty Images*

Left: Jonah Lomu repeats his 1995 World Cup demolition of England with another brutal performance in the 1999 World Cup group game that consigned England to a quarter-final play-off game and the prospect of facing South Africa in the quarter-final. *FotoSport*

Below: Jannie de Beer kicks one of his five drop-goals that sent England out of the 1999 World Cup. 'You learn from experiences like that,' said Dallaglio, 'and over the following seasons, Clive never let us forget how we felt on the journey home from Paris… He touched a raw nerve and when he saw us wince with pain, he touched it again and again.' *Getty Images*

Above: The moment many have marked as the true turning point in England's fortunes during the Woodward years: the team celebrate beating South Africa in Pretoria in the summer of 2000. 'We had come to South Africa and drawn the Test series 1–1 but we all knew we should have won it 2–0,' said Dallaglio. 'That tour convinced us all that Clive was the right man… We felt like we were part of an elite group.' *Getty Images*

Below: It takes twenty seconds to score. With the clock ticking deep into injury time against the Wallabies at Twickenham in November 2000, Iain Balshaw chips to the corner and Dan Luger gains enough downward pressure to score the winning try. *Getty Images*

Above: Austin Healey celebrates scoring against Italy at Twickenham. England dominated in the spring of 2001 before the foot-and-mouth outbreak delayed the completion of the Six Nations until the autumn. 'You'd wake up on a Saturday morning and no matter who you were playing, you were just so excited about the game,' said Woodward. 'It was real Jim Greenwood stuff, because you just knew your team was going to go out and play; you just knew.' *FotoSport*

Below: Jason Robinson shows the Twickenham crowd just how electric he is after coming off the bench against Scotland in 2001. 'There was a bit of negativity around Robinson when we brought him across from rugby league,' recalled Woodward. 'But after a couple of games you had about four hundred people sitting around you shouting, 'Bring on Robinson! Get Robinson on!' *Getty Images*

Above: Jonny Wilkinson was hounded throughout the 2002 Six Nations clash with France by Serge Betsen, which cost England yet another Grand Slam. When England met France the following year, they would always ensure that the pressure on Wilkinson was eased by having a second playmaker alongside him in the midfield. *Getty Images*

Below: Ben Cohen makes a break against New Zealand at Twickenham in November 2002 and flies in to score as England go on to record a famous 31–28 victory. *Getty Images*

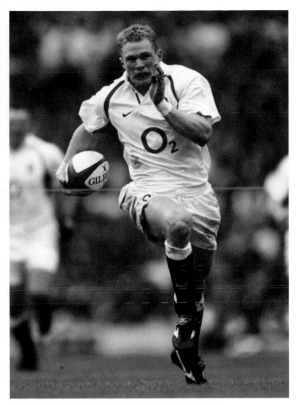

Left: Josh Lewsey returns to the England fold in dramatic fashion against Italy at Twickenham in the 2003 Six Nations and shakes up the back-three options available to Woodward just months before the World Cup. *FotoSport*

Below: Jonny Wilkinson hammers Justin Bishop during the 2003 Grand Slam decider. 'Jonny Wilkinson was magnificent,' said Greenwood of his fly-half's performance. 'A man who leaves nothing to chance, he was awe-inspiring that day. We had our tactical differences, but after that match I vowed to always back him up. If he was willing to put that much effort in for a team then the rest didn't matter.' *FotoSport*

Above: After five heart-wrenchingly close attempts, Woodward finally achieved his first Grand Slam as a coach. 'Had we lost this game the ramifications would have been huge,' he said in the aftermath of the match. 'People would have said again that this is a team that cannot win the big games. If we hadn't nailed this one, it would have been tough to recover and it would have made the months going into the World Cup even harder. We responded with a colossal performance.' *Getty Images*

Below: The brains trust. Woodward, Dave Alred, Phil Larder and Andy Robinson with the Six Nations trophy. *Getty Images*

Above: Captain fantastic. Martin Johnson powers into space against the All Blacks in Wellington in the summer of 2003 as England record a famous win against the odds, playing with just thirteen men at one stage of the game. *Getty Images*

Below: Will Greenwood, the man Woodward described as 'the best player I have ever seen play in the centre for England', scores in the crucial pool game against South Africa at the 2003 World Cup. With all his troubles at home it was a remarkable performance. 'If you watch the replays you can see a smile on my face,' said Greenwood, 'because for a short time rugby had pushed the worry from my mind. There are not many jobs you can say that about.' *Getty Images*

Above: Nature versus nature? Manu Samoa perform the Siva Tau before their World Cup pool game against England. *Getty Images*

Below: 'Too old?' Neil Back asked when questioned about the Dad's Army moniker. 'You're either good enough or you're not. If people say you're not good enough, then fair enough. But too old? That doesn't mean anything.' He proves his point as part of a magnificent England performance against France in the semi-final of the World Cup. *FotoSport*

Left: After having suffered uncharacteristic inconsistency with his kicking early in the World Cup, Wilkinson was deadly in front of goal in the semi-final. He kicked five penalties and three drop-goals (two of which he struck with his weaker right foot) to collect all of England's twenty-seven points and consign France to a third-place place play-off match against the All Blacks. *FotoSport*

Below: Just as he had done in the opening minutes of the First Test for the Lions in 2001, Robinson tore down the left-hand touchline without a finger being laid on him to score against Australia in the final. *FotoSport*

Above: Matt Dawson delivers the ball to Wilkinson for his drop-goal attempt. 'Dawson was my number one scrum-half – primarily because of his brain,' said Woodward. 'The way I saw it, this was the biggest pressure moment of all our lives, why would I take off Dawson for someone who I don't think would handle the pressure as well?' *Getty Images*

Left: The kick that reverberated around the world. *Getty Images*

Above: Will Greenwood collapses with joy at the final whistle. *Getty Images*

Below: England's finest ever back-row combination, the Holy Trinity of Neil Back, Lawrence Dallaglio and Richard Hill, celebrate reaching the promised land. *FotoSport*

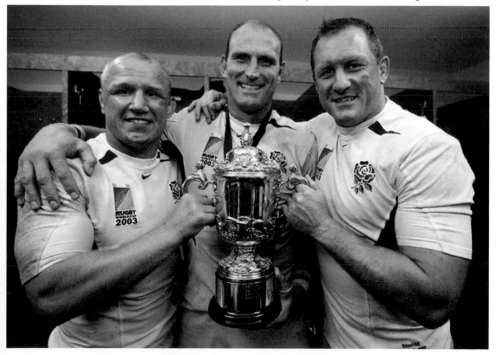

Above: World Champions. *FotoSport*

Left: The players take part in an open-top bus parade through the streets of London. The RFU estimated that some 20,000 spectators might turn up to watch the team show off the World Cup but more than 750,000 people came out to celebrate. *FotoSport*

SIX

THE ANATOMY OF BUILDING A WORLD-CLASS TEAM

'Some people dream of success… others stay awake to achieve it.'
Anonymous

DESPITE ALL HIS efforts to the contrary, Woodward confessed, in his review of the World Cup to the RFU management board, that the team were still working in a 'fingers-crossed environment'. He had begun a process in 1997 to eradicate the 'what ifs' of sport as much as he could so that the team could exist in an environment of no excuses. But the process was not finished and there was still a lot more that could be done. The structure of the tournament had not helped – after the loss to New Zealand they had been set on a path from where victory in the tournament would have been nigh on impossible – but he accepted that this was true for every team involved. What he didn't want to accept was that, despite their preparation, the team could not cope under the most severe pressure. He laid out his recommendations for moving the team forward, which included requests for the RFU to negotiate with the clubs for greater access to the players and with the IRB over the structure of the World Cup and the scheduling of fixtures.

'The 44–21 World Cup quarter-final loss to South Africa in 1999 was my most significant defeat as England coach,' wrote Woodward in the *Daily Mail* some fourteen years later. 'We were pummelled. After that loss I compiled a bullet-point plan of how to create success from setbacks. Go home, shut the door and get it out of your system. There were no positives, you got smashed. Grieve for forty-eight hours – then come out fighting. When things go well you credit everybody else. When things go wrong the only person you look at is yourself. This is a "mirror moment". Take full responsibility, make sure everything you do is geared towards winning the next Test match and nothing else should be in your head. Look at the personnel around you – players, coaching staff and back-room staff. Do not be scared to admit you should have done things differently. Make tough calls and make them quickly. Analyse every key decision, not just during the eighty minutes but during the week. This is the perfect time to see who really fronts up to problems and who hides. Do not use age as an excuse as you select the team. Don't forget perspective. Concentrate on successes, not failure, and go back to what made you a good team – while realising you must reach another level to win at the very top.'

He delivered a twenty-six-page report to the board and it was largely well received – but not universally so. Just a few days later the report was leaked to a national newspaper and Woodward's efforts to push the organisation forward were picked apart as nothing more than excuses for the team's disappointing campaign. For several weeks the calls for his head were intense.

But the RFU held fire. Woodward was contracted until the end of the summer of 2000. While they made no promises to extend his contract beyond that, they were throwing him a lifeline. He had the 2000 Six Nations and a summer tour to South Africa to convince them that he was the man to guide the team through to the 2003 World Cup. He was backed by Fran Cotton, who was now running the Club England organisation within the RFU, Francis Baron, who understood that the success of the national team was the most important element for the success of the RFU as an organisation and who bought into Woodward's philosophy entirely, and by the players themselves, who publicly endorsed his continued involvement.

The target for 2003 was to arrive at the tournament with the best prepared group of players, as the No.1-ranked side in the world, and as favourites to lift the trophy. The four-year cycle before the next World Cup would be focused on achieving exactly that status.

After the humiliating defeat in the quarter-final, the RFU were desperate for the situation not to repeat itself and were willing to listen to Woodward's demands for change – and to action many of his plans.

In the middle of December, Woodward announced the move from England's traditional base at the Petersham Hotel in Richmond to Pennyhill Park in Bagshot, Surrey. Pennyhill Park was just thirty minutes from Twickenham but it seemed like a world away. Set in 130 acres of immaculate estate land, the five-star ivy-covered hotel was a truly exclusive location. On entering the grounds, a long driveway snakes up to the hotel, passing a golf course to the right, while off to the left a purpose-built rugby ground had been constructed for England's use.

The previously established pattern for a Test week would see the team arrive on a Tuesday and be based at the Petersham, because it was relatively close to Twickenham. But as there were no training facilities at the hotel they would be bussed to some nearby pitches owned by the Bank of England and ferried back and forth throughout the day for training, meals, meetings and further training sessions. All the travelling to and fro was a waste of valuable time – especially when, because of the structure of professional rugby in England, the players spent such limited periods in the national set-up. They were also only allowed on the pitch at Twickenham the afternoon before a Test match for a light run-through. All this had to change.

The move to Pennyhill Park ensured that the logistics of training days and Test match weeks ran much more smoothly and with fewer distractions.

Every player was assigned his own room and Humphrey Walters had worked closely with Woodward on the finer details. The players had their name on their door, pictures of them in action for England adorned the walls and they were always allocated the same room so that there was a sense of familiarity whenever they came into camp.

The Pecorelli family, who owned the hotel, were incredibly open to the team's demands. Not only did they upgrade their gym facilities, but they converted a large lawn into a full-scale rugby pitch so that the players had only a three-minute walk from the hotel to the pitch. The larger hotel allowed for a much bigger war room and because there was no travelling between the training ground and their accommodation as had been the case at the Petersham Hotel, the team were able to keep all their kit and training equipment permanently set up in one place.

Jason Leonard, who was by now the longest serving member of the squad, said at the time, 'Everything is laid on, everything is beautifully organised, down to the last detail. But what that creates is a no-excuses environment. Before in England teams, people might say that the beds were uncomfortable or the food didn't agree with them or that their back was playing up. All that has gone. The back-up and the coaching and the medical assessments and treatment are spot on. The perks are nice but if you don't perform, you are out.'

Other changes were also made. A deal with a bus company was struck so that the team had their own luxury coach emblazoned with the England red rose. They would take this bus to and from Twickenham and would even bring it over to France with them so that they could arrive at Stade de France in it – making a statement as to who they were and the lengths that they would go to to demonstrate their professionalism.

Woodward conducted a review of his first two years in charge, analysing every aspect from off-field preparation to the team's performances on it. Despite losing in the World Cup to South Africa's cold and calculated tactic of scoring drop-goal after drop-goal, and discovering a new resolve that winning really was all that the team would be remembered for, he did not abandon his lifelong passion for attacking rugby and his desire to inspire the nation with their style of play. The problem had been that with such a short period of time with the players he and Brian Ashton had had very little opportunity to develop the England attack in the way that a club coach could. When they had encouraged the backline to stand flatter, edging towards Woodward's own ideal for a completely flat backline, they had caused teams all manner of problems – as they had done against New Zealand in the second Test in the autumn of 1997. 'It was a milestone game for Clive,' said Will Greenwood of that New Zealand Test, 'not just in terms of the result and the self-belief it engendered, but also because he tried a different game plan in which Paul Grayson and myself played flat rather than very deep like England midfields in the past. The idea was to get us to probe and test the opposition from close quarters, and it seemed to work very well.'

A major issue – which would not be resolved during his tenure – was that his midfield players all lacked out-and-out pace. But they were clever footballers, were strong in contact and could all play an offloading game. Dave Reddin could, and would, work on their speed and footwork, but he wouldn't be able to transform them into Olympic-standard sprinters. This didn't necessarily preclude the players from playing a flat backline attack because the key to its success was based on handling skills, angles of running, dummy runners and off-loading. But if they didn't also possess the ability to burst with real speed on to the ball or accelerate swiftly from a standing start, then defences would, in time, work them out and stifle their attacking play.

So a hybrid attacking system would have to be conceived, something that conjured some elements of an Ella-inspired flat attack and a more traditional staggered backline. Ashton got down to work.

*

England's first match of the 2000 Six Nations saw them face Ireland at Twickenham. The game featured debuts for centre Mike Tindall and wing Ben Cohen, two hugely powerful young players who would go on to become almost permanent fixtures in the team over the next few years.

It was a performance that exorcised many of the World Cup ghosts, a physically dominant, brilliantly creative and free-flowing annihilation. The team scored tries through Tindall and two each for Cohen on one wing and Austin Healey on the other to record a 50–18 victory.

'Clive approached the 2000 Six Nations with a nothing-to-lose attitude,' said Matt Dawson, 'taking risks and making all the selections he really wanted to make. His game plan combined razor-sharp attack with rock-solid defence... We came into the Six Nations as probably the fittest side in the world. And we played like it. We were relentless. Speaking to the Irish boys afterwards it was obvious they were very down, but they had to admit they had been run ragged because we attacked them from every area of the pitch.'

What was also significant in that game was Mike Catt's performance. It was his fortieth cap but one of his few forays into the centre, having also played at fly-half, full-back and wing. But placed as a second playmaker beside Wilkinson, he was a revelation. His handling skills, speed and kicking game not only allowed for a new attacking dimension in the midfield and offered another creative option in broken play, but also gave Wilkinson an ally outside him – another player who could call plays, tell him where to kick or to shoulder the responsibility for both should Wilkinson find himself under pressure. It was a partnership that would bear considerable fruit over the coming years.

From an analysis point of view, one might have thought that there would be little of real significance to look at following such a decisive win: the eighteen points conceded, perhaps; poor discipline in range of their own posts; handling errors or mistakes made at set-pieces. But what Tony Biscombe picked up when he watched the tape was more abstract – it was a worrying trend that he had been aware of for several matches.

Noticeably against the All Blacks and Springboks during the World Cup and again against Ireland, England had started strongly for the opening quarter and built up an early lead. As both teams settled into the first half, the game would even out – as could be expected against top opposition. But England tended to have a lull in concentration and effort immediately after half-time, which would often last through the third quarter of the match, before they came back into the game and attempted a late fight back.

'I watched Pete Sampras playing at Wimbledon and he changed his shirt on court,' Humphrey Walters told Alison Kervin. 'And, bloody hell, he suddenly looked fresh as a daisy. I watched and realised that Sampras almost always picked the moment when his opponent thought he was about to win.'

Walters discussed this with Woodward and they decided to give the tactic a try at half-time. They called it 'the reset' and psychologically it gave the players a shift in focus. They completely reworked the half-time routine so that the change of shirt became a catalyst for what they would term 'Second Half Thinking'. As soon as the referee blew for half-time, Woodward wanted his team to run off to the tunnel – preferably leaving the field ahead of the opposition. When they entered the changing room he wanted absolute silence for two minutes while the players reflected on the first half while removing their shirts, towelling off and then pulling on fresh shirts. The coaches would then give their feedback on the first half and issue their instructions for the second while the players took on food and fluids. The captain would then have his say and there would be a further two minutes of silence as the players focused on the second half, mentally resetting the scoreboard in their heads to 0–0 and preparing themselves to begin the second half as they had begun the first.

They first instigated the practice at Stade de France and the change in shirts and attitude had as powerful a psychological impact on the French as it had on the England players. Just as with Sampras, England suddenly looked and seemed fresh and when the whistle blew they tore into Les Bleus. France, who had dismantled the All Blacks in the semi-final of the 1999 World Cup in one of the greatest matches ever played, before losing to Australia in the final, were fielding one of their largest ever packs of forwards – which is really saying something. But England cleverly shifted the gargantuan French eight around the field, smashing into them with their flat midfield, looking to set a platform for the forwards or to offload to the outside backs and thereby pressurise the home team into conceding penalties. During the match, Wilkinson performed one of the most iconic tackles in the game's history when he smashed France's huge winger Émile Ntamack, who accelerated on to the ball and then crashed into Wilkinson. England's fearless fly-half lifted the huge man off his feet, spun him in the air and buried him back into the turf. It was a defining moment in Wilkinson's career. If the rugby world hadn't yet woken up to Wilkinson's talents, it did now. And in the same moment it redefined what was expected of fly-halves in the professional game; no longer were No.10s expected just to create – they were now expected to destroy.

Wilkinson kicked five penalties and, even though they were reduced to just thirteen men at one stage when both Austin Healey and second-row Simon Shaw were sin-binned, they clung on to record a famous 15–9 win.

'It was a slim margin,' said Woodward. 'Just one score by the French, one intercept try, was all it would have taken to reverse the result… If we had lost that game I have no doubt I would not have been allowed to carry on even if I wanted to.'

Next they faced Wales at Twickenham. The first half was a tight affair with England hooker Phil Greening's score all that separated the sides at half-time. But aided by their new half-time routine, England cut loose in the second period, scoring tries through Ben Cohen and one apiece for the marauding back-row trio of Dallaglio, Hill and Back to win 46–12.

The fourth game of the championship saw them travel to Rome to play the new boys of the tournament, Italy. The Azzurri had shocked defending champions Scotland in the first round and there was a carnival atmosphere in the Eternal City. But England spoiled the home team's party with a 59–12 win, thanks to a hat-trick from Austin Healey, two tries each from Ben Cohen and Matt Dawson and a penalty try.

And so it was to Edinburgh for the final game of the tournament – with a Grand Slam once again on the table.

After a relatively mild start to the year, the heavens had opened and a chill wind swept across the east coast of Scotland as the plane carrying the team touched down at Edinburgh airport. For twenty-four hours the rain fell, covering the city in a thick, swirling miasma. In the hours before kick-off the rain at last relented and watery sunlight filled the cavernous bowl of Murrayfield. But by two o'clock, just as the anthems were drawing to a close, the clouds had gathered once more, pressing in over the Firth of Forth and rolling out over the city, bringing with them a light but persistent drizzle that set in over Murrayfield towards the end of the first half. By the the second half that drizzle had developed into a downpour. Very soon it became a deluge. Despite conceding a try off the back of a scrum to Lawrence Dallaglio, Scotland were succeeding in their tactics to stifle quick English ball and slow their backs' attack at its source. England had thrown the ball around at will in their previous matches but the rain and a determined Scottish defence were hindering their attack – and to make matters worse, they began to struggle at the line-out.

Scotland's stand-off, Duncan Hodge, was keeping his side in the game with his goal-kicking – and it was he who sealed the game late on when he dived over the line after a series of pick-and-go drives from the forwards. His conversion made the score 19–13 and the Calcutta Cup was in Scottish hands for the first time in a decade.

For the second consecutive year, England had stumbled at the final hurdle. They had looked to play too much rugby in the wrong areas of the field and, despite the appalling conditions in Edinburgh, they had stuck to trying to play an expansive handling game, while the Scots had adapted their tactics perfectly to the weather.

Just as they had done against Wales in 1999, the team played desperation rugby in the final minutes as they chased the winning score. But it had been largely headless stuff – wild passes, lone running, hit and hope tactics rather than composed and methodical play that would build towards the score.

It was not a question of ability. It was a question of mental strength and composure. The lessons of the Marines echoed all around the video analysis suite at Pennyhill Park.

As further proof of the lengths that Woodward would go to to develop and hone a winning culture for his team, he flew to Israel to meet a man named Yehuda Shinar, who had developed a computer program for identifying leadership characteristics in individuals and testing their ability to perform in high-pressure situations – and subsequently training them to do just that.

Many of the players were sceptical – and some even outwardly critical – of the program. 'It was this ridiculous Mossad thing,' said Martin Johnson. 'All the young guys who played computer games were amazing at it, the older guys like me were rubbish. We couldn't believe it when Clive said he would base Test match selection on how we did in it.' But one principle of Shinar's that was effectively adopted was 'Correctly Thinking Under Pressure'. This was adapted by Woodward first to 'Thinking Correctly Under Pressure' and from there shortened to T-CUP. It became an acronym that would be repeated time after time at team meetings, video analysis sessions and during matches themselves – a reminder of moments when the team had buckled under pressure in the past, a keyword that focused their thoughts and altered their mindsets so that they could force an element of control over proceedings and decide with clarity the best course of action for the situation they were in – be they attacking or defending. 'It is the ability to control aggression, to know when to push the referee, when to slow the ball down or have your prop fake an injury,' said Will Greenwood. 'It is knowing when to take the points, play for territory or unleash the blitz. It is a catch-all phrase that sums up a player's ability to stay cool and do the right thing. In short, it is knowing how to win.'

*

In total, eight new players had been handed Test debuts during the Six Nations. The summer tour would provide an opportunity to hand out some more and to bed the new players into the Test environment. It was also the final spin of the dice for Woodward to convince the RFU that he was deserving of a contract extension to the 2003 World Cup.

At the conclusion of the Six Nations, John Mitchell returned to his native New Zealand and Woodward moved swiftly to appoint his old partner from his England Under-21 and Bath days, Andy Robinson.

'Andy was the last piece in the jigsaw in creating a group of world-class coaches in all areas of the game,' said Woodward. 'Andy is the most competitive person I have ever met. Once he was on board, I believed winning the World Cup was a very real possibility. His coaching ability is significantly ahead of any other coach working in the sport, but what made him such an important person within our team was his ability to transfer this expertise to all the players.'

Also added to the back-room team was Nathan Martin, a former Marine Woodward had met during the pre-World Cup training camps in 1999. Martin assumed the role as England's first full-time team manager.

The players flew to South Africa in business class and Woodward made it clear that their wives and girlfriends were welcome to come on tour if they wished. He wanted his players to be as comfortable as possible and for there to be no excuses for them not to perform when it came to the business-end of their jobs.

It was a five-match tour with midweek games against Western Transvaal Leopards, Griqualand West, Gauteng Falcons and two Tests against the Springboks – at Loftus Versfeld in Pretoria and in Bloemfontein. Martin Johnson was back to lead the side after missing the Six Nations through injury.

It had been a long season by that stage – from the tour to Australia the previous summer to the World Cup training camps and warm-up games, the tournament itself, club league and cup games, the Six Nations and then the conclusion to the club season. The last thing that the players needed was another Couran Cove-style hard slog through South Africa as they had experienced in Australia a year earlier. Woodward and Reddin appreciated this and tailored their training loads accordingly. They knew that the only chance they had for a successful tour was to keep their players fresh and injury-free, so they backed off from intense training and instead concentrated on improving the analysis of their performances and the strengths and weaknesses of their opposition. They focused on making sure the players believed that they could win in South Africa and they tapped into the experience of the Lions players who had been there and done just that in 1997.

'You can really feel the change around the England team on our summer tour to South Africa,' wrote Wilkinson in *Jonny*. 'Everything feels so professional – where we are training, how we are training. Clive wants to lead change in international rugby, rather than waiting and following. We are not copying anyone. The desire now is to set the pace.'

The team based themselves at the five-star Westcliff Hotel in Johannesburg for the duration of the tour to reduce the disruption of constantly moving hotels, and flew in and out from there for their matches. Three months before the tour, Dave Reddin was sent on a recce of the hotel to ensure that the facilities were up to scratch. Nothing was going to be left to chance. 'The hotel is ideal,' said Wilkinson. 'But the point is that this is no longer about touring. It's about winning.'

They won their first midweek game 52–22 to get the tour off to a positive start and move on from the defeat to Scotland.

Wilkinson had to withdraw from the side on the morning of the first Test after suffering food poisoning and was replaced at fly-half by Austin Healey. Tim Stimpson, who had been brought in on the wing after Healey's change of position, was cruelly denied a try by the video referee and a late penalty sealed the match 18–13 to South Africa. 'It was pretty disappointing,' said Johnson. 'But given what had happened in the World Cup and the fact that we were playing in such a hotbed like Pretoria, it was a good performance.'

Dallaglio also made a startling discovery after the match. He left an England dressing room of disappointed and frustrated players who felt disgusted at themselves for letting such a golden opportunity to record a win in the southern hemisphere pass them by. Dallaglio wandered down the corridor to the South African changing room to swap shirts with his opposite number, Andre Vos. The sight that greeted him was not what he had expected. 'There were bodies everywhere,' he recalled, 'bandages being taken off, ice-packs on knees and heads, players having wounds checked and everyone too shattered to talk… They were completely gone whereas I felt we still had 20 to 30 per cent of our energy left. At that moment I knew we would take these guys the following week. I also knew that in their bruised and smashed state, they now respected us. With that thought came the certainty that we were no longer the old England.'

During the week the second-string side ran out 55–16 winners against Griqualand West before the squad flew up to Bloemfontein for the second Test.

The first team squad had enjoyed a light week, with a night out together on the Sunday after the first Test and two rest days before beginning their preparation for the second Test. They arrived in Bloemfontein refreshed and ready for another brutal encounter.

Before the first Test, Woodward and Tony Biscombe had taken Wilkinson aside. They sat in the war room at the Westcliff Hotel and picked over England's attack in the opposition 22 when the defensive line was set and well organised. It was Wilkinson's mindset to always go for the try, to keep working through the phases until a chink emerged in the defence.

'But statistically, that's the wrong decision,' said Woodward.

'Why?' asked Wilkinson.

'Look,' said Woodward, and Biscombe started a montage of England attacks that ended with a dropped ball, a turnover from the defence, a penalty given away by England or the ball going out of play.

'Every time the opposition keep us out, it's a victory to them. Their chests puff out, their shoulders square, they're jacked up on adrenaline, patting each other on the back. Their team spirit rises. And what happens to us? We grow more desperate. The next time we're down there we feel we have to score a try, we have to prove we can do it, we feel we have to make up for our previous failure to score.' Up flashed the final moments from the Grand Slam decider against Wales and Scotland. 'There is no composure,' continued Woodward. 'We are chasing the game rather than controlling it.'

A new montage popped up. Jannie de Beer's five drop-goals against England at the World Cup; Stephen Larkham's extra-time winning drop-goal against South Africa in one World Cup semi-final; Christophe Lamaison's two drop-goals against New Zealand in the other that put them ahead against the All Blacks; finally, Jeremy Guscott's winning drop-goal against South Africa for the Lions in 1997.

'If we come up against a brick wall, I don't even want you to think about it,' said Woodward. 'I want you to take the drop-goal. I want us to keep the scoreboard ticking over as much as we can. Every time we are down in the opposition 22, I want us leaving with points. Preferably tries, but if that's not going to happen, I want three points. That's a victory for us.' He rewound the tape to a moment after de Beer's fourth drop-goal and paused it. The camera frame was frozen on the dejected faces of the England defence as they watched the ball sailing between the uprights. 'And that's what we want to do to them. And the more we do it, the more relentless we are at scoring, the more they will desperately try to stop us – which will lead to them giving away penalties or opening up gaps in their defence. Teams will fear us.'

Wilkinson's withdrawal from the team before the first Test meant that he hadn't had the chance to put Woodward's plan into action. But he had locked it in his memory for the second Test.

The match was fast and furious and the atmosphere at the ground in Bloemfontein was as hostile as it was in Pretoria.

'And then it happens,' recalls Wilkinson. 'I take the ball one way to attack and then, as if a lightbulb's suddenly flicked on in my head, I stop. I'm right in front of the posts, not far from the 22. I take the drop-goal. It flies through the posts.'

Wilkinson claimed all of England's points in a famous 27–22 win.

'Without doubt, it was a turning point in the development of the team,' said Dallaglio. 'We had come to South Africa and drawn the Test series 1–1 but we all knew we should have won it 2–0… That tour convinced us all that Clive was the right man. For one thing, his attention to detail meant that the logistics of the three-week tour could not have been better. We felt like we were part of an elite group and had someone at the top who wasn't going to be messed around.'

The last midweek game was against Gauteng Falcons, which was also won to complete a record of four wins out of five.

The tour had been a huge success, but Woodward and his back-room staff had no intention of resting on their laurels. Just a few weeks after their return from Johannesburg, they were on a flight across the Atlantic for a group study of the methods employed by the University of Colorado and the Denver Broncos. After this, they travelled to Agen in France to observe the club for four days at their pre-season base in the Pyrenees. 'When I first went to Denver I came back with a load of ideas and hugely excited by what I had seen,' said Woodward. 'When I went back with Andy Robinson, Brian Ashton, Phil Larder, Dave Reddin and Dave Alred, I felt reassured that what we were doing was right. When I first went I was there just to observe and pick up what I could, but when we went back there was a genuine exchange of views between the coaches on both sides. It was tremendous. But what was really interesting, however, was that in many ways I was really disappointed by that second visit – because nothing had changed. They were still doing the same training drills, the same practices. The other guys really enjoyed it because they hadn't seen it before, but when I compared it to what we had done in that time it was astonishing the changes we had made. I remember sitting there thinking, *Wow, we're now as good as you guys. In two years we've caught up with you and in many ways we're now doing things better than you* – in terms of the staff we were employing, the attitudes we had, the way we were always thinking and looking to evolve and improve what we were doing. And that became a mantra that we developed – that we wanted people to be talking about us on the world stage, that we wanted people asking to come to see *us*.'

Following this, Woodward made an excursion to Paris on his own to meet the France coach, Bernard Laporte. 'Rugby nations working together should not be unthinkable,' wrote Woodward in a 2013 article for the *Daily Mail*. 'We were enemies in the eyes of the media and our teams but in private we spoke often and got on well. I went to see him because I wanted to start having regular training sessions with the French. I made it clear that if England were not to win the World Cup in 2003 then I wanted a northern hemisphere team to win it. New ideas are always a challenge, so I spoke with a few of my players. They did not jump up and down with joy at the prospect but also nobody said "no".

'Bernard was supportive of the idea, but he could not get the support of his players for something so radical. He eventually called me saying it would be too difficult logistically! For me it was just common sense. Can you imagine the scrummaging, the defensive and attacking sessions – or the fitness competition on show in the gym?

'I wanted to create an intensity in training that was greater than any Test match. Most importantly, training with the French would have left the southern hemisphere teams wondering what we were doing. If someone told me New Zealand and Australia were training together ahead of the World Cup, it would just reinforce my feeling that they were once again leaving nothing to chance and their collective mindset was ahead of their northern rivals.'

*

As the players and management gathered at the beginning of the 2000–01 season, they were all well aware of how gruelling the next two years would be. There was an autumn series, the 2001 Six Nations, a Lions tour to Australia for those selected, a tour to North America for the remainder of the England squad, another autumn series and then the 2002 Six Nations, with intense club matches filling the spaces in between.

The congestion of fixtures brought into sharp focus what the players were about to put their bodies through for club and country – and the financial remuneration they would receive for doing so. At the time the players received £6,000 a match when they represented England. Considering the money that was pouring into the RFU coffers through TV rights, sponsorship, ticket sales, corporate hospitality and replica kit sales there was a strong feeling that those the circus revolved around weren't getting their fair share. It was decided by the playing group that three senior players – Martin Johnson, Lawrence Dallaglio and Matt Dawson – would represent their collective interests in negotiations with the RFU.

'We were being paid less than 5 per cent of the turnover,' said Matt Dawson. 'All we wanted was fair recompense. We didn't want to be like Premiership footballers earning millions of pounds a year and bankrupting the sport, but neither were we prepared to undervalue ourselves when we have probably not got even ten years at the top.'

The players wanted a new deal with two-thirds of a revised match fee guaranteed to them, with the final third paid as a bonus based on the result. The RFU wanted it staggered in reverse – but the players contested that any man who played for England would play his heart out no matter what and in a game that could be decided by the finest margins, it was wrong for the payments to be weighted in that manner.

As well as match fees the players argued that the image rights of the players, which had been sold by the RFU to its sponsors, were not the RFU's to sell. There was no contract in place assigning the RFU that right, so the players demanded compensation.

Added to this was compensation for other players in the extended squad who committed time and effort at training weeks but didn't make the Test match twenty-two. 'You would have thirty players in the England squad in the week of an international but by Saturday afternoon, the squad was reduced to twenty-two,' said Dallaglio. 'The eight people left out had to cope with the disappointment of not making the match-day twenty-two and they weren't getting anything for their time with the squad. We argued that they had to be paid.'

The negotiations lasted throughout the summer and into the autumn and had still not been settled by the time of the first fixture of the autumn series, against Australia, which was then followed by matches against Argentina and South Africa.

Australia, the world champions, arrived in London amid much fanfare. After the win against South Africa in Bloemfontein the question that was hanging in the air was whether England possessed the consistency to beat the southern hemisphere giants on a regular basis, or whether they could manage only one-off triumphs.

A month before the autumn series kicked off, Ben Cohen's father was attacked outside a nightclub in Northampton. He was hospitalised but, after several weeks in intensive care, he appeared to be making a recovery. The week before the Australia match, however, he passed away. 'Clive was brilliant with

Ben,' said Austin Healey. 'He took him to one side, broke the news in the best way he could and arranged for him to go home. He told him not to worry about England – if he felt up to playing, the shirt would be waiting for him.' But Cohen couldn't muster the strength to play and withdrew from the match squad on the Thursday before the game. His place in the team was taken by Healey and the squad resolved to do everything in their power to support their stricken teammate, knowing that a win would prove a fitting tribute.

As part of the preparation for the autumn series, Tony Biscombe had analysed the statistics of England's play in the 'red zone' (the opposition's 22) and in key moments of the game (the opening ten minutes, the five minutes before and after half-time and the last ten to fifteen minutes of the match). One fascinating revelation that Biscombe made was that it took, on average, twenty seconds to score a try. In the build-up to the 2000 autumn series he showed the team a montage of tries that showed this. The point was, if England were behind going into the final minutes of a match, there was no need to panic – as they had done at Wembley and Murrayfield – because the clock was running down. They just had to be aware of their field position and their time management. If they stayed patient, they could construct a means to score. It was a theory that was to prove significant against Australia.

The game was a tight, physical affair. Australia seemed to have broken the English stranglehold when Joe Roff lanced off his wing, stepped past Austin Healey and then passed to full-back Matt Burke to score. But the game-changing moment was still to come in a final, extraordinary denouement. Late in the second half Woodward decided to make a tactical change, sending on Iain Balshaw, the twenty-one-year-old full-back/winger from Bath. Balshaw was tall and willowy in build and in possession of incredible speed. He had won his first cap against Ireland in that year's Six Nations and had been a bench player for every Test match since then. He was electrically quick and desperate to prove himself. In the short time that he was on he made a huge impression, twice breaking through the Wallaby defence, but his key contribution came eight minutes into injury time. Gathering the ball to the left of the Wallaby posts he noticed that the defensive line was completely flat and was drifting across the field to close down the attack. He had two men outside him – winger Dan Luger and further out flanker Neil Back. With the drifting defence there was no room for the attack to go anywhere but into touch if Balshaw passed the ball to Luger.

But there was space in behind. Very little, but space nevertheless. He chipped the ball over the defensive line and Luger rushed on to it, just forcing downwards pressure on the ball as it skidded over the try-line and barely moments before he himself slid into touch. The decision on whether or not it was a try was referred to the video referee who, after several minutes of examination, awarded the score. Wilkinson stepped up to take the conversion from the touchline and coolly slotted the kick to give England a 22–19 victory.

'Never once in those dramatic last few minutes did I doubt we were going to win. There was no panic,' said Wilkinson. 'To turn a game we could have won against a top side into a game we did win was an important step in our development.'

It was momentous – back-to-back victories over two of the top three sides in the world. But unfortunately the celebrations did not last long. In the week that followed, when the sole focus should have been on preparing to face Argentina, the contract negotiations with the RFU turned bitterly sour.

'Lots of people say things like, "I'd walk over broken glass to represent my country" and "I'd play for England for nothing". I understand those sentiments,' said Martin Johnson. 'But I think people forget that many of us *have* played for England for nothing. We virtually have walked over broken glass, too… The fact is we would go through all the pain and the stress for nothing again if we had to. We would do so gladly because we want to play for England, because we know it is an honour and because we recognise that we are very privileged to have been chosen to do it. But if you want us to do it for nothing, don't charge £50-£200 a ticket at Test matches, don't demand millions in TV revenue and don't look for massive sponsorship deals using us.'

The players felt that they had two options – to threaten to strike or to refuse to take part in any commercial activities, such as signing autographs, wearing sponsored kit and appearing at sponsors' dinners. In the build-up to the Australia match they informed the RFU that they would be taking the latter option. Woodward was desperately worried that their actions would cause too much of a distraction before the Australia match and told them that if they did that, he would just pick a new team of players; he convinced them to hold fire, which they did.

'After speaking with all the players and getting confirmation of their intent to strike, I asked them to leave the team hotel since they were not there to prepare for a Test match,' said Woodward. 'I also advised them that if they wanted to play for England they should be back at Pennyhill Park by 11 o'clock on Wednesday morning ready to train, or not bother coming back.'

'Clive's role in the dispute upset me a little because I felt he shouldn't have got involved,' said Dallaglio. 'He took our threat to strike personally, as if we were letting him down... Clive's interference drove a wedge between the players and the coaching staff. A lot of things were said that didn't need to be said.'

But following that win there was still no movement from Francis Baron. The players felt that they had little option but to take as drastic a measure as they could; Johnson, Dallaglio and Dawson informed the RFU that the squad intended to strike for the Argentina match.

'We all knew Johnno was a great rugby captain from the 1997 Lions tour,' said Mike Catt, 'but away from the pitch he had always come across as a quiet guy who never pushed himself to the fore in anything. All that changed with the strike, during which he was brilliant. In fact, magnificent... He never flinched. He wasn't intimidated by anyone.'

There was a stalemate for two days until, at last, the RFU relented. They didn't concede to every demand made by the players but the two parties eventually reached a compromise that they were happy with and things got back on track. Sort of. In many ways it was similar to the moratorium year that the RFU announced after the game went open in 1995. 'The moratorium year was a case of the RFU panicking and holding the floodwaters at bay,' said Jason Leonard. 'It may have seemed like a good idea at the time – to hold fire and think about things for a year – but it meant that the rest of the world and the clubs moved ahead of England. It meant that while all the world's leading nations had centrally contracted players, and had begun working on a way forward for the sport, we were all sitting around waiting to see what would happen.' The contract negotiations that led to the strike continued into the spring, by which time the Premiership clubs had signed blanket agreements with the players; with such a strong position they negotiated as a group for player release to the England set-up, which costs the RFU several million pounds a year. The RFU once again failed drastically to improve the chances of England's success as they continued to lack the control of their players that other unions around the world enjoy. The true consequences of this would be revealed only much later.

Despite the disruption to their preparation, England went on to defeat

Argentina 19–0, the team welcomed Ben Cohen back into the fold following his father's funeral, and the young wing paid tribute with a fine performance that included a try.

'I was impressed by the way Clive regained the trust of the players after the strike threat,' said Dallaglio. 'He regained lost ground by talking about the situation, and we all accepted that he genuinely believed what he was doing was the right thing… everyone seemed to realise it had been a strange, one-off situation, and should not be allowed to destroy what we were trying to achieve.'

'By the time the chapter had been concluded we, as a group of people, were a truly united force, not just on the pitch but off it,' said Catt. 'As a squad of players we had taken the action on, provoked a major scandal, and reacted to it as one… It is no coincidence England went from strength to strength after the strike.'

Refocused and with a full week of uninterrupted preparation, the team readied themselves for the Springboks and the inevitable physical onslaught of the South African team determined to avenge their defeat in Bloemfontein. But for all their efforts, the Springboks just couldn't cope with the power of the English forwards combined with the speed and attacking width of the backs – or the unerring boot of Wilkinson, who kicked six penalties and a conversion of Will Greenwood's try, which he had also helped to set up. After a huge driving maul from the England forwards, Wilkinson had received the ball on the run, shimmied to sidestep, turned his head as if readying himself to switch the ball to a late runner, but instead delicately placed the ball into the arms of Greenwood as the centre hit a flat line off him. Greenwood carved right through the South African defence and skipped past full-back Percy Montgomery to score.

'That was a moment of beauty in a fierce contest,' said Wilkinson. 'A lot of blood was spilt but I didn't think it was a dirty game – in fact, I thought it was a good one.' For all that Wilkinson may have relished the brutality of the battle, the casualty list was high by the time the game was over. Wilkinson himself had his head cut, both Richard Hill and Neil Back required stitches – the latter totalling thirty-one – and Phil Greening broke a finger. But all four men were still on the field at the final whistle to celebrate the 25–17 victory.

*

As Woodward continued to tweak and build his team, so too did he continue to shuffle the cards behind the scenes. At the beginning of 2001, Nathan Martin moved to become performance services director and his role as team manager was assumed by Louise Ramsay.

Ramsay had spent several years working for the British Olympic Association in a planning and organisational role for the Summer and Winter Olympics, including Sydney 2000. She finished working for the BOA in the spring of 2001 and shortly afterwards, driven by her interest in rugby, applied to the RFU to see if there might be an opportunity for her there. She timed her application to perfection as someone with her skill set was exactly what Woodward had been looking for – someone who understood the level of intense detail required to create and optimise an environment for elite athletes, who was prepared to work the long hours required to deliver on these requirements and who was obsessive in ensuring each was delivered on time and in the correct manner. For Woodward, Ramsay was like a gift from the heavens and helped enormously as England prepared for the 2001 Six Nations opener against Wales.

The game against their old rivals was England's first at the Millennium Stadium. Much had been made of Graham Henry's impact as head coach; the New Zealander had been nicknamed 'the Great Redeemer' as he turned around the fortunes of the Wales team – with such success that he was named as head coach of the Lions tour to Australia that summer. Although Wales had been heavily beaten at Twickenham the previous year, their tails were raised after their heroics at Wembley in 1999 and the team, the press and the fans in the Principality were desperate to lay down a marker against England in their new home.

As the teams gathered in the tunnel the noise from the crowd was deafening. The roof had been closed and the thunder of 75,000 roaring voices bounced off the lid of the stadium to reverberate through the air.

Martin Johnson stood at the front of the England line; a trickle of sweat ran down his forehead and gathered on his glowering brow as he stared straight ahead at the field before him. An official appeared at the head of the tunnel and gave him the signal that it was time for them to run out. Johnson nodded and then turned to the men behind him. 'Hear that?' he growled, gesturing over his shoulder. 'Let's silence it.' Then he turned and began striding out into the glow of the floodlights.

And silence it they did. They scored six tries that afternoon, including a hat-trick from centre Will Greenwood.

'It was almost as if someone had suddenly flicked a switch and sent us into overdrive,' said Richard Hill. 'Suddenly we were playing out Clive's dream of heads-up rugby, feeding off each other so well that the numbers on our backs became almost irrelevant.'

'We were cock-a-hoop with our display, as any team would be,' said Greenwood. 'But it was even more special because for so many decades Cardiff had proved to be a barren hunting ground for England. To thump them by a record score [44–15] was deeply satisfying.'

The team played host to Italy for game two, and continued with the attacking brilliance they had displayed in Cardiff, tearing through the Italian ranks almost at will, scoring a total of ten tries, including a stunning length-of-the-field effort by quicksilver full-back Iain Balshaw, while Wilkinson kicked thirteen of his fifteen attempts at goal and also scored a try in the thumping 80–23 victory. England ran rampant across the park, the backs were given the ball on a plate time and time again and the back-row, in particular, seemed to be everywhere. The trio of Neil Back, Lawrence Dallaglio and Richard Hill were beginning to be recognised as the most formidable unit on the planet – and were soon dubbed the Holy Trinity.

'By 2001 or so, we were probably starting to think as a unit,' said Hill of the back-row triumvirate. 'I'm not sure it was telepathic but we could read each other's games perfectly. When we first got together, we used to walk through our moves every week but as time went on we knew each other's positions off by heart.'

The most notable feature of that match against Italy at Twickenham, however, was that it marked the debut of Jason Robinson. Robinson was a legend of rugby league, having enjoyed a stellar career for Wigan and Great Britain before crossing the code divide by signing for Sale in 2000. He made an immediate impact for the Manchester club and just four months later received a call-up to the national side, becoming only the second player in history to play rugby union for England and rugby league for Great Britain.

'Just when you think you might be learning the game, when you think you know what the best looks like, how to get there and how the game works, along comes someone who breaks all the rules,' wrote Wilkinson in *Jonny*. 'Here is a guy who forces me to reassess what I thought was possible in the game… His ability to beat players both ways and make ninety-degree direction changes without losing speed totally obliterates what I believed were the limits for footwork and speed.'

Robinson's dazzling athleticism impressed every player in the squad. One particular moment, which occurred during a training session on the 2001 Lions tour, also revealed the hunger that Robinson possessed and made more of an impact on his teammates than anything he did while winning his first caps for England. It was during one of Phil Larder's defensive sessions. The ball was being passed along the line and, as the defence pressed up, one of the attacking players thought there was space on the outside for Robinson. He threw a long looping pass towards the diminutive figure on the wing. As it sailed towards its target, Iain Balshaw shot out from the defensive line and easily plucked the ball from the air before it could reach Robinson. Everyone in the squad knew how fast the Bath full-back was and they stopped in their tracks to watch Balshaw cruise in for the try. Everyone except Robinson. As Will Greenwood recalled in *Will Greenwood on Rugby*, 'It was like a cheetah hunting down a gazelle, the short powerful sprinter against the languid, graceful, suddenly-terrified beast. For the first time, there was fear in Iain's eyes – he was thinking about the abuse he would cop, he was worried his gas would be deemed flat – and to counter it, he put his foot to the floor. It was to no avail. Jason had Balshaw's ankles in sight and ten yards out the blonde Lancastrian was grounded. Jason Robinson had arrived. He had let his feet do the talking and we had witnessed a truly remarkable piece of pace and desire.'

Pace and desire. It was the hallmark of Robinson's play. He had electricity in his feet, piston-like drive in his legs and the upper-body strength of a powerlifter. Wherever he played, every time he touched the ball, spectators would be on their feet as defences scrambled desperately to shut him down; they rarely could. It is remarkable that he started for the Lions in the summer of 2001 before he won a starting shirt for England, but Woodward had monitored him very closely and knew just what a potent weapon he could be. Robinson was a born match-winner but Woodward played his hand carefully and didn't rush to introduce him into the starting line-up. Instead, he began by bringing him on towards the end of games, when opposition defences were tiring and suddenly had to try to find a way to cope with Robinson's explosive pace. After playing for thirty-four minutes against Italy and failing to receive a single pass – as the England midfield tore through their opposition and the ball seldom needed to go any further out – it was the Scots in the third match of the tournament who would become Robinson's first true victims.

The home Calcutta Cup clash threw up a raft of new records: the biggest winning margin, the highest score and the most tries in an England–Scotland match. 'On the night before the game, Clive gathered us all together for a team meeting,' said Wilkinson. 'His tack was straightforward. Last year we had let ourselves down; this year we had the chance to put it right. We were shown a few video clips of the previous season's game, highlighting the despair we felt at the end. *Remember the feeling,* was the underlying message, *and make sure it does not happen again.*'

England were merciless throughout, with their play orchestrated brilliantly by Matt Dawson, Jonny Wilkinson and Mike Catt and gilded by the pure pace of Iain Balshaw and the power of Ben Cohen on the wing. Wave after wave of England attacks brought two tries for both Balshaw and Lawrence Dallaglio and one each for Will Greenwood and Richard Hill, while Wilkinson added a further thirteen points from the boot. It was in the last quarter of the game, however, when Woodward introduced Robinson, that the Twickenham crowd witnessed a global superstar in the making. Robinson twice received the ball deep in the England half, shimmied and arced and split the Scottish defence like a lightning bolt; on the second occasion he swept upfield on a forty-metre run before drawing the Scottish full-back Chris Paterson and putting Greenwood away for an easy canter to the posts.

'There was a bit of negativity around Robinson when we brought him across from rugby league,' said Woodward, 'but after a couple of games I remember sitting in the stand at Twickenham and as soon as half-time started, you had about four hundred people sitting around you shouting, "Bring on Robinson! Get Robinson on!" And then when he came on everyone would just go nuts. He brought a real superstar factor to the game whenever he touched the ball.

'I remember a great quote from Andy Nicol in 2001 when we played Scotland at Twickenham: "There were twenty minutes to go," he said, "and we're getting stuffed, we're out on our feet, and there is a stop in play – and they bring on Jason Robinson. And you're just thinking, *give us a break!*"'

'It was pace as much as anything that beat the Scots,' said Wilkinson of the 43–3 win. 'As well as the six tries we scored, one of the most pleasing aspects of the victory was keeping them out from our try-line. We had conceded two tries on our first two matches of the championship and knew we had to improve. We placed a lot of emphasis on defence in the build-up and it showed, particularly at the end when we could have leaked a soft try and it would not have mattered. Instead, the discipline remained right until the final whistle.'

England were on fire. Next they were due to travel to Dublin, but the match was postponed because of the outbreak of foot-and-mouth disease across mainland Britain. The rescheduled match wouldn't be played until the autumn. 'It was massively frustrating because we were on a roll,' recalled Richard Hill. 'But we took out those frustrations on France.'

England scored six tries against Les Bleus at Twickenham, including an audacious set-up by Austin Healey when, with his back to the French posts, he chipped the ball over his shoulder for Mike Catt to run on to and score. No try epitomised the confidence of England's attack more than that one move, executed to absolute perfection. The other scores came from Balshaw, Greening, Greenwood, Hill and Perry, while Wilkinson kicked all six conversions and a further two penalties for a 48–19 victory.

'You'd wake up on a Saturday morning and no matter who you were playing, you were just so excited about the game,' recalled Woodward. 'It was real Jim Greenwood stuff, because you just knew your team was going to go out and play; you just knew. And you could see how excited the guys were to play together and to play with the style that we had developed. It would have to take an incredible performance from the opposition to stop them winning. I used to say that in the team meetings, "If anyone can beat you, good luck to them. The only thing that will stop us playing is us." It really was a magical time.'

By the end of those four games, England had scored an incredible 215 points, which included a record twenty-eight tries, and had conceded just sixty points. 'Twenty-eight tries, an average of seven per game, tell the story of a golden period of fifteen-man, free-flowing rugby that had the crowd standing on their seats,' said Woodward.

'The other big thing that year – actually, it was probably another of those defining points in the team's progress – was the fine-tuning of our style,' said Richard Hill. 'We realised we had to be adaptable. Different conditions would demand a different approach. So would certain opponents. We had to be able to play whatever game was required on the day.'

With the conclusion of the Six Nations postponed until the autumn when Ireland would play their remaining fixtures against Wales, Scotland and England, attention turned to the Lions tour to Australia. Martin Johnson was named captain, the first player to captain a Lions tour twice, and seventeen of his countrymen were selected alongside him in the tour party, a fair reflection of their total dominance of the Six Nations in the spring. It was a source of extreme pride to Woodward that so many of his charges were recognised by the Lions selectors, but little did he know how heavy a toll the tour would take on them all.

As well as the large number of English players selected, the back-room staff was also thickly populated by members of Woodward's team – yet another testimony to the quality that he had assembled behind the scenes at Twickenham. Andy Robinson was forwards coach, Phil Larder was defence coach and kicking guru Dave Alred was joined by Jonny Wilkinson's mentor and fitness expert Steve Black.

On paper, the squad looked extremely powerful, with many critics regarding them as one of the finest touring sides ever to leave the British Isles. The Wallabies were the world champions and were playing at home in front of their own supporters, but for all that it was felt that the Lions were favourites to claim the series. The tour itself was short, with just ten matches in total and head coach Graham Henry and his back-room staff felt that the players needed to put in as much work off the field as they did on it to prepare for the series.

'We made big mistakes on that trip,' said the Ireland hooker and captain Keith Wood. 'We overtrained heavily and I remember having conversations with Martin Johnson about it and we challenged Graham. We said, "Listen, we're overtraining, we're knackered, every one of us, we're wrecked." And he said, "We're going to stop in a week's time and that'll be all the really hard work done." But by the time we stopped it had taken too much out of the players.'

'Looking back,' said Donal Lenihan, the tour manager, 'I would accept 100 per cent that we worked the players too hard early on but there were reasons for it. England as a professional entity were two years ahead of the other three countries at the time. England had a defence coach. Ireland, Scotland and Wales didn't have one. So you had Phil Larder who demanded more time because defensively he would say the other fellas didn't have a clue. This was a whole new set-up for three-quarters of the players. So Larder demanded more time and, in fairness to Graham, because it was largely an English management team that were used to working with each other, he was trying to find common ground and so he was keen to give them the time they needed for their specific aspects of responsibility. As a result of that, I'd put my hand up and say we trained too long.'

Lenihan's observations about the superior fitness and professionalism of the England players over their Celtic rivals is interesting as it corroborates the progress being made towards achieving Woodward's ambitions for his team to become the fittest in the world and for them to be the best prepared and most professional outfit in the game. It also reveals just how effective Dave Reddin's programmes were proving and the commitment that the England players were showing in adhering so rigidly to them. Even two years out from the World Cup, they were a long way ahead of their British and Irish rivals. Indeed, in the face of all the complaints about being overworked, Lawrence Dallaglio took a different attitude than many to the heavy training routine imposed on the tourists. 'Contrary to many reports which emanated from the tour,' he said, 'I believe that the fact that the Lions stayed in contention right to the final whistle of the final Test was in no small part attributable to the huge workload we put in as a squad in the first three weeks of the trip. I don't accept the criticism that the training was far too hard and there's been a lot of rubbish spouted on the subject. This is the modern professional era and the players are paid to do a professional job. I firmly believe that the two main coaches, Graham Henry and Andy Robinson, did a first-class job.'

While the English players naturally, because of their number, formed the bedrock of both the midweek and Saturday side and were central to much that was great and good in the Lions' play, two of their more celebrated number also courted considerable controversy. Matt Dawson and Austin Healey both wrote damning newspaper columns which, in Dawson's case, undermined the coaching and management of the tour and, in Healey's, insulted the Australian players and the nation at large.

Despite the criticism of the training schedule and the way the teams were selected (many players felt that the Test team had been pencilled in long before the squad had even left Heathrow and that there was little or no chance to stake a claim for a Test berth if a player was outside that predetermined side), the Lions played some astonishingly good rugby throughout the tour, picking up where England had left off in the spring and augmenting that attacking style with the best of the best from the other home nations. In the First Test at the Gabba in Brisbane, Jason Robinson showed all his magic in his first start in a union Test by scoring a sensational early try, rounding Wallaby full-back Chris Latham with barely a metre of space to work in. His try sparked a blitz from the Lions and they went on to take a crucial 1–0 lead in the series.

The Second Test started well for the Lions and after a try from Neil Back they led 11–6 at half-time. But then the tour imploded. Jonny Wilkinson, playing at fly-half, wafted a looping pass to his outside backs that was intercepted by Australia winger Joe Roff, who cruised in to score. Roff's try was the start of a twenty-nine point blitz that left the Lions ragged. To make matters worse, Richard Hill, who had been one of the most outstanding players in the series up to that point, was poleaxed by a stiff-armed challenge from centre Nathan Grey just before half-time and was concussed out of the series.

By the time the Lions reached Stadium Australia in Sydney for the series finale, the team was being held together by sticking tape. Exhausted and battered, they had been unable to stage a single training session with the starting team throughout the week building up to the Third Test, with Graham Henry later revealing that if the game had been scheduled just two days earlier, five players from the starting line-up would not have been able to play.

Despite all this, the Lions remained in the game until the final seconds, with Wilkinson, who had been an injury doubt during the week, scoring a total of eighteen points, including a try, to go alongside Jason Robinson's second touchdown of the series. Trailing 29–23, the Lions had one last roll of the dice but Martin Johnson was beaten to the ball on the Lions' own throw at a line-out and their last attacking opportunity was lost.

Desolate and beaten, the Lions players had to return home to deal with the loss of a series that had been there for the taking while also trying to pick themselves up for the conclusion to the postponed Six Nations, the autumn series, and the next stage in their cycle towards the 2003 World Cup.

*

As Woodward welcomed his troops back into camp before the rescheduled match with Ireland in Dublin, he believed that he could nurse his players back into form and fitness in time for the final hurdle in their Grand Slam crusade.

His team had played with such confidence, power and uninhibited skill in the spring that he felt sure that just gathering the players together once more under the red rose banner would be enough to get them all back on track. But he had not foreseen quite how severe the remedial requirements were – or how other obstacles would emerge that would have significantly debilitating effects.

For one, their preparation was almost non-existent. The England players were battered and downcast after the Lions tour. Some, like Dallaglio, had been injured and ruled out of action in Australia and were still to return to full fitness, while Martin Johnson was also unavailable because of injury. Iain Balshaw, who had been sensational in the spring, had lost his confidence in Australia and his form had disappeared. Furthermore, all of the team's arrangements in terms of player release, hotel bookings, fitness and training sessions had been based on the upcoming autumn Test series, not this rescheduled match. They now had to shoehorn in an extra fixture and all the procedures that went with it. 'We were horribly unprepared,' said Woodward. 'There was no way we could negotiate any additional players' release from their clubs in that time. And Ireland would be playing Scotland and Wales on successive Saturdays before playing us, which gave them a huge advantage… I also totally underestimated what the Lions tour had taken out of the players, and got selection badly wrong.'

'The mistake we made,' said Matt Dawson, 'was to think we could play the way we did in the spring in a one-off game, when Ireland had two games already under their belts and had ironed out the creases in their game, and we'd not had even one.'

Ireland's captain, Keith Wood, looked at the England team-sheet and realised there was a chink in England's armour beyond their lack of preparation, or the form and fitness of some of their key players. Having been pitched into battle alongside Martin Johnson and Lawrence Dallaglio with the Lions in 1997 and in the summer of 2001, he knew that they were a different opposition without those two men in their ranks. Dallaglio was the beating heart of the team, a giant ball-carrier and a complete nuisance at the breakdown. As well as being one of the finest players on the planet, Johnson had an aura that galvanized those around him, that inspired and drove them to the limits of their ability – both individual and collective. If Johnson and Dallaglio were playing it wouldn't much matter what else was set against England, they would always be in with a shout. With them gone, Ireland had a real opportunity.

In celebration of Wood's iconic status, huge numbers of the Lansdowne Road crowd were decked out in masks bearing the visage of the home team's talismanic captain. And it was therefore fitting that after Ireland tore into the visitors with a ferocious appetite from the first whistle, it was Wood who would score a try, peeling off the back of a line-out and charging over Neil Back.

England were soon fighting back, with Wilkinson keeping them in the hunt with his boot. Wood's try aside, the pivotal moment in the game came when Dan Luger sliced off his wing and straight through the Ireland midfield. The whole pitch opened up before him and as he scorched away a try seemed certain. But the Ireland scrum-half Peter Stringer dived desperately for his ankles. A flailing hand made contact with one of Luger's trailing boots and slapped it sideways, tripping the England wing and sending him sprawling to the ground, where the chasing cover defenders enveloped him and swiftly extinguished the danger.

As the match reached its final minutes, Austin Healey, who had come off the bench, scythed in for a try, which Wilkinson, surprisingly, failed to convert. At 20–14, England needed a converted try to claim the Slam, but the Irish defence were dogged and fought like mad men to keep them out. When the final whistle blew, England were Six Nations champions but the Grand Slam had once again slipped through their fingers and the millstone of 'chokers' continued to hang heavy around their necks. While the press went to town once more with this label, Neil Back looked back on those Grand Slam-costing defeats quite differently. 'We lost to Wales, Scotland, Ireland and France because we played badly and the other side, at home, played well,' he said philosophically. 'That happens in sport. It is just a coincidence that, on three occasions, we were going for the Grand Slam. It is insulting to the other sides, in my opinion, to suggest that if only the real England turned up on the day it would be a foregone conclusion. These are proud, talented, international rugby sides and they are going to beat us from time to time.'

'We always felt we were learning something from each of our losses,' reflected Richard Hill. 'It may sound strange, but I really think each one helped us. There were always little details that you picked up on and stored in the memory bank. That Lansdowne Road defeat definitely influenced our preparations for the next time we played there.'

'Champions learn from their mistakes and grow stronger as a result,' said Woodward. 'They don't feel inhibited by the fear of failure, but are stimulated and motivated by it.'

After Dublin, the 2001 autumn Test series saw Australia, Romania and South Africa entertained at Twickenham over three consecutive weekends. Sandwiched in between the Tests against two giants of the rugby world was Romania, a once-proud rugby nation that had last been truly competitive in the late '80s and early '90s. The side that represented the Mighty Oaks in 2001 were a shadow of their forebears and duly fell to a humiliating 134–0 scoreline. The fixture did neither side any good.

The real tests for England would be provided by the Wallabies and Springboks, whose scalps they had claimed twelve months earlier. With Johnson and Dallaglio still unavailable, there was every chance that the Wallabies would have the power and nous to regain the Cook Cup.

The Wallabies arrived in London as the holders of the World Cup, Tri Nations championship and with a Test series victory against the Lions in the bag. But Woodward and his team were looking for a reaction to Dublin – and they got one. It was a game in which the momentum swung back and forth, with England surging into a 15–0 lead at the break only for the Wallabies to punch back in the second half. But Wilkinson was as metronomic as ever and his powerful forwards set the platform for him to target the Australian posts and England pushed on to win 21–15.

The final game of the year against South Africa was a typical pitched battle between the sides. Once again it was Wilkinson who was the critical figure for England. While Mike Catt grabbed a drop-goal and Dan Luger sealed the deal with a late interception and a length-of-the-field sprint to score, it was Wilkinson's boot that had doused the fire of the Springboks' fight. England had many heroes, notably Jason Robinson, who caused the Springboks defence no end of difficulties, but it was Wilkinson's seven kicks out of nine attempts that tolled the bell for South Africa. 'That was a great day to be in the stands at Twickenham,' said Woodward of the 29–9 victory. 'It was our third straight win over South Africa and our fifth successive win against a Tri Nations side – the first European nation ever to do so.'

'We saw off Eddie Jones's side without the injured Johnno, Lawrence and Daws, which made a statement,' said Richard Hill. 'It was also back-to-back wins over the world champions. Johnno was back for the Springboks and made an even bigger statement after that match, saying that it was no longer such a big deal for us to beat southern hemisphere sides.'

SEVEN

THE ANATOMY OF
EXCELLENCE

'You don't win once in a while, you don't do things right once in a while,
you do them right all the time. Winning is habit.'
Vince Lombardi

THE SUCCESS OF the autumn series put the disappointment of the
Lions tour and the Grand Slam loss to Ireland to one side and spread
a feel-good factor within the England squad so that they went into the
2002 Six Nations Championship with a great sense of optimism.

England's first game was away to Scotland in Edinburgh. To maximise
their preparation time, Woodward kept the team at Pennyhill Park until
the Thursday before the match before flying north. It was a gritty game, but
England showed their class and won 29–3, scoring four tries through Mike
Tindall and Ben Cohen while Jason Robinson crossed twice.

*

A few days later, in the video analysis suite at Pennyhill Park, Tony Biscombe
sat transfixed at his computer as he put together a series of clips from the
Calcutta Cup match. While sitting in the stands at Murrayfield, he had noticed
something but hadn't wanted to raise it with Woodward until he had had a
closer look at the footage after the game. Now he had confirmation of what he
had seen, evidence to back up his initial impressions. He finalised the clips and
burnt them to a DVD, then went to find Woodward.

The two of them sat down in Woodward's room and went through
Biscombe's findings. While Will Greenwood, Austin Healey, Ben Cohen and
Jonny Wilkinson all featured in the montage, the main footage that Biscombe

had gathered had been of Jason Robinson. Now playing full-back, Robinson had scorched in for two tries but there had been several occasions when he had made a half-break through the defensive line and was hauled down only because a Scottish defender had managed to get hold of his baggy shirt.

'If his shirt was tighter,' said Biscombe, pausing the action as centre Gregor Townsend reached out a desperate hand towards the breaking Robinson, just managing to grab the back of his flapping jersey, 'Townsend wouldn't have even laid a finger on him. And even if he had, he wouldn't have had enough purchase to bring Jason down. He probably wouldn't have even slowed him down.'

Woodward's brow was furrowed but his eyes were bright. Tighter shirts. Why not? It made perfect sense. Tighter and lighter. Surely that was possible.

Within an hour he had sent an email to Nike, the kit suppliers to the team, with Biscombe's clips attached. It was an email that became something of a company legend as it passed from department to department at Nike and the challenge to design the new shirt was enthusiastically accepted. It took eighteen months of development but in the end they had just the product that Woodward was after – and from that moment on, rugby shirt design never looked back.

*

In round two of the Six Nations, England welcomed Ireland to Twickenham and more than made amends for their performance against Keith Wood's men in the autumn by sweeping the visitors aside 45–11. Will Greenwood scored two tries and he was joined by Wilkinson, Cohen, Joe Worsley and lock Ben Kay, who scored after a spectacular forty-metre charge through the Irish defence. Wilkinson mercilessly added a penalty and six conversions. It took England's results at home to fourteen consecutive victories, a record.

All eyes turned to Paris and a French team that was firing once again. With England due to entertain Wales at Twickenham and Italy considered little more than a formality, even in Rome, this match seemed destined to decide the championship and England's tilt at the Grand Slam.

England trekked across the Channel with confidence, having not lost to Les Bleus since 1998, but the trip to Paris got off to the worst possible start. Woodward thought it would be a good idea if the team caught the Eurostar and travelled on their own rose-emblazoned bus. It would make a dramatic statement to turn up at Stade de France in the bus – *we are England, we think of everything*. But they hadn't thought of everything; in fact, they had forgotten a rather unfortunate hazard of travel by bus: traffic. This and a delayed train conspired to make the journey to the team hotel a gruelling eight hours.

Matters did not improve at the Stade de France, where England were treated to a physical onslaught led by a fearsome new back-row combination of Serge Betsen, Imanol Harinordoquy and Olivier Magne. The French had recently employed Dave Ellis as defence coach. He was an Englishman who had played rugby league in England, Australia and France, before becoming involved with rugby union when Jacques Fouroux persuaded him to join Racing Metro. With the New Zealand-born centre Tony Marsh controlling the defence in midfield alongside Damien Traille, France put up a robust wall across the park and Ellis charged Betsen with the task of single-handedly – and single-mindedly – hunting down Wilkinson.

'Jonny won't mind me saying it was probably one of his poorest games,' said Woodward. 'Betsen focused his energy on putting Wilkinson under as much pressure as possible. Occasionally he'd take himself away from the rucks entirely, place himself in the midfield and go for Wilkinson from the outside, putting his pass under pressure. Then at the appropriate time he'd come from the other direction to shut down Wilkinson's kicking game, forcing him to miss touch or restrict his distance significantly. Wilkinson's mistake was that he decided to take on Betsen. He let it become a personal battle and started flying into rucks to clear out Betsen, to show him he was not intimidated, but you do not want your No.10 flying into rucks, you want him playing quarterback. Betsen won that battle only because he got Wilkinson playing in a way England didn't want him to play. Both myself and Wilkinson learnt a lot that afternoon. The next time we played France, I put Charlie Hodgson outside Wilkinson to offer him a get-out route and we won the game comfortably.'

'Usually, if a guy flies out of the line like this, it's brilliant because it means that they are defending individually and you've got opportunities elsewhere,' recalled Wilkinson in *Jonny*. 'But when Betsen goes, the reaction of everyone else in their team is so urgent. They come out so fast it's like their lives depend on it... I had Clive in my head – *build the score, direct the game*. But we can't build anything because, at home in front of their passionate fans, they are too good at preventing us from doing so. They play very, very well, and it's actually in attack where they really win the contest. They exploit a couple of minor lapses in our defence and score two tries.'

'They spotted weaknesses in our game and were clinical in exploiting them,' said Richard Hill. 'For years the England team had prided itself on playing pragmatic rugby, but we failed to live up to that. Johnno made exactly that point afterwards; we needed to go back to those roots in crunch games, playing it tight where necessary… We had been developing an "all-singing, all-dancing brand of rugby" but the method was not always working when we were put under pressure. For years, under previous coaches, England had gone through an era of rolling mauls, so Clive had concentrated on taking us to the other extreme. To be successful, though, we knew we had to marry the two approaches.'

'I'd been France defence coach for a couple of years under Bernard Laporte,' said Ellis, 'but it was in that game when we spotted a weakness in the England team that people really sat up and took notice. Working with Mike Catt a few years later, he told me how that match changed their game plan and made them realise that Jonny could be isolated, and it's no coincidence Catt or Hodgson always came into the team to face France.'

'Regrettably, our chances of the Grand Slam perished again,' said Jason Robinson in *Finding My Feet*. 'We had promised much as a team and, again, we had come up one game short. Yet there remained a sense of optimism. There was more right than wrong with England's rugby. Once the disappointment of the moment had passed, I am sure, like me, the other players in the squad looked forward to the future with optimism, keen to rise to the fresh challenges ahead.'

After that Paris defeat the team regathered themselves at Pennyhill Park and, as had been expected, they bounced back with comfortable wins against Wales and Italy – 50–10 and 45–9 respectively. Thanks to the points difference, England were in the hunt for the Six Nations title right up to the final game, but France finished the tournament undefeated to pick up the Grand Slam that had so eluded Woodward's team.

A further shuffle of staff behind the scenes occurred during the Six Nations when Brian Ashton stepped down during the middle of the championship owing to issues at home. He moved sideways within the RFU and became national academy manager. Woodward felt that it would be too disruptive to the team to bring in another attack coach so close to the World Cup, so he assumed the role himself. It is fair to say that while he was undoubtedly competent in this area, he was not as inventive as Ashton and an analysis of England's attack over the next eighteen months showed that the élan with which they had torn defences to shreds while Ashton was there fell away somewhat after his departure. But having said this, some in the team felt that there was already a general decline in the team's play that had begun even when Ashton was involved. 'The worst thing for me was that as well as losing to France we'd also shown that we'd gone backwards as a squad,' said Jason Leonard. 'We weren't as good as we had been the previous year… There were lots of reasons for our loss of form but the main one was sheer exhaustion. It was the end of an awfully long season – the Lions tour had taken up the previous summer and we'd rolled straight into a tough autumn international season, the delayed Ireland match and then straight into the Six Nations… We didn't have the zip and snap of the year before. There was an irony in the fact that while we were all tired and needed a break, we also needed more sessions together as a team.' The recognition of the team's fatigue was one of the main reasons why the England management rested many of the leading players and took a second-string side to Argentina for a one-off Test in Buenos Aires in the summer of 2002.

With the front-line players rested, Woodward was keen to develop some more selection options for the team going into the biggest season of his career.

The previous summer, while the Lions were in Australia, England had taken five hookers on tour to North America to work on strengthening their reserves in a key area of the team and, as part of their squad development programme, had employed Simon Hardy as a specialist line-out coach to work with them. Among their number was a young man from Northampton called Steve Thompson. Born in Hemel Hempstead, Hertfordshire, Thompson moved to Northampton when he was three, around the time that his parents split up. His relationship with his father soon became distant, something that never really recovered, and he grew up with his mother, who eventually remarried. Thompson was adopted by his stepfather and he changed his name to Steve Walter. He spent much of his childhood playing sport and no matter what he turned his hand to, he did it well. He was a useful footballer and represented the Midlands at basketball, but rugby was his big love. Then, when he was seventeen, his world shifted on its axis. He was sitting at breakfast with his mother and stepfather one morning when they turned to him and said, 'We'd like you to leave.'

Thompson recounted this story in a heartbreakingly frank interview with David Walsh of *The Sunday Times* in 2004. 'I thought, "I'm not going to start arguing here", and I just left,' Thompson said. 'I didn't see that anything was wrong. I hadn't done anything. I was never a kid that got in trouble with the police or anything like that. I was just sitting there and they walked in and said, "Look, we want you to leave." Just like that... My mum kicked my sister Heidi out when she was fifteen or sixteen. I didn't want to give them the satisfaction of seeing I was taking it badly. So I was just fine with it. "Right, OK then. I'll go."

'I am not very forgiving in situations like that. I will never forgive them for it. Where my sister still speaks with my mum, I don't. I never went back. I will never forgive them.'

Thompson moved in with his sister, and while Heidi offered him physical refuge with a new home, rugby offered him an emotional one. He played flanker for Northampton School for Boys, then the Old Scouts junior teams and was finally signed as a professional for Northampton Saints. He played in the back-row for Northampton and changed his name back to Thompson as he worked his way through the traumas of his personal life. Then, aged twenty-one, Northampton's head coach Ian McGeechan and his assistant, Colin Deans, suggested that a career change might be in order. Deans had been one of the finest hookers of his generation for Scotland and the Lions and he saw something he liked very much in Thompson. They suggested that he could make a name for himself at the highest level if he changed his position. 'I loved playing flanker,' said Thompson. 'I'd played in the European Cup for Northampton in the back-row, I'd scored tries, played well there... But there's something about being a hooker. That one-on-one battle is the heart of the game. Looking people in the eye, knowing you have got them, that's the best feeling in the game.'

McGeechan and Deans, a combination made in Scotland, had created a new force for England. Coincidentally, it was against Scotland in the 2002 Six Nations that Thompson made his debut and, while newspaper hacks north of the border crowed that the converted flanker was an obvious weakness in the England juggernaut, Thompson proved that he was anything but. After an assured debut, he played in every match in the campaign, adding both size and ball-carrying dynamism to the front-row where previous candidates in the position had offered either one or the other. As Woodward prepared his squad for Argentina, he wanted to know just how far Thompson could go. Was he going to be as key an element in the World Cup squad as his early form in the team had promised? Time would tell. But if his mettle was ever going to be truly tested, it would be done in Buenos Aires.

There were a number of other fringe players that Woodward was interested in looking at while his established stars were resting. He wanted to see whether lock Ben Kay and flankers Lewis Moody and Joe Worsley could continue the progress they had been making when opportunities had come their way, and whether Phil Vickery could show leadership skills to guide this young and inexperienced squad against one of the most powerful teams in the world.

An unpleasant atmosphere greeted the team upon arrival in Buenos Aires. England were never popular opposition in Argentina and the tour was unfortunately timed so that it coincided with the twentieth anniversary of the Falklands War. To make matters worse, the country was in the throes of an economic crisis, with banks collapsing and demonstrators taking to the streets; and to add to the uneasy feeling, England had just knocked Argentina out of the football World Cup.

Amid the furore of the game itself, with the crowd going wild behind twenty-foot metal fences, England played a simple but direct game, refusing to cower in the face of an aggressive Argentinian pack or the pressure pouring down from the crowd. In a remarkable demonstration of the depth of talent England now had at their disposal, Vickery's men won 26–18. 'I felt so proud,' said the stand-in captain. 'We won the match and it sent a message back to the guys who weren't there that they had competition for their places. This was a valuable thing for them to hear, because it ended up lifting the whole squad and making everyone play to the best of their ability. A lot of guys said, "I'm good. I'm ready for this", and when we returned to England Clive must have realised that he had far more players to choose from than before we left for Argentina.'

The victory was indeed significant and kept up momentum within the squad. However, of more significance was an agreement made that same summer between the RFU and the Premiership clubs that created the new Elite Player Squad. The EPS allowed England to identify a squad of players at the start of the season and essentially buy training time with them from their clubs. It gave Woodward a full twenty days of training before the 2002 autumn internationals and the 2003 Six Nations and handed the players over to England full-time from the end of May until the end of the World Cup in November. This gave him a total of an incredible eighty days with the players in the World Cup calendar year. After years of craving quality time with the England players to prepare properly within the international camp, Woodward finally had his wish granted. And what a difference it would make.

It was estimated that to bring the side to a peak in time for the World Cup would cost the RFU in excess of £20 million. Woodward continued in his determined crusade to ensure that no stone would be left unturned as they prepared for the sport's blue riband tournament – and so it was that Sherylle Calder was appointed visual awareness coach in the autumn of 2002. Calder was a former South Africa hockey international and captain, who had become an expert in visual perception. Originally employed for the Six Nations and the summer tour, she so impressed Woodward that she was kept on for the World Cup. Calder, who would go on to work with the World Cup-winning Springboks team of 2007 and the Australia cricket team before becoming part of Team GB's back-room staff for the London 2012 Olympics, specialises not only in improving hand-eye coordination but also in developing peripheral vision. Just as Woodward had first imagined an Ajax-styled Total Rugby philosophy in a pub when he was a young Harlequins player, he had never given up on his ideal of players playing 'heads-up rugby', with every member of the team a potential attacking weapon. In order to achieve that, the players needed first to be totally comfortable on the ball and within the team itself, but they also needed to understand space and timing and opportunity. They needed to see, absorb and react to all the visual information available to them on the pitch at any given moment. That was exactly what Sherylle Calder was able to hone and refine.

'When I first brought in Sherylle Calder,' said Woodward, 'I remember some of the players saying, "What on earth is this all about? How can you train your eyes?" She was brilliant. And look at her career, she's won two Rugby World Cups, has worked with both the English and Australian cricket teams, she was on the 18th green with Ernie Els when he won the Open at St Andrews, she was part of Team GB at the 2012 Olympics… She is just fantastic.

'I think the idea of getting in touch with her came from one of the players, who had read an article about her working in cricket and about how you can weight-train your eyes, and gave it to me. And at first I was literally imagining small dumbbells on your eyelids. And so I tracked her down and I liked her immediately. She had played international hockey for South Africa, and she explained over the phone that the eye is a muscle and you can make your eyes stronger by doing things on computers, doing exercises with balls, you can do all these things that make the muscles in your eyes stronger. I had no clue scientifically if it all stacked up, but to my common-sense way of looking at it, it sounded plausible. So I brought her over for a couple of months and she did various sessions with the players and then I employed her full-time.

'I remember introducing her to all the players in the team room and then we went outside and I said she was going to do the first session. So she went up to the players, with one finger raised which they would track as she approached them, and she touched them on the bridge of their nose – and could instantly tell which of their eyes was the stronger. She then handed out eye patches that they all had to wear over their stronger eye. It was hilarious, all the players were falling about laughing, taking the piss out of each other, and even I was thinking, "Oh my god, what is this?" And then she turned to me and said, "Clive, I just want you to run the session as normal and we'll see what happens." So we got them all in position to receive a kick-off and one of the guys dinked a kick to the forwards – and it was just a little lofted, gentle kick. And Danny Grewcock shouted, "Mine!" and jumped up to catch it – and the ball landed about three feet to his left. It was hilarious, all the guys were killing themselves laughing. But it showed how much your depth perception can be worked on and they were eventually able to do all these training sessions with the eye patches on, catching and passing and so on, with as much accuracy as they did with unrestricted vision.

'What was also great was that normally when you have injured players, they just hang around on the side, but Sherylle would take them off and get them working on computers, which was fantastic from my point of view because there was no wasted time.'

'I work on visual motor performance – how accurately you use the information you see and put it into your hands to respond,' said Calder, who uses a specially designed computer program called EyeGym which develops reflexes, testing how quickly users react to games on a screen. EyeGym works to develop skills such as hand-eye, foot and body co-ordination, better peripheral vision and spatial awareness. Peripheral vision and spatial awareness are crucial in rugby and being adept at reading as much information as possible from what is around you on the pitch significantly aids decision-making in both attack and defence. 'What it really teaches,' said Calder, 'is the ability to see accurately and to process that information correctly.' Calder's work was just another cog in Woodward's obsessive plan to cover all the bases possible; it was a 'one per center', another area in which his players might be able to improve by even a single percentage point. Cumulatively, these areas would give them an advantage over their opposition. Above all, Calder's skills had a psychological impact – as many of the critical non-essentials tended to have – because not only did they improve the players' vision but they also stimulated a greater self-confidence in them as they appreciated that they were part of an environment in which everything possible was being done to help them succeed.

While many coaches around the world focused on picking teams with their thoughts on the future, particularly during a World Cup cycle, Woodward stuck by a simple mantra that flew in the face of this perceived wisdom: the next game was the most important so always pick the strongest side available to you. Not only did this mean that his team was more likely to win, but that the central core of the team built up experience together – units were well established, each player knew instinctively what those around him would do, and they learnt to win together. While this would prove costly if the team began to break up with retirements, injury or loss of form, for the process of working towards a winner-takes-all tournament like the World Cup, it made perfect, logical sense.

As we have seen with Jonny Wilkinson's development into a phenomenal striker of a rugby ball, thanks to thousands of hours of deliberate, high-quality practice, so too can we see the development of the entire team in this light. Each component player within the team – as they trained and played together year on year – accumulated successful decision-making characteristics and skills and acquired the complex knowledge of how to win games, no matter the situation, which can be built up only through deep experience. It is no coincidence that every team that has won the World Cup since its inception in 1987 has had many years of development together and experienced as many bitter lows as they have highs. It is also no coincidence that there has yet to be a back-to-back winner. Rugby World Cup dynasties have not, as yet, come to pass. By the time a team has had a chance to accumulate the necessary skill and knowledge to triumph in a World Cup the core of the team tends to be at an age when another World Cup cycle is beyond them. This may change in time. A country may be able to blood a core of players young enough to build up the necessary experience to win a World Cup and then continue their development for a further four years to do it again, but it would no doubt also require the assistance of chance and the form of opposition teams, particularly for the first triumph, to allow this to happen. In sport nothing is impossible, but the chances of such an eventuality occurring are slim.

*

When the squad gathered again at Pennyhill Park to prepare for the 2002 autumn internationals, they had, at last, entered World Cup year. Standing at base camp and staring up at the peak of Everest, every player and member of the back-room staff knew that they had a gruelling climb ahead of them. From October 2002, if they made it through to the World Cup final in November 2003, they would play twenty Test matches – each of them, including the games against the 'minnows' in their World Cup pool, huge encounters of staggering significance. The challenge that Woodward set down was for the team to be the No.1-ranked side in the world by the time they entered the tournament and favourites to lift the Webb Ellis Cup. In order to do that they needed to stamp their authority on every game they played – and win. No matter how, they had to win.

And their first challenge was considerable: an autumn series against the best three sides in the world on consecutive weekends.

'Looking back, they were about as close as you could get to the last three phases of a World Cup,' said Richard Hill of the scheduled games against New Zealand, Australia and South Africa. 'Quarter-final, semi-final and final, one after the other.'

Even though the stakes were high and there were fewer than twelve months to go before the World Cup kicked off, Woodward was still tinkering with the make-up of the team, with Cornishman Trevor Woodman making his debut start for England in the front-row. Woodman was raised in a village near Liskeard in south-east Cornwall and played his early rugby for Liskeard Looe before moving to Plymouth Albion, then to Bath and finally to Gloucester. There he teamed up with Phil Vickery, a player he had first encountered as a twelve-year-old when his school played against Vickery's Bude. Little did the two young props realise how intertwined their careers would become. 'Who would have believed when we were slogging it out in eight inches of mud down in Bude that we would be running out to play the All Blacks together?' said Woodman.

At the start of the 2002 season, Gloucester were dominating the Premiership thanks in no small part to the power, speed and dynamism of their two props. While Vickery was often very effective in the wide channels and the cornerstone of the scrum, he acknowledged that Woodman was the faster and stronger of the two. The injection of pace that Woodman could put on the ball when in open space created a potent new attacking dimension for Gloucester and it was one that Woodward was keen to incorporate into the England team – and it pushed him ahead of his rivals for the No.1 shirt, Jason Leonard and Graham Rowntree.

In the twenty-three matches that had taken place between England and New Zealand, England had managed to secure just four victories. While Kyran Bracken, Jason Leonard and Martin Johnson had been part of the famous 15–9 victory in 1993 and Leonard and Johnson had won the second Test with the Lions in New Zealand that same year, the closest most of the squad had come had been the 26–26 draw at Old Trafford in 1997. Every other encounter had ended painfully for the men in white.

The 2002 game provided a return to Twickenham for Woodward's former right-hand man, John Mitchell, who was now head coach of New Zealand. Mitchell knew all about the strengths of his former charges and was aware that the All Blacks side that he had brought on tour had an experimental flavour to it. He cleverly stated at a press conference that, with twenty capped players left at home, his team was extremely inexperienced – and in so doing set himself up in a no-lose situation. If his side lost, he could blame it on the fact that it was a second-string line-up. If they won, it showed both the strength in depth of his squad and his ability as a coach. And the statement also turned the pressure up on England.

But even with so many front-line players left at home, there was still more than a sprinkling of stardust in the All Blacks ranks. Doug Howlett and Jonah Lomu were on the wings, Tana Umaga was in the centre, the mercurial Carlos Spencer was at No.10 (with Andrew Mehrtens poised to replace him from the bench) and Taine Randell was in the back-row.

England's first-choice XV had not played together since defeating Italy in Rome in the spring. Woodward sprung some selection surprises of his own by picking Lewis Moody ahead of Neil Back, with the young tyro pulling on the No.6 jersey while Richard Hill moved to the open-side. Dallaglio was back in harness at No.8 after eighteen months out with an horrific knee injury suffered in a club game for Wasps.

Woodward's introduction of Moody was just reward for the young flanker, but he also wanted to show the old guard that no player's place was assured.

For the All Blacks, Lomu was making his first appearance after a torrid few years out of the international set-up, during which he had suffered from kidney problems and a loss of fitness and form. Of all the players selected for the tour, Mitchell publicly stated that Lomu was the only one picked on reputation alone. The press in both the UK and New Zealand leapt on the story, highlighting Lomu as a weakness – possibly for the first time in his career – in the All Blacks backline.

The England players, however, knew enough about Lomu not to accept reports of his decline as gospel. 'Lomu has always produced when it counts, and especially against us,' said Johnson before the game. 'His was an amazing performance in the 1995 World Cup semi-final, and his try in the 1999 World Cup group game sank us when we'd fought hard to get back into the game. It's easy to say from a broadcasting booth that Lomu's not the player he was, but they don't have to tackle him.'

But while Johnson was wary of the threats the opposition posed, he was still bullish in his assessment of where England were. 'This is one of those must-win games,' he said. 'We haven't beaten them since 1993 and if we are to be taken seriously as World Cup contenders then we have to put that record right.'

In the event Twickenham was treated to a breathless, exhilarating and intensely entertaining match. Defence coaches on either side would have been pulling their hair out while the attack coaches alongside them were purring loudly.

Lomu, spurred by the criticism levelled at him, had two early touches and with each one he reminded the world just what a potent force he could be. His first was a crash ball off Spencer, straight down Wilkinson's channel. The fearless fly-half, who prided himself on the solidity of his defence, could do nothing in the face of physics and was swatted aside. The giant winger's second touch was even more significant as he again took the ball at pace, this time on England's line, and charged straight through the challenges of Mike Tindall and Jason Robinson. The try and Ben Blair's conversion cancelled out two Wilkinson penalties to make it 7–6 to the visitors.

But England lost neither their shape nor their composure. They knew that whenever they were deep in New Zealand's territory, in the 'red zone', they had to come away with points. It was a strategy and a mantra that had been established in the team's game plan since the 2000 summer tour to South Africa. And so it was that as England pressed near the New Zealand posts, Wilkinson received the ball from Dawson at a ruck and thumped over a drop-goal to regain the lead.

England looked as if they were getting into their stride when calamity struck. Richard Hill, dependable, solid Richard Hill, threw a wild pass out of a tackle that was intercepted by Tana Umaga, who swiftly transferred the ball to Doug Howlett. The winger put on the afterburners to race forty metres to the posts without a finger being laid on him.

With two minutes left on the clock before half-time, Wilkinson kicked another penalty. England then began to work their way methodically upfield and a chance presented itself. Wilkinson switched direction and took the ball down the blindside, fixed Lomu and fed James Simpson-Daniel. The young Gloucester winger's burst of speed put him free and he drew the last line of the All Blacks defence before passing to Lewis Moody, who scored in the corner.

Will Greenwood had to be withdrawn at half-time with a dead leg and there was concern that, with such an important player now missing, England might be exposed in the second half. But it was not to be. Just five minutes after the match resumed, England had worked their way back into the red zone.

Any thoughts that Wilkinson might have had about dropping a goal, however, were dashed when Dawson was collared by All Blacks flanker Marty Holah as the England scrum-half dug into the ruck in search of quick ball. On this occasion, though, Wilkinson showed his versatility and his ability to play the game in front of him. With the New Zealand defence fanning out to cover the danger, he spotted the lack of cover behind them, shaped for a drop-goal and then executed a delicate chip that floated the ball over the onrushing defenders. Before the All Blacks hooker Andrew Hore knew what was happening, Wilkinson had slipped past him and had regathered his chip. Twickenham exploded as he dived in under the posts. It was an incredible score.

And it didn't stop there. After another period of sustained pressure during which the England forwards and backs combined to progress relentlessly upfield, Wilkinson flicked the ball cleverly to Ben Cohen and the Northampton winger raced clear to score, celebrating the moment with a swan dive as he crossed the line. As Wilkinson added yet another conversion, England completed an astonishing fourteen-minute blitz in which they had scored twenty-one unanswered points to push them into a 31–14 lead. It looked as if the under-strength All Blacks were on the verge of humiliation… but the New Zealanders then roared back into contention.

Lomu scored an even more impressive try than the one he picked up in the first half, crossing the whitewash after bullocking his way through challenges from Tindall, Cohen, Robinson and Johnson. Andrew Mehrtens, on for Spencer, converted and the veteran fly-half began to pull the strings commandingly. Prop Joe McDonnell almost scored but was held up by his opposite number, Vickery. But the black tide kept coming and with ten minutes to go, replacement scrum-half Danny Lee slipped the England defence to score, with Mehrtens again converting.

The All Blacks were trailing by three points and, gathering the ball from the kick-off, continued to surge their way back downfield, hunting the winning score. And they almost got it. Howlett made a break and drew Jason Robinson, releasing full-back Ben Blair down the touchline. Ben Cohen had tracked the All Blacks' sweeping attack from the opposite wing and he was the last man standing able to stop Blair. He timed his tackle to absolute perfection, slowing his run enough to ensure that Blair was forced to aim for the corner flag rather than trying to step inside Cohen, and it became a flat-out foot race. Just a few yards short of the line, Cohen leapt and collared Blair, bundling him into touch. It was a magnificent tackle that saved the game for England. 'It's my job to do that,' said Cohen self-deprecatingly afterwards. 'I wouldn't have played for England again if I hadn't made that tackle.'

In the final few minutes New Zealand continued to batter the lines. They had one final chance with a line-out near England's try-line, but Ben Kay read the placement of the ball and managed to get a hand to it, stealing possession. Wilkinson cleared their lines and Twickenham rocked with joy at the victory.

*

In the build-up to the Australia Test, Clive Woodward revealed a little secret at a press conference. He showed a video montage to highlight to the officials and the press what he considered to be blocking lines run by the All Blacks backs during set-plays. The material had been collected using a program called Prozone, which had been part of England's video analysis for the previous two years. While the blocking moves were of concern to him and Phil Larder, what Woodward was actually doing was showing his rivals just how advanced their analysis was. 'I wanted to highlight what the New Zealand backs were doing, but more importantly I wanted them to see that we had this new technology which could transform the way you approach a game.'

Footage was gathered for Prozone from twenty cameras placed around the ground and showed the movement of players throughout the game, calculating their speeds and work rates, as well as monitoring the team's defensive patterns. Ever since he had joined the back-room staff, Phil Larder had continually hammered home the importance of defence to any trophy-winning team – and demanded a 95 per cent successful tackle rate from each game. The program allowed Larder to easily map out the pitch with player positions, thereby facilitating clear and concise feedback that allowed him to explain various defensive systems, failings and opportunities to the players. Prozone allowed him to collate the information, analyse each player and send them individual statistical reports after every match.

The players knew that with Prozone gathering information on their every move, there were absolutely no hiding places. 'By 2002 we had used Prozone for two years,' said Woodward. 'It was being used by four or five Premiership football clubs. The biggest thing in coaching is in the debriefing after the match. This system allowed you to go way beyond what you do immediately after the game. You show could players clearly how much they were working and not working. From the moment they walked down that tunnel, we had them. We knew every step they made and how fast and how hard they were working. They knew it too. They called it Big Brother. I also wanted the rest of the rugby world to see that we had this technology which, when used well, could transform the way we analysed training and a match. I knew that twelve months out from the 2003 World Cup our rivals wouldn't have time to implement it. We could analyse ourselves but more importantly we could analyse the opposition as never before.'

While Woodward cites the main benefit of Prozone as being the ability to study the opposition better than ever before, his observation that the players and coaches could study themselves with greater insight is even more significant. As we have looked at with Carol Dweck's theory of growth mindset and K. Anders Ericsson's 10,000-hour rule – together showing that skill is coachable and that world-class standards can be achieved with thousands of hours of deliberate, dedicated practice – a further vital component to the development of skill is through feedback. And that was exactly what Prozone offered the coaches. Every aspect of each player's game could be analysed, which gave the coaches specific, information-rich data on which to base their training sessions and how to improve the individual components within the team. Furthermore, it allowed Dave Reddin access to incredibly detailed statistics that he used to tailor individual fitness and biomechanics programmes. The value of Prozone, particularly as no other rugby country on the planet was using it, was inestimable.

*

The Wallabies arrived in London on the back of a loss to the Irish in Dublin, their first to the men from the Emerald Isle since 1968. They were a wounded animal, desperate to salvage some pride and to reclaim the Cook Cup, which had eluded their grasp since November 2000.

Trevor Woodman, who had made such a good impression against New Zealand in both the scrum and in the loose, had to withdraw from the team with a minor neck injury and his place was taken by Jason Leonard, who would win his ninety-eighth cap.

While Woodman's absence and Leonard's progress towards one hundred caps filled several inches of newspaper columns, it was nothing compared to Woodward's decision to drop Lawrence Dallaglio to the bench for the first time in seven years – on an occasion that would have seen the No.8 claim his fiftieth cap. Just as Woodward had done with Neil Back the week before, he was making a statement that no player could rest on his laurels. 'We pick on what we see, not reputation,' said Woodward. Back returned as the open-side flanker, Moody was retained at No.6 and Richard Hill shuffled sideways into Dallaglio's No.8 shirt.

In the backs, Ben Cohen was selected on the wing just as he had been two years earlier before withdrawing after his father's death. 'Australia was the big game for me because of all that had happened,' said Cohen. 'I'd never played against them but I would have done had it not been for my father's death. That chance was taken away from me. After the All Blacks game I spent an anxious couple of days waiting for the announcement of the team to face Australia. I didn't tell Clive Woodward because I didn't want him to be concerned about my emotional state. I kept my thoughts to myself but I was very relieved when I got the nod. It was the chance to lay a ghost to rest.'

Forty-eight hours before the Test match Cohen drove to Northampton to visit his father's grave. He placed a photograph of his swan-dive score against the All Blacks on the gravestone, inscribed with the words: *Dad, this one is for you.*

Australia made several changes to the team that had lost in Dublin and the side was packed full of World Cup winners and players who had tasted victory over the Lions. The forwards were menacing and the backline posed a threat in every position, with the likes of half-backs George Gregan and Stephen

Larkham, Daniel Herbert in the centre, Matt Burke at full-back and the recently converted rugby league superstar Wendell Sailor on the wing.

It would prove to be another thrilling match. Having moved into a ten-point leads thanks to Wilkinson's boot and a coolly taken try by Cohen, which the winger celebrated with a point to the heavens, England were hit by an Australian blitz as the Wallabies scored twenty-five points in a seventeen-minute period on either side of half-time. After fifty-six minutes the home side were 31–19 down, with Elton Flatley crossing twice, followed by Sailor, but crucially they held their nerve and their shape. While the England forwards were dominant, the defence was surprisingly fragile at times and the tactical kicking of Wilkinson, Tindall and Greenwood was occasionally wayward, but their tenacity to keep fighting was hugely impressive.

Standing in the shadow of their posts as Burke lined up the conversion of Sailor's try, Johnson pulled his men together. 'This is what great teams are made of,' he said, 'to come back from this.'

Think Correctly Under Pressure. And that was exactly what they did. They were calm and controlled. They knew exactly what to do in each area of the pitch and they went about their work efficiently and effectively. 'We dominated, we led, we were overhauled and we went behind – but we never panicked, we never lost our shape and we showed the Australians that this generation of England players competes until the final whistle,' said Jason Robinson. 'Martin Johnson kept the team focused, with one eye on the big electronic clock, one eye on the game plan. His message to the team was plain – if Australia can rack up points in no time, so can we. When you are behind and the clock is against you, it is easy to panic and stray from the game plan. We stuck to the task and, in doing so, staged a comeback that had never before been achieved against a team of the stature of Australia, the reigning world champions… It's games like this that illustrate how far you have come as a team.'

'Our ability to adapt, our knowledge of how to construct scores and win games was tested to the full,' said Wilkinson. 'Clive had been telling us it takes just twenty seconds to score. So we didn't panic, we started chipping away at the gap with penalties, and then, when we were within striking distance of the win, we launched Ben Cohen for his second try.' Cohen scored out wide, leaving a tricky conversion for Wilkinson to win the game. As the Wallabies gathered along the try-line, readying themselves to sprint out and try to put him off, Wilkinson collected his kicking tee and began his ritual. With the seam lined up to the centre of the posts, he stood two paces off to the right and eased himself into his comfortable crouch, hands lightly touching in front of him, his centre of gravity completely balanced. He glanced at a point between the posts, imagining the woman with the Coke can, then returned his eye to the ball. He exhaled, stepped forwards and struck. The ball boomed in the silent stadium and for a few moments he could hear it fizzing through the cold evening air before the sound of its flight was drowned out by an eruption of noise as euphoric England fans burst into life. The game was won, 32–31, and England retained the Cook Cup for the third game in a row, took their winning run against the Tri Nations teams up to seven and in doing so established the longest spell of dominance over Australia, and the whole southern hemisphere, in the history of the game.

*

Two down, one to go. South Africa arrived at Twickenham having lost to both France in Paris and Scotland in Edinburgh. They were in a deep slump, their Super 12 teams struggling domestically, their proud Springboks insipid and uninspiring. In less than a year they were due to face England in Perth in the most crucial game in their pool at the World Cup. They had to make an impact – but no one in the England camp had any expectation of what was coming their way.

It was always going to be a brutal match. The Springboks have a tradition of huge physicality, but they took that to the edge at Twickenham.

'We can all accept being boomed by Jonny Wilkinson or run over by Jonah Lomu or rucked out of the back by the French pack for being on the wrong side,' said Matt Dawson. 'That's all part of the game. But the Boks went way beyond that.'

Right from the kick-off the Springboks piled into the English players, digging knees into ribs during rucks, dropping sly punches off the ball, hitting with just their shoulders or with straight arms in the tackle. Things came to a head when lock Jannes Labuschagne was sent off after just twenty-two minutes for a late tackle on Wilkinson after the fly-half had made a clearance kick. The referee, Paddy O'Brien, had no option but to show Labuschagne a red card and to try to settle the rising tide of violence. While the sending-off stopped some of the more overt violence, it did not extinguish it entirely. Springbok captain Corne

Krige was particularly culpable as he barrelled around the pitch like a one-man wrecking ball, successfully taking out both Jason Robinson and Richard Hill with straight-arm challenges. Wilkinson and Lewis Moody were forced from the field with injury before the end and Robinson discovered after the match that he had a perforated eardrum after being kicked in the head. But England had come through the brutal trial and with magnificent effect. As the weary, bloodied figures in white trooped off the field, Twickenham stood in admiration not just at the astonishing 53–3 scoreline but at a sensational three weeks that had witnessed rugby at its coruscating best. Phil Larder would have been disappointed that the try-line had been breached so easily against New Zealand and Australia, but it had been watertight against the Springboks and they had conceded just five penalties. England had scored twelve tries that autumn and the Total Rugby played by every man who represented England over those three weekends had Woodward grinning like a Cheshire cat. What was significant, however, was that the players and the management didn't feel satisfied.

'Our general improvement was obvious from the 2002 autumn campaign,' said Dallaglio. 'We won all three matches and yet didn't feel like we had done anything fantastic.'

'You couldn't forget,' said Hill, 'that we had home advantage and played them at the end of their seasons. Some of their top players weren't available and the first two wins had been by narrow margins. We knew we were not the finished article.'

On 18 December 2002, for the first time in rugby history, England were ranked No.1 in the Zurich world rankings. The challenge now was to stay there.

*

On 27 January 2003 the squad gathered for their first session at Pennyhill Park to begin their preparations for the Six Nations.

Woodward set his stall out early to the squad. The Grand Slam had eluded them for five campaigns. If they were serious about winning the World Cup they had to carry the momentum from the autumn into the Six Nations and they had to prove that they were the best team in the northern hemisphere. They had to win the Grand Slam.

The first match was against France at Twickenham and both sides knew how important the result would be to deciding the outcome of their respective championship challenges. 'I'm expecting it to be tough and to go down to the wire because there's very little between us,' said Martin Johnson at the time. 'We're favourites, but only because we're playing at Twickenham. That, I hope, will give us the edge. But nobody should bet too much money on either of us. It's going to be too close for that.'

To counter the threat of Serge Betsen hounding Wilkinson out of the game as he had done the year before, and in the absence of the injured Mike Catt, Woodward promoted Wilkinson's fly-half understudy, Charlie Hodgson, into the No.12 shirt to assist Wilkinson with his kicking and distribution duties.

Jason Leonard was set to lead England out for the France clash to celebrate reaching his one hundredth cap – an extraordinary achievement for any player, but all the more so for one in as attritional a position as the front-row.

It should have been a day of joy and optimism, but a dark cloud hung over the England squad. On the eve of the match, Mark Evans of Harlequins had visited the camp at Pennyhill Park to break the news that young England scrum-half Nick Duncombe had died suddenly from a rare bacterial infection while at a training camp in Lanzarote. It was a devastating shock – all the more so for his Harlequins teammates, particularly Dan Luger. 'Nick and he were very close friends, almost like brothers, and he took the loss harder than anyone,' said Matt Dawson. 'I can only imagine how horrendous it must have been for him to be told his best friend had died and then to have to run out at Twickenham and take on France. In the same circumstances, I don't know that I could have gone out onto the pitch, I really don't.'

Over the previous few years, tragedy had often surrounded the camp. In September 2000 Will Greenwood had lost his prematurely born son, Freddie, and just a few weeks later Ben Cohen lost his father. Martin Johnson's mother died of cancer in 2002, Mike Catt's infant daughter had narrowly escaped death after heart surgery and now this: one of their own taken from them. 'When you've been through personal shit it's a game of rugby, nothing more,' said Will Greenwood of the perspective that the squad had gained through such terrible adversity. 'Losing a game of rugby doesn't even come close to what some of the boys have been through. We were so much tighter as a group due to the sad times.'

It was an element of growth in the team that Woodward would never have wished for, but the misfortunes that struck the players individually had a unifying effect and they became more than teammates because of them. These events swept away the macho bravado that is so often present in team sport, particularly at international level where players come from a variety of different clubs and backgrounds and which can present an obstacle to collective success; instead the petty, parochial differences were stripped away and their shared humanity was exposed by raw, painful emotion. Within the confines of the England camp there was a structure that existed that allowed the players to escape, for a time, the burden of their personal tragedies. The game may have been revealed to be nothing more than a game, but it also offered them solace and an escape from what they were dealing with.

The match against France saw a relatively poor performance from England, but with the news of Duncombe's passing could it have been anything else? What is most impressive is that, despite the shock of the news and the effect it had on the players, the team were still able to pay tribute to his memory by overcoming their Gallic rivals. England lost the try count 3–1 but Wilkinson outgunned his opposite number, Gérald Merceron, and England were able to emerge 25–17 winners.

England's second match of the tournament was away to Wales, who were smarting from an opening-round loss to Italy in Rome. Once again there were very few fireworks from England, but they produced a cool, calculating and assured performance. Wilkinson was again deadly with the boot, scoring two penalties, two drop-goals and two conversions to complement tries from Will Greenwood and young flanker Joe Worsley, and they left Cardiff with a 26–9 win.

In the build-up to the Italy match, Jason Robinson sustained a minor injury that Woodward was unwilling to risk against a side that England were expected to beat convincingly. It would have been natural for him to turn to either Iain Balshaw, Austin Healey or Tim Stimpson to fill the full-back role. But Woodward's thoughts strayed elsewhere, to a player that he had not considered beyond the A team for more than five years – Wasps full-back-cum-wing-cum-centre, Josh Lewsey.

Lewsey was a product of Watford Grammar School for Boys, where he had played fly-half. Sport had come easily to him, academia less so, but he had worked hard and earned a place at Bristol University to read physiology. Concerned by the strain the cost of his university education would place on his parents, Lewsey applied for a commission to the Royal Military Academy at Sandhurst. He was accepted and received a bursary in return for a promise to attend Sandhurst for his officer training upon graduation. During his second year at university he joined Bristol, made the club's first team and, as the sport was now professional, began to earn a decent salary from the game.

He wrote to Sandhurst and requested to defer his entry for a year. The academy accepted and he signed professional terms with Wasps. After his first season he wrote and deferred again, but he was aware that he would have to make a decision soon – either to quit professional rugby or to repay his bursary.

In 1998 he was selected for the Tour of Hell. While he endured the ignominy of the 76–0 loss to the Wallabies, he also suffered the embarrassment of Clive Woodward picking him out in a team meeting as a physical role model for the other players to aspire to. At a relatively modest 5ft 10in, Lewsey had long been professional in his attitudes to diet and training, knowing that he would not survive long in the professional game on his speed and skill alone, and in terms of physical conditioning he was years ahead of many of his teammates. He did not want for bravery either. In the second Test against New Zealand, Jonah Lomu made a break and seemed certain to score. Only Lewsey stood in his way – a blonde-haired speed bump, giving away seven inches in height and five stone in weight. Lewsey felled the big man and the try was averted.

Lewsey seemed to be proving himself with England, but it didn't last. On the squad's return to London, he dropped off the international radar.

He spent several frustrating years seeing others selected for England squads ahead of him and became increasingly disillusioned with life as a pro rugby player. He spoke to his club's director of rugby, Nigel Melville, and they concocted a plan whereby he would continue to play for Wasps while finally fulfilling his promise to Sandhurst.

'Combining officer training with my rugby career at Wasps was incredibly hard, because I was determined to do precisely the same as everyone in my year at Sandhurst,' said Lewsey. 'What attracted me to the Army was that it was all about leadership. It was something that challenged me physically and mentally.'

There was a twist to this tale, however. Lewsey had graduated from Sandhurst in 2001 and then served for two years as an officer in the Royal Artillery. He had given up on his dream to play for England but Woodward, despite plenty of evidence to the contrary, had not forgotten about him; the caveat was that Lewsey had to return to full-time rugby. Lewsey could have continued on in some capacity in the Army, with a desk job of some kind, but the prospect didn't sit well with him. 'I just couldn't feel comfortable taking the same pay and rank as friends and peers who could be dodging bullets while I swanned about west London playing rugby.'

So he made the decision and resigned his commission. 'Leaving the Army was the hardest decision I've ever made,' he said. 'I hold my head up because while I was there, I did the same as every guy: no favours, got the extra tuition, passed the same exams. I have only good memories from my time in the Army.'

Lewsey was on a tour with Wasps in Cornwall when Jason Robinson went down injured and the call came from Woodward.

And so it was that Josh Lewsey made his home debut for England in the 40–5 win over Italy, scored two tries and ran with such balance, poise and incisiveness that the rugby world was forced to sit up and take notice that a new star appeared to have been born. Despite the searing ability of Jason Robinson, such was the command of Lewsey's play that he made the No.15 shirt his own – unequivocally. Robinson, when he returned from injury, was moved back to the wing. Woodward now had an embarrassment of riches at his disposal. But looking at the new back-three combination of Robinson, Lewsey and Ben Cohen, he knew that he had an exquisite balance of pace, power and guile. The World Cup jigsaw pieces were falling into place.

The Italy match had also seen Jonny Wilkinson named captain while Johnson was rested, further developing the leadership core within the squad. But it was not all good news. Charlie Hodgson, the primary back-up to Wilkinson in the fly-half position, cruelly suffered a cruciate ligament injury that would rule him out of England contention until 2004. It was a tragic blow for the young Sale player, but it saw the return of an old England favourite in his place. Paul Grayson, who had last played for England during the 1999 World Cup quarter-final loss to the Springboks, was reintroduced to the squad.

The fourth game of the tournament was against Scotland at Twickenham. Martin Johnson returned to the team and the familiar triumvirate of Dallaglio, Hill and Back lined up once more in the back-row, while Jason Leonard prepared himself for an unprecedented fourteenth Calcutta Cup clash.

England's performance against Scotland was their best of the championship so far. They scored four tries through Robinson (with two), Cohen and Lewsey, while Wilkinson added a devastating seven kicks from seven attempts in a crushing 40–9 victory.

Not only did the win seal the deal on a Grand Slam showdown with Ireland in Dublin (with the Irish also making it four from four after seeing off the Welsh in Cardiff thanks to a last-minute drop-goal from fly-half Ronan O'Gara), but the successful defence of the Calcutta Cup took England's consecutive winning tally at Twickenham to an astonishing twenty-one matches. When Humphrey Walters had spoken of his dream for Fortress Twickenham back in 1997, even he wouldn't have imagined that it would come to fruition in quite so emphatic a fashion.

And so it was on to Dublin, the graveyard of England's 2001 Grand Slam hopes, where they would be competing for the Slam, the Six Nations title, the Triple Crown and the chance to exorcise some demons.

*

Bright spring sunshine leaked through the oak-framed windows of an anteroom at Pennyhill Park. This was the war room.

At one end of the room, a semicircle of chairs had been arranged around a whiteboard that was covered in notes and diagrams. Woodward was standing by the board, pen in hand, deep in discussion with those sitting: Andy Robinson, Phil Larder, Dave Alred, Phil Keith-Roach, Tony Biscombe, Simon Hardy and Louise Ramsay.

Although the group had moved on from the subject, and were now discussing the logistics of their training day in Dublin on the Saturday before Sunday's Grand Slam showdown, Dave Alred's eyes kept drifting to a word that Woodward had written in capital letters near the top of the board. Not only was it written in capitals, but it had been circled and underlined. Twice. It read: *CHOKERS*.

Chokers. The albatross around their necks; the elephant in the room. Five years. Five Grand Slam attempts. Five missed opportunities. France had denied them twice during the course of the tournament, but on three occasions it had come down to the final weekend and England had bottled it on each occasion.

Alred smiled to himself. The subject had been discussed by the group and the point had been hammered home that, this time, there could be no excuses for choking. The team had to deliver. The pressure to win the Grand Slam was greater than ever. So why was Alred smiling? Because this year it all felt different. The team had matured. They had all experienced the agony of defeat, of having the Grand Slam snatched from them time and time again. But they had embraced that pain and they had learnt from it. And Alred, who was at that time in the middle of a PhD at Loughborough University examining performance under pressure, knew better than most the mental tenacity of the

England players that surrounded him.

'The most fundamental change,' he said, 'has been looking at the whole issue of mental preparation, trying to ensure players always perform at or very near their potential whatever the interference. If there's anything I can do to get a player to go where he's never been before in terms of the level of his performance, that's my job.'

Alred had taken on the role of the team psychologist to such an extent that he was individually coaching them in ways to cope with pressure situations – from playing crowd noises over the speaker system at Twickenham while the kickers practised or the forwards went through their line-out routines, to establishing trigger words for each player to help calm them in moments of extreme stress (something they were encouraged to do for a teammate as well).

'When the bullets start flying it's useful to have someone alongside you who can prompt you,' said Alred. 'It's not something you ram down people's throats, it's something you offer. If there's one thing I can help them with, it's worth it. How do you know that one thing is not the difference between a ball being caught or dropped?'

Once again it was about marginal gains, ensuring that no stone was left unturned. At this level, Alred knew, the difference between winning and losing was often down to mental attitude. Who wanted it the most? Who was prepared to put themselves through the most pain? Who could keep coolest under pressure? And although he would never have wished for it, he, like Woodward, realised that the personal tragedies that had befallen the squad had provided them all with valuable perspective. If they were able to remember that it was just a game, then there was much less chance of them becoming overwhelmed by an occasion; if they could retain a sense of perspective then they had a greater chance of remaining calm and controlled. *Control the controllables, be in charge of your own destiny.*

'Yeah, there is pressure,' said Josh Lewsey at the time. 'But it pales into insignificance when compared to bigger, more important things. What kind of pressure were the guys who fought in the world wars under? We get to play rugby now because they were prepared to fight for our freedom. I've got mates in Iraq. They text me before the games; I text them. I don't want to sound like I am belittling the game, but how can I compare the pressure I'm under with the pressure they're under? All I've got to do is play eighty minutes of rugby. I don't have to dig a trench, I don't have to turn up to a bombed building and pick up dismembered bodies. There are countless people – not just soldiers – who work incredibly hard for average rewards, and I realise how privileged I am to be playing this game for a living.'

Yes, reflected Alred, this year everything felt different.

*

With the Grand Slam showdown scheduled for Sunday, 30 March, Dublin boiled with anticipation.

In the build-up to the game, Martin Johnson was candid about the importance of victory to the England squad and his openness spoke not only as a searing statement of intent, but also of the no-excuses environment that now epitomised the camp. 'Either side would take a 3–0 win right now, I can promise you. In fact, I'd grab a one-point victory any day. Whatever it takes: penalties, drop-goals, anything. All we have to do is win. Nothing more, nothing less. I don't care how we achieve it. I don't care how badly we play, just as long as we emerge the winners. People use the phrase, "must-win games" all the time, but this is just about as "must-win" as you can get. It would be a massive relief to win and a huge weight off our shoulders. No matter what this side have achieved over the years, we've never won a Grand Slam. That's a huge failing to our name. We're absolutely desperate to win it this time. Above all else, we want to win it for ourselves.'

Woodward was equally blunt about the importance of securing the result. The time for learning lessons was well and truly over, now was the time for the team to start delivering. 'Defeat?' he said before the team flew to Dublin. 'It's not even entered my mind. Next Monday doesn't exist as far as I'm concerned. The World Cup doesn't exist. All our thoughts are focused on Sunday. This match is the culmination of four years' work. That's what it's boiled down to. The pressure to win this match and this Grand Slam comes from within. There are no more learning curves. Winning against Ireland is all that matters. I've not even thought of the ramifications if it weren't to go our way.'

It had been fifty-five years since Ireland's last Grand Slam. Despite the closeness of their win over Wales the previous week, what had been most impressive had been their claiming of the result despite playing poorly. In the previous games they had swept past Scotland 36–6, Italy 37–13 and France 15–12 before pipping Wales 25–24. Ireland had two fantastic playmakers at their disposal in Ulster's David Humphreys and Munster's Ronan O'Gara, who covered Humphreys from the bench. The fly-halves could both play a delicately controlled territorial game, keeping play deep in the opposition half where their well-drilled forwards would batter away like a green wave, setting up time and space for the outside backs, where Ireland's captain Brian O'Driscoll, considered by many to be the world's best centre, lurked with perpetual intent. This was the acid test of England's quality that Woodward had longed for.

'I think in previous years when we dropped the odd game that cost us Grand Slams it was because we weren't so much focused on winning as we were on really playing,' said Woodward. 'But by the time 2003 came around I changed things and I wanted to put the pressure of winning on the guys. I said that if we were to have any chance of lifting the World Cup, we had to win the Grand Slam – it wasn't about entertainment any more, it was about results. I wanted to put that pressure on them to see how they handled it.

'The night before we played Ireland, Tony Biscombe put together a montage of clips to the Eminem track "Lose Yourself", with the lines, "If you had one shot, or one opportunity, to seize everything you ever wanted, would you capture it or just let it slip?" And I really rammed home that unless we won the game and won it well, we had no chance in the World Cup. I really turned up the pressure – which is the exact opposite of what you're meant to do as a coach, but I felt it was really important to do it. And the players responded magnificently.'

There was a wild, carnival atmosphere around Lansdowne Road that bright Sunday afternoon. But right from the moment that Martin Johnson led his team on to the pitch, England refused to give an inch – causing considerable controversy before the first whistle had even been blown.

Leading his side out of the tunnel, Johnson turned right, where England would be playing the first half, and lined his men up along the red carpet for a pre-match greeting from the Irish President, Mary McAleese. As the Ireland team prepared to follow them out there was a delay – the side that Johnson and his men now occupied was Ireland's 'lucky end' and a groundsman was dispatched to ask England to move to the other side.

Neil Back broke ranks and marched along the line shouting, 'Stand firm, stand firm!'

Johnson glowered down at the groundsman. 'This is our end,' he said. 'We're not moving.'

England didn't budge – and nor did Ireland accept the situation, which led to the bizarre sight of O'Driscoll and his team lining up on the grass even further to the right of England. Neither side were willing to concede even a sliver of an advantage to the other.

'If we'd moved we would have given Ireland an immediate psychological edge,' said Back later. 'In the frame of mind that we were in, we weren't prepared to give them anything. Not during the game, and not before either.'

And so began one of the great Grand Slam encounters. Ireland, full of pride and ambition, played magnificently; a David Humphreys drop-goal and penalty meant that they trailed England 13–6 at half-time after two Jonny Wilkinson drop-goals (both struck with his weaker right foot) and his conversion of a Lawrence Dallaglio try. Ireland were a great team full of great players who would all go on to have great careers, some of the most celebrated in Irish rugby history – but in the second half they just couldn't live with England. Even O'Driscoll could do nothing to conjure any serious opportunities to reverse the tide.

'For myself and Phil Larder, it was his attacking threat that was our big concern,' said Woodward of O'Driscoll. 'We worked on a plan to man-mark him with three players, so the tackler was not exposed by O'Driscoll's footwork and pace in a one-on-one situation. That's how big a threat we believed he was – he needed three men to handle him. Ireland were going for a Grand Slam, but none of the players around Brian were in the same league. Whenever he had the ball we wanted one player opposite him and one man either side – it would usually be Wilkinson, Will Greenwood and Mike Tindall. The trick was to get on to him quickly and shut him down, give him no time or space in which to run. For the first quarter of that game the scores remained close, but Ireland had the bulk of the ball. Wilkinson got on top of O'Driscoll more than any other player, making twenty tackles in the first twenty-five minutes. Shutting down O'Driscoll shut down Ireland.'

Playing into a strong wind in the first half, England had been delighted to push their noses in front, especially as Ireland had dominated many of the early exchanges. But in the second half there was never any doubt as to England's superiority.

England scored four more tries, with Wilkinson weighing in with a penalty and two further conversions while Paul Grayson converted England's fifth try of the day after replacing Wilkinson late in the game. For all of Ireland's committed and often highly skilled play, the final scoreboard read 42–6 to the visitors. Had a Grand Slam ever been sealed in such an emphatic fashion? They had scored second-half tries through Tindall and Luger and Greenwood had gone over twice. The second of these was from an intercept and after a clear run to the line he mischievously veered right and dotted the ball down near the corner flag to ensure the conversion was as challenging as possible for Wilkinson.

'Thanks, mate,' said Wilkinson drily as he collected the ball from Greenwood. It was almost like a preconceived scene from a magic show; Wilkinson placed the ball just inside the touchline, lined up the kick and delivered for the crowd: the ball sailed straight and true between the posts.

'Jonny Wilkinson was magnificent,' said Greenwood of his fly-half's performance. 'He was awe-inspiring that day. We had our tactical differences, but after that match I vowed to always back him up. If he was willing to put that much effort in for a team then the rest didn't matter.'

The effort that Greenwood refers to was not just Wilkinson's immaculate goal-kicking or his orchestration of England's attack, but the bone-crunching nature of his defence. Late in the first half, Ireland's bullocking centre Kevin Maggs had charged on to the ball near England's line and had been smashed to the ground by Wilkinson. The England fly-half made several more telling tackles, but none more dramatic than his second-half hit on Justin Bishop; the Ireland winger had burst on to the ball near the halfway line, looking to use his pace to burn through the English defence, but he was met by Wilkinson, who stopped him dead in his tracks, lifted him horizontally and slammed him into the ground, just as he had done to Émile Ntamack three seasons before. Roars of delight echoed from the English supporters within the Lansdowne Road crowd.

After five heart-wrenchingly close attempts, Woodward had finally achieved his first Grand Slam as a coach and he was justifiably delighted. 'Had we lost this game the ramifications would have been huge,' he said in the aftermath of the match. 'People would have said again that this is a team that cannot win the big games. If we hadn't nailed this one, it would have been tough to recover and it would have made the months going into the World Cup even harder. We responded with a colossal performance.'

*

After the glories of the autumn and the triumph of the spring, the summer tour Down Under was a potential bombshell. Both New Zealand and Australia had wounds they had been licking for nearly eight months; they were desperate to right the wrongs of November 2002 and shove the results at Twickenham back down English throats with interest. The danger for Woodward and his team was that this wish would come true and England would suffer two humiliating defeats, just as they had done in 1998 on the Tour of Hell. And if that were to happen, the team's confidence, which was now somewhere up in the stratosphere, could be shot to pieces just months before the World Cup kicked off.

It was a three-match tour with fixtures scheduled against the Maoris, New Zealand and Australia. The temptation might have been to wrap the core of the Grand Slam-winning team in cotton wool before the World Cup, but Woodward was having none of that. 'What happened five years ago was a very low point in the history of the game,' he said, in reference to the Tour of Hell. 'It was a total mismatch and I was determined it would not happen again… There are risks involved but this is the right thing to do. We're prepared to put everything on the line. If your mindset is to be worried about losing, then you might as well not play Test match rugby.'

Martin Johnson, as ever, had his feet planted firmly on the ground. 'Let's be honest about it, they lost by only three points at our stadium at the end of their long season. They had big names missing but still beat us on the try count by three to one. We have the Grand Slam, which is a huge weight off our shoulders, and we're very hungry to prove to the world that we can win in places like Wellington. If we're close to our best, we can win. If we're not, we'll be taught a harsh lesson.'

'We felt we could play against anybody anywhere in the world,' said Woodward. 'We'd won big games away from home and we'd lost a couple of big games. We looked forward to playing those away games. If you want to be the best team in the world, you've got to get a win away from home. There's no point being able just to win at Twickenham.'

The first tour match, against the Maori in New Plymouth, was played in a tempest. The Maoris were a true force to be reckoned with, even though the game didn't have Test match status. Until they lost to a full-strength Wallaby side in 2001, the Maoris had gone undefeated for an extraordinary seven years and twenty-four matches, and had defeated twelve international teams, including the 62–14 humiliation of England in 1998.

The New Zealand media foresaw a similar result as England fielded a second-string side, but the tourists set down an impressive marker with a thoroughly deserved 23–9 victory. England controlled the ball and the territory to near perfection in the dreadful conditions.

There were some big-name omissions from the All Blacks squad for the first Test of the tour as John Mitchell shaped his team in advance of the Tri Nations and World Cup: Jonah Lomu's kidney condition, which he had been battling for several years, had worsened to such a point that he would soon begin dialysis and eventually require a transplant; Christian Cullen, the full-back whose try-scoring rate was the best the world had ever seen, with forty-six tries in just fifty-seven Tests, was now considered surplus to requirements; and Taine Randell had been supplanted as both captain and flanker by Reuben Thorne. With the Auckland Blues having won the Super 12 in glorious fashion just a few weeks earlier, Carlos Spencer was again chosen ahead of Andrew Mehrtens at fly-half and his electric Auckland teammate Joe Rokocoko was on the wing.

Woodward stuck by the squad of players that had won him the Grand Slam for the Test at Wellington's Westpac Stadium, the only change occurring when Matt Dawson withdrew due to injury on the Wednesday before the game. His place was taken by his perennial rival, Kyran Bracken, and Andy Gomarsall was promoted to the bench.

The rain was falling steadily and a wicked wind was whipping in from the Cook Strait on the evening of the match, swirling around the stadium that had been nicknamed 'the Cake Tin'.

Every England player put his hand up that day to be remembered for ever in the country's rich rugby history, but Martin Johnson, Lawrence Dallaglio and Jonny Wilkinson, in particular, bolstered their positions in the pantheon of all-time greats of the game.

Wilkinson's goal-kicking, superior to that of Carlos Spencer, ultimately decided the outcome of the match, but the story of the game was so much more complex than that. Spencer created a try for Doug Howlett with a kick into space but, this moment of inspiration aside, the dominant stand-off on the pitch was wearing white. With four penalties and a drop-goal, Wilkinson's points haul took England home – in quite a different fashion to his last experience in New Zealand.

'I didn't enjoy it,' he said of the Tour of Hell, 'but the experience helped me speed up my improvement. Going through such an intense range of emotions allowed me to progress quicker than I would have otherwise. In terms of my education, it was vital. I thought I was getting somewhere in the game until I went on that tour. It was as if someone was saying to me: "You think you've done well, but hold on. You've got a long way to go to even get close to this level." I raised my standard and set out to reach a level I would be satisfied with. In one respect I've been distancing myself from the experience, but I have always maintained that it taught me more than anything else I have gone through, or ever will.'

But the real turning point in the game, which will be referenced for decades to come, occurred shortly after half-time. Stuart Dickinson, the referee, had repeatedly warned both sides about continued infringements around the breakdown and finally his patience wore out. In the forty-sixth minute he sent Neil Back to the sin bin; just sixty seconds later, Dallaglio committed a similar offence and followed his teammate into the bin for ten minutes. England, away from home, were down to thirteen men against a full complement of All Blacks. Then it got worse. From the penalty that Dallaglio had conceded close to the England line, only halfway between the posts and the touchline, the All Blacks opted for a scrum instead of a shot at goal. With only six forwards against New Zealand's powerful eight, a try seemed a foregone conclusion.

Johnson gathered his men around him, his sharp dark eyes glaring beneath his furrowed brow. 'Push,' he growled. 'Just push.'

Four times the ball was fed into the scrum. Four times England held firm. They twisted and turned, they rose and they fell, but they did not move backwards. After another reset scrum Dickinson penalised England's front-row for standing up. Rather than pack down again Rodney So'oialo, the All Blacks No.8, tapped a quick penalty and drove for the line. He thought he had made it but the video referee decided that he had grounded the ball before the line and had committed a double-movement in his attempt to score. England cleared their lines and, even more extraordinarily, Wilkinson kicked a penalty to move England three points further ahead before Back and Dallaglio rejoined the fray.

Asked afterwards what had been going through his head during that scrummaging sequence, Johnson answered drily, 'My spine.'

It was an heroic back-to-the-wall effort, but it was also one that England had planned for. For more than a year Phil Larder had regularly introduced drills in which they had to cope with defending while a man down. 'We try to think what we will do when certain players get a yellow card,' said Woodward. 'That effort in Wellington doesn't just happen by luck, but by experience and practice.'

England went on to record a 15–13 victory, only the second ever by an England side on New Zealand soil.

As a testament to the standards now set and expected within the camp, there was, incredibly, a palpable sense of disappointment with the way they had played. 'The dressing room was like a morgue afterwards,' said Johnson. 'I had to remind everyone that winning away in New Zealand is a great achievement.'

After the game, Dallaglio made an interesting observation about one of the key differences between the teams. He had been up against the somewhat unknown quantity of Rodney So'oialo, so he and Tony Biscombe had spent hours poring over videos of the young No.8 playing for Wellington in New Zealand's National Provincial Championship and the Hurricanes in the Super 12 competition as well as the few run-outs he had had for the All Blacks. It seemed obvious, however, that with the exception of Wilkinson and Johnson, the All Blacks – and even the New Zealand press corps – seemed to know nothing about any of the England players, their strengths and weaknesses as a team or even their style of play. The New Zealanders had clearly forgotten one of Sun Tzu's most fundamental lessons from *The Art of War*: 'Know your enemy.' It was an accusation that could never be levelled at Woodward's team.

*

Less than twenty-four hours after their Wellington heroics, England were on a plane to Melbourne. They had six days before they had to face the Wallabies at the Telstra Dome.

With the roof of the stadium closed, there couldn't have been a greater contrast in conditions to those experienced in New Zealand. England had proved that they could beat the best in the wind and rain, and now they had the chance to prove that they could beat the best on a dry, hard pitch unaffected by the elements.

Australia began the game with the odds stacked slightly against them as fly-half Stephen Larkham had been forced to withdraw with injury and his back-up, Elton Flatley, was stood down from the squad by coach Eddie Jones after missing a recovery session the day after their win over Ireland the previous week. In their absence, centre Nathan Grey was handed the pivotal No.10 shirt.

But even if Larkham or Flatley had been available, it is debatable whether it would have made the slightest difference, such was England's almost unerring dominance throughout the eighty minutes. England scored three breathtaking tries, each a demonstration of the wide variation available in their play.

The first, finished by Will Greenwood, was a celebration of continuity through phase play. There were fourteen phases, the ball skilfully retained and recycled time and time again between incisive running angles and deft offloads.

The second was a combination of quick thinking, quick hands and even slicker continuity than had led to Greenwood's try. Johnson peeled off a line-out and fed Dallaglio, who popped the ball to the rampaging Woodman. As the prop was felled, the ball was almost instantly recycled. Back acted as a scrum-half and fed the ball to Wilkinson, who offloaded to Thompson. He slipped a pass to Greenwood, who in turn flicked the ball to his centre partner, Tindall, to slide over the line. The ball had flashed through each pair of hands as the outside runners hit the line flat and at full pace; it was the Mark Ella-inspired flat backline attack at its very best, come back to haunt the Australians.

The third and final try, which killed off the Aussie challenge, came from a set-piece play, executed to absolute perfection. The forwards won a line-out just over the halfway line and drove the ball on to the Australian 10-metre line. As Dawson, on as a replacement for Bracken, released the ball to the backline, Wilkinson shaped to pass to his centres, who were arcing towards the wide outside, when out of nowhere Ben Cohen appeared from his blindside wing, slashing back against the run of play. Wilkinson dropped a soft pop pass to Cohen and the giant wing lacerated the Aussie defence. Travelling at full speed, he rounded Chris Latham to score.

Australia, as is seemingly imprinted on their DNA, refused to buckle and fought back with a late try from Wendell Sailor, but England played for territory, bossed the forward collisions and won Wilkinson a further two penalties to build on their lead and push them out of sight.

But the drama did not end there. As the game drew towards its conclusion, there was a spat between the full-backs, Mat Rogers and Josh Lewsey. The two had to be separated and play continued, but it was clear that both were livid with one another. A few minutes later, Australia looked to break out from their 10-metre line. The ball came to Rogers, who looked to attack down the left wing. But just after he received the ball, a blonde-haired meteor smashed into him. Lewsey's tackle was a moment of defensive perfection. He came at full pace, from just on the edge of Rogers' peripheral vision, sprung like a tiger and clattered Rogers at chest height. The entire stadium let out an exhalation at the impact. Lewsey leapt to his feet, point proved, while Rogers lay writhing in agony for several minutes. While the match proved to any remaining doubters England's mantle as the best team in the world, that tackle demonstrated the savage pride that coursed through the team. 'I've taken a fair few hits in my time, but that one was like getting run over,' recalled Rogers several years later. 'I think that hit will take the crown as the biggest ever. I just remember lying there writhing in pain, unable to breathe. It left me with broken ribs and for months afterwards I couldn't go surfing because my rib stuck out on the board!'

The 25–14 win signalled a tenth successive victory over the southern hemisphere giants – a record that completely outstripped anything done before in the history of the game. The variation in England's play was shown to outstanding effect that night – power, finesse, tight attack, wide attack, deep attack, flat attack, expert kicking – the full gamut. 'The greater the pressure, the better our guys perform,' said Woodward the next day. 'We have no fear now about playing anyone, anywhere. We relish the pressure on us.'

After the tour Woodward insisted that the squad stop off in Perth for a few days. Not only did it give them some well-deserved downtime, but they were staying in the same hotel where they would be based for their opening World Cup pool games and they had a couple of light training sessions at Perth High School, which would serve as their World Cup training ground, and wandered around the Subiaco Oval where their games would be staged. Woodward understood the importance of familiarity when away from home and how distracting an alien environment could be. It was another marginal gain notched up for his team.

EIGHT

THE ANATOMY OF PREPARATION

'The fight is won or lost far away from witnesses – behind the lines, in the gym,
and out there on the road, long before I dance under those lights.'
Muhammad Ali

AFTER THREE WEEKS off, the squad met up again for pre-season training in late July. But even while they were away from the England camp, the players hadn't been idle.

'We weren't due to reconvene until 21 July, but we were all given personal fitness programmes to follow during the break,' said Richard Hill. An extended squad was selected for the pre-World Cup training camp and every player would be vying with several others for a place in the final squad that would leave for Australia. There could be no time for complacency, no time to rest. Every player understood the need to hit their straps and impress as much as they could – or else face the very real possibility of missing out on their dream of competing at the World Cup.

The team had three warm-up games scheduled for the end of August and the start of September: Wales at the Millennium Stadium and France in Marseille and at Twickenham. They were three Tests that would get them match-ready and were a world away in class to the warm-ups arranged before the 1999 tournament. But in many respects, as rigorous a workout as those matches would be, they paled into insignificance when compared to the physical torture the players would endure at the hands of Dave Reddin and the other coaches at Pennyhill Park.

Woodward arranged for a temporary pavilion to be erected beside the pitch at the hotel and for all the gym equipment to be transferred there from Twickenham. This meant that all their training facilities were in one place; the temporary gym would soon be dubbed the 'House of Pain' by the players.

At the start of the season Woodward had introduced 'nine winning behaviours' to the team – defence, basics, contact, pressure, kicking, team attack, self-control, tactics and leadership. All nine had been taken to world-class levels throughout the season and had made significant contributions to their success. Arguably the most crucial, and the one that held all the others together, was the last: leadership. Over the course of six years, Martin Johnson, Lawrence Dallaglio, Matt Dawson, Phil Vickery, Jonny Wilkinson, Jason Leonard and Neil Back had all captained the side. The collective knowledge, cumulative experience of performing under pressure and the charisma of these men was not only reassuring for the other members of the team but also a source of intimidation for opposition teams. These players had all been there and done it and would be able to respond positively to any situation thrown at them either on or off the pitch. Martin Johnson epitomised the maturity of a squad that had been together for years, had endured so much both collectively and individually, and had gained a valuable perspective on what they were doing. 'We weren't good enough to win it last time, it's as simple as that,' said Johnson during the training weeks at Pennyhill Park. 'And I'll tell you one of the main reasons why this was so: we were all guilty of getting it out of proportion; the players, the management, everyone involved. We got it out of kilter, we made it too big. I can tell you now that most guys didn't even enjoy the 1999 tournament, and not just because we were dumped out of it by the Springboks.

'Now, I just think the whole team's managed to put some perspective on life, especially those who have suffered private grief in recent times. A lot of the guys have been through some tough times off the field and it's helped us all to understand that, as desperate as we are to win the World Cup, life goes on whatever. Whether I return as captain of the world champions or not, I'll still have my wife and my daughter, hopefully my health and the rest of my life to look forward to. I'm not saying I won't be bothered – I've put my heart and soul into winning this World Cup – but I've gained some perspective in my life which I maybe didn't have four years ago.'

When the team had been Down Under for the summer tour, Woodward had had the pitch at Pennyhill Park dug up and relaid by the groundsmen from Twickenham. Not only did it serve their purposes to be training on an international-standard surface, but it also reduced the risk of rolled ankles or other soft tissue injuries caused by running on an uneven surface.

'In my estimation,' said Woodward at the time, repeating an assertion that he had long believed in, 'the top four or five teams at the World Cup will be of roughly the same ability, and will be coached roughly as well as each other. The key factor could be which team can find that extra edge somewhere.'

Woodward was still obsessed with the philosophy of marginal gains and understood that constant small improvements might prove to be the difference between his team's performance and that of the opposition. It was revolutionary in rugby at the time, but it was a well-recognised practice in other disciplines and has since become a staple of elite sport. From Roger Federer only ever using his best racket for Wimbledon to the Team GB cycling team putting away their bikes after the Beijing Olympics and pulling them out of storage only in the build-up to the London Olympics, modern sport is awash with stories of athletes depriving themselves of the best equipment outside of the most important events in order to give themselves a crucial edge when it matters most. The art of critical non-essentials and marginal gains begun by Woodward was taken to a new level by Sir Dave Brailsford and the Team Sky and Team GB cycling teams that he oversaw.

Brailsford's teams have become a global force, winning thirty medals over three Olympic Games, eighteen of them gold, while in 2012 Sir Bradley Wiggins became the first British rider to win the Tour de France, followed into the maillot jaune by Sky teammate Chris Froome in 2013.

As well as a meticulously planned training regime for each athlete, Brailsford and his team have obsessed over 'the aggregation of marginal gains': from spraying alcohol on tyres to remove dirt, to visored aerodynamic helmets; heated shorts that keep muscles warm, to studying the sleep patterns of the athletes to determine the best positions for them to lie in bed to achieve the deepest sleep, and even specialist guidance on washing their hands to reduce the risk of illness.

In many respects these make Woodward's obsessions look tame, but it serves to emphasise that he was a thinker ahead of the curve rather than simply a mad dreamer. 'In professional sport, everybody is looking for the edge,' said Woodward, 'It's getting smaller and smaller the more competitive the world of sport becomes. Take Tiger Woods. If someone asks him why he's better than the rest of the world, he talks about his fitness; he doesn't talk about his golf swing. He talks about feeling mentally stronger and that comes down to believing he's the fittest. He's an athlete. He's as fit as the 100-metre champion. He thinks he's fitter than any athlete in the world. He has massive mental strength.'

'Winning in rugby is all about tiny percentages,' said Phil Vickery. 'That was one of the key messages from Clive. It's not about making huge leaps forward – it would be great if it was, but at elite level no one makes huge leaps forward. It's the tiny little differences that separate the best from the rest. You have to be able to do everything you possibly can as frequently as you possibly can to make those tiny improvements.'

'I remember Steve Redgrave coming to talk to the team on one occasion,' said Jason Leonard. 'And one of the things he said was that in all his years of training, he had one clear goal – to make that day's training session just a bit better than the day before's. If he could make tiny improvements every day, he would improve enormously over the course of the weeks, months and years.'

Looking back over Woodward's time in charge of the team up to that point made impressive reading. In Woodward's sixty-eight matches as England's head coach, they had won forty-nine, lost seventeen and drawn two. Since losing to South Africa in the 1999 World Cup, they were undefeated at Twickenham and had won thirty-five out of the forty matches they had played. But he knew that if they didn't return from Australia with the World Cup he would be deemed a failure, and the players would be forever remembered as chokers rather than for their glorious achievements. But the failures of the past were valuable lessons that they had all learnt a huge amount from. As they approached the foothills of Everest, the entire squad had bought into the unequivocal importance of preparation.

'Our preparation immediately before the World Cup was quite different from the preparation we did in 1999,' said Jason Leonard. 'There were no army assault courses or complicated team-building sessions. I think Woodward had learnt the lessons from 1999 and our training was quite specific to the task in hand and less harsh than it had been. We didn't feel we had the natural enthusiasm trained out of us – we went into the tournament feeling fresher and fitter.'

'As candidates for World Cup selection we wanted for nothing,' said Matt Dawson. 'The pitch outside was a beautiful surface, the gym inside as comprehensive as I'd ever seen. There were three lanes of equipment and never any wait to get on the machine of your choice. With no contact work scheduled, it was a great chance to get in really good shape.'

Woodward was well aware of the need to strike a balance between training and rest. With three weeks spent in camp at Pennyhill Park working on strength and fitness, three weeks of Test matches, a week off and then departure for Australia, plus the tournament itself, the players were looking at between fourteen and fifteen weeks together – so it was important that a balance was struck between spending time together and getting away from the cocoon of the camp to spend time with friends and family away from rugby.

'The training was intense and tough but incredibly well structured, planned and orchestrated,' said Josh Lewsey in *One Chance*. 'Weekends were a welcome break in which everyone bomb-busted away from captivity back to their wives and girlfriends. The Friday feeling was heightened when we had team Olympics – a series of team-based fitness competitions designed to knacker everyone just before a couple of days' rest and before it started all over again the following Monday morning.'

'Getting the balance right is vital for a squad's morale,' said Will Greenwood. 'And I thought it was spot on to give us time apart, back with our families and friends. This was also when the decision to make that reconnaissance run to Perth in the summer paid off because it meant that we could delay our departure that little longer. Although we were the last team to arrive in Australia, we settled in as if our Perth hotel was a second home.'

'It was like training with a club side because we all knew each other so well,' said Phil Vickery in *Raging Bull*. 'You knew other people's scrum machine settings and what they liked and didn't like about training, just like you would in a club environment. I knew the system, the techniques and the personalities. It was Club England, which is exactly what Clive had been keen on achieving. There's no question that he did that. We were all part of a club that felt very familiar and were all very confident.'

One of the criticisms that had been levelled at the squad, particularly on their tour Down Under in the summer, had been that a number of key players might be too old to endure the rigours of the World Cup and that they had perhaps peaked too early in the year. 'Dad's Army' became the watchword for England's detractors and, on paper, they may have had a point. By the time the tournament kicked off, Martin Johnson would be thirty-three, Neil Back thirty-four and Jason Leonard thirty-five. Dorian West was thirty-six. Richard Hill, Lawrence Dallaglio, Will Greenwood, Mike Catt and Matt Dawson were also all in their thirties.

'That always makes me laugh,' Dave Reddin said of the 'Dad's Army' moniker. 'There are many examples of athletes over-performing in their thirties. I would back our fitness against anybody. One argument is that as you get older, there is more potential to develop certain aspects of fitness, like strength levels.'

'Too old?' Back had asked when questioned on the Australian leg of the summer tour. 'You're either good enough or you're not. If people say you're not good enough, then fair enough. But too old? That doesn't mean anything.'

In 1999 Reddin came into possession of fitness reports from the All Blacks camp. 'I put the figures up on a screen for the England players. Jaws dropped. *No way.* I knew we were miles behind. So we gave them the most uncomfortable eighteen months of their lives. It was a constant source of amusement to me that the Dad's Army tag kept on being levelled at us in Australia. I knew that our guys were an incredible group in terms of their work ethic, their need to achieve, their will to win. They knew they were better than anyone else in every single area because they had worked consistently well every single day.'

Woodward thought little of the 'old timers' jibes. He had deliberately worked to build a squad full of experienced players who knew how to win Test matches. His attitude was similar to Neil Back's – if the player could perform to the standards that he demanded, age had nothing to do with it. And he refused to countenance any discussion about his older players retiring after the World Cup. The suggestion that the tournament might be some kind of send-off for the senior players might detract attention and focus away from the job in hand, and he was adamant that this would not be allowed to happen. 'If any player thinks he's going to the World Cup as his swansong, I don't want him,' said Woodward at Pennyhill Park. 'No bullshit, I expect Martin Johnson to captain the team in the Six Nations in February. And if he's not, it will because I've made that decision in February. Now's not the time to say he's retiring because I don't want him going through this World Cup with the wrong mindset. The same with Backy and the other older guys. I expect to see them playing for England in February.'

While the players may have scoffed at the Dad's Army jokes and Reddin and Woodward publicly decried it, Reddin was nevertheless acutely aware of the age and career stage of each member of the squad and he tailored their training programmes accordingly. 'Organisation skills were better with the older group so we have to be far more precise in the way we do things with the younger men who have never known anything other than professional rugby,' he said in an interview in 2004. 'But we can be more adventurous on the technical side. Weight training, for instance. A lot of the younger guys have grown up with that so they have a better technique but their training volume is less. The training background you accumulate over the years gives you a tolerance to work at the highest level… You have to be careful how often and how heavy you load the young players so that they don't get over-fatigued. But you could probably hit Jason Robinson with anything and he'll be fine – he, though, has more than a decade of work behind him.

'We work on the Olympic lifts, which are excellent ways of developing power, but I would never have tried to teach someone like Martin Johnson how to do a snatch. His body had become fairly battered towards the end and it would have been a pointless exercise; he would have become frustrated.

'Take a prop like Matt Stevens; very powerful, very quick, learns lifts very well. He has physical attributes which Jason Leonard never had but he needs the toughness, the attitude to hard work that Jason had.'

The programmes were all designed with a single purpose: for the team to be as physically fit and strong as possible, but also fresh for the rigours of a Test match tournament. It was all about peaking at the right time.

'There was a lot more notice taken of the players' vibes than in the previous World Cup campaign,' said Matt Dawson. 'As a result the players were more honest with themselves and the management over injuries. If I said, "my legs are fucked" nobody doubted that.'

'By the time we get to Australia,' said Woodward at Pennyhill Park, 'the amount of coaching we want to do is minimal. The heavy work will be done here. We want the load to be light in Australia, precise, and the players to be fresh in body and mind.'

Lorries loaded with ice would make regular drops at the hotel. Whenever the players ran, lifted weights or took part in an arduous training session, they would tear thousands of microfibres in their muscles. This is perfectly normal and part of increasing muscle size and strength as the muscles repair and regrow in the aftermath. By plunging into large bins of icy water after training, the microscopic bleeding in the players' muscles is halted; when they emerge, blood rushes back into their muscles and aids recovery, which reduces stiffness, pain and inflammation. This then allows the players to increase their capacity to train at maximum intensity a short time later. Submersion for several minutes in the ice baths is a painful process for the players, even in the sweltering temperatures that baked England that summer, but the benefits of doing so were enormous. The practice has been developed with more sophistication using cryotherapy chambers, particularly in the Olympic training facility in Spala, Poland, where athletes spend time in chambers with the air temperature cooled with liquid nitrogen to around -166°F (-100°C). England had a more prosaic approach with the ice baths, but the effects were the same.

'The main thrust of his programme is to get you to go absolutely flat out from the outset,' said Will Greenwood of Reddin's training. 'He wants you on your knees by the end. He wants you to leave nothing on the pitch when you walk off it.' By plunging the players in the ice baths after such training sessions, Reddin improved recovery rates so that the coaches could squeeze in more training, strength and fitness sessions per day than they otherwise would have been able to.

The player who worked harder than any other, unsurprisingly, was Jonny Wilkinson. 'He had always impressed us as a player but this was the first time we had spent such a long time training together and it was a real eye-opener,' said Richard Hill. 'Everybody knows he is meticulous with his practice routines, but it was even more impressive when you saw it first-hand. As for his fitness levels, they were just as mind-blowing, particularly in the running exercises. I thought I worked hard but Jonny pushed himself to the very limit. He was out on his own. There was one exercise where you had to run as far as you could in a minute, sit down for a short break, then repeat the exercise twice more. Jonny would be way off in the distance somewhere. Nobody else got near him.'

As Pennyhill Park basked in the sunshine, the coaches felt that the heatwave was a blessing for their preparation as they believed that their games would be played in sweltering heat – little did they know at the time that the weather that would greet them in Australia would be dreadful – but, typical of Woodward's regime, they had considered every aspect of the conditions they would face. 'We are increasing our knowledge about hydration,' said Woodward at the time, 'about how to produce peak performance in heat and how to plan rest. But we're also talking about the effects of dew. Our games begin at 8 p.m. and dew will be coming down hard. The fields may be quite wet by then.'

At this stage the patterns of play that the team practised out on the Pennyhill Park pitch were like second nature. 'All the repetition in training and our collective experience on the pitch means that instinct takes care of us,' said

Wilkinson. 'We know our jobs and our roles and when it doesn't quite go as expected, we just alter and shift a little. We hang in the game because we have a structure for our game-breakers to come in when the time is right. It feels as though we are permanently moving forward and waiting. The team performance becomes a springboard from which any player can launch at any time. In defence, the support is like a white wall round each player; in attack, it is the decoy runners, the unselfish options. It means that week in, week out, we're seeing the best of each other.'

As Daniel Coyle discusses in his book, *The Talent Code*, every human skill is enabled by chains of nerve fibres carrying tiny electrical impulses to the brain. Neurological scientists have discovered a neural insulator, called myelin, which some consider to be the holy grail of acquiring skill. 'Myelin's vital role,' writes Coyle, 'is to wrap those nerve fibres the same way that rubber insulation wraps a copper wire, making the signal stronger and faster by preventing the electrical impulses from leaking out. When we fire our circuits in the right way – when we practise swinging a bat or playing a note – our myelin responds by wrapping layers of insulation around that neural circuit, each new layer adding a bit more skill and speed. The thicker the myelin gets, the better it insulates, and the faster and more accurate our movements and thoughts become... Skill is a cellular insulation that wraps neural circuits and that grows in response to certain signals. The more time and energy you put into the right kind of practice, the more skill you get, or, to put it a slightly different way, the more myelin you earn.'

While Wilkinson and other world-class goal-kickers have acquired their phenomenal skill levels through thousands of hours of quality practice, the England squad as a whole had acquired knowledge of how to react and perform in hundreds of different scenarios around a rugby pitch – so much so that in certain areas of the pitch or at certain times in a match, they would almost go into autopilot so well did they know the pattern of play that was required of them.

Take the 'zig-zag' play as an example – a pattern designed to move Wilkinson into a position to score a drop-goal, which they had first developed after the 2000 tour to South Africa. From a line-out they would take the ball up in midfield and the scrum-half would then pass short balls to the forwards, or instruct them to pick-and-go around the fringes until they were close enough to the posts to make the drop-goal attempt as straightforward as possible for their fly-half. When the play was called – or any other similarly well-rehearsed pattern was called – the players knew exactly what to do, where to run, how to hit, everything. They had practised it so many times, literally hundreds of repetitions, that it was almost second nature. The hours of practice that they put in 'earned' them myelin, as Coyle would put it, so that they ran like clockwork in their precision and accuracy. It was the result of hundreds of hours of hard work and the consistency of Woodward's selection over much of his six-year period in charge – the team had built up their experience and skill together and functioned as a single unit that understood one another perfectly.

By sticking with experienced players familiar with each other's game, when play broke down and became unstructured – from a turnover, a kick gathered in space, a break through the defensive line – creating or supporting a quick change in broken play had become second nature. The beauty of what Woodward had created was that it wasn't just the first-choice starting players who had this instinctive understanding – the enlarged squad had spent so much time together, had had their play and training broken down and analysed by Tony Biscombe, the coaches and the other back-room experts so often, and the feedback delivered to them on such a regular and consistent basis, that they all knew what was required of them. Details like the black book meant that every player in the squad knew what was expected of them – there were no elite cliques that knew more about the way England played than anyone else, no rookie to the set-up who felt unsure of his role. It was a testament to Woodward's planning and forethought, and it had all been born out of the trauma of the 1999 World Cup. 'A lesson from 1999 was that we weren't confident enough to use our squad fully,' said Woodward at Pennyhill Park. 'Since then, however, we have been able to improve our strength in depth immeasurably. Looking back, we hadn't tested ourselves enough mentally, put ourselves on the line enough, in the build-up four years ago. That had to change.'

But this club-like approach to selection, where everyone had been working closely together for years, also meant that when a player was dropped, it was a painful experience for the entire group, not just the individual. 'It is the toughest part of the job,' said Woodward at the time, 'when I have to tell them they're not good enough to play for England any more.'

It was a dilemma that Woodward would have to face in the coming weeks. While he was not dropping the players for ever, he had to make his choice on the thirty players that he would take to the World Cup. For a man who valued loyalty as highly as any other quality, it would be heart-wrenching to dash the dreams of a host of players who had served him faithfully for many years.

But before he and his fellow coaches had those decisions to make, there were three Tests to be played. The first of these was against Wales at the Millennium Stadium; another game, another historic milestone. England won at a canter against a full-strength Wales side and the victory brought England level with their old rivals in terms of the number of games won between them, the dominance of the men in white finally matching that enjoyed during the halcyon days of Gareth and J.J., J.P.R., Gerald, Phil Bennett and Barry John, the King, when the Dragon lorded it over the world.

What was most remarkable about this victory, away from home, was that it was achieved by a second-string England side. They missed seven shots at goal and still emerged with a 43–9 scoreline. Those on the fringes of the squad were determined to give Woodward the mother of all headaches as to who would fill the final places in the World Cup squad.

Next they were off to France, to the Stade Vélodrome in Marseille, a fortress for French rugby where Les Bleus had never been defeated.

Again Woodward fielded his second string. 'Bernard Laporte and I arranged two England versus France matches before the World Cup because I felt the need for really strong warm-up opposition,' said Woodward. 'As part of this gentleman's agreement, I fielded my second team in the away leg and Bernard put out his second side at Twickenham a week later.'

Up against France's strongest selection, England's understudies almost achieved what had seemed impossible. In the bear pit of the Vélodrome, they lost by a single point, 17–16. England's run of consecutive wins had been halted at fourteen and while Woodward and his coaching crew moaned about the loss, seemingly oblivious to the fact that their second XV had almost beaten the French first XV, the French did a lap of honour – apparently equally oblivious to the evidence just presented.

The game was notable for the fact that it saw the introduction of the new skintight shirts. As Nike was the kit supplier to France and South Africa as well as England, both sides at the Vélodrome were bedecked in the revolutionary new shirts and all three teams would appear in them at the World Cup.

'The detail is terrific,' said Dan Luger after the game. 'It really is hard to hold on to a player in the tackle now. The forwards, for instance, have a looser part on the shirts so they can get a grip in the scrum. Everything is thought through.'

The return fixture at Twickenham featured a role reversal – England's firsts versus France's seconds. The gap in class was palpable as England romped to a 45–14 victory.

Throughout the three fixtures, players who had served England and Woodward with great pride and towering performances throughout much of his six-year reign were now shifting nervously, unsure whether they would make the cut for Australia. Only thirty could go. Every player in the wider squad knew that there would be some big-name casualties – they just had to pray that they would not be among them.

In the event it was Simon Shaw, Graham Rowntree, Austin Healey and James Simpson-Daniel who were the biggest of the names to miss out. All except Simpson-Daniel were triumphant Lions and all had been key figures in some of England's most momentous victories during Woodward's tenure. There is no doubt that each of them would have walked into just about every other Test side on the planet. But they were surplus to requirements for now – only injury or some other twist of fate could see them called out to Australia as a replacement.

On the flip side, there were some players counting their lucky stars. Iain Balshaw's form had crumbled on the 2001 Lions tour and it had remained in the doldrums for two years. But he had rediscovered his sparkle during the warm-up games and he was in. So too was Mike Catt. After two years out with injury, he had returned to action just in time, and his class had advanced with age and perspective. Martin Corry, who had been a revelation as a late replacement on the 2001 Lions tour, had fallen down the pecking order since then but had shown enough in the preceding months to stake a claim as a valuable utility player who was capable of playing in the second-row or in any of the three back-row positions. His selection cost Shaw his place. 'He would be in any other international team in the world and not to pick him is the hardest decision I have had to make in my six years as head coach with England,' said Woodward of Shaw's omission. 'I told Simon that there was nothing more he could have done. The same is true of Graham, but I had to make a decision. And they weren't necessarily the ones I would have made six weeks ago. That's why I'm delighted we had these warm-up games.'

In the early years of Woodward's reign, Austin Healey's versatility had made him an invaluable member of the squad, but with only thirty players able to travel to Australia, Woodward wanted specialists in the backs rather than utility players. And when measured against the scrum-halves, fly-halves and wingers that were vying with Healey, the Leicester dynamo – who had been struggling with injury that season – was not technically superior, man-on-man, to any of the others.

'I asked for a reason and Clive didn't really give me one,' said Healey in *Me and My Mouth*. 'He just said he thought it was the best way to go… So I just accepted it, and wished him good luck. "I'm really disappointed," I said, "because I know we're going to win it."'

Mike Catt, on the other hand, had class and experience and offered a different option at centre to the incumbents, Tindall and Greenwood – even if he too had been battling all season with injury problems.

'I always believed that we would need an experienced team to win a World Cup, especially playing down in Australia,' said Woodward. 'So I was very keen to get Catty involved. But my concern was that he was a long way short of physical fitness. I took a decision not to name him in the preliminary World Cup squad, nor in any of the warm-up games. I just believed that at that stage it was best for him to stay at Bath and work non-stop, rather than undergo all the squad sessions with us.

'Catty hadn't done himself any favours the previous season. He played for Bath when he wasn't right physically and that showed in his form. What I told him was to take the whole summer off and go away and get in physically great shape. Then he'd have a chance. I told him that he had nothing to prove to me in terms of his playing ability, so he didn't need to play in those warm-up games. I knew he'd been there and done it.'

So that was that. The squad was picked. Six years of effort, planning, preparation, perseverance, failure, comebacks and at times glorious, beautiful, magnificent rugby had come to this. Next stop: Australia.

PART THREE
ASCENSION

NINE

THE ANATOMY OF
THE CLIMB

'Show class, have pride, and display character.
If you do, winning takes care of itself.'
Paul Bryant

CLIVE WOODWARD WAS sitting having breakfast in the lobby-level restaurant of the Sheraton Hotel in Perth. He was gazing out of the window at the sparkling water of the Swan River drifting by in the distance, the morning sun dappling its surface and the cityscape stretching out into the distance beyond.

He paused for a moment to finish his breakfast – an egg-white omelette prepared by the England team's chef, Dave Campbell, who was now ensconced in the Sheraton's kitchen. Ever since Jonny Wilkinson had fallen ill with food poisoning in South Africa in 2000, Woodward had decided that no risks could be taken with his players and the food they ate while they were in the England camp. Backed up by an assertion from various sources within the All Blacks camp that their players had had their food tampered with on the eve of the 1995 World Cup final – which they went on to lose to South Africa – Woodward had employed Campbell as the team's official chef. Ever since his introduction, he had been in charge of the players' meals while they were at Pennyhill Park and Louise Ramsay had always ensured that Campbell was allowed full access to the kitchens in hotels that the team stayed in while playing away matches. Over the course of several years Campbell had worked with Dave Reddin and nutrition specialist Matt Lovell to develop an optimal menu for the players, which varied depending on the stage of the season.

It was 7 a.m. and the tables around Woodward were filled by the players, who were tucking into similar omelettes and plates of bananas and fresh fruit, while protein shakes adorned their place settings like large strawberry milkshakes in a burger joint.

Woodward poured himself a fresh cup of tea from a small white china pot, and as the steaming liquid swirled through a strainer, his thoughts turned to Georgia, England's first opponents at the World Cup. He had made the decision to field his strongest side for this opening match long before they had departed from Pennyhill Park and nothing had occurred since they had arrived in Perth to alter his thinking.

'The majority of those players have only played once in four months, so it is important that we start strongly,' said Woodward of his selected team. It was vital that the cobwebs were blown away by the time they played South Africa six days later in what was clearly the key encounter in the pool stage. England's route through the rest of the World Cup would be made considerably more challenging if they lost that match, just as had been the case when they lost to New Zealand in the 1999 pool.

'It's a huge match for us,' said Neil Back of the Georgia game. 'It's about us showing the rest of the teams in the tournament what we're made of and that we mean business. It's about us being physically ruthless. It's about us making the world and his wife sit up and take notice. It's about us laying down a marker about the way we can play rugby. Anything less will give our rivals reason to doubt us, our critics ammunition to fire at us, and the Springboks cause for confidence ahead of next week's game. I don't want Georgia crossing our line, I don't want us coming off the Subiaco Oval at the end of eighty minutes feeling that we underperformed. That has been my message to the team in the build-up.'

It was quite a statement of intent. The Georgians were never considered a serious threat to England, all the more so when the privations that their squad had to endure were publicly revealed in the build-up to the match. Like many of the tier two and three countries (those outside the top eight to ten IRB ranked sides), their best players plied their trade as professionals for clubs in England and France. It was rumoured that English and French club owners had attempted to keep as many of their foreign Test players from vanishing to the World Cup by offering them two contracts – one if they withdrew from the tournament and one if they did not. The latter was said to be significantly less lucrative. For players hailing from the likes of Samoa, Tonga, Fiji, Romania or Georgia, who were often supporting families back at home, it was a dreadful choice. Fulfil your dream of taking part in your sport's showcase tournament, or accede to your responsibilities as a breadwinner in a short-lived career. It seemed that many of the French-based Georgian players had felt compelled to eke what they could from their professional careers and had withdrawn their availability to the national team.

But the disadvantages did not stop there. According to Zaza Kassachvili, the Georgian Rugby Union's vice president, there was only one scrum machine for the team to train with – in the whole of Georgia. And to compound matters, the pre-tournament training camp planned for the Caucasus and a warm-up tour of Canada were both cancelled when funding was withdrawn by the Georgian government. The team therefore turned up both under strength and underprepared. The differences between the haves and the have-nots in world rugby remained as big as ever, and with the financial largesse that had been poured into preparing England for their campaign, the disparities could not have been more acute.

In the event the Georgians were brave and passionate, as had been expected, but they were completely blown away by the power, speed and accuracy of the England team, who barely broke sweat in an 84–6 victory. England scored twelve tries, nine conversions and two penalties and held their line resolutely intact. Amid the flood of tries a world record was broken as Jason Leonard came off the bench to win his 112th cap. He had had harder games before that day, but few as special. And as for his team as a whole, they were up and running. It had not been an arduous workout but it was an important one to get the players' minds focused and their bodies ready for the battles ahead of them.

*

There were several injury concerns during the run-up to the Springboks match. All three of England's scrum-halves were struggling – Kyran Bracken had pulled up with a back spasm during the warm-up to the Georgia game, Matt Dawson had limped off with a dead leg after thirty-eight minutes and Andy Gomarsall had a heavily bruised shin. On top of that, Richard Hill had pulled a hamstring, Mike Tindall had been replaced during the game after taking a heavy knock and Danny Grewcock had broken a toe in training when Ben Cohen stood on his foot, though Woodward was relatively unconcerned by this latter injury, stating that the Bath lock could still be pressed into service in an emergency.

An analysis of the Springboks team named to face them revealed further proof of the turmoil that South African rugby had been through in recent seasons. Constant chopping and changing of playing personnel in the Springboks squad thanks to injury, fatigue, loss of form and the vagaries of selection had given the South Africans a listless look. With the exception of captain Corne Krige and scrum-half Joost van der Westhuizen, South Africa were desperately short of experience, with the rest of the team averaging a paltry ten caps each. England's experience, meanwhile, totalled 580 caps. While youthful exuberance is often a great positive, and the information available to Tony Biscombe on many of the Springboks was limited, there was no hiding the gulf in Test match experience between the teams.

The demolition of the Springboks at Twickenham the previous November was still fresh on everyone's minds as the game approached, but every participant understood that a repeat of that scoreline was not going to happen in such a high-stakes game. For Woodward and his medical staff, however, the biggest fear was that the game might bear witness to the violence that had dogged the Twickenham encounter.

Krige, South Africa's captain, was quick to try to dispel those worries, knowing that if his players gave even a hint of such misdemeanors again, the referee and his assistants would take swift action and the challenge to topple England would be even greater. 'When you are in a situation like we were you've got one or two decisions to make,' said Krige of the infamous November 2002 match. 'You can either say, "We're getting a hiding, I might as well give up," or you can say, "I'm going down but I'm taking a few guys with me." It wasn't the right attitude to take and I apologised to the people I needed to, and since then I haven't played like that again. As a South African and a Springbok, losing by that margin is totally unacceptable. It took me a long time to recover from that.'

England were equally aware of the importance of maintaining discipline and reducing their penalty count. As ever with Woodward, he went the extra distance and employed international referee Steve Lander to join the back-room staff as an adviser. Lander offered thoughtful insight into the transgressions that the referees would be looking to pick up on, particularly around the breakdown. 'The work Steve does for us is tremendously important,' said Phil Larder. 'His work at full-contact sessions has been essential. I'm sure his presence has made a massive difference.'

'We have had a very intense four years since losing the 1999 World Cup quarter-final to South Africa,' said Martin Johnson in the final press conference before the match. 'Everything has moved on – our preparation, fitness levels, Test experience as a squad. By hard work we have become very difficult to beat. There have been some notable high points, such as beating South Africa in Bloemfontein, France in Paris, Ireland in Dublin, New Zealand in Wellington and Australia in Melbourne. But none of these games was as big or as important to England as our next game. It's absolutely massive for both countries… Like New Zealand, South Africa are historically the giants of world rugby. They have lost only one World Cup game in the three tournaments they have been allowed to enter, including this one. That is the calibre of what we face on Saturday. And both camps are realistic enough to accept that it will be pretty difficult for the losers of this game to go on and win the World Cup.'

While England were publicly walking the walk and talking the talk, behind the scenes things were not running as smoothly as they seemed. Neither Dawson's nor Hill's injuries were responding well to treatment and both were ruled out of the game. And for centre Will Greenwood, there was a development at home that had completely taken his thoughts away from the match.

In September 2002, Greenwood and his wife, Caro, had lost their son, Freddie, after he had been born eighteen weeks premature. Just days before the South Africa match, Greenwood received a call from Caro telling him that she was being rushed into an emergency operating theatre as the tragic scenario seemed to be happening again with her second pregnancy. Greenwood went straight to Woodward to tell him.

'Will came to see me at the start of the week to tell me there had been complications,' said Woodward. 'He knew how big the South Africa match was and didn't want the team worrying about him. He wanted to keep it to himself – but he also wanted to stay and play if he could.' Woodward instructed Louise Ramsay to provisionally book Greenwood on every flight out of Perth and back to the UK between that moment and the day after the game. If things worsened with Caro, Greenwood would be on the next plane heading north; if she remained stable, he would be heading home to be by her side as soon as the final whistle sounded.

'I spoke to him almost on an hourly basis before the match,' said Woodward. 'He wanted to play and Caro wanted him to play, but we prepared in the knowledge that if her condition worsened, he would be on the first flight home. It had been a tough week for Will but he handled it brilliantly. He didn't want the rest of the team to get worried about it so we only told them in the changing room after the game. Caro was also fantastic.'

'Twelve thousand miles away with your missus in intensive care, it's very difficult to know what to do with yourself,' said Greenwood. 'What do you do with your time? You think you should be back at home and then you think, *what can I actually do if I'm back there?* So rugby training and the games were a break from the constant thinking.'

'What he did, playing that game and playing as well as he did, was phenomenal,' said Martin Johnson. 'I don't think I would have been able to do it.'

'During the match I even scored a try,' said Greenwood. 'And if you watch the replays you can see a smile on my face, because for a short time rugby had pushed the worry from my mind. There are not many jobs you can say that about.'

Greenwood's determination to stay and play the key group game was a testament to his dedication to the team and the iron-willed support of his wife and family back home. His importance to the team, as far as Woodward was concerned, could not be overstated.

The son of former England flanker and coach, Dick Greenwood, Will followed in the footsteps of England great Will Carling first at their alma mater, Sedbergh School, then in the colours of Harlequins, England and the Lions. His career had been fascinating; while still uncapped by England, he had been selected for the 1997 Lions tour to South Africa and had played with great aplomb until he suffered a near-fatal injury playing against Orange Free State. Carrying the ball into contact he had been hammered in the tackle and his head and shoulder had been swung on to the hard ground, knocking him unconscious and dislocating his shoulder. The danger had been that as he was knocked out his tongue had blocked his airway. Only swift intervention by the veteran Lions doctor James Robson saved Greenwood's life.

Upon his return to the UK he had a shoulder operation, but the joint troubled him for the rest of his career and he would have periods out of the game as a result. He won his first cap under Woodward in the autumn of 1997 against Australia, but his career began to falter as injury plagued him and his form dipped at Leicester, where he was playing at the time. He was released by coach Bob Dwyer and was signed by Harlequins, where he experienced a renaissance in his career and soon established himself as a key member of the England team. 'Greenwood was Jonny Wilkinson's secret weapon,' said

Woodward. 'He was absolutely key to the success of the England team while I was in charge. Was he the best passer? No. Was he the best kicker? No. All round was he the best player? By a mile. His big thing was hitting the line flat and being able to offload the ball. He had everything. In terms of his communication skills and understanding of the game, his offloading ability, he was the best player I have ever seen play in the centre for England.'

And so with Greenwood in place and only Richard Hill and Matt Dawson unavailable, Woodward had virtually his strongest team available to face the challenge of the Springboks. After the carnage at Twickenham the previous November, there was great anticipation that another bloody battle would ensue at the Subiaco Oval. In the event, none of the dark play that had so blighted the most recent encounter emerged as both sides let their rugby do the talking.

In what was still a ferociously physical confrontation, Jonny Wilkinson played a typically calm and controlled game, keeping his team on the front foot with booming punts that pinned the Springboks back in their half and keeping the scoreboard ticking over with four penalties, a conversion and two beautifully struck drop-goals.

The huge Springboks pack were causing difficulties for England at the scrum and around the breakdown and Martin Johnson's team were clearly missing the influence of Richard Hill. Lewis Moody was a tenacious replacement but he had a difficult night, spilling ball, losing turnovers in the face of the bigger South African forwards at the breakdown and conceding one soft penalty with a high tackle that gifted the Springboks three points. Woodward had long espoused the qualities of Hill and now the man who had been ever present for England since Woodward had taken over was showing just how important he was with his absence.

Despite the strength of their forwards, South Africa struggled to assert much authority on the game, not helped by their fly-half, Louis Koen, who missed four attempts at goal. His evening was made all the worse when Moody, in a moment of redemption, charged down a Koen clearance kick in the South African half. Greenwood was the first to react and he skilfully shepherded the ball over the line to score the game's only try. From there England never looked back and they went on to win 25–6.

The day after the game, Greenwood was on a flight back home. He arrived to find Caro in good spirits, her condition stabilised. She had a minor operation to help carry her pregnancy through its full duration and then, a week later, she sent her husband back to the airport.

He missed only one match – against Samoa – and was back on the bench for the final pool game against Uruguay. Caro had sent him away with one message: don't come back without the Webb Ellis Cup. 'A lot of people have inspiring stories,' said Greenwood. 'But I felt like I was a man with an extra mission after that.' Just over three months later, on 3 February 2004, Archie Frederick Lewis Greenwood was safely delivered.

*

In many regards the victory over the Springboks had been a disappointment in terms of performance. England had turned over a lot of ball, their scrum had come under some pressure and the service of Kyran Bracken to Wilkinson had been notably below par, which had placed the fly-half under unnecessary strain and interrupted the flow of ball to his outside backs. But England had won and won well against one of the superpowers of the world game despite playing relatively poorly.

Phil Vickery held his hands up for the poor scrummaging performance, having been given a particularly hard time by South Africa's monstrous prop Christo Bezuidenhout. 'I had given everything I had, couldn't have wrung one more ounce out of myself, and, even though we'd won, it hadn't gone that well for me,' said Vickery in an interview with Stephen Jones, recounted in *On My Knees*. 'At the end of the match, you hold your hands out but there's nothing there. You've given 110 per cent and you've got nothing to show. Everyone goes away from the game and they start going through the performances: "Ah, Vickery. Looked slow, a bit sluggish, a couple of dodgy scrums, a couple of good ones, average performance." God, it can be demoralising. Because then you've got to go back and face your teammates. There is no hiding place in this squad. *You haven't had a good game, why haven't you had a good game?* There's none of this, "Ah, it'll be all right next week." No, it's *how many times were you a fraction late getting to the rucks, why were there twelve minutes between tackle number five and tackle number six?* Everything is on the video; every excuse you try can be checked. So you front up, and this is why not everyone plays for England.'

'We are so relieved,' said Woodward after the game. 'But it was nowhere near the level of performance we can achieve.' For the rest of the big guns in the tournament, it was an ominous warning.

'For me, England are the best,' said Bernard Laporte when the France coach was asked his opinion of England's performance. 'They have hardly lost for three years. They are the most complete team and far more mature in their rugby. Besides, what won the last World Cup? Defence. Australia had one try scored against them four years ago. Who has the best defence now? England. It is the best part of their game.'

'I would always pick a team to attack but modern players love the physicality of defence,' recalled Woodward. 'With England, we did a fifteen-minute defensive drill on a Tuesday called "murder-ball". It was brutal, aggressive stuff – full-on tackling. The players wanted to do it, I wanted to keep them fit and I eventually negotiated with defensive coach Phil Larder to bring it down to ten minutes. The idea was that if your body wasn't ready for this, you weren't ready for Saturday. We used to put Jonny Wilkinson in a yellow vest and say "nobody touch him", but of course he would go flying in smashing somebody because he wanted to get involved.'

'The collisions are very fierce in a Test match and the only way to prepare for that is to train with the same ferocity,' remarked Phil Larder. 'We do a lot of organisation, we do a little bit of technique that is only 60 or 70 per cent intensity, then we do ten minutes or so of Test match ferocity work. There are three areas of defence that I look at. There's technique and you can improve technique at 50 per cent intensity, but some of it can only be improved when you work at 100 per cent. So throughout a Test week we will build from 50 per cent to 100 per cent ferocity. The second thing is organisation. We can do organisational strategy at 50 or 60 per cent intensity, but then the thing that really makes a defence as good as ours is the third thing: enthusiasm and desire. The only way to get that enthusiasm and desire is to go full-on. Obviously there is a danger of picking up injury, so we keep it short. But it's essential. The fear of being unprepared is greater than the fear of picking up injuries – and that comes from the players as well. They want to feel that they are 100 per cent prepared to play at the highest intensity that they possibly can when they step into the Test arena.'

England's defence would have to be primed and ready for their next game, against Samoa in Melbourne. Samoa, like Georgia, were missing some front-line players – in their case twelve – for the tournament, who had opted instead to stay with their clubs in England and France. They too had meagre financial resources. The All Blacks side at the World Cup were fielding no less than six players who could have been playing in the blue of Manu Samoa – backs Mils

Muliaina, Tana Umaga and Ma'a Nonu and forwards Keven Mealamu, Jerry Collins and Rodney So'oialo.

To the uninitiated these impediments suggested that England would sweep the islanders aside just as they had done with Georgia. But the uninitiated would have no appreciation of the physical magnificence of the Samoans, the dazzle of their attacking play, the bone-crunching force of their defence or the unabandoned joy with which they played the game. Perhaps certain technical aspects of their play could be flawed, notably around the set-piece, but they remained a clear and present danger to England.

*

In terms of the scientific analyses of performance that have been discussed in this book, it is interesting to hold the England–Samoa match up to the light of two contrasting scientific hypotheses. The first, as discussed previously, is the theory that England's developing excellence under Woodward was, in part, thanks to the 10,000-hour rule, obsessive organisation and preparation, first-rate medical resources, deep financial backing and dedicated programmes to achieve world-class levels of strength and fitness.

The second is the theory of natural genetic advantage. It is arguable that there is nowhere on the planet where a people are more naturally suited to the game of rugby (particularly the modern game and the physicality of its collisions) than the Pacific islands. Underfunded and under-resourced and with a comparatively tiny pool of talent to draw from, the players who represent Samoa, Tonga and Fiji are among the most talented athletes in the game. While wielding a broad brush is obviously dangerous for any study, it is probably fair to state that the players representing these teams at the 2003 World Cup were big, strong and fast. They could also, to a man, display incredible dexterity with the ball in hand, were possessed of balance and poise when running at full tilt, and they could – and would – throw their bodies into contact with frightening intensity.

In 2003, in collaboration with the Australian Institute of Sport, Yemima Berman and Kathryn N. North conducted a variety of studies that examined skeletal muscle α-actinins, the results of which they published in their article 'A Gene for Speed: The Emerging Role of α-Actinin-3 in Muscle Metabolism' in the *Journal of Applied Physiology*. Their studies, conducted across a wide spectrum of ethnic groups, examined the presence of the non-mutated version of the alpha actinin skeletal muscle isoform 3 gene in elite athletes. In layman's terms, the ACTN3 genotype is associated with high-level sprint/power performance. 'The large number of human studies that have been performed to date show that the ACTN3 R577X polymorphism represents an important genetic factor associated with variations in muscle performance in humans,' they wrote, 'with the presence of α-actinin-3 associated with improved sprint and power performance.'

The presence of skeletal muscle α-actinin proteins is encoded in the human gene sequence. The α-actinins bind to a glycolytic enzyme to affect the efficiency of skeletal muscles. Skeletal muscles are composed of muscle fibres and there are two types: slow twitch and fast twitch. Fast twitch fibres trigger more rapidly and generate more force than slow twitch and are responsible for human speed and power.

While no study was made of the Polynesian players taking part in the 2003 World Cup, it is not unrealistic to suggest that the majority of them, if not all of them, carried the ACTN3 genotype. In the build-up to the 2012 Olympic Games a study examining the fastest sprinters in the world revealed that they all possessed the ACTN3 genotype.

'There is a bloodline there,' said John Boe, the Samoa coach. 'These guys are born to play rugby. They develop physically earlier than Europeans and enjoy the smash element of the game. They have a natural instinct for the ball and are athletic on the move. Remember that rugby is not just a game in Samoa. It is a central part of their culture. It is one thing they have contributed to the world.'

And so England's third Pool C clash, against Samoa, threw up an interesting case study. Could the natural athleticism of the islanders and their broad range of skills compete with the more finely tuned and specifically developed talents of the England players? While the England team contained some outstanding athletes and the Samoan team contained some highly dedicated professionals, the match nevertheless pitched the theory of nature versus nurture on the rugby field. It would be fascinating to see which would prevail.

*

There were several changes to the England team that had defeated South Africa. Jason Robinson was moved to full-back to accommodate Iain Balshaw on the wing, Stuart Abbott filled Greenwood's position in the centre, Matt Dawson came in at scrum-half, the whole front-row changed with Jason Leonard, Mark Regan and Julian White winning the starting shirts, and while Richard Hill continued to recover from his hamstring injury, Joe Worsley replaced Lewis Moody on the blindside flank.

Even in the face of their limited resources, the loss of their front-line players and the widely-held belief that they would be unable to live with the fitness and efficiency of the England players, Samoa began the game by ripping up the pre-match script. At the end of the first quarter they had enjoyed 90 per cent of possession and were quickly on the scoreboard thanks to an Earl Va'a penalty before a sweeping move from deep in their own half saw the ball pass back and forth between forwards and backs and possession retained deftly through eleven phases and for more than forty passes before the captain Semo Sititi burst through the last line of English defence to score a truly glorious try.

And the brilliance of the Samoans did not stop there. As was their wont, they brought a thundering brutality to the tackle area. Brian Lima, the veteran centre who was playing in his fourth World Cup, showed that Father Time had still not caught up with him and that he was still thoroughly deserving of the nickname of 'the Chiropractor' (thanks to his penchant for rearranging bones on a rugby field) with two thumping hits on Jason Robinson and Jonny Wilkinson. The thud of each collision could be heard all around the feverish stadium.

Amid the storm of Samoa's early play, Wilkinson had an opportunity to get England on the board with a penalty – but missed. White-shirted fans in the Docklands Stadium and all around the world shifted uncomfortably in their seats. A few minutes later he tried again and the ball ricocheted off an upright. For any other kicker in the world this would have been a disappointment but not necessarily an anomaly. For those who had watched even a handful of Wilkinson's career performances, the two misses from relatively simple kicks felt like the world was shifting on its axis.

Samoa were treating the spectators to an exhibition of powerful running rugby, with even their huge props and second-rows dancing and spinning and accelerating through gaps like centres. In the end the great leveller was fitness. England had built up deep reserves of energy thanks to years of work with Dave Reddin, while Samoa's beleaguered troops eventually ran their tanks dry of gas. As the game wore on and the islanders' legs grew weary, England surged back into the game.

From a well-controlled rolling maul following a line-out, Neil Back burrowed over to score and Wilkinson finally found his kicking boots. He and

Va'a exchanged penalties and Samoa managed to just keep their noses in front at half-time, 16–13.

Woodward made some key personnel changes during the break, with Steve Thompson, Phil Vickery and Lewis Moody replacing Mark Regan, Julian White and Joe Worsley respectively. The replacements made an almost immediate impact as England set a scrum on Samoa's line and turned the screw. The white-shirted pack shunted mercilessly forward with a destructive power akin to an advancing steamroller. The Samoans tried to resist but were ultimately powerless to do so. As they collapsed under the pressure, referee Jonathan Kaplan signalled a penalty try. Wilkinson added the conversion and England were at last ahead.

But still the Samoans battled. Va'a added two further penalties and as the game moved into the final quarter, they were back in the lead, 22–20. 'There was no real panic,' said Martin Johnson. 'We just knew that we had to cut out the penalties, dominate territory and possession and we'd get there. It was simple but we knew it was an effective route out of trouble.' It was time for the real England to turn up. After his early wobbles, Wilkinson took the game by the scruff of the neck. England worked themselves into Samoan territory, the fly-half scuttled forward to retrieve the ball from a ruck and quickly snapped a drop-goal over to regain the lead. Then a few minutes later, in an appreciation of the open spaces available on the periphery of the field that would have Sherylle Calder grinning from ear to ear, he sent a deft cross-field chip off to the far wing. Iain Balshaw streaked after it like a cheetah, leapt gracefully to gather the ball and touched down without a Samoan defender laying a finger on him.

Mike Catt joined the fray and England's attack picked up fresh speed just as the Samoans began to fade from the game. England moved the ball around with precision and then Catt's fizzing pass found Vickery and the big tight-head barrelled over the line to score. The final score stood at 35–22, but England had been well and truly tested. It had been a magnificent encounter.

England's victory had been achieved with the team once again not firing on all cylinders. 'It's the sign of a good team: not panicking,' said Mike Tindall. 'That's what we've learnt over the years. We had a phrase that developed over time called the "win ethic" – it's just a ruthlessness to try and win no matter what we face.'

While their lack of accuracy and the concession of a number of costly penalties would have irritated Woodward and his team, they also knew that they had room to improve significantly – a comfortable position to be in while still notching up victories. Of more concern was an incident that occurred just before the final whistle that posed a greater threat to England's campaign than anything they had faced on the field. Mike Tindall had gone down injured and was receiving treatment just off the pitch. Dave Reddin was in charge of the England replacements and, with Woodward barking at him down his radio to make a swift substitution, he sent on Dan Luger to cover for Tindall. But Tindall, aware that England were short defensively but unaware that Luger had come off the bench, returned to the field. For thirty-four seconds (until the mistake was realised) England had sixteen players on the field. Referee Jonathan Kaplan was alerted to the incident and Luger was ordered from the field. In the aftermath England faced the very serious threat of a points deduction and even expulsion from the tournament. To make matters worse, Reddin had got into a heated argument with touch-judge Steve Walsh about the substitution. Things were spiralling out of control.

Fortunately, Woodward had, once again, thought of everything. Among the back-room staff that he had brought to Australia was Richard Smith, Q.C. During the Test match in Wellington four months previously, Ali Williams, the All Blacks lock, had stamped on Josh Lewsey's head, causing an injury that had required stiches but could have been much more serious; Lewsey had been lucky to get away with just a cut. The England camp were convinced that Williams would receive a lengthy ban – but the domestic citing officer reviewed the incident and felt that Williams had no case to answer. The matter was dropped. The team – and the media at home – felt that this decision represented a gross miscarriage of justice and Woodward had decided there and then to always travel with a legal adviser so that his team could be represented fairly should any such disciplinary matters arise again.

So it was that while the team moved on to the Gold Coast to prepare for their final pool match, against Uruguay at the Suncorp Stadium in Brisbane, Woodward, Reddin and Smith flew to Sydney for the disciplinary hearing.

'In court, Richard Smith was brilliant,' recalled Woodward in *Winning!* 'Even to my non-legal brain it was obvious he was simply destroying their argument… he was worth his weight in gold. The disciplinary hearing showed him at his best and he never thought about charging the RFU for his services. He was just delighted to have seven weeks as part of the England rugby team.'

In the end England were fined £10,000 and Reddin was banned from the touchline for two weeks – but no points were deducted and the threat of expulsion from the tournament was dismissed.

With Uruguay among the weakest sides at the World Cup, the management ordered the players to have a night out and the following day's training consisted of a game of football. It was in direct contrast to the intensity that had surrounded every move in the camp during the 1999 tournament – but the expectations were also markedly different. The management had complete faith that they would be in Australia for the full seven weeks, so they knew how important it was for the players to have some downtime when they could.

England's second-ever century of points was delivered against the South Americans, with seventeen tries scored, five of which came from Josh Lewsey, making him only the third Englishman to achieve the feat in more than a hundred years of Test rugby. Albeit against severely limited opposition, the true glory of England's attacking ability was finally unleashed. With Wilkinson being rested, Paul Grayson stepped into the No.10 position and played with aplomb, converting eleven tries along the way, but it was Mike Catt outside him who really pulled the strings, orchestrating the irresistible running lines of the outside backs and forward runners with pinpoint, clever passing. He made a splendid partnership in the centre with Wasps' Stuart Abbott, while out wide Lewsey's electric performance had almost been matched by Iain Balshaw and, in the second half, by Jason Robinson when the Sale man appeared off the bench. Lawrence Dallaglio, who had been singled out by Woodward in the build-up to the game as having performed quietly at the World Cup up to that point, was back to his prowling, rumbustious best.

On the negative side of the ledger, Woodward was concerned to see that both Balshaw and Danny Grewcock had been injured in the demolition of Los Teros and Dan Luger had still to show any real form despite his best efforts to involve himself in the game. And while there was no question of England's dominance or the chance of the result going any other way, Phil Larder was still furious that Uruguay had managed to breach his defensive line to score a try – such were the standards expected of his charges.

But with Balshaw and Grewcock's injuries considered minor and Luger's career bedecked with stardust, there was very little to be disappointed with in the result. England had topped the group and would now face their old rivals Wales in the quarter-finals, while South Africa had the much more challenging route to the final ahead of them, with a match against New Zealand awaiting them in the next round. For Georgia, Samoa and Uruguay, the journey was over.

*

While there had been some cracking encounters thus far in the World Cup, none came close to the searing excitement and brilliance of the final Pool D match between New Zealand and Wales. With both sides having secured qualification for the quarter-finals the fixture was seen as something of a dead rubber, even if the winner would seal the top spot in the group. With Wales having endured several long seasons of disappointment and New Zealand being many pundits' favourites for the tournament, the result seemed to be a foregone conclusion. Steve Hansen, the Kiwi head coach of Wales, certainly seemed to think so as he fielded an under-strength side against a powerful All Blacks line-up. But his reserves made a mockery of the facts and played with huge skill, bravery and a refreshing freedom that had not been seen from the men in red for many, many years. Shane Williams, who would go on to be named World Player of the Year in 2009, break try-scoring records, play an instrumental part in three Welsh Grand Slams over the following decade and establish himself as one of the game's greatest wingers, had been selected by Hansen as the third-choice scrum-half in his 2003 World Cup squad. This match, which saw Williams pressed into action on the wing, signalled a sea change in the direction of his career. Alongside back-rowers Jonathan Thomas and Colin Charvis, centres Mark Taylor and Sonny Parker, and Gareth Thomas, who came off the bench, Williams and Wales took the game to New Zealand and cut their defence to ribbons. The All Blacks, in turn, showed their attacking genius and the world just had to sit back and watch running rugby at its finest.

When Shane Williams skipped over for his try in the final quarter, following Taylor, Parker and Charvis over the whitewash, and Stephen Jones kicked the conversion it moved Wales into a 34–28 lead and an upset as great as France's defeat of New Zealand in the semi-final of the 1999 World Cup appeared to be on the cards.

But New Zealand ultimately showed their finishing qualities and greater stamina. First Carlos Spencer slipped through for a try before Doug Howlett crossed for his second of the match; Leon MacDonald kicked a penalty and then Aaron Mauger broke through the exhausted Welsh defence for his side's eighth try. The final score stood at 53–37 and it revealed much. For those that would face New Zealand it showed that the All Blacks could be placed under severe pressure by an impassioned defence and by a side willing to attack from any quarter. For England, it showed that the Welsh Dragon was roaring again and that all their recent encounters against them counted for naught. Forget the recent hammerings and remember Wembley 1999. That was the kind of Welsh performance that England had to prepare for.

But there was further bad news in the England camp. Not only was Richard Hill still unavailable, but Danny Grewcock had had an X-ray on his injured hand and discovered that it had been broken. His World Cup was over and an S.O.S. was sent back to England to summon Simon Shaw as his replacement. Then, on the eve of the match, Josh Lewsey and Iain Balshaw had to withdraw from the squad with hamstring and knee injuries. Dan Luger, who had not even been in the originally selected match-day twenty-two, was handed a wing berth and Jason Robinson was moved to full-back. 'For all the rugby league Test matches I've played for Great Britain,' said Robinson before the game, 'for all the internationals for England's union Test team, this is the biggest thing I've been involved in… Wales stand between us and a semi-final. We're well aware that if we underperform we're on the plane home. The truth is, we haven't hit our best. That's still to come, but it is at this stage that the big performers start to perform. Cometh the hour, cometh the man, as they say. I know this is the biggest game of my life.'

For the first forty minutes of the game, England looked like a different side to the one that had been playing with such width and speed for the previous four years. They were tight around the ball, the backs standing bunched together with no wide options for Wilkinson to exploit. Wales, meanwhile, played a superb tactical game, pinning England deep in their half just as England had been doing to opposition teams for years. Because England were always so compacted as an attacking unit, Wales could afford to drop their wings and stand-off back to cover Wilkinson's territorial punts. This gave Wilkinson very few kicking options whenever he stepped outside his 22 and as he probed for space he would invariably find one of the Welsh sweepers, who would either fire the ball back into England's territory, or would look to counter-attack – which they did with the same devastating effect as they had shown against New Zealand. The World Cup would signal a renaissance in Welsh rugby that would grow with increasing momentum over the next decade, re-establishing their place as one of the top sides in the world. The performance they were putting in during the first half of that quarter-final was not one that England had expected or prepared for, even after studying the video of the New Zealand game a week earlier. There was no way Wales could do it two weeks in a row, they thought. But Wales were doing just that and they were putting England to the sword in the process.

'Whichever daft sod thought we were going to beat Wales by forty points needs shooting,' said Will Greenwood after the game. 'Wales–England in a World Cup quarter-final was always going to be close.'

'I think we played the World Cup well enough, but the one game we really did stuff up was against Wales – we *really* stuffed it up,' said Woodward. 'I think that was partly because we looked at the fixture and were already focused on playing France in the semi-final. We were up in Brisbane and all week things felt wrong, you could just tell people's heads weren't right. And that is the worst part of being a coach because you try all sorts of things to turn it around to make it a good week, to make training better, to change the atmosphere in the camp, but it just wasn't happening. Training was flat – I put my hands up and say we probably overworked the players – but we were just trying to do things to lift them and it didn't work. I woke up on the day of the game and I didn't feel like I normally did, I didn't think, *Oh wow, great, we're ready to go*, I thought, *We're just not right*. And it is a horrendous feeling. You always look in the mirror and blame yourself at those moments.

England were panicking and Wilkinson was again struggling with his kicking. He missed his first shot at goal from a penalty and a drop-goal attempt didn't even come close to the target. The malaise spread through the team, affecting decision-making all over the field – they were forgetting the basics of T-CUP, none more so than Ben Cohen, who grabbed the ball at a penalty that was within range of the posts and sent a poorly executed cross-field kick wide to Neil Back that missed its target and bounced harmlessly into touch. This tactic was repeated a few minutes later by Mike Tindall – but to much more costly effect. The centre fired the ball wide to where lock Ben Kay was roaming in open space, but the ball was gathered instead by Shane Williams, who continued the dance he had started against New Zealand. He weaved his way downfield, fed the ball to scrum-half Gareth Cooper, who carried for thirty metres before slipping a pass to Gareth Thomas, who returned the ball to Williams. As the last-ditch England defence tried to haul the diminutive Williams to the ground, the little winger juggled the pass and then flipped the ball delicately to fly-half Stephen Jones to score.

'We saw errors from the team that we'd never seen before,' said Woodward, 'and suddenly Wales were running through us like we were an under-10s side.'

Just four minutes later, England imploded again. Cohen fielded an up-and-under, but he was isolated in the tackle and conceded a penalty. Wales nudged the ball into the corner and from the resulting line-out they drove to the line and formed a ruck from which Welsh captain Colin Charvis pounced to score. Stephen Jones was unable to convert either try, but Wales were more than deserving of their 10–3 half-time lead.

'We came in at half-time and the boys looked tired. I felt tired,' confessed Martin Johnson. 'The humidity was draining us and I thought, *we could be in trouble here*. It almost felt like we had pushed ourselves out.'

Woodward strode into the changing room and stared around at his troops. He was pleased to see that, despite ignoring virtually every tactical principle they had built their game around for the past few seasons in the first half, they were at least going through their usual half-time routine. When chaos threatens to overwhelm you, it is important to have reference points to return to, islands on which they could seek shelter from the storm. The half-time routine was one of these and, as the players silently changed their shirts and took on fluids, Woodward could sense a semblance of calm returning. A few moments later the players gathered into their forwards and backs units to discuss how to address the problems they were facing on the field. Then the captain addressed the team.

'Johnno just let fly,' recalled Woodward. 'He really lost it in the changing room – which he needed to do. He needed to make a statement to the team.'

'What are you going to do?' recalled Johnson of his outburst. 'You're not going to pack it in. You have to go back out there and go for it. If that was going to be our last forty minutes in the World Cup, then we were going to make it a good one.'

Then it was Woodward's turn to speak.

'Calm,' he said. 'Just stay calm out there. We need to relax. We know we're not playing well but we know how to fix that. I haven't ever seen this side play the way we have just played in that half. So now we go back to doing what we do best. I want width on the ball. I want to stretch them across the field. At the moment, we're easy to defend against. We should never be easy to defend against. Trust our systems, trust our fitness and trust each other.

Don't overcommit at the breakdown – we don't need so many bodies in the rucks. We should be able to win our own ball cleanly and quickly with fewer numbers, let's just make sure our technique is spot-on.'

He glanced around the room. 'Luges,' he said to Dan Luger. 'Thanks for your work, but you're off. Tinds, I want you on the wing instead. Will, you're moving to outside-centre. Catty, you're up.'

Then he turned to Martin Johnson and nodded. He had made the tactical changes he thought necessary – Mike Tindall on to the wing, Mike Catt into inside-centre, Will Greenwood to outside-centre. Now it was up to the players.

'The shuffling of the back-line was a big call, but those are the ones that you're proudest of when you look back,' recalled Woodward, 'because it worked. I think most coaches would have left it ten or fifteen minutes into the second-half to make that call. And if someone went down injured we would have been stuffed but I just felt it was a change that we had to make at half-time to give us a change in momentum as soon as we left the changing room. That was a T-CUP moment, we had to make the big changes, make the big statements.'

As he watched them wander out for the second half, Woodward was pleased to see Catt talking animatedly to Wilkinson, his arms cutting running angles and kick trajectories in the air. He was even more pleased to see the calm focus on Wilkinson's face. The fly-half had played poorly in the first half, he had been rattled. But now that Catt was there, he looked serene. He was computing exactly what was needed to haul England back into the game and what was needed for them to push on for the win.

Catt's presence seemed to add reassurance to the whole team. As soon as England got possession of the ball in the second half, they looked like a different side. The distance and variation of Catt's passing stretched the Welsh defence across the field, forcing the back-three defenders and fly-half Stephen Jones to push flatter, while his accurate, long, diagonal punting moved England into the areas of the field where they needed to be.

'Mike Catt came on and was inspirational in what he did,' said Wilkinson, 'which he is as a person not just as a player – but this time he came on and really added to the game enormously.'

Both sides knew how crucial it was to be the next to score – Wales to push further ahead, England to bring them back into the game.

The width of Catt's passing game meant that the Welsh defence was spread across the field like a string of pearls. They were being forced to stand further apart from one another than they had in the first half, but they were still harrying and pushing up fast and defending furiously.

Then came another moment of pure magic in an already scintillating game. After Wales had won an English line-out in their 22, Gareth Cooper hoisted a thumping clearance kick that soared deep into the England half. Ben Cohen tracked its path, gathered it on the bounce near the left-hand touchline and immediately fed the ball infield to Jason Robinson. Robinson looked up. The Welsh defensive line was racing up after the kick. Their organisation was impressive – a red wall was swiftly closing in, every chasing defender holding the line to ensure there were no dog-legs, every man evenly spaced so that there was no hint of a gap. Robinson would have to kick, there was no other option.

Robinson began to run.

He set off, shuttling on a diagonal towards the midfield where three defenders awaited him. As he closed in on them they began to push together, shutting down the space – three on one, with two sweepers just behind them. There was no way through. Robinson was travelling at full pace and as he approached the defence he gave a little hop and then stepped off his right foot, cutting a jagged line between the first two defenders. Normally a step like that would take the momentum out of a player's run, but Robinson was still sprinting and, incredibly, had even more speed in reserve. He put on the afterburners and accelerated through the traffic, using a powerful hand-off to repel a despairing tackle. He arced his run to the right and then honed in on full-back Gareth Thomas, the last line of defence. Another little half-skip and feint of balance change fixed Thomas in his tracks. Screaming up outside Robinson was Will Greenwood, who, alone among some 70,000 spectators in the Suncorp Stadium and twenty-eight other players on the pitch, had read Robinson's intentions from the moment he had touched the ball. With Thomas committed to tackling Robinson, the little magician floated a delicate pass out to Greenwood, who strode in to score in the corner.

'It is my natural ability to just go and run,' said Robinson. 'And the way I see it, if I don't know where I'm going, the opposition defence certainly doesn't know where I'm going… It's a rush when you do create those opportunities, when you do beat men, and you can sense the crowd on their feet… that's why you play the game.'

'You can see what he's trying to do,' recalled Greenwood in *Will Greenwood on Rugby*. 'But you just don't believe it is possible that someone can cram all that skill into a split-second of natural athleticism and instinct. I can honestly say that I was disappointed to score the try he made against Wales – Jason deserved to finish that off on his own.'

'Will's ability to read the game is probably second to none,' said Matt Dawson. 'It's like watching a snooker player and wondering how he knew where he needed to be four shots earlier. He could read the game so well and he had obviously thought, *Jason could make a break here and if he does, he's probably going to be running to the outside, so I need to be there.* For me that was the defining moment of our World Cup.'

The score took Greenwood's Test try tally to thirty, equalling Jeremy Guscott and leaving him second only to Rory Underwood on the all-time list for England.

Wilkinson, who had endured a torrid time with the boot up to that point, slotted the touchline conversion perfectly. The tide was turning. With Wilkinson's confidence restored and Catt expertly dictating play alongside him, England returned to their formidable best throughout the rest of the game – and as Wales desperately tried to slow them down and hem them in, they began to concede penalty after penalty. Although they would score another try through Martyn Williams in the closing minutes, Wilkinson had already pushed clear daylight between the sides with five more penalties. Then, with the last kick of the match, he sealed the result with a drop-goal to take his side through to the semi-finals, 28–17.

'Clearly, we were not at our best today,' said Woodward at the post-match press conference, 'and we made some fundamental errors, but I am also confident that we can sit down, have a clear-the-air meeting next week and beat France. We are disappointed with how we played, but it's far nicer to be flying to Sydney than flying back home to London. We are not playing well, but we are winning these games through sheer bloody-mindedness.'

*

England flew south from Queensland to Sydney, settled themselves in the Manly Pacific Hotel and began to prepare for the semi-final – against another old rival, France.

The margin of victory in the quarter-final had flattered England. How Woodward and his team handled their analysis of the game and their preparation for the semi-final would be critical if they were to stand any chance of success. They held a clear-the-air meeting behind closed doors. 'There were some pretty serious bollockings handed out,' said Tindall.

While England had stuttered through the tournament, France were widely considered to be the form team. Les Bleus had blown away every opposition they had faced. They had dispatched Fiji 61–18, Japan 51–29, Scotland 51–9 and the USA 41–14. In the quarter-final they had faced Ireland and been just as merciless. If the final scoreline of 43–21 suggested that Ireland had put up something of a good fight, it was misleading. Ireland did indeed make a late rally, with two well-worked tries from Brian O'Driscoll and one from Kevin Maggs, but that was only after France had pushed themselves into a 37–0 lead and taken their foot off the gas. Frédéric Michalak, the young darling of French rugby, played magnificently outside his equally impressive captain, Fabien Galthié, the half-backs pulling the strings of a powerful French team with an otherworldly grace as they blew Ireland away. The French forwards completely dominated their Irish counterparts in the set-piece and in the contact areas, allowing their audaciously talented back-row trio of Betsen, Harinordoquy and Magne to cause complete mayhem in the open spaces.

To a casual observer – and even the professional pundit and bookmaker – France, playing so brilliantly, were odds-on favourites to overcome England. In a pre-match press conference, Martin Johnson was as pragmatic and forthright as ever about the way his team had been performing and the challenge that awaited them. 'It's much better to be talking about a disappointing victory than to be sat at home talking about being beaten. We won a World Cup quarter-final and people are saying, "Oh dear, you're not playing very well." I'll tell you this – Wales would love to have won that game and be able to say that. As for France, they have a lot of class and a lot of speed in there. They are the form team of the World Cup. It's a tough challenge. We could play well and still lose. We're not going to be able to play poorly and pull off a win. France are too good for that. But it's not a game we're now expected to win. So winning by a point will do.'

While England had had a shaky time at the tournament, their campaign was built on stronger foundations than any other team's. The players also felt that they had over-trained in the build-up to the Wales game and that heavy legs and the general sluggishness that permeated the entire team had been to blame for their poor first-half showing – a condition that had not been helped by the humidity in Brisbane. The senior players broached the subject at the post-match debrief the following day and the week that preceded the semi-final was dramatically different to that which had preceded the quarter-final. Training was light and organisation-based and the players were given plenty of time off to relax away from the field. As they all accepted, there was little more that they could do to improve their well-honed game and drills in the space of a week, but they could certainly disrupt their chances in the same space of time by over-training and exhausting themselves.

*

On the Saturday, Australia played New Zealand in the first semi-final. So far, New Zealand had been magnificent, cruising through their pool – with the exception of the fright against Wales, but even then they had scored eight tries – and had then completely dismantled their old rivals South Africa in the quarter-final. Their back-three were electric, Carlos Spencer at stand-off had more tricks up his sleeve than Merlin and in Richie McCaw at open-side they had one of the finest players the game had ever seen. But they had a problem that had not been challenged since a wet and windy night in Wellington a few months earlier when they had succumbed to a thirteen-man England: the forwards, as a unit, were poor. The team had claimed a dramatic clean sweep in the Tri Nations after that loss at the Cake Tin, running in tries for fun away from home. But when the Wallabies and the Springboks had come to New Zealand and played more pragmatic, forwards-orientated rugby, the All Blacks had only just scraped past them. And when the pressure came on up front and Spencer's time and space were cut down, the fly-half struggled to pull any rabbits out of his hat.

And so it was that New Zealand's World Cup dreams unravelled once again. McCaw remained a giant and the back-three were still a constant threat, but the Australian tight-five turned the screw on their opposite numbers and Phil Waugh and George Smith – two natural open-sides playing either side of No.8 David Lyons – roamed menacingly around the breakdown and hunted down Spencer, while the muscular figure of Stirling Mortlock in the centre was like a brick wall. And it was Mortlock who broke Kiwi hearts as he intercepted a loose Spencer pass to sprint almost eighty metres to score. Although the All Blacks claimed a try back through their captain, Reuben Thorne, Elton Flatley kept the Wallaby score mounting until his team closed out the game 22–10. The hosts had reached the final and were one game away from being the first side to retain the World Cup.

The next day would see who was going to face them. The trans-Tasman match had been played on a balmy evening, but the next day the weather began to change – quite dramatically as it would turn out.

Wind and rain – a lot of both – thundered over Sydney. Although both semi-finals were played in the same stadium, the difference in the conditions from one day to the next made it seem as if they were played in different hemispheres.

'We looked at the rain and we thought, *Fine, we don't mind this, we can play in this*,' said Mike Catt. 'But I'm sure the French were probably cowering, thinking, *Why does it have to rain on this particular day?*'

To say that the conditions suited the style of one team significantly more than the other was nonsense. Both England and France had powerful players and clever tacticians and both sought to play a Total Rugby game involving all fifteen men on the field running comfortably with the ball. In these regards, the teams were evenly balanced. The difference, as it would transpire, was a mental one – it would come down to who could better control the ball and the run of the play in the conditions. It was rugby's equivalent to a game of chess – and the lessons learnt from playing at Murrayfield in 2000 and in Wellington in June suddenly came to the fore.

Woodward was pleased with how the week had gone. He could sense a calmness among the players; even though they hadn't been playing to their best, every player knew that they had it in them – individually and collectively – to play leagues better than they had been. Now was the time to turn up the heat. The biggest game of their lives was on the horizon and it would be the coolest heads that would emerge triumphant.

Part of that calmness, he knew, was instilled when it was announced that Richard Hill had finally overcome his hamstring injury and was ready to rejoin his brothers in arms in the back-row.

'Mentally we were where we wanted to be,' said Catt, 'partly because Richard Hill was finally fit, partly because everyone, it seemed, had written England off.'

'You can't overstate how important Hilly was to us,' said Matt Dawson. 'In my eyes he's the best player England have ever had. He was so important to how we played. We stuttered through against South Africa, Samoa and Wales and there was a big, big difference to the way we played the game against France when Hilly came back – not only because of what he could bring to things, but also what he enabled other players to do, particularly the back-row.'

With Hill back in the team, Woodward had some other decisions to make around selection. With everyone back to full fitness he was able to name his strongest XV and bench for the match. Trevor Woodman replaced Jason Leonard at loose-head and Josh Lewsey came back in at full-back. The only real surprise was the role reversal of Mike Catt and Mike Tindall, with Catt taking the starting position and Tindall moving to the bench. Memories of the Paris clash of 2002, when Serge Betsen had hunted down Wilkinson, were still vivid; while Tindall offered a stronger defence and was a more powerful and direct runner, Catt's distribution and kicking skills would help offset that tactic if the French sought to employ it again.

'It was a big surprise when Catty was selected because I thought we were fine in the midfield,' said Dawson. 'But the big thing that he brought was that he took the pressure off Jonny. His distribution was obviously great but we knew that we would have to play a territorial game against France and Catty definitely had the ability to do that. And with Hilly coming back into the side, we knew we would get a bit more dominance up front and with the way the weather went it was always going to come down to who controlled the territory and possession the best.'

Mike Tindall epitomised the resolve in the squad that the team performance and the result were the most important things – not personal disappointment. 'You haven't got time to be feeling sorry for yourself,' he said when he learnt that he was to take up a bench position. 'It's tough and it hurts but there's nothing I can do about it. You can't afford to be disappointed, otherwise you won't be able to do yourself justice when the time comes. Besides, there's some reasoning behind it in that Mike bossed the game when he came on against Wales. He helped Jonny and kicked superbly. If people are targeting Jonny and pressurising his kicks, it gives us an option.'

'We had no fear of the French – they were a team that we wanted to play against,' said Woodward. 'We felt that we were fitter, faster, stronger and more mobile than them all around the pitch.'

'We have a confidence born out of what we've achieved,' said Neil Back. 'We've won nineteen of our last twenty games, the one defeat by one point to a full-strength French side, in France, against our second string. If that doesn't give you confidence, I don't know what will.'

Bernard Laporte stuck to the starting XV that had demolished Ireland and played with such flair throughout the pool games. Laporte had transformed the French team from a side that could be flaky and hot-headed into an efficient, well-disciplined team that still retained the basic cornerstones of the

French game: brutal forwards and mesmeric backs. But if the France coach thought he had worked hard to remodel and reshape his team, it was nothing compared to the work that Woodward had put in over the previous six years. On the eve of the match, Woodward spoke of the confidence he had in his players, knowing that he had done all he could to change them from spirited also-rans into the best side in the world.

'I strongly believe England will beat France,' he said. 'We have an outstanding set of players, outstanding leadership, we're fresh, we're very experienced and we know how to win games. Just a look at our track record will confirm this. I have absolutely no doubt that England will step up to the plate. We came here to win the World Cup and we will not be leaving the field until we've made it to the final. Of that we are absolutely determined.'

On the day of the game, the downpour from the heavens was formidable. A strong wind whipped through the Telstra Stadium and the temperature plummeted – but on the field there was a different kind of tempest and the temperature was fiery. Both teams erupted out of the blocks with fierce intensity. Wilkinson knocked over a right-footed drop-goal after a period of sustained pressure before France gained a foothold of their own. As can often happen in a game that is so structured, the unexpected can create space and chances to score opportunistic tries – be it from a knock-on or a bouncing ball, one side's defensive line can be pulled out of joint and open up a gap for the opposition. In this case it was a poorly executed French line-out that caused havoc for both sets of forwards; Raphaël Ibañez threw the ball in, but Jérôme Thion was not lifted properly and the ball spilled wildly into space behind him. Serge Betsen was the quickest to react and grasped the ball from the air before racing through a space between Dallaglio and Hill to score.

As the England players waited for Michalak's conversion, there was no sense of panic among the ranks. It was an unfortunate score to have conceded, but it had come from a lucky spill. France hadn't threatened their line in any other way and Johnson's men knew that hard graft and accurate application of their skills would get them into the right areas of the pitch from which to score points. 'The guys basically said, "Forget about it, and let's move on,"' said Johnson. 'I was confident that we'd stop them scoring after that.'

After Betsen's try, Johnson began to marshal his forwards around the field, placing the emphasis for gaining momentum back squarely on their shoulders. He knew that if the French tight-five could be squeezed, their back-row would have to commit themselves to the contact areas of the game and couldn't play the roving style at which they had been excelling in earlier matches. For the remainder of the game England were clever, calm and relentless. The forwards picked around the fringes, they rolled mauls and they were solid in the scrum and the line-out. And France, unable to withstand the onslaught, collapsed under the pressure. 'The forwards were absolutely awesome that day,' said Catt. 'The amount of ball they gave me and Jonny to do whatever we wanted with was phenomenal.'

With possession in short supply and with England's defensive line pressing up hard, France began to lose the rhythm of their game. Michalak was young and relatively inexperienced on the Test stage and he struggled to adapt his previously free-flowing game to deal with the pressure of England's defence; he was the leading points-scorer in the tournament but after his successful conversion of Betsen's try, his radar abandoned him and he didn't hit another successful kick at goal. And as he started to lose control, so too did the rest of his team. As the game wore on, the Frenchmen became increasingly ill-disciplined; they began to stray offside, giving away needless penalties, their defensive line started to dog-leg, their defenders around the breakdown grew lazy and their set-piece began to creak horribly. Both Betsen and winger Christophe Dominici pressed the self-destruct button and were sent to the sin bin – Betsen for a late hit on Wilkinson, Dominici for recklessly throwing out a leg to trip Jason Robinson after the England winger had stepped inside him. On the hour mark, France were in freefall and substituted two of the players deemed before the game to be central to their chances of success – Betsen and Michalak.

It seemed that France had believed the hype that had built up around them, while England's troubles had steeled their resolve. And while the England forwards strangled the life out of the French pack and Catt and Greenwood dictated play in the midfield with precision kicking, clever passing and a solid defence, it was the man in the England No.10 shirt that made the biggest difference.

After having suffered uncharacteristic inconsistency with his kicking earlier in the tournament, Wilkinson was deadly in front of goal in the semi-final. He kicked five penalties and three drop-goals (two of which he struck with his weaker right foot) to collect all of England's twenty-seven points and consign France to a third-place place play-off match against the All Blacks.

England, meanwhile, had a date with destiny against the host nation. 'It's a dream final,' said Woodward. 'We came here to win the ultimate prize and now we're one match away. We'll have to play the game of the tournament to beat Australia.'

TEN

THE ANATOMY OF
THE SUMMIT

'He that wrestles with us strengthens our nerves
and sharpens our skill. Our antagonist is our helper.'
Edmund Burke

WOODARD STOOD AT the window of his room at the Manly
Pacific, watching long rivulets of water streaming down the glass
and occasionally blooming into flower as fierce squalls from the sea
blasted against the pane. A pot of tea was steeping on the nearby desk, where a
lamp illuminated a pile of notes in the slate grey morning light. He looked out
over the promenade to the roaring waves beyond and let his mind drift. Here he
was back in Manly and it felt like things had come full circle.

Manly had reinvented him. He had pushed himself out of his comfort
zone in Leicester by coming to Australia and his business career had benefited
hugely from the lessons that he had learnt there. He and Jayne had married
and their first two children had been born in Manly – the suburb whose rugby
club had inspired him to apply business techniques to a sporting environment,
where he had first seen flat backline play up close, and where he had grown
to understand the winning mentality at the heart of the Australian sporting
psyche. Australia and Australian rugby had played a pivotal part in his life.
His experience at the Institute of Sport had galvanized the idea of cross-sport
expertise, the sharing of knowledge and the utilisation of specialist coaches in
elite sport. His first steps towards coaching a flat-line attack had been aided by
the introduction of two imported players from Manly, his first game in charge
as England coach had been against Australia and the humiliation on the Tour
of Hell had spurred him to never accept second-best – or to feel the horror of
such heavy defeats again. And after three straight wins against the Wallabies

at Twickenham he had masterminded the first victory for England in a Test match on Australian soil.

Woodward recalled sitting on the rocks outside his old apartment down the road almost twenty years earlier, enjoying an early-morning cup of tea and watching the rolling surf tumble on to the golden sands. His mind wandered across those long-ago breakers to downtown Sydney of today where, somewhere out there, Eddie Jones and his Wallabies were also preparing for the biggest match of their lives.

Eddie Jones. The antagonist. The pantomime villain of world rugby – at least from an English perspective. Ever since he had taken over from Rod Macqueen to lead the Wallabies in 2001, Jones had seemed to relish playing England more than any other side in the world. It was as if his raison d'être was to try to wind up Woodward and his team in the build-up to a match. During games he would yap endlessly at the referees, trying to highlight some new ploy or deficiency in England's armoury. The sniping and sledging was nothing new in sport – particularly between England and Australia – but the media lapped it up and pitched the two coaches against one another whenever they could.

The Australian media, in particular, loved the rivalry and had taken the sledging up a level or two during the 2003 summer tour when the term 'Dad's Army' had first been coined; a poll in one newspaper had even found that Woodward was more unpopular with the Australian public than the perennial English villain, Douglas Jardine – the England cricket captain who secured the 1932–1933 Ashes series thanks to his controversial Bodyline tactics. When he heard this, Woodward had been delighted by the comparison. Jardine had, after all, won the series.

Things had escalated steadily since England's arrival in Perth for the World Cup. *Is that all you've got?* read a headline in *The Australian* after England had defeated South Africa thanks largely to Jonny Wilkinson's boot – never mind the fact that England had crushed a world power without playing particularly well. John Eales, the double World Cup-winning former Wallaby captain, had made lengthy analyses of England's apparent illegalities in the rolling maul; Toutai Kefu, the injured Wallaby No.8, had appeared on television calling for England to be kicked out of the tournament after the incident with the sixteenth man; and Eddie Jones had endlessly criticised England for being a one-trick pony with their tactics: *keep the ball tight until the opposition give away a penalty and Wilkinson will kick the goal.*

But Woodward knew that this caricature of his team was grossly inaccurate. England had scored twenty-nine tries in the 2001 Six Nations, twenty-three in 2002 and eighteen in 2003 – an average of 4.6 per game over those three years. 'You cannot go into big games resting on the comfort of having a top goal-kicker and hope he kicks you to victory,' wrote Woodward later. 'This type of conservative approach means victory is out of your own hands. If a team simply plays smart, they will not give you a kick at goal. In fact, you have a greater chance of kicking penalties if you are playing to score tries. It is when presented with such an attacking threat that defences opt to kill the ball and are forced into making the mistakes which give away penalties. It happened on many occasions, including the 2003 World Cup itself. We were outscored in tries in the quarters and semi-final by teams who conceded penalties to stop our attack.'

Woodward had nothing against Eddie Jones personally – whenever they met at post-match functions they got along well enoughc – it was the public pronouncements, the clear attempts to influence the referees in Australia's favour, that irritated him. After the victory in Melbourne in June, Woodward had had enough. He told a gathering of journalists, 'The team didn't need motivation from me, Eddie Jones did the job. You get labelled by the opposition coach but you just have to get on with winning. I don't believe in pressurising the referee. It was premeditated and it was not good for the sport. I'm just pleased that we've made it four wins out of four against Jones. We'll wait until the World Cup in October in Australia and the next anti-English media campaign orchestrated by him. We'll thrive on it.' And then, at the post-match press conference, he rounded on the journalists that had called England boring before the match. 'I must be missing something here,' he said coldly. 'I thought sport was all about winning. Everything seems to have changed here in Australia, certainly seems to have with respect to rugby union since I lived here. I thought you Aussies were all about winning and not about marks out of ten for performance. Eddie Jones and the Wallabies have been trying to wind us up all week about what an old, tired, slow and boring team we are. Well, all that's bullshit. You guys all asked us both whether we wanted to play with the roof open or closed. I wanted the roof shut so that the game could be played in perfect conditions, giving us the best chance for a great running game. Eddie

Jones wanted it open and to introduce the uncertainty of weather conditions. And you call us boring?'

Woodward appreciated the idea of trying to get an edge for his team, but he felt that Jones's tactics went beyond the pale. Jones tried to defend his actions before the final by saying, 'I love mind games, they are a part of rugby: you can look to get a result by messing up the heads of your opponents. England are probably the hardest nut to crack, but that does not stop you trying. Part of your remit as national coach should be to create interest. You are not going to get exposure if you sit at a press conference and say nothing, but there are some who prefer not to get into trouble. Clive Woodward is not one of those and I like that. He plays the game extremely well and he knows that he has the support of the English rugby hierarchy, which is important. When things blow up it is nothing personal: I have met him after games and we have had a quiet chat, but the nature of the beast these days is that you do not get to know your opposite numbers very well.'

Woodward may have understood the sentiments, but he felt that the barbs were unnecessary. Australia were one of the best sides in the world – and as an ancient rival of England's the match-up between them had set up a dream final. They had stars throughout their team. The back-three were all ex-rugby league icons: Mat Rogers at full-back, Lote Tuqiri and Wendell Sailor on the wings; each offered a different kind of threat, but all were proven winners. Stephen Larkham at stand-off and George Gregan at scrum-half were two of the most experienced half-backs in rugby history and had guided Australia to victory in the 1999 World Cup, a series victory over the Lions in 2001 and Tri Nations titles in 2000 and 2001, while also winning the Super 12 with the ACT Brumbies in 2001. Outside them they had the clever footballing brain of Elton Flatley and the monstrous figure of Stirling Mortlock. The pack was seen as the weakness in the team, but they were wily and they had set enough of a platform to get the Wallabies to the final. What they lacked in bulk they made up for in speed and skill. All three front-row players were comfortable on the ball and were backed up by intelligent line-out operatives in Justin Harrison and Nathan Sharpe, while the back-row trio were an interesting combination of power in David Lyons at No.8 and foraging skill and link-play in George Smith and Phil Waugh, two natural open-side flankers.

The Wallabies would be ready – but so too would England. This game had been six years in the making. More than that, it was the coming together of a lifetime of experiences. The influences of Kirton, Greenwood and White had all contributed to the shaping of the England team that was about to play in the final; so too had the revolutionary backline play of the Ella brothers and Woodward's coaching career at Henley, London Irish and Bath. Was there anything more he could have done to prepare the team? Thanks to the philosophies of Paddi Lund and Humphrey Walters, he knew that there was not. Every possible stone had been turned.

His thoughts wandered back to the two semi-finals and the contrasting attitudes of the victorious teams at full-time. The Australian players had leapt in the air with joy, bear hugged one another and then set off on a lap of honour to thank the home crowd for their support. It had been a titanic battle against the All Blacks, a side that many pundits had named as tournament favourites, and the Wallabies had made it to the finishing line with their noses in front. The home fans were ecstatic and the joy that the players felt was writ large on their triumphant faces.

The England players, meanwhile, had barely uttered a cheer of congratulations to one another when the referee called full-time against France – and this was after a devastatingly effective performance, undoubtedly their best since the summer tour. They had recognised the game for what it was – a hurdle that they had to get past on their way to the final, where they would face one last challenge on their journey to rugby immortality. The job was far from done. Yes, they were pleased, but the dance had not yet finished.

Had Australia, in contrast, played their metaphorical final in that victory over New Zealand? Would they be able to raise themselves both mentally and physically for another brutal test of their mettle and their skill?

Woodward took a seat at the desk in his hotel room and poured himself a cup of tea, carefully straining the leaves and thoughtfully watching the milk as it clouded, spun and dissipated in the almond-coloured water. Australia had, like England, failed to really hit their straps until the semi-final. In the last four encounters with them, England had found a way to win. Every Wallaby player in that side feared England. They would never admit it, but deep down Woodward knew it to be true – he had seen it on their faces at full-time in Melbourne a few months earlier. And despite the mental strength that they would harvest from defeating the All Blacks, he knew that there would be a lingering anxiety in the backs of their minds at the prospect of facing Martin Johnson and his men. The final difference between the winner and the loser would be mental. *Think Correctly Under Pressure*. The team with the strongest mental steel would win. Of that he had no doubt.

All he had to do now was pick his team. The physios – Phil Pask, Richard Wegrzyk and Barney Kenny – had worked wonders with the players and Woodward had a full roster to choose from. The most difficult decision was to decide which eight players would miss out on the night altogether. Only twenty-two of the squad of thirty could be involved. For those eight, there was a heart-breaking disappointment to come.

He looked down at the piece of paper on which he had scrawled the twenty-two names he wanted. There had been a few choices to consider; who would start in the centre alongside Will Greenwood – Mike Catt or Mike Tindall? Who would sit on the bench – Lewis Moody or Joe Worsley, Andy Gomarsall or Kyran Bracken? But he had finally made his decisions and he was happy with his team. Tindall had won the nod over Catt – in part because Catt felt too battered after the semi-final to feel comfortable that he would last the distance. Catt had come to him and told him of his worries and that he had been pleased with the way he had contributed to matches coming off the bench. If it made the team selection easier, he would be happier with the bench spot. Woodward appreciated the honesty – and it was a testament to Catt's desire to put the interests of the team first that he would give up the chance to wear the starting shirt in a World Cup final. The only concern that Woodward had was that Jonny Wilkinson wouldn't have a foil outside him to help with tactical kicking; the flip side of that was that with Tindall and Greenwood in place, the midfield had the strongest defensive combination available – and the Wallabies were likely to repeatedly throw their biggest runners down those channels. But thinking back to the way the quarter-final had developed, Woodward knew that if Wilkinson began to struggle with his tactical kicking, he had Catt in reserve to come on and help address the issue. That decision made, the rest of the team virtually picked itself.

Josh Lewsey, a deadly strike-runner, as tough as they come defensively and a totally uncompromising competitor, was at full-back; Jason Robinson, a man with dancing feet that couldn't be matched by any other player on the planet, was on one wing with Ben Cohen, arguably the best winger in the world in 2003, with speed and size that made him virtually unstoppable, on the other; Tindall and Greenwood were a combination of power and brains in the centre, both were quicker than many would give them credit for, and they were outstanding footballers; Wilkinson and Dawson were the controllers, the talkers, the strategists at half-back, the men who would move the team around the field, with Wilkinson the tackle-hungry points machine; Woodman, Thompson and Vickery were the finest front-row in the game, they were big and powerful, quick in open space and blessed with soft hands; in the engine room Ben Kay was the line-out master while Martin Johnson alongside him was Captain Fantastic – hard, obdurate, grounded and an incredible athlete who would walk into any team in any era; and then there was the Holy Trinity of Back, Dallaglio and Hill in the back-row, who would run themselves into the ground and never, ever admit defeat.

It was one hell of a team.

*

The week leading up to the final would require careful planning. The main job was to keep the players focused without overwhelming them with the enormity of the occasion that awaited them. Woodward knew that the players would be hounded by sponsors, agents and fans, who would all want a piece of them – special appearances, new deals and endorsements, autographs by the thousand. He discussed the matter with Martin Johnson and then they called a meeting with the entire group. Johnson stood up and asked his players to shelve all of the peripherals for a week – just one week. After that they could do what they liked. But after all they had been through, it would be criminal for them to lose their focus when they were so close to achieving something incredibly special.

In just a few days' time they had a chance to right the wrongs of the 1991 World Cup final, when Will Carling's side had lost to Australia at Twickenham.

During this final stage, Woodward was unwilling to risk exposing his team to any disadvantage. During the 2001 Lions tour there were suspicions that the Lions' training sessions had been watched – even filmed – by the Australians and that their hotel rooms might have been bugged in order to reveal their game plan and codes. It was felt, in the aftermath of the deciding Third Test, that the Wallabies had come into possession of the Lions' line-out codes, so well did they read where the ball was going to be thrown throughout the match.

Woodward was not prepared for the same thing to happen again, so he hired security guards to keep any spectators from lingering too long while the team were training, had barriers erected around the Manly Oval and had their hotel rooms swept for bugging devices. 'I took a fair bit of stick for it,' said Woodward, 'and people called me obsessive but it was all part of creating a world-class environment where security and secrecy were high on the agenda. I wanted to give the players the impression we were under siege, that they were in a rarefied environment available only to them.'

They kept training light throughout the week and after assessing the physical condition of the team, particularly the front-row players, after the battle with the French, it was decided that they wouldn't hit a single scrum in practice – something unheard of in preparation for a Test match.

'We had short sessions on Tuesday, Wednesday and Friday and that was it,' said Martin Johnson. 'You'd think, with the World Cup final just a few days away, that we'd all be nervous wrecks but I had never seen the boys so relaxed. They were full of life and energy. I guess partly it was because they were in the final and partly that they could see light at the end of a seven-week tunnel. No matter what the occasion, you want to get home after that length of time. It was strange: I caught myself thinking, *This is the World Cup final*, and wondering why it felt like any other week, why I wasn't more jittery.'

'Johnno was excellent that week,' recalled Woodward. 'To be fair, he was always excellent, but he was especially good that week at keeping everyone calm and focused. His line was "everyone do your job." If I did my job, the players did theirs, the other coaches and the physios and so on did theirs, then we would win. We would go to the game, win, and go home. It was as simple as that – and that was as simple as it needed to be. He said that, unlike when England played in the World Cup final in 1991, it wasn't the time to change anything. We had to do everything exactly as we always did, train exactly as we always did (although a little bit lighter), play the way we always played, and we would win. Everyone had to stay away from all the peripheral stuff going on, stay disciplined, do their job, play well and we would win. It was therefore a fairly normal week and I was immensely proud with how everyone handled themselves.'

Striking the right balance was a precarious job – get too relaxed and the players might not be able to get their focus attuned correctly; go overboard and they could choke.

The phenomenon of 'choking' in sport is one that has been pored over obsessively by journalists, sportswriters, scientists, pundits and fans since time immemorial. Why do some of the most talented, gifted and experienced sportspeople choke when the stakes are at their highest and they are on the edge of sporting greatness? Why does one of the world's greatest golfers fluff a three-foot putt that costs him a major? Why does a top-five-ranked tennis player double-fault in a crucial tie-break in the final of Wimbledon? Why does one of the highest-paid strikers in the world hoof the ball over the crossbar during a World Cup penalty shoot-out? One of the clearest studies of its occurrence can be found in Matthew Syed's *Bounce*. Syed writes how a lifetime of practice allows sportsmen and women of all gifts and talents to 'automate' their skill sets: 'Many hours of practice have enabled him to code the stroke in implicit rather than explicit memory,' writes Syed. He examines the work of Russell Poldrack, a neuroscientist at the University of California in Los Angeles, who conducted a number of brain-imaging experiments to trace the transition from explicit to implicit monitoring that occurs over many hours' practice. Poldrack discovered that the prefrontal cortex is activated when a novice is learning a skill, but that control of that skill switches over time to areas such as the basal ganglia, which is partly responsible for touch and feel. 'This migration from the explicit to the implicit system of the brain has two advantages,' explains Syed. 'First, it enables the expert player to integrate the various parts of a complex skill into one fluent whole, something that would be impossible at a conscious level because there are too many interconnecting variables for the conscious mind to handle. And second, it frees up attention to focus on higher-level aspects of the skill such as tactics and strategy.' He then goes on to reference Sian Beilock, a psychologist at the University of Chicago: 'It is not the pressure in a pressure situation that distracts us into performing poorly,' said Beilock. 'The pressure makes us worry and want to control our actions too much. And you cannot think your way through a routine, practised action, like making a three-foot putt. Compare it to quickly shuffling down a flight of stairs. You could do that without thought. But if I asked you to do it, and at the same time think about how much you bend your knee each time or what part of your foot is touching the stair, you would probably fall on your face. That's what happens when people choke. They try to think their way through the action.'

Tactically Woodward knew that his team had to get their decision-making spot-on. But he had known this for a long time, which was why he had stuck with tried-and-tested combinations as much as he could throughout his reign – the players had spent so long in each other's company, had trained and played together so much, that they had instinctively come to understand how those around them played. They could read running lines, feints of movements, the shaping of passes, and each others' body language.

The problem with choking is that it is individual. If the occasion got too much or a player wanted to overtly stamp their authority on the game, then everything could fall out of sync. And with a highly structured team game like rugby union, if one cog begins to malfunction, the whole machine can run into catastrophic difficulties.

Martin Johnson made it his mission to ensure that no heads drifted into the clouds and that no player developed ideas of pressing his cause too forcibly in the limelight. The team, the performance and the result had to come above everything else. 'We've won nothing yet,' he said at a press call during that final week. 'We've not achieved our goal yet. We have one single aim, and we've had it ever since we lost in the quarter-final four years ago. That defeat has haunted me ever since. Not just the fact that we lost, but how we lost, by five drop-goals to which we had no answer. So now it's only ever been about winning the World Cup. To go home as losing finalists is not what it's all about, and never has been. It should be an incredible occasion, an incredible game, and I have complete respect for the Wallabies. It will be tight, will probably be decided only in the final quarter, maybe even in the last ten minutes. But we're as ready as we can be. We're going to give it our all, every single one of us, and I'm hoping – and expecting – this to be enough. We know we can beat Australia, but we also know we'll have to be at our best.'

*

Twenty-four hours until kick-off.

All the players and back-room staff were gathered in the team room at the Manly Pacific. The room was darkened and on a screen at the front of the room the second of two motivational videos was just coming to an end. The films were short but spine-tingling: highlights of the team's best pieces of play and motivational messages, all set to music. The films were Tony Biscombe's last gift to the team before the final.

The film finished and the lights went up. Clive Woodward rose to his feet and cast his eyes around the room. He fixed each pair of eyes for a moment – connecting with the twenty-two men he had selected for the biggest match in English rugby history and the eight devastated but resolutely loyal men whom he had had to cut from the side; Julian White, Mark Regan, Simon Shaw, Joe Worsley, Andy Gomarsall, Paul Grayson, Dan Luger and Stuart Abbott had come to the highest reaches of Everest, but they would not be pushing on to the summit. 'Telling those guys that they wouldn't be involved was one of the worst things I've ever had to do,' said Woodward. 'But they were all magnificent throughout that week. They trained just as well as everyone else and they supported the guys in the team. It was a testament to them as individuals and to the values we had set down about being One Team.'

For the other twenty-two, they knew they were on the cusp of history. Jason Leonard was alone among them to have experienced the high of playing in a World Cup final and the crushing low of defeat. He had spoken privately to every player and made it clear that this was their chance to set their names in rugby lore for ever... or be simply known, once again, as the also-rans.

Woodward cleared his throat. 'England versus Australia,' he said. 'It doesn't get any bigger or any better. Playing them in Sydney is one of the biggest challenges any rugby player can ever face. But we know that we have the measure of them. And so do they. We are bigger, faster, stronger, fitter. We have the superior pack. Our backs can shred theirs to pieces. I wouldn't swap one of their players for ours.' He pointed to a large whiteboard on which both squads had been written down side-by-side. 'Man for man we are better than them in every department. Not one of their players would get into our team.

'What we must not do tomorrow night is go into our shells. No one has attacked Australia during this World Cup. That is what we have to do for eighty minutes – attack, attack, attack. We need to mount the pressure on them time and time again. If we do that, they won't be able to live with us. That is how we have beaten them that last four times we've met. We have never given up, never given them space to breathe. We have to be relentless throughout the entire match. We build a score any way we can – tries, penalties, drop-goals, anything. Just like we did against France, whenever we get near their posts we are scoring. We get our noses ahead and then we push on. We never give up, we never think the job is finished. Australian teams above all others know how to stage a comeback – so we don't give them a sniff. We crush them physically and then we crush them mentally on the scoreboard. Our destiny is in our hands. We control everything.'

He looked over at Martin Johnson and nodded. Johnson pushed back his chair and walked to the front of the room.

Johnson towered, upright and powerful, his deep-eyed gaze panning around his teammates. He wasn't one for Churchillian orations. He preferred concision. The way he saw it, rugby was a simple game. It didn't require overly complicated thinking and if the men around him couldn't psyche themselves up for an occasion like Test match rugby, let alone a World Cup final, then they were in the wrong place, in the wrong team. 'Let's play our normal game,' he said. 'Let's not force things, try to do things we wouldn't do in any other match. Let's do the things we would always do. Don't let the occasion get to you. If you start thinking *it's the Rugby World Cup final* as you receive the ball the likelihood is that you'll end up paralysed by the moment. We've got all the guts and courage we need. It's big, yes, but let's just go and play our game. It's just another game. It could be at Twickenham; it happens to be in Sydney but that stretch of grass is the same as anywhere else. It has two sets of posts and it has white markings. We know what to do on a stage like that – so let's do it.'

And that was that. It was much the same routine and speech that both men had made dozens of times before a Test match. The fact that it was a World Cup final didn't mean that they should change their routines. The routines had helped make them the best side in the world – this was not the time to change anything. And so it was that the team left the team room and went off for dinner. Often there would be options for the starter and the main course, but the dessert was a tradition and never changed: bread and butter pudding. Familiarity is a comfort, a reassurance – like the same bedrooms at Pennyhill Park, or playing in a thirtieth Test match with your mates.

Woodward's words had been simple, but his assurance that they were the best in the world had filtered down into the deep subconscious of his players over the preceding years. They believed it; the next game's day would simply prove it. Will Greenwood summed it up perfectly. 'We found ourselves honestly believing that we would not have swapped one of our players for anyone else in the world. That takes some saying, but I know all my old teammates would agree. A team like that is an amazing place to be. There is no feeling like it in the world; not arrogance, just total belief in one another.'

*

After dinner, Matt Dawson was sitting in the team room with Paul Grayson watching TV, killing time before going to bed and trying to sleep.

'How are you feeling?' asked Grayson.

Dawson smiled. 'I'm all right. Just hope I get some kip tonight.'

Grayson laughed. 'Unlikely, even for you.' Dawson was notorious for sleeping any time, anywhere he could – the team room, buses to training and games, the floor of the physio room, even quiet corners of the changing room.

'A World Cup final, mate. Can you believe it?' said Dawson.

'We deserve it. All of us.'

'What do you reckon, a late entry from P. Grayson to snatch the victory? A 79th-minute drop-goal?'

Grayson smiled ruefully. 'Jonny or Catty will have to have both their legs broken overnight for that to happen.' He paused. 'Where's that baseball bat?'

'Ha!'

Grayson smiled, but then his face grew serious again. 'I'll tell you one thing, Daws. If it's on for a late drop-goal to win it, you've got to take it on yourself. No one will be looking at you. All eyes will be on Jonny.'

'Or you, Grays.'

'No, I'm serious. All eyes will be on Jonny. And the gap will be there. You take it and you make history. I can see it already.'

A short time later, Grayson retired to bed. Dawson was too jacked up. He knew he should get some sleep but adrenaline was coursing through his body. Fortunately, because the game wasn't until the following evening, they would have a late start to the day. The players would all try to sleep for as long as possible before heading down to breakfast. There would be a final light team run and then there would be lunch and an opportunity for a nap. Finally there would be a meeting with the coaches and a chat between Wilkinson, Greenwood and himself to reaffirm tactics and then it would be time to get ready to head to the stadium. A carefully scheduled day, but a long one waiting for the kick-off.

There was no rush to go to bed, but eventually Dawson realised that it really was time. He hauled himself from the team room and made his way back to his room.

As he pushed open his bedroom door he heard a rustle against the base of the door. He looked down and saw a letter with the handwritten scrawl of *Daws* on the envelope. He recognised it at once as Grayson's handwriting.

The opening lines were jovial but the tone quickly changed. Grayson wanted him to know what a good friend he was and how important Dawson was to his family – his son, James, was Dawson's godson. And then he moved on to the match.

Today is your day. All your growing has been done, don't do it on the field. You're in control of the World Cup final. This is where you belong. Enjoy it. The rest of the world can rejoice in Matthew Dawson the finished article... Win the World Cup. It will happen... They'll be looking at you and you'll go... You'll make the difference.

Dawson blinked back tears. Grayson would later tell him that the only way he could have expressed those sentiments was through a letter – it would have been too emotional in person. For Dawson, it struck just the right chord. So overcome was he that he couldn't bring himself to read it a second time.

'Once was perfect,' he said.

*

5.15 p.m., Saturday, 22 November 2003.

The England players lurched gently in their seats as their coach pulled away from the Manly Pacific. They were on their way. In an hour's time they would arrive at the Telstra Stadium, with two hours to prepare themselves for kick-off. They would get into the dressing room, change, get any strapping required from the physios, and then begin their individual warm-ups. Some players would get massages, others grab a few extra winks of sleep, and the rest might flick through the match programme while music blared from a stereo. The kickers would go out first, then the rest of the team. The forwards would go through some line-outs and then they would come together for some handling drills and defensive work to get their bodies ready for the collisions. The whole warm-up was designed to get their bodies and minds prepared. It was simple stuff. The team had already had a light run-through that morning – in a downpour, the air cool, just like a Six Nations morning back home.

Then it would be back to the changing room to put their match kit on plus tracksuits to keep them warm throughout the anthems. Fluids would be taken on board, energy bars would be consumed. Some would fall silent, focused; some would prowl and scream and beat their chests, eyes popping, sweat pouring down their faces.

'You get ready and you've just got to think about your own performance and the whole team thing,' said Woodward on the atmosphere in the pre-match changing room. 'If you do that, you're fine. The moment you start thinking about the enormity of what we're trying to do, that's when you won't think correctly. That's when it could all go pear-shaped… We have to keep our thoughts clearly on the first kick-off, our first moves, the first tackle, the first offence. You just want to visualise the start of the game.'

*

Changed and ready for the warm-up, Lawrence Dallaglio liked to take a few minutes to read through the match programme before heading out to the pitch. He held the glossy brochure in his hands and admired the cover title: *IRB World Cup Final*. He had never held a programme like this before. He began to flick through the pages and as he neared the centerfold he saw the individual profiles of the players on each team. At last he stopped at his own: Lawrence Bruno Nero Dallaglio.

Dallaglio. And he thought of Francesca. This was the greatest day of his life. This was a chance, at last, to ensure that the world would always remember the name Dallaglio. A lump caught in his throat and he quietly shut his eyes and remembered the graceful ballerina that had been lost to the world fourteen years ago. This one, as it always was when he played, would be for her.

Pat, pat, pat, pat. Jonny Wilkinson sat, hunched forward, lightly flicking a ball back and forward from hand to hand in front of him. Ever since he was a teenager, he and Dave Alred had worked on visualisation techniques. *See what you want to do, how you want to play, how you want to pass a ball, how you want to fly a kick – focus on those images and make them happen. Make them real.*

Pat, pat, pat, pat, pat. He knew that the Australians would fly out the blocks, looking to play with width and tempo. They didn't have the same muscle that England had up front, so they would look to shift England around the pitch as much as possible. But if the defensive line held firm, Gregan and Larkham and Flatley would be forced to kick. They would hand possession back to England. It would then be his job to orchestrate what England did with the ball. The Aussie back-three were all dangerous runners, but they were relatively new to rugby union. If Wilkinson kicked poorly to them he knew that they could cause all sorts of difficulties for England. But if he could kick well, if he could turn them, pin them deep in the corners and give them no room to run… then that back-three would become a weakness, an achilles heel. If Wilkinson could bury the ball in the Wallaby 22 he knew that his forwards could squeeze the life out of any side in the world. There would be opportunities to score – tries, penalties, drop-goals. They would all be on the cards. But first it was up to him to control where the game was played.

Wilkinson's feet were fidgety, the studs in his boots drumming on the hard floor of the changing room with a clackety-clack. He needed to get outside and start his kicking routine. He knew that Alred would be out there already, waiting for him with a pile of balls. He reached into his bag and retrieved a kicking tee, then stood and flicked the ball to Will Greenwood before heading for the door.

Greenwood gathered the ball in one hand and tucked it under his arm as he watched Wilkinson disappear out of the changing room. *Good old Jonny*, he thought. If there was one player on the planet that you wanted in your team, it was Jonny. Then he saw the towering figure of Johnson striding across to the physio bench to retrieve some tape. Or Johnno. Yeah, every team would want Johnno in their side. Or Hilly. Or Lol. Or Backy. Who wouldn't want a front-row with the size, strength and speed of Vicks, Thommo and Woody? Who wouldn't want a line-out professor like Benny Kay, or a gobby wee controller like Daws at scrum-half, or a bulldozer in the centre like Tins, or a back-three like Jason, Josh and Benny Cohen?

Clive was right, Greenwood mused, *I wouldn't swap a single one of them.*

They were here, in the final, and despite the heartache that so many of them had been through, they were ready. Greenwood felt that he was as ready as he had ever been in his life – even with flights across the world and back and all the worry at home, he was ready. And he thought of what Caro had said to him before he had flown back out to Australia: 'Don't come home without that trophy.' In all his sporting career, he had never had as emotive a line to inspire him before a match. He was going to go out there to play for his family and all his mates; for all the teachers and coaches that had helped him get to this point; for the doctors, the physios and the surgeons that had repaired and healed his damaged body, and had even saved his life. But most of all he was going to play for Caro and their unborn child. And he was going to play for Freddie.

All around Greenwood, his teammates were experiencing similar thoughts of personal motivation, remembering loved ones no longer with them, of those that had helped and inspired them to reach this moment, of all the hardships and the joys that had driven them here. The cool calculation required to deliver the win would come in due course, but first the fires within had to be roaring. And in England's changing room they were burning like an inferno.

*

A capacity crowd of 82,957 were packed into the Telstra Stadium. Twenty giant cylindrical figures representing each competing nation billowed around the periphery of the pitch. Each was a Cyclops, representing the one-eyed nature of each nation's fans. One by one, the figures collapsed and were gathered away until just two remained behind each set of posts: the English and Australian Cyclops glaring menacingly at one another across the length of the pitch.

The atmosphere in England's changing room was electric. The players were awaiting the knock on the door from the referee, signalling that it was time to walk down the tunnel. They were gathered in a big circle, arms locked around shoulders, squeezing together, relaxing, squeezing together, studs rapping on the floor, chests heaving as they breathed in the smell of sweat and liniment in the air.

'This is it, lads,' said Neil Back. 'Get yourselves ready for the pain. It's going to hurt. But no pain, no gain – let's go through the pain together.'

'Look around you,' roared Dallaglio. 'Look in the face of the guys next to you. We've been through hell to get here – now's the time to unleash hell on them. They've got no respect for us. No fucking respect. Today we shove that down their fucking throats. We show them just how good we are, how hard, how skilful. Let them know who you are, where you're from, what you're about. Get right in their fucking faces all game and let's take the win. That's all there is – the win, the win, the win!'

Johnson drew the huddle tighter. 'It's all been about this moment, boys. All the work, all the pain. All about now. Your whole life has been focused on a single moment and place: here and now. It's time to deliver. There are no second chances.'

'Let's remember to build the phases,' said Wilkinson, his voice steady. 'We play the game where we want to play it. We move them around, give them no space to move, no space to breathe. Every tackle is huge.'

'Every tackle says, "Fuck you!"' spat Dallaglio. 'You fucking bury them out there!'

'Build the phases,' repeated Wilkinson. 'We control the pace and the space. We build the phases and we build the points. Everything is ours to control.'

Then came the knock from referee Andre Watson and a jolt visibly shot around the entire circle. A hush fell over them.

'This is it, lads,' said Johnson. 'No second chances.' He stared around them all, bore his dark eyes into each of the faces around him and nodded. 'Let's get on with it.'

The teams gathered in two long lines side by side in the tunnel, waiting for the signal to run out. Steam was rising from each and every man as they shifted from foot to foot, ready to explode out on to the field.

Mike Tindall, one of the youngsters of the team, looked down the line and he could see the edge of the pitch just beyond where Martin Johnson and George Gregan were standing. Then he looked to his left and saw that he was standing beside Stirling Mortlock. The huge Wallaby centre was staring straight ahead, veins bulging on his neck, a thunderous look etched on his face.

'Hey,' said Tindall.

Mortlock didn't react at first but then the salutation seemed to register with him and he turned to see Tindall grinning at him. 'This is what we play rugby for, isn't it?' said Tindall.

Mortlock blinked and then his face creased into a smile. 'Yeah, mate,' he said. 'I suppose it is.'

As the teams exited the tunnel they were greeted by an ocean of white and gold in the stands, and a tumultuous roar.

After a typically emotional set of national anthems, the teams were ready.

'Enjoy it, guys,' said Andre Watson. Then he blew his whistle and as Wilkinson sent a high hanging kick into the night air the stadium exploded with camera flashes.

The opening minutes were played at a frenetic pace and Australia seemed determined to run England ragged in the first quarter. Twice they won kickable penalties but spurned the attempts at goal in favour of territorial advantage. Their line-out was functioning smoothly and they looked well in control.

Then came the first scrum – an area of the game in which England expected to have a significant advantage. In the build-up to the game, Andre Watson had spoken about his reluctance to give penalties at the scrum. He wanted there to be a contest but he knew how easily scrum infringements could blight a game. He didn't want that to happen and he expected the two competing packs to play as hard and fair as they could. This was music to the ears of Woodman, Thompson and Vickery – all the more so because the Wallabies had lost their first-choice tight-head during the semi-final.

The incident had occurred at a scrum. The Wallaby tight-head Ben Darwin thumped into his opposition and instantly knew something was seriously wrong as a searing pain shot down his spine. 'Neck, neck, neck!' he screamed out. To his eternal credit, the All Blacks loose-head Kees Meeuws immediately reacted to Darwin's cry and stopped pushing. The force of a scrummaging pack can measure up to 7,000 newtons and Meeuws's reaction prevented a tragic – and potentially fatal – accident. Darwin suffered a prolapsed disc in his neck and he was extremely fortunate to be walking around within a matter of days – but his rugby career was finished. It was wretched in so many ways, all the more so because Darwin had to withdraw from playing in a World Cup final in front of his home fans, but it could have been so much worse.

Darwin's replacement was a young buck by the name of Al Baxter. He was green in the extreme at Test level and his task – to contain the monstrous England pack – was an arduous one. At the first scrum Baxter collapsed under the pressure from Trevor Woodman and the outlook for Australia looked ominous. But the interpretation of the scrum by referee Watson favoured, often inexplicably, the weaker Australian eight rather than the clearly dominant white-shirted pack. With touch-judge Paul Honiss also chipping in with advice on scrum misdemeanours, the officials kept Australia in the game by overlooking the clear superiority of England's scrummaging ability. Even Baxter himself would admit that he had been taught a huge lesson out there and that he had a lot to learn if he was to survive as a Test match tight-head. For everyone involved in England's campaign, the fact that Watson and Honiss were overlooking the clear evidence before their eyes was a source of incredulity and enormous frustration.

'When you consider the difference in size, power, experience and ability between our front-row and the Wallaby one, it was mystifying to me that the referee could imagine that we would be scrummaging illegally,' said Martin Johnson. 'Why would we need to? Vicks and Trevor were taking them apart as it was.'

The scrummaging issue would hound England throughout the game – and come back to haunt them at the denouement.

But the ball was in open play again now and both sets of backs looked dangerous whenever they spun it wide. But the World Cup final was pitching the two best defensive sides in the tournament against one another and only a moment of inspiration and a perfect execution of skill would be able to unlock the defensive lines. And the Wallabies produced just that in the fifth minute.

The Australian pack secured the ball from a scrappy scrum. David Lyons had recovered well as his tight-five were being marched backwards and he was able to set up a ruck on the right flank. Gregan quickly swept the ball away to his left where Larkham was standing deep. The fly-half turned his body and sent an inch-perfect cross-field kick to the left-hand corner. The ball hung delightfully in the air, allowing Lote Tuqiri on the left wing plenty of time to race up and arrive just as it was making its descent towards the scuttling figure of Jason Robinson as he raced to cover the kick.

Tuqiri was a good six inches taller than Robinson and had been on fine form in the tournament. He rose like an Aussie Rules footballer, easily clearing Robinson's leap, collected cleanly and dived over for a beautifully executed score.

'It was a great kick and it worked perfectly,' admitted Robinson. 'I'm just surprised that they didn't do more of it. The night was wet and horrible and those kinds of kicks are always 50–50 – in fact more than that for the attacker as they are going forward and have the momentum to take them over the line if they have the ball – and he had a big height advantage on me. But from our point of view there was no panic, we just thought, *Right, let's get back into doing what we do. Let's focus and play to our patterns.* And that's how we went about it.'

From the touchline, Elton Flatley struck the upright with his conversion attempt.

'In most of our World Cup matches, we went behind early and when Tuqiri scored, it was a case of, *Well, here we go again,*' said Dallaglio. 'There was no panic.'

Just as they had done against Samoa, Wales and France, England held their nerve despite the early setback. They pressed and they probed and they muscled their way into the Australian red zone, forcing them to concede penalties. Just a few minutes after the try had been scored, David Lyons went off his feet at a ruck and Wilkinson put England's first points on the board with the resultant penalty.

After seeing the accuracy of Larkham's kick to Tuqiri, the English back-row made it their mission to do everything they could to disrupt the Wallaby fly-half. They hit him hard, they hit him late, they tugged his jersey, they got up in his face time and time again. They were like a pack of dogs, intent on doing everything they could to unsettle him, to put him off his rhythm. And it worked. The tactic of the cross-field kick wasn't repeated and then, just a few minutes after a crunching hit from Richard Hill, Larkham rushed out of the defensive line and took Ben Cohen out without the ball. In so doing, he both conceded a penalty and gashed open his lip, which required him to leave the field for treatment. As Wilkinson kicked the penalty, Larkham's blood replacement, Matt Giteau, joined the fold, and England were in the lead.

Over the next ten minutes, England made two sixty-metre incursions into the Wallaby half from broken play. The first was from a kick downfield after Wilkinson had forced a turnover from Giteau with a crunching tackle, which was only just rescued by Tuqiri; the second saw Richard Hill hack the ball downfield and chase brilliantly to put pressure on the covering Giteau, who knocked the ball on as he dived to secure it. Quick as a flash, Hill was over the ball, followed immediately by Steve Thompson and Neil Back, who slung the ball right to Josh Lewsey. The full-back sensed the space and saw that he, Matt Dawson and Ben Kay had a three-on-two overlap against the scrambling Australian defence. Lewsey drew Gregan and flicked the ball on to Dawson, who stood up Waugh and then popped the ball to Kay, who was arcing round towards the corner flag. There was all of a yard or two to go and Kay simply had to catch and dive for the score. But in the excitement of the moment, the blood rushed to Kay's head and he fumbled the ball forward, losing control. It was a terrible error.

'His are normally the safest of hands and I couldn't believe my eyes,' said Martin Johnson. 'A definite try, gone begging. He'd probably made the fatal mistake: thinking about it.'

'It was just one of those things,' said Richard Hill. 'Ninety-nine times out of a hundred he would have caught it and scored.'

'Ask Ben Kay about dropping the ball in the World Cup final,' said Will Greenwood. 'Even ten years later he says there is not a day goes by that he doesn't think about it.'

From the resultant scrum Australia cleared their lines, but England were still very much in the ascendancy. In the twenty-eighth minute, Wilkinson stroked over his third penalty to make it 9–5 and just ten minutes later he was involved again as England went for the jugular.

George Gregan was lifted and thumped into touch by Mike Tindall and from the line-out England spun the ball into midfield, where Will Greenwood carried it strongly up the middle of the park. Greenwood hit the contact high and pumped his legs, carrying three defenders with him until they forced him to the deck. Running from right to left, Lawrence Dallaglio swept around the shadow of the ruck and took a pop ball from Dawson. The Wallaby defenders to the right of the ruck hadn't seen Dallaglio coming and the No.8 surged through the gap and into open space. He was running around Mortlock and, just as the centre was about to haul him down from one side and Wendell Sailor was about to crash into him from the other, Wilkinson ran a switch line from left to right and Dallaglio flicked the ball inside to him. Wilkinson took it on, gave a shuffle of movement to fix full-back Mat Rogers and then spun the ball back out to the left where Jason Robinson was searing up outside him. Just as he had done in the opening minutes of the First Test for the Lions in 2001, Robinson tore down the left-hand touchline without a finger being laid on him. He dived in at the corner as Rogers desperately lunged for him, then leapt to his feet, punched the ball away and roared, 'Come on!' to the delighted English fans in the crowd.

It was a spectacularly executed try.

Wilkinson missed with the conversion but England were more than deserving of their 14–5 half-time lead.

In a calm changing room, the team talked through a few technical points; line-outs, scrummage and how to adjust our game plan for the slight breeze they'd now face.

Johnson looked around his team and could feel the energy surging through them. They had played well in the first forty minutes. The early try had been a setback, nothing more, and they had responded magnificently. They were all over the Aussies. They had spurned at least one golden try-scoring opportunity but they hadn't let their heads drop. Instead, they had created another opportunity and they had taken it.

'We keep them moving,' he said. 'I want the intensity lifted another level or two now. We fucking bury them out there.'

England started the second half strongly, the forwards rumbling powerfully,

Mike Tindall punching holes in the midfield, Wilkinson thundering long touch-finders deep into Australian territory. Ben Cohen seemed to have busted his way through for another score, but play was brought back as the officials deemed an obstruction by Richard Hill had illegally opened the gap for the big winger.

But the Wallabies were displaying the national characteristic that Woodward had first come to understand back in his playing days with Manly – Australian sportspeople do not give up. The Wallabies clung on with every fibre of their beings and slowly began to crawl their way back into the game.

The wind was behind them now and there could be no denying the class and experience of the half-back pairing of Larkham and Gregan (the latter would go on to become the most capped player in history), and the clever footballing skills of Flatley. These three expertly returned the ball into England's half and the gold defensive wall pressed hard.

England conceded a penalty that Flatley gratefully nudged over to make the score 14–8.

The downpour grew heavier and both sides began to make an increasing number of handling mistakes. At the line-out, both hookers were struggling with the slippery ball and there were several overthrows that completely missed their targets. The net result of all these errors was scrums. England should have been delighted, but it was Australia who had won the referee's ear and they were surviving as Andre Watson saw several misdemeanours by the England front-row for which he awarded penalties.

Their frustration was evident – and was no doubt the reason Phil Vickery, in an effort to atone for his scrum penalties and to try to put his side back into the ascendancy, handled the ball on the ground at a ruck. The shrill sound of Watson's whistle broke the air and his arm swung up on the Wallaby side. Flatley was coolness personified as he knocked over the kick to make it 14–11.

England had a mass of possession and were playing a strong, controlled game, but the scrum penalties were killing them. With the rain pouring down and both sides absolutely fanatical in defence, there were dropped balls and knock-ons aplenty. England's pack were without doubt the superior scrummaging unit, but they were penalised time and time again for scrum infringements.

'We were the stronger, more physical side but every time we got pressure on them it was the same old story,' said Johnson. 'A dropped ball, a needless penalty, allowing them to claw back six precious points. Jonny tried a couple of snap drop-goals but they slid wide to raucous Australian booing and we stayed scoreless in the half as the minutes ticked away.'

'The ball was pretty greasy but we were playing with width and moving it about,' said Richard Hill. 'Perhaps we overdid it and didn't look after the ball enough. For whatever reason, we just couldn't get our game going again after the break. We were also getting penalised in the scrums, which was difficult to understand. We clearly had the stronger scrum but the Aussies worked it well and managed to get the ref on their side.'

Astonishingly, for all their dominance, England didn't score a point in the second half. But as the clock ticked down towards the 80th minute, they were still three points clear. All they had to do was hold on and they would do it. They would win the World Cup.

The ball died in play on England's 10-metre line, some fifteen yards in from the touchline. Andre Watson, correctly, awarded a scrum to Australia, who had been in possession. It was the seventy-eighth minute of the game. England needed to see out the scrum, defend for their lives, keep their discipline and Australia would run out of time.

The packs engaged and England surged forward; Baxter collapsed under the pressure. The ball had appeared out the back of the scrum and George Smith had comfortably controlled it, but Watson wasn't happy. He blew his whistle and demanded that the scrum was reset and replayed. Martin Johnson was incensed. 'You've got to ping three!' he shouted. 'He's on the ground every fucking time!'

Watson did not appreciate being told how to call the infringement. 'I'll ping what I see. Don't test me.'

Watson walked down the line between the two front-rows, then turned and called 'Engage'. The packs collided but Woodman hadn't been ready.

'I just missed the engagement and Baxter came in underneath me and I couldn't engage,' he explained. 'Often the ref will just reset it but this time he gave them the penalty.'

Seventy-nine minutes on the clock. It was do-or-die time for the Wallabies. Gregan pointed to the posts and Flatley walked to the spot to await his kicking tee. If Flatley missed the World Cup was England's. But if he kicked it the game would go into extra-time – and all bets were off.

Practice, as we have discussed, makes perfect and players develop skills to such an extent that they no longer think about their execution. This is called expert induced amnesia. But when they are faced with a huge pressure situation they can, as has also been examined, choke. As Matthew Syed explains in *Bounce,* 'Choking happens when a sportsman gets so anxious that he seizes conscious control over a skill that ought to be delivered subconsciously. Suddenly, he is at the mercy of the conscious system. The highly sophisticated skills encoded in the subconscious part of his brain, built up over years of practice, count for nothing. He is striving for victory using neural pathways he last used as a novice.'

Woodward's greatest fear had been that his players might choke at the summit. Looking at Flatley, he hoped that this would be the moment the Australian would bottle it, would get the yips and slice the kick wide under that welter of pressure.

Flatley threw his scrum-cap to one side and placed the ball on the tee. He rose, checked his alignment and then took three steps backwards and one to the side. He hunched his shoulders forward and jutted out his strong, square chin, setting his eyes on the posts in front of him and the sea of gold and white shirts behind. He took a deep breath and began his run-up. And in that moment he displayed just what an iron will he had as he landed a perfect penalty and threw his team a lifeline.

'The key was that as soon as he slotted the kick over, the guys didn't dwell on anything,' said Johnson. 'We didn't talk about what could have been or that we had just let the World Cup slip through our fingers.'

'We just thought, *what do we have to do in the next twenty minutes to win this game?*' said Mike Catt, who had replaced Mike Tindall with just four minutes of normal time left on the clock. 'That was the great thing about it.'

The players gathered in a circle on the field, took on fluids and spent a few moments gathering their thoughts. Woodward appeared from the stands and headed over to meet them. He was about to address the group when Johnson pulled him to one side. 'We've got this, Clive,' he said. 'Leave it to us.'

It was player empowerment as he had always hoped – but it was also a moment of agony for Woodward. After all his years of hard work and dedication, he wanted to be there to help steer the team through to the end. But he knew that Johnson was right. It was the players who would win the game, not him. It was all on their shoulders now. He nodded. And then a thought occurred to him. 'I want to speak to Jonny,' he said.

'That's fine. Thanks, Clive,' said Johnson and then he turned back to his men.

Woodward approached Wilkinson. 'Don't pass the ball,' he said. 'Just smash it down into their half, behind their wingers, and make them play from there. We need to play territory – nothing in our half at all. Keep them pinned back. This isn't going to be won by tries.'

Wilkinson was nodding vaguely, his eyes on the posts in the distance. 'I need to go and do some kicking,' he said.

Woodward realised that his fly-half hadn't listened to a word he had said, so as Wilkinson disappeared off to practise his goal-kicking, he tracked down Mike Catt and relayed the message to him instead.

'Got you,' said Catt with a smile, as cool as ever. 'That's what I'm here for.'

'Johnno got the tone just right at that point,' recalled Richard Hill. 'There were around 83,000 fans in that stadium, all in a state of hyper-excitement, yet that huddle was one of the coolest and calmest environments I've ever experienced during a match. "We know what we have to do and we don't have to change much to win this," he told us. It was just a matter of tightening up and concentrating on what we did well. Johnno knew we were going to win, you could just feel it.'

With Catt now on the field, Woodward made another substitution that would prove crucial. He took off Phil Vickery and replaced him with Jason Leonard. 'I wasn't told to defuse the situation when I went on, or not to scrummage, but just to make sure I didn't give away any more penalties,' said Leonard. 'I jogged on and just ran past the ref and said, "Look, you know what I'm like, and you know how I scrummage. I won't go up and I won't go down. I might go backwards and forwards, but you won't have any bother with me, all right?" And he said, "That's all I'm asking, thanks Jason."' That was 114 caps of experience talking and Watson appreciated the effort. Tellingly, England weren't penalised again at the scrum throughout the remainder of the game.

'Bringing Jason Leonard on was massive,' recalled Woodward. 'He was disappointed because he felt he should have started the match, but his impact off the bench can never be overstated. We could have done things differently, we could have made a raft of changes – as a lot of coaches would do – but there's every chance that if we had done that, we might not have held our composure. I think it's ridiculous nowadays that everyone in the squad gets on the pitch – and with pre-planned substitutions being made on the hour mark. I never worked like that; I always used my eyes and made judgement calls depending on how the game was going. Take Matt Dawson and Kieran Bracken, for example. Kieran didn't get on the pitch in the final. I looked at Matt and I could see he was fine, so there was no way I was taking him off. I had people saying to me, "Get fresh legs on," but Dawson was my number one scrum-half – primarily because of his brain – and he was settled and playing well and he was fit enough to last the distance. The way I saw it, this was the biggest pressure moment of all our lives, why would I take off Dawson when I knew he was going well and I knew he had the experience to handle the pressure?'

The game restarted and within two minutes England were awarded a penalty. Wilkinson, who had not enjoyed anywhere near his usual standard of accuracy with his kicking, showed just how important those few minutes of extra practice had been by slotting a monstrous effort from fifty metres out, taking the score to 17–14. It was a magnificent strike.

England played with tremendous ambition in Australia's half, with Mike Catt coming to the fore. One short ball off Wilkinson saw him bust a hole right through the Wallaby midfield before slipping a delicate offload to Dallaglio.

Minutes later he did the same off a short pop from Dawson and England swept forward through the phases. They worked their way down to the 22 and Catt attempted a drop-goal but was charged down by Justin Harrison. As the ball fell loose, Phil Waugh dived to secure it but knocked it on.

England set the scrum, Leonard shoring up the right-hand side. The ball came wide and Catt took it up again; Dawson slung the ball back to Wilkinson who went for a drop-goal… but it slid wide.

The Wallabies recovered the ball and looked to settle the frantic pace. From the drop-out they launched the ball back into England's half and the danger was averted. The ball eventually died in play and the first period of extra-time came to an end.

Ten minutes left in the final to end all finals.

Three minutes into the second period, Australia launched an attack on the England 10-metre line. The ball swept through the backline and Tuqiri hit the ball at pace on the wing. He carried it for twenty yards until he was met by Robinson, but again the Australian's size and weight won the contest and he barrelled over the England winger. Only the intervention of Cohen put Tuqiri to ground. The ball squirted infield and Wilkinson pounced on it, just a matter of yards from his line. The forwards poured over their fly-half and Dawson kicked the ball into touch.

The sides continued to spar back and forward. Punch, counter-punch, punch. Then came a moment of madness in a ruck on England's 22 and Andre Watson spotted the hands trying to wrestle the ball back on the deck. Penalty to Australia.

Flatley, shoulders hunched forward, slowly approached the ball and stroked the kick over. 17–17.

From the restart, Wilkinson rifled the ball long down the middle. George Smith gathered and set off upfield, where he was met by the kick-chase defensive wall. The Wallabies set up a ruck and Gregan fed Mat Rogers.

Phil Larder had spent dozens of hours drilling the players on effective charge-down techniques as a means of triggering counter-attack opportunities. Lewis Moody had shown the worth of his exuberance and willingness to throw his body in harm's way during the pool match against South Africa when he had charged down Louis Koen's clearance and Will Greenwood had scored. Now, fresh after arriving on the pitch for Richard Hill, Moody was haring around, ready to do it again. As soon as Gregan's fingertips were on the ball, Moody was out of the traps. He belted towards Rogers and as the full-back drew back his leg to kick, Moody launched himself through the air. Rogers' boot connected with the ball and he managed to clear the charging figure of Moody, but he sliced the kick into touch.

Woodward was prowling back and forth along the touchline, his hand rubbing his forehead. 'T-CUP, T-CUP, T-CUP,' he muttered.

'Call zig-zag, Jonny,' shouted Andy Robinson. 'Call zig-zag!'

Woodward stared at the stadium clock. There were just a few minutes left. Statistics began to fly through his mind. *It takes twenty seconds to score. If we can retain the ball for five phases our chance of scoring a try, a penalty or a drop-goal increases to 85 per cent. We know how to win these games.*

'Call zig-zag,' said Dave Alred under his breath, his eyes burning on his protégé.

Gathering themselves just outside the Australian 22, Steve Thompson listened for the call from Ben Kay. When he heard it, he sniffed but displayed no emotion on his face. The call was to go long to the tail to Moody. Thompson knew that Moody's heart rate would be up after chasing down Rogers and that he would be trying to get his head around the occasion having just come on to the field – now he had to prepare himself for the line-out jump and take. But the call had been made – and before Moody would even be involved there was the small matter of Thompson delivering the ball to him.

Memories of watching the final agonising moments of the 2001 Lions tour flickered for a moment through Thompson's mind. It had been the Lions' throw. It was meant to go to Johnson, the safe option at the front of the line, but the call had been anticipated and the ball intercepted and won by Wallaby lock Justin Harrison. Harrison was again in position alongside Johnson, watching the body-language of the England players, trying to read their movements, hoping that the same thing would happen again. Kay had obviously had the same thought. The front and the middle of the line-out were the safe bets and Kay knew that the Aussies would guess that that was where the ball would go. The tail was a gamble – but it would also be unmarked. The only problem lay in the throw – in the rain and the wind, the ball could slip and fall short, or go too long, or deviate left or right.

Thompson raised the ball above his head and focused. Since coming into the England set-up he had been working with two dedicated specialists: Simon Hardy and Sherylle Calder. Hardy had honed his technique, Calder his spatial awareness. They had spent hundreds and hundreds of hours working together and he had spent hundreds more back at Northampton with Colin Deans, the man who had been the inspiration for his move to hooker. Was this the moment that all that time and dedication would pay off, or would he falter at the crucial moment? He took a steadying breath, drew back his arm and threw. The ball spun smoothly away from his outstretched fingers and spiralled in a perfect arc. Fifteen yards away he saw a shuffle of movement and then Moody's blond mop of hair rose above all the others. The young flanker reached skywards as he was propelled up and at the apex of the jump the ball landed safely in his hands. It had been a perfect throw. Indeed, the whole line-out operation had been executed to perfection.

Like a well-oiled machine, thought Andy Robinson with a sigh of relief.

As the ball came down to Matt Dawson he heard the call of 'Zig-zag, zig-zag!' from Wilkinson. He spun the ball wide to his fly-half and then repeated the call to the forwards.

Ten thousand hours of practice, of repetitive drills to hone skills to world-class standards. Now was the time for all that dedicated practice to come into its own.

Mike Catt hit a flat line to set up the first phase. He knew there was no chance of breaching the Aussie line on his own like that, but the ruck would set up field position. His contact skills would have to be perfect and he repeated the actions he had been through countless times with Andy Robinson barking in his ear: shoulder into contact, pump the legs to buy time for your support to reach you, pivot your torso, hit the deck, place the ball back towards your scrum-half at full stretch, steady the ball with your hands.

Catt crashed into the line and was thumped in a double tackle by Larkham and Flatley. As he twisted his body to lay the ball back, the forwards piled in over him to retain possession. But too many went in and Dawson suddenly found himself with very few options. He looked up for Wilkinson, who had dropped back into the pocket for the drop-goal. He could sense the Australian defenders lining up, ready to charge Wilkinson as soon as he passed the ball. They were more than forty yards out from the posts and Wilkinson had already missed two drop-goal attempts. The risk was huge but time was running out.

'I'll tell you one thing, Daws. If it's on for a late drop-goal to win it, you've got to take it on yourself. No one will be looking at you. All eyes will be on Jonny.'

Paul Grayson's words echoed through his thoughts. Dawson glanced out of the corner of his eye – and there, as Grayson had predicted, he saw a gap. He snatched up the ball, shaped to pass to Wilkinson, stepped off his left foot and slipped through the hole. He carried the ball for fifteen, twenty yards before he was hauled down by Mat Rogers and George Smith. Jason Robinson and Will Greenwood had been the first English players to react to the break and they bridged over the top of Dawson before Smith could attempt to steal back possession.

Again, Wilkinson dropped into the pocket. Neil Back stepped into scrum-half and readied himself for the pass. But Johnson, as cool at that moment as he had been throughout the match, knew that Wilkinson needed Dawson's whip-fast pass to buy him as much time as possible to strike the drop-goal cleanly. He screamed for the ball from Back and charged up the right-hand flank of the ruck, carrying his team a further two yards forward. At this range the Wallabies didn't want to concede a penalty, so they didn't contest the ball on the ground and Johnson was able to lay it back cleanly for Dawson, who was back on his feet and back in position.

George Gregan, acutely aware of the danger his team now faced, began yelling, 'Field goal! Field goal!' and Australian defenders spread out across the line, crouched like sprinters in the starting blocks ready to burst off the mark to close down Wilkinson. Some of them were too eager and, as Dawson set himself for the pass, the Wallaby defence kept creeping forward offside and then retreating. Forward and back, forward and back. But Dawson wouldn't be rushed. Then, when he was ready, he let the ball fly.

Wilkinson was set to kick but Dawson's pass was poor and as the ball arced through the air towards him it swung left to right, forcing him to change his body angle, shifting his balance away from his favoured left foot. A wall of gold-shirted defenders desperately raced up to hit him, the barrel-chested figure of Phil Waugh springing ahead the fastest, screaming at Wilkinson as he approached.

The ball hit Wilkinson's outstretched fingers and he drew it down, adjusting its angle to open the sweet spot for his right foot. He released it from his grasp. His leg drew back and Waugh was almost on him, his bellowing scream rising high above the roar of the stadium. *Head down, eye on a stitch, harden the toes, lock the ankle, strike with the inside-arch, follow-through.* For the white-shirted warriors around him on the pitch, those on the sidelines and the management in the stands, for all the players that had played a role in Woodward's six-year campaign and for those whose lives had influenced each and every protagonist in this story, this was the moment of truth. And for Wilkinson, this was the moment when a life of tortured, unrelenting dedication and obsession would either mean something… or nothing.

His foot struck the ball. Waugh leapt forward, his arms stretching out to charge down the kick.

The ball spun end over end, up and over the Australian flanker's clawing fingers. All around the stadium the crowd rose to their feet, faces craned forward, hearts in mouths, breath caught…

And the stars aligned.

The ball sailed through the posts.

20–17.

Twenty seconds remained on the clock. The players scrambled back into position and the Wallabies grasped the ball for one last roll of the die. And an opportunity presented itself. As Larkham raced back to the halfway line to take a quick kick-off, he noticed that there was a space in the midfield. In their excitement, England hadn't aligned properly for the restart. Larkham hoisted the ball – but his intentions had been read by Trevor Woodman, perhaps the most unlikely of eleventh-hour saviours, who darted over to fill the space at the last moment.

'From the coaches' point of view, I was out of position,' said Woodman. 'But I was in a place where I thought they might kick. They looked at me, a prop, and I mean if you saw a short fat bloke, you'd kick it to him, wouldn't you?

'At the time I felt like I'd jumped two feet in the air to make the catch when in fact all I'd done was jump three inches.' Woodman made a good catch, two arms above his head, and then braced himself for the impact of the chasing Wallabies. He rode the storm just long enough for his support players to help him out.

Matt Dawson bent to retrieve the ball. He looked up and saw Mike Catt in the first-receiver position. Good old Catty. As Dawson spun the ball back, he yelled, 'Kick it to the shithouse!'

And Catt duly obliged. His booming punt sent the ball spiralling into the crowd. Andre Watson checked the time and then whistled for the end of the game.

England were world champions.

PART FOUR
HUBRIS

ELEVEN

THE ANATOMY OF
THE THEREAFTER

'Do not go gentle into that good night,
Old age should burn and rave at close of day;
Rage, rage against the dying of the light.'
Dylan Thomas

I F THIS WAS a movie, we would fade to black and the credits would start to roll. But no retrospective study can end at the moment of glory – there has to be an examination of what happened to the protagonists after they had scaled their Everest.

For the rest of 2003 all was well in the garden of English rugby – the red rose was in stunning bloom. Ben Cohen had made a special history of his own in following his uncle, George, who had played right-back in the England football team's historic victory over West Germany in 1966, in becoming a World Cup winner. The victory was nevertheless tinged with poignancy, as Cohen knew how much his father would have wished to have been there to see his son's greatest triumph. Cohen was not alone in experiencing those feelings. It was perhaps Johnson who summed up best what the victory meant to the players, many of whom had experienced tragedy of one sort or the other over the previous few years. 'I can't remember what I was thinking as I picked it up,' he said of raising the World Cup after the medal presentation. 'Pride in the boys, pride in my country, relief that we'd finally done it. Most of all, I wished my mum had been there to see it; she would have loved it.'

The team flew home on a plane renamed *Sweet Chariot* by British Airways. While the players mingled with fans on board and showed off their winners' medals and the Webb Ellis Cup, Mike Tindall attempted to break Aussie cricketer David Boon's record of drinking fifty-two beers on the journey back, a feat that had stood unbeaten since 1983. Some accounts say Tindall managed it, others say he passed out a long way shy.

They landed at Heathrow Terminal Three at 5 o'clock on a cold, wet winter's morning – and were greeted by the astonishing sight of more than 10,000 fans who had made an early-morning pilgrimage to welcome their heroes home.

In the following days the players took part in an open-top bus parade through the streets of London. The RFU estimated that some 20,000 spectators might turn up to watch the team show off the World Cup; more than 750,000 people came out to party.

Weeks of celebrations followed. They met the Queen at Buckingham Palace and the Prime Minister at Downing Street. Woodward was named UK Coach of the Year at the Sports Coach UK awards, the team was named Team of the Year at the BBC's Sports Personality of the Year awards and Jonny Wilkinson picked up the main gong, before Woodward and four members of England's coaching staff – Andy Robinson, Phil Larder, Dave Alred and Dave Reddin – were inducted into the UK Sport Hall of Fame. Finally, every player and the senior coaches were appointed MBEs, Johnson a CBE, Wilkinson, Robinson and Leonard OBEs, and Woodward was knighted. But perhaps the greatest legacy was that all over the country, thousands of children were standing over rugby balls in a half-crouch, hands held out in front of them, mimicking the golden boy Wilkinson as they readied themselves to kick for glory.

The rugby landscape was now changed for ever – tight shirts became the norm, as did expanded playing squads, bloated back-room staff, military off-field planning, the utilisation of critical non-essentials, specialist coaches, and freakish fitness and strength levels. This latter point was to become an issue in later years as the size and power of the modern professional player gave rise to greater risk of serious injury. After the brutal 2009 Lions Test series against South Africa, veteran Lions doctor James Robson voiced his concerns for the modern rugby player. 'I hope, at some point, that welfare will become a bigger part of player management,' he said. 'There's a lot of talk and rhetoric but, for the players' sake, I hope more action is taken. We're reaching a level where players have gotten too big for their skill levels. They've become too muscle-bound and too bulky… These have been the most physical three Test matches I've been involved in.'

England had set the pattern and they knew that they would now have an even bigger target on their back than ever before. Other teams would focus on matching and then overtaking them. In 2004 New Zealand developed their own version of Prozone called Verusco Analysis – and the rest of the top nations would shortly follow suit. By 2013 it had become regular practice for all professional clubs and international teams to wear heart monitors at training, GPS chips in their shirts (even on match days) and to have their every movement on a training field or in a match filmed and pored over by video analysts. Woodward, the pacesetter, the mastermind, had started a revolution and it had gone global.

*

But all things in life are transient. In *The Golden Bough: A Study in Magic and Religion*, the anthropologist Sir James George Frazer examines the ancient tradition of the sacred king in a multitude of cultures around the world. The king rises in the spring, an all-powerful deity able to control the elements and, crucially, the growth of crops. But when the crops fail he is sacrificed, to be reincarnated once again in the spring – and so the cycle of life continues. Nowhere is the symbol of the sacred king more obviously present in modern Western society than in the world of sport. Football is undoubtedly the dominion of sacred kings where the firing and hiring of club and international managers dominates newspaper and TV news headlines throughout the year – every year; but Woodward was soon to experience the phenomenon in rugby union. From 2001 until the end of 2003 he was flawless, untouchable; and then the crops began to fail.

In January 2004 Martin Johnson announced his retirement from Test rugby. 'When I look back now,' said Johnson in 2006, 'I think, *you lucky, lucky bastard.* I don't think I ever played in a team that lost more games than it won, and that's from the age of 11 to 33. And look at the guys I played with. People like Graham Rowntree, Darren Garforth and Neil Back were there almost all the time. The World Cup was great, but the best thing was the guys you were with.

'I find the bad memories fading, leaving the good. I appreciated what we had at the time but I appreciate it more now. I couldn't stand the moaners, the people who said it was hard. We were playing sport. We'd train for a few hours, then we'd sit in a hotel. Some things in life are hard. That wasn't.'

Over the course of the next few months he was followed into the international twilight by Jason Leonard, Neil Back, Kyran Bracken, Dorian West and Lawrence Dallaglio (although Dallaglio would later reverse his position and return to play for England, and both he and Back were selected for the 2005 Lions tour, where Back became the oldest player to wear the Lions' red in a Test match). Injury woes struck many more. Jonny Wilkinson underwent the first of many operations that would plague his career, and Iain Balshaw, Mike Catt, Matt Dawson, Lewis Moody, Mike Tindall, Phil Vickery and Julian White all suffered injuries that kept them out of the game for extended periods. For those who played in the World Cup and remained fit, there was a noticeable tail-off in their performances the following season – so much so that, despite depleted resources, Will Greenwood, Ben Kay and Jason Robinson were given the summer off to rest and recuperate in the hope that their form would return.

In a simple analysis, this was always going to happen. The team had been built to win the 2003 World Cup and the target had always been for that team to peak at the tournament. Woodward, Dave Reddin and all the other coaches achieved exactly what they set out to do – and Woodward now had four years to do it again. There should have been no surprise that, with the team breaking up after the tournament, a lean period would follow before the rolling success started up again. But sport is fickle and the bigger picture is often easily lost.

The World Cup was won because England had a squad of pure quality, that had grown together over a number of years – years that had been filled with morale-boosting victories and ambition-galvanizing losses. The players had played together over dozens of Test matches, they had learnt how to cope with pressure and they had learnt how to win, no matter who or what they faced. That had been facilitated by meticulous attention to detail, by sparing no expense, and by going to every length possible to give the players an edge over their competitors. So Woodward knew that if England were to achieve a feat never managed before and successfully defend the World Cup, then they would need to do that all over again – but with an even greater attention to detail, with even more effort and with increased financial investment. Woodward needed more money, more time with the players, more support. If he could have that then he knew that he could create a dynasty.

But from the moment the team returned to the UK, it was clear that no one else in the RFU hierarchy was focusing on the future like Woodward and his coaching team were. After the 1999 World Cup exit, Woodward had been hauled before the RFU to review what had gone wrong and how he planned to improve things. After their 2003 triumph, it seemed that to many in the RFU the journey was complete. When you reach the top, where else is there to go? For Woodward, it was to return to base camp and then look to scale the heights again – only this time faster, better, stronger. There was no formal tournament review, but Woodward did his own. He had been given a new four-year contract in the summer of 2003 that would take him through to the World Cup in France in 2007; so he laid out a four-year plan, detailed in the extreme. 'I came back from the World Cup and within days I was back in the office getting ready to plan for the next cycle,' said Woodward. 'I wanted to put in place a blueprint for where we needed to go from here.

'I presented all of my ideas to the board but they just didn't understand the necessity or the urgency with which they needed to be made. The problem was that the board members, outside of Baron, had no idea how we had won the World Cup. They thought this success would just continue.

'There was a belief that we had won simply because we had great players, and yes, that was the number one reason. But it also took a lot more than that – after all, all of our competitors had great players as well. It was a very frustrating time and I couldn't help but feel that even though we had got it right for so long and everyone had been brilliant, Baron was brilliant, and the team were given everything we needed leading up to the World Cup, we still only won the World Cup by a drop-goal in the last seconds of extra time. We now needed to do more and as England it is even tougher because everyone wants to knock your block off. Although England winning the World Cup proved very popular in England, I knew it would prompt a huge response from our rivals and that every other rugby playing nation would be figuring out how to take their teams to the next level to beat us.'

In the summer of 2004, Woodward appeared on Radio 5 Live's *Sportsweek* programme. The presenter, Garry Richardson, asked him whether he would receive the same support from the RFU for the defence of the World Cup in 2007 as he had in the build-up to 2003. 'I'm convinced that myself and a few people know exactly why we won it,' said Woodward. 'The only thing I'm a little cranky about is that there are one or two people in influential positions to make things happen for the England team who possibly, and rightly so, don't understand why the team won. We've got to increase the number of training days, increase the investment, but it's my job to make sure people understand that.

'Sometimes you have conversations with people and you walk away shaking your head, as they seem to think we won the World Cup because we had a few good players. Well, we've got more than a few, we've got world-class players, but they'll be the first to admit you don't win World Cups because you've got good players, you win them because you prepare properly.

'I'm making it quite clear that England won because of the investment, and that's fantastic. Everyone invested hugely in me and the team and that's why we won, but we can't just expect that to happen every four years. It has to happen every year, and I'm determined to keep driving that investment through. I'm here to represent the players, and people like Johnson and Dallaglio have created huge role models, and we want people to step into those shoes and win. To do that, though, we have to understand why we won.'

The RFU's lack of vision infuriated him and he often felt like he was banging his head against a brick wall. For all his achievements, they still weren't listening to what he had to say. 'After the Rugby World Cup win in 2003,' he wrote in *The Sunday Times* in 2012, 'the England management devised plans for what we called a Pressure Dome. I had favourable funding discussions with Tessa Jowell, then secretary of state for media and culture. It was to be a dedicated performance centre for England rugby (all teams) where we could coach players to play under pressure, where we could scientifically monitor individual development programmes and develop coaches and referees – a true centre of excellence, in other words. Those in authority at Twickenham, however, decided to build a hotel instead.'

In an effort to begin building for a new era, he announced in January 2004 that any player not available for the summer tour to New Zealand wouldn't be selected for the Six Nations. This decision pushed several senior players to call time on their Test careers earlier than they perhaps might have done. While this certainly signalled a new dawn for the team it also robbed them of one of its most precious commodities – and one that Woodward had been carefully developing for years: experience. It is easy for a new player to come into a team of seasoned campaigners, easy to step into a team of winners when all you have to do is play your natural game. It is so much harder to come into a team and be surrounded by players who are as wide-eyed as you are. When the cauldron of international rugby really begins to boil, when backs are to the wall and the pressure is like a lead weight on your shoulders, where do you look for leadership and guidance through the maelstrom? With that experienced core stripped out and the senior players who *were* there struggling for form, that was exactly the problem faced by the England players during the seasons directly following the World Cup.

But there were other factors too.

England played a New Zealand Barbarians side at Twickenham at the end of 2003. For the RFU, it was to be a showcase celebration match; for Woodward it was a chance to show the world that nothing stood still in sport, that he was intent on continuing the journey; but for the clubs it was yet another intrusion into their already disrupted season. They had lost their stars for the entire summer and the first quarter of the season. Now that they were back, and victorious, their most valuable commodities were even more valuable. They didn't want their England stars swanning off to play in a meaningless exhibition match when they had serious league games to play and their presence could guarantee a bumper crowd.

In the face of yet another club versus country row, an agreement was reached whereby Woodward could select only three players from each club – and, even then, he would often find that his first-choice picks from those clubs were unavailable. 'I think it's a wonderful fixture,' he said of the Barbarians game, 'provided I can play it with a full-strength side. It's hard to get excited about a game with a decimated squad.'

'The break-up of the England team post RWC 2003, due to retirements, injuries, player fatigue and loss of form, would have been all more manageable if we actually had more control over the players and worked in the same way as the southern hemisphere teams are run,' he would later say. 'England will win if we are allowed to prepare properly and compete on a level playing field, but currently we are not and never have been since the game went professional. That is what makes winning the World Cup even more remarkable.'

His disillusionment was palpable, yet his focus remained intact. His thirst for success had been barely quenched by the World Cup success and he refused to rest on his laurels. Going into 2004, his new mantra was to go 'Beyond No.1'. He had already made history, he had already reshaped the rugby landscape, but he wanted to make it permanent.

With Johnson's retirement, Woodward made Dallaglio captain once again for the Six Nations and the No.8 led England to an impressive 50–9 win over Italy in Rome and a 35–13 win over Scotland in Edinburgh. But Woodward's time with the players had been stripped right back to the minimum demanded by the IRB rules for international windows, and the sponsors and other corporate interests were muscling their way into the players' time, even in Test weeks. In the build-up to England's third game, against Ireland at Twickenham, the team managed only a paltry two training sessions. And the outside interference finally took its toll as England not only lost 19–13 to an inspired Irish side, but surrendered their unbeaten run at home, which had stood at an incredible twenty-two consecutive wins.

They recovered to beat Wales 31–21 at Twickenham but then travelled to Paris, where they lost 24–21, handing France the Grand Slam and relinquishing their position as the No.1-ranked team in the world. Beyond No.1 this was not.

The summer tour to New Zealand and Australia sunk this new England side still further. Owing to injury, retirements and fatigue, Woodward was able to take only twelve players who had been in his World Cup squad. They were humiliated 36–3 and 36–12 by the All Blacks and 51–15 by the Wallabies. It was the Tour of Hell all over again.

When they returned home Woodward was greeted with the news that the RFU and the clubs had come to a new arrangement for player release throughout the season. An injury to an Elite Player Squad member would allow for his replacement in the programme, but form would not. So if a player was selected for the EPS at the start of the season, but went on to have a stinker for his club, there was no removing him while he remained fit and healthy. It was deeply restrictive – but the worst part was the access England would have to those EPS players. While accounting for the fact that the 2002–2003 season featured a World Cup, Woodward had still had his players for twelve weeks. Under the new EPS deal, he would have them for sixteen days.

'I realised when I came back that the clubs felt they had done their stuff and that now it was their turn,' said Woodward. 'I realised, when I put in a World Cup report with some serious recommendations that were completely ignored, that people were listening to me less than they had before the tournament. I found that very strange and disturbing... I understand that the players are the property of the clubs, but if we had them under our control, then think what we could do. We could manage them properly as a squad. We could manage their fitness and we could manage things like their welfare, their retirements, even their testimonials. But we have no control over our elite athletes.'

*

By the late summer of 2004, Woodward was world-weary. The mid-table position that England had achieved in the Six Nations, the brutal summer tour and the ongoing battle with the clubs and the RFU were taking their toll.

There was too much opposition, too much infighting, too many individuals and organisations sucking the life out of English rugby. The World Cup honeymoon was well and truly over.

On 2 September 2004, he announced his resignation as England's head coach and was succeeded by Andy Robinson. It was the end of an era. 'It wasn't a snap decision, it was something I had considered for some time and probably settled on whilst on tour in New Zealand and Australia. I did not believe the England Team was being made the priority which I found very hard to understand because it drives the rest of the game in England.

'It all revolved around the feeling that we couldn't continue in the same way and I didn't feel I had the support of the board for my new ideas – which I didn't. And I couldn't continue in that environment. I regret the way I left – the press conference was not my finest hour. It was a sad day because being the England head coach is the best job in the world, and I had been able to work with truly remarkable individuals and together achieve something very special. But I just felt my position had become untenable.'

In the days that followed his resignation he publicly vented his frustrations with the RFU and the battle that he had fought throughout his seven-year reign at the head of England rugby. 'Control of the players is everything and you can't control them through directors of rugby,' he said. 'It's like trying to run a business without a workforce. You cannot take any shortcuts... These are young men who are not at their best, and to be an elite performer you have to control the athlete all the time. The England head coach has to have more control of his players. We sat around the negotiating table with people who, with respect, have no idea about elite performance. When your job and career is involved in winning, you look at what is going on and you can't accept it. I haven't accepted it and it has come to this. You end up with a compromise agreement and you don't win World Cups by compromising. If you want to win the World Cup, and get behind this England team, you have to have something very special. You can't take shortcuts or compromises if you are trying to be the best in the world and win by an inch...

'It was fantastic to win the World Cup but it was clear to me from the moment that plane landed [back in the UK] I felt totally out of control. My mindset was we had a clear plan of how we were being successful, and that has been watered down. I went into the same meetings with the same faces and heard the same things. I wanted more and we have ended up with less... We won the World Cup by inches. You cannot compromise. We won the World Cup because we had an outstanding set of players. We prepared properly. But agreements have taken place between the RFU and clubs that on paper look great. They're not in reality.'

*

In February 2004, Woodward had been selected to lead the 2005 Lions tour to New Zealand. He was the candidate that had stood head and shoulders above all others and his resignation from the RFU seemed to suggest that he had done the Lions a favour as he could now concentrate 100 per cent on the challenge of touring New Zealand. And this is where we encounter one of the great elements that makes sport so special, so intriguing, so wonderfully varied. For even within a game like rugby union, which is highly structured and where the elite players are often of a similar standard and mindset and, in the home nations in particular, capable of playing in a certain uniform style, Woodward looked at previous Lions tours (including his own experiences) and was convinced that the blueprint he had drawn up for England would work for the Lions. But in sport no blueprint is ever directly transferable. There are too many nuances, too many exceptional circumstances with regards to the physical and mental states of the players, too many individual character traits that must be considered before any kind of structure is put in place. The management of a Lions tour, by the very nature of its variety, the paucity of preparation time and the fickleness of any player's form, has to be fluid in its approach. General styles and tactics can be laid out but they cannot be draconian. The Lions is a melting pot of four rugby nations and the way that one country approaches things cannot be foisted on the three others – not if the tour is to be a success. And so it proved in 2005. Woodward tried to make the Lions an extension of England in the way he approached the squad size, match preparation, accommodation, leisure time and team selection. And it was a disaster. As one leading English player said in the aftermath of the tour, you cannot take a system and a culture and an environment that had been developed over a number of years with England and cram it into seven weeks with the Lions. It just doesn't work. 'I'm big on building teams and I got it wrong with the Lions,' said Woodward. 'I said, "This is what I did with England and I know it works" – but you can't apply that to a scratch team in six weeks.

It is a tough, tough place to tour and the injuries just wrecked us. People talk about the size of the squad being an issue, having central bases being an issue, the splitting of the team being an issue, having Alistair Campbell there being an issue, but in all honesty, it's bullshit. If you prepare properly – and we did, we had absolutely the best coaches and medical team that were available – then it comes down to fifteen versus fifteen on the pitch and they were just better than us. We got thumped.'

On the face of it, a Lions tour is a near impossible challenge for a coach. Gather the best available players from four countries who go for each other's throats on an annual basis in the Six Nations, occasionally in World Cups and regularly throughout each season for their clubs, patch them together as best you can at the end of an arduous season, spend ten days (at most) in a training camp introducing them to one another, trying to dissolve the ingrained national barriers and hostilities, give them a brand new playing style, defensive system and set-piece codes, then fly them to the furthest reaches of the earth for a brutal six-week tour that culminates in a three-Test series against one of the best sides in the world, who have had months and sometimes years of preparation for your visit. It is for all these reasons and myriad more that since the Second World War there have been only five victorious British & Irish Lions tour parties in eighteen attempts – 1971, 1974, 1989, 1997 and 2013.

While it must be remembered that the Lions faced an All Blacks side considered by many to be one of the greatest of all time, and that their challenge was severely hampered by savage injury, there is no escaping the awful humiliation that they suffered in the Test series, losing 3–0 with barely a shot fired in anger. 'Leading the Lions is an incredible honour but in no way an easy job,' wrote Woodward in 2013. 'I have listened to many people's opinion about the Lions tour I led in 2005, especially concerning my selection. It is always a controversial subject. All I can say is that I did everything I believed was right and in the interests of the team. You can analyse it however you wish. We were up against one of the finest All Blacks sides I've ever seen and we lost to a superior team after we were depleted by injuries to some key players, including Brian O'Driscoll and Lawrence Dallaglio.'

With Woodward no longer in the driving seat at Twickenham and the wreckage of the Lions tour being picked over by every rugby pundit in the world, it seemed as if the Woodward Way would be consigned to history. Never mind that it had brought England several years of unprecedented success and delivered the World Cup, something that they have not managed to accomplish since; no, as time passed it seemed to many that Woodward was just lucky – a crank who was fortunate enough to have a team of outstanding players who did the business for him.

'Obviously, we all put in the work, lots of hard work to do it,' said Jason Leonard of the long run of success that led to the World Cup triumph. 'But there's no point pretending that all that set-up just fell naturally into place, because it didn't. It needed someone in there who knew what he was up to and who could have the arguments and stand his ground in order to get it. Clive took the long-term view and put things together so that if we did things right, applied ourselves and concentrated on what we were doing and where we were going, we could become world champions. He did his job, the team did theirs and as a unit we were good enough to do it.'

Woodward's rugby legacy will, unfortunately, always be tarnished by the Lions tour. He made an astonishing, highly criticised and ultimately unsuccessful move into football coaching with Southampton in 2005 and from there he went into a role with the British Olympic Association, but he has never been able to lay the ghosts of that Lions tour to rest with a successful rugby comeback – despite repeated attempts to claim the role of performance director at the RFU.

His work with the BOA, however, saw the phoenix rise from the ashes. On 6 September 2006 he was made director of elite performance for the BOA before acting as deputy chef de mission at the 2008 Beijing Olympics, where he reviewed the practices at the Games in preparation for London 2012. He took his England rugby blueprint, adapted it with a host of necessary tweaks and applied it to Team GB. Critical non-essentials became watchwords all around the country as Woodward brought his obsessive attention to detail to Team GB's preparations. He pushed hard for the utilisation of specialist coaches, encouraged and facilitated cross-sport cooperation and the sharing of ideas, and successfully managed to inspire 541 athletes across twenty-six sports to buy into the One Team philosophy, which they demonstrated with aplomb at London 2012. And he even brought his old muckers Dave Reddin, Dave Alred and Sherylle Calder along for the ride, each of whom had a significant impact on what would turn out to be a glorious summer for British sport, with Reddin in particular proving a star recruit as he built unquestionably the finest medical and training facilities in the Olympic Village.

And even though his tenure with the BOA would come to something of an acrimonious end in 2013, there is no doubt that the achievements of

Team GB's athletes at London 2012 were due in no small part to Sir Clive Woodward. If ever there was to be further vindication of his methods and practices this was certainly it.

*

In July 2009 England won the rights to host the 2015 Rugby World Cup. Home advantage, which had failed to push them over the finishing line in 1991, might just give England the edge to re-enter the pantheon twelve years after Jonny Wilkinson's drop-kick to glory in Sydney.

After a fairly miserable campaign both on and off the field at the 2011 World Cup in New Zealand under the management of Martin Johnson, there was a coaching and player clear-out at the RFU and Stuart Lancaster was brought in as a temporary head coach before securing the job outright in March 2012. Lancaster's new broom swept England to second place in both the 2012 and 2013 Six Nations and saw his team earn a notable Test series victory over Argentina in the summer of 2013, although the most impressive performance of his tenure came when England dismantled the world champion All Blacks at Twickenham 38–21 in December 2012.

The target for Lancaster and his squad is to repeat the triumphs of the class of 2003. Many of Woodward's ways have been swept out since his resignation, but some still remain: Pennyhill Park, specialist coaches, an environment of no excuses. Lancaster is diligent, down-to-earth and a source of steady reassurance for his players. He is not a visionary or revolutionary in the mould of Woodward, but he has ambitions to build a team that can take on the world. Whether he is able to achieve this remains to be seen. While the ghosts of Woodward and the 2003 team still stalk every movement of their successors and the world awaits the flowering of another golden period for the red rose, it is important that the achievements of the Woodward years are seen as a benchmark to aspire to rather than a millstone around the incumbent's neck. For now the triumphs of those years remain isolated in their splendour, but eyes must ever be on the present and the future – just as Woodward's always were.

BIBLIOGRAPHY AND FURTHER READING

BOOKS

Winning! The Autobiography of Clive Woodward by Clive Woodward

Mind Games: Inspirational Lessons from the World's Finest Sports Stars by Jeff Grout and Sarah Perrin

Bounce: The Myth of Talent and the Power of Practice by Matthew Syed

Outliers: The Story of Success by Malcolm Gladwell

The Talent Code: Greatness Isn't Born, It's Grown by Daniel Coyle

Mindset: How You Can Fulfil Your Potential by Carol Dweck

Building the Happiness-Centred Business by Paddi Lund

A Social History of English Rugby Union by Tony Collins

A Game for Hooligans: The History of Rugby Union by Huw Richards

Sport in Britain: 1945–2000 by Richard Holt and Tony Mason

Clive Woodward: The Biography by Alison Kervin

Think Rugby by Jim Greenwood

FitzSimons on Rugby: Loose in the Tight Five by Peter FitzSimons

Will Greenwood on Rugby by Will Greenwood

Jonny: My Autobiography by Jonny Wilkinson

Will: The Autobiography by Will Greenwood

Finding My Feet: My Autobiography by Jason Robinson

Martin Johnson: The Autobiography by Martin Johnson

Me and My Mouth: The Autobiography by Austin Healey

One Chance by Josh Lewsey

Raging Bull: My Autobiography by Phil Vickery

Richard Hill: The Autobiography by Richard Hill

Nine Lives: The Autobiography by Matt Dawson

Size Doesn't Matter: My Rugby Life by Neil Back

Full Time: The Autobiography by Jason Leonard

Landing on My Feet: My Story by Mike Catt

Lions and Falcons: My Diary of a Remarkable Year by Jonny Wilkinson

It's in the Blood: The Autobiography by Lawrence Dallaglio

In Your Face: A Rugby Odyssey by Richard Hill with Michael Tanner

Agony & Ecstasy: My Diary of an Amazing Rugby Season by Martin Johnson

Graham Henry: Final Word by Bob Howitt

Blackie: The Steve Black Story by Steve Black

Team England Rugby: World Cup 2003, The Official Account by Team England Rugby

Grand Slam Champions: The Official Story of England's Undefeated Season by Team England Rugby

Sweet Chariot: The Complete Book of the Rugby World Cup 2003, edited by Ian Robertson

Chasing the Chariot by Mick Collins

On My Knees: The Long Road to England's World Cup Glory – A Harassed Hack's Homage by Stephen Jones

Thirty Bullies: The History of the Rugby World Cup by Alison Kervin

Triumph and Tragedy: Welsh Sporting Legends by Peter Jackson, foreword by Clive Woodward

Alumni Montium: Sixty Years of Glenalmond and Its People by David Willington

Goodbye to Glory: The 1976 All Black Tour of South Africa by Terry McLean

Behind the Lions: Playing Rugby for the British & Irish Lions by Stephen Jones, Tom English, Nick Cain and David Barnes

Behind the Thistle: Playing Rugby for Scotland by David Barnes and Peter Burns

MULTIMEDIA

Time of Our Lives: World Champions 2003 England Rugby. Sky Sports.

Inside England Rugby: Sweet Chariot (DVD)

Rugby World Cup Glory 2003 (DVD)

Rugby World Cup 2003: England's Story (DVD)

Jonny Wilkinson: The Perfect 10 (DVD)

Jonny Wilkinson: How to Play Rugby My Way (DVD)

www.hmsconway.org

ARTICLES AND JOURNALS

'Woodward in a world of his own', by Paul Ackford. *The Sunday Telegraph*, 20 August 2000.

'Woodward's back-seat drivers', by Paul Rees. *The Guardian*, 3 October 2003.

'Inside Clive's World', by Nick Greenslade. *The Observer*, 4 December 2005.

'Woodward: Impulsive, but a man of principle', by Peter Jackson. *Daily Mail*, 23 November 2000.

'We didn't win in 1999 because we weren't ready to', by David Walsh. *The Sunday Times*, 14 August 2011.

'Art of statistics gives you an edge', by Sir Clive Woodward. *The Sunday Times*, 11 November 2012.

'It's time to go on the attack: Why England's humbling defeat must lead to new approach', by Sir Clive Woodward. *Daily Mail*, 17 March 2013.

'England must play a brand of attacking and thrilling rugby that will wake up the world', by Sir Clive Woodward. *Daily Mail*, 31 January 2013.

'Rugby's great underachievers no more', by Kevin Mitchell. *The Observer*, 5 October 2003.

'The Big Interview: Steve Thompson', by David Walsh. *The Sunday Times*, 4 January 2004.

'The Big Interview: Josh Lewsey', by David Walsh. *The Sunday Times*, 16 November 2003.

'A genius made by lonely moments', by Richard Williams. *The Guardian*, 24 November 2003.

'Woodman clears path into England reckoning at last', by David Hands. *The Times*, 8 November 2002.

'Long shot! Andy's back from the sun for final bid with Northampton', by Chris Foy. *Daily Mail*, 11 May 2012.

'My Life in Rugby', by Dave Ellis. *The Rugby Paper*, 18 April 2013.

'Farrell must learn from Jonny's mistake when the French come to town', by Sir Clive Woodward. *Daily Mail*, 21 February 2013.

'It took three of our best to stop the genius of O'Driscoll in 2003', by Sir Clive Woodward. *Daily Mail*, 6 February 2013.

'Mat: Lewsey ran me over', by Gary Payne. *The Sun*, 8 October 2008.

'The power behind England', by David Hands. *The Times,* 5 February 2005.

'Secret of success', by Nick Cain. *The Sunday Times*, 25 May 2003.

'Fit and ready', by Gary Jacob. *The Times*, 4 October 2003

Functional Path Training Blog: Dave Reddin interview.

'Training has been brutal and we're ready to do battle', by Sir Clive Woodward. *Daily Mail*, 13 March 2013.

'A Gene for Speed: The Emerging Role of α-Actinin-3 in Muscle Metabolism', by Yemima Berman and Kathryn N. North in the *Journal of Applied Physiology*. © 2010 The American Physiological Society.

'2013 v 2003', by Sir Clive Woodward. *Daily Mail*, 14 March 2013.

'Greenwood summons up the spirits of old glory', by William Fotheringham. *The Guardian*, 19 November 2003.

'I love playing mind games', by Paul Rees. *The Guardian*, 30 October 2003.

'Pick your Lions on merit... anything else is dangerous', by Sir Clive Woodward. *Daily Mail*, 14 February 2013.

'Rugby: Key is quality, not quantity', by Sir Clive Woodward. *The Sunday Times*, 1 July 2012.

'I hadn't a clue what to do when it ended', by David Walsh. *The Sunday Times*, 21 August 2011.

'What Johnno did next', by Stephen Jones. *The Sunday Times*, 17 September, 2006.